In this concluding volume of J. Murray Beck's biography of the great Nova Scotia tribune, Joseph Howe extends his horizon well beyond his native province and in the climactic period of a tumultuous political career accepts the union of the British North American colonies and "becomes a Canadian."

Professor Beck shows how, in Churchillian fashion, this final resolution was preceded by a series of setbacks and disappointments in Howe's public life. These were the result of a bold though abortive colonization scheme encompassing an intercolonial railway between Halifax and Quebec; a cloak-and-dagger mission of recruitment in the United States for the British armies in the Crimea; the embattled leadership of an unstable provincial administration in the early 1860s; and the hard-fought campaign to prevent the passage of the British North America Act and later to secure its repeal. Professor Beck believes that Howe's resistance to Confederation was not self-serving, but was rooted in his conviction that no such union should be imposed upon Nova Scotia without consultation with its people, and in his longstanding advocacy of a refurbished British Empire in the government of which colonial leaders, himself included, would share. Disillusioned by the indifference of British politicians to his vision of empire, Howe turned his energies to making the new Canadian federation work, especially in Nova Scotia, where as a Dominion cabinet minister he played a major role in "pacifying the Antis" and preserving the union. A wholehearted supporter of Confederation in his last years, Howe displayed in this as in every other facet of his life the irrepressible vitality that Professor Beck sees as the trademark of the man.

J. Murray Beck is Professor Emeritus, Department of Political Science, Dalhousie University, and is the author of *Joseph Howe: Conservative Reformer 1804–1848*.

# Joseph Howe

*Volume II*
The Briton
Becomes Canadian
1848–1873

J. MURRAY BECK

McGill-Queen's University Press
Kingston and Montreal

© McGill-Queen's University Press 1983
ISBN 0-7735-0388-9

Legal deposit 4th quarter 1983
Bibliothèque nationale du Québec

Printed in Canada

This book has been published with the help of a grant from the Social Science
Federation of Canada, using funds provided by the Social Sciences and Humanities
Research Council of Canada. Publication has also been assisted by the Canada
Council under its block grant program.

---

**Canadian Cataloguing in Publication Data**

Beck, J. Murray (James Murray), 1914–
Joseph Howe

Includes bibliographical references and indexes.
Contents: v. 1. Conservative reformer, 1804–1848 – v. 2.
The Briton becomes Canadian, 1848–1873.
ISBN 0-7735-0387-0 (v. 1). – ISBN 0-7735-0388-9 (v. 2)

1. Howe, Joseph, 1804–1873. 2. Politicians –
Nova Scotia – Biography. I. Title.

FC23221.1.H68B43      971.6′02′0924      C82-904676-1
F1038.H68B43

*Cover* Joseph Howe, lithograph by C.G. Crehen, 1854, apparently
from a portrait of 1851 by T. Debaussy. Courtesy Nova Scotia Museum

*Frontispiece* Joseph Howe, daguerreotype by T.C. Doane, possibly about
1855. Courtesy Nova Scotia Museum

# Contents

# Preface

Before 1848 Joseph Howe talked of the "infernal feeling" which impelled him to pursue "something ahead ... viewless and undefined." That feeling remained with him to the end of his days, indeed, continued to be the source of the unrelenting drive which was his most notable characteristic. The difference after 1848 was that he extended many of his activities beyond his native province and in doing so discovered that, master publicist though he was, he could not influence public opinion in Britain and the United States to the same extent as he had done in little Nova Scotia.

It is not surprising, therefore, that most of the criticism of Howe by academics relates to his later life. One of his major biographers even suggests that "once [responsible government] was achieved his main work was done. Dullness succeeded enthusiasm, cynicism succeeded faith; and from now on, his history is one of fading day and falling night." A contemporary historian states that in 1864 Howe was "entering the last tired and disillusioned decade of a career that had never been quite what he had hoped it might be."

None could deny, of course, that the British Empire he proposed and advocated could never have come into existence during his lifetime. It is somewhat puzzling, however, that his critics, in dealing with their favourite target, the Confederation issue, have seldom discussed the tactics used to bring Nova Scotia into the federation, or wondered if a liberal, as Howe undoubtedly was, could have been expected to accept those tactics unquestioningly. Because he failed to prevent the Canadian union or secure its repeal, are they justified in labelling Howe himself as a failure? Would not this kind of criterion downgrade any person of unimpeachable motives who makes a strong fight against impossible odds? As Professor R.G. Trotter once observed, there is "no justice in that sort of *ex post facto* verdict on political opinions." But perhaps I have already condemned myself, either as a Nova Scotian or as an admirer of Howe, or as both.

Elsewhere I have examined in some detail the viewpoints of Howe's academic critics. In this volume I am content to let his career unfold largely through his own words and to offer my interpretation of his conduct as the occasion warrants it.

Again, my first thanks must go to Dr Phyllis Blakeley, the Provincial Archivist, and the staff of the Public Archives of Nova Scotia, for helping to make my research activities both pleasant and fruitful. I have also benefited greatly from the many scattered bits of information provided by Allan C. Dunlop, the Assistant Provincial Archivist. I am grateful to Mrs Doris Boyle for typing the manuscript.

My enthusiasm for working with McGill-Queen's University Press continues undiminished and I repeat my earlier comment that the Canadian academic community is fortunate that such an institution exists and that it performs an invaluable function so capably.

I alone am responsible for the shortcomings of the book.

Mrs Joseph Howe, 1860s. Notman photograph. Courtesy Public Archives of
Nova Scotia

Sir John Harvey, lieutenant-governor of Nova Scotia, 1846–52. Courtesy Public Archives of Nova Scotia

Sir Gaspard le Marchant, lieutenant-governor of Nova Scotia, 1852–8. Courtesy Public Archives of Nova Scotia

Sir Fenwick Williams, lieutenant-governor of Nova Scotia,
1865–7. Courtesy Public
Archives of Nova Scotia

Sir Hastings Doyle, adminis-
trator of Nova Scotia, 1863–4
and 1865, and lieutenant-
governor, 1867–72. Courtesy
Public Archives of Nova Scotia

William Annand, Liberal
politician and publisher.
Courtesy Public Archives of
Nova Scotia

William Young, Liberal politician and chief justice. Courtesy
Nova Scotia Museum

J.W. Johnston, Conservative
politician and judge in equity.
Courtesy Nova Scotia Museum

Martin Wilkins, Conservative
politician and anti-Con-
federate. Courtesy Public
Archives of Nova Scotia

Charles Tupper, Conservative
politician and Confederate.
Courtesy Public Archives of
Nova Scotia

William J. Stairs, merchant
and vice-president of the
Anti-Confederation League,
1866–7. Courtesy Public
Archives of Nova Scotia

# MORNING CHRONICLE.

## HALIFAX, JULY 1, 1867.

### CANDIDATES OF THE NOVA SCO-
### TIA PARTY.

### COUNTY OF HALIFAX.

*For the House of Commons of the Dominion
of Canada :*

A. G. JONES, Esq.,        P. POWER, Esq.

*For the House of Assembly of Nova Scotia:*

HENRY BALCAM, Esq., JAMES COCHRAN, Esq.,
JEREMIAH NORTHUP, Esq.

---

## DIED.

Last night, at twelve o'clock, the free
and enlightened Province of Nova Scotia.
Deceased was the offspring of old English
stock, and promised to have proved an
honour and support to her parents in their
declining years. Her death was occasioned by unnatural treatment received at
the hands of some of her ungrateful sons,
who, taking advantage of the position she
had afforded them, betrayed her to the
enemy. Funeral will take place from the
Grand Parade this day, Monday, at 9
o'clock. Friends are requested *not* to
attend, as her enemies, with becoming
scorn, intend to insult the occasion with
rejoicing.

---

*Morning Chronicle,* July 1, 1867. Courtesy Public
Archives of Nova Scotia

Joseph Howe, late 1860s. Notman photograph. Courtesy Public Archives
of Nova Scotia

*Joseph Howe*
1848–1873

# A Normal School for the Colonies

Change was everywhere as the Reformers took over the government of Nova Scotia in 1848. With nothing short of fascination Joseph Howe watched "the downfall of ancient dynasties [in Europe], the violent disruption of the relations of established society, and sanguinary Civil conflicts."[1] But in its own way even little Nova Scotia was having its taste of revolution, since, in releasing its tight hold over the colonies, the British government did not confine itself to the political realm. The dismantling of the empire's protective system, largely accomplished in 1846, would be completed by 1855, and steps were well under way to making the Nova Scotia post office entirely independent of the British postmaster general by July 1851. In the communications field the electric telegraph would be completed to the New Brunswick border by November 1849 and the building of railways was finally proceeding beyond purely theoretical discussion. In all of these developments Howe would display a keen interest, in some play an active role, but throughout 1848 and 1849 his major concerns were still political.

In reviewing the events in Europe with a kindred spirit, the advanced English reformer, Charles Buller, Howe – the conservative reformer par excellence – compared the Germans and the French to the latter's disadvantage. The two agreed that the French, in the "Established Communism of Paris," were seeking, even before they learned self-government, to make changes in the social system which would fail even in Britain and the United States;[2] in contrast, the German evolved slowly: "you must hit him hard to knock any fun out of him, but he is an honest, industrious, fellow ... There may be a Thirty Years' War in Germany, but there will come out of it a vast political as there came out of the old one a great religious reformation."[3] Closer at hand, Howe was delighted that Queen Victoria had bestowed on his native province a constitution which left "nothing to fear and nothing to demand,"[4] and even more pleased that Nova Scotians had played such an "elevated, intelligent, steady, peaceful" part in these political gains. It was now up to his Reformers to ensure that the province reaped all "the practical fruits" of the new system[5] and in the process to make her "a 'Normal School' for the rest of the Colonies."[6]

Although by no means naïve in these matters, Howe did not foresee the kind and number of obstacles that would be strewn in the Reformers' path. Perhaps he should have, since J.W. Johnston, the Tory leader, had always contended that the Reformers' principles would be implemented no less effectively by the presence of one responsible minister in the assembly than by that of half a dozen. More than that, Johnston and the Tory press had never acknowledged that the pre-1848 administration was an out-and-out party government or that the entire governmental establishment was Tory to its very core. He by implication, his newspapers more explicitly, had suggested that the nonpolitical office-holders were an experienced, efficient, public-spirited elite, whose talents contrasted sharply with the ignorance and incapacity of the ragamuffin groups that had gathered around Howe. For the Tories these reasons were sufficient in themselves to justify opposing major changes in the status quo every step of the way.

Because the Tory Executive Council did not resign until voted out by the assembly, the Reform ministry assumed office only eleven days after the legislature opened, without having had the opportunity to prepare a legislative program. In the absence of a precedent to guide them,[7] the Tories could hardly be blamed for not resigning; not nearly so easy to excuse, however, was the conduct of those individuals who resigned their executive councillorships but not their specific offices and hence necessitated "a [vast] volume of correspondence and the usual amount of special pleading, ... [only] cut short ...by the forcible removal of certain obstructives."[8] No less blamable was the Tory tactic of opposing Attorney General J.B. Uniacke, Solicitor General W.F. DesBarres, and Provincial Secretary Howe at their ministerial elections, since it delayed the introduction of major government bills two to three weeks longer. When Uniacke and Howe ran up unprecedentedly large majorities, the *Novascotian* had good reason to call Johnston a "blundering obstructive."[9]

In the ministers' absence from the assembly only one measure designed to introduce the new order saw the light of day. That was the judges bill, which permitted a justice of the Supreme Court to be removed on the joint address of the legislature, but allowed him six months to appeal to the Privy Council. It could be proceeded with, however, only because, as an exact transcript of an earlier act of the Parliament of Canada, it required no preparation, and even so it needed the return of Howe to the assembly and the use of all his skills to get it through the legislative mill.

For him the bill was much more than a symbolic gesture. Remembering with some bitterness how the wheels of justice had been made to revolve in favour of the Tories earlier in his career, he wanted the judges to know that they too operated under checks. When Johnston conjured up all sorts of "vain imaginings," Howe told him he had "one prominent fault as a statesman – he is very apt to be startled at a shadow."[10] When Johnston suggested that it would be "a *bold* man indeed who hereafter accepts a seat upon the Bench," Howe laughingly rejoined that "it would be rather difficult ... to find *one coward* at the Bar" who would refuse the emoluments of a judge. Derisively he dismissed the contention that the bill would permit judges to be removed without a fair trial. Could Johnston really believe that "this Assembly of fifty-one gentlemen would jump to the conclusion that the accused was guilty, and proceed at once to pass condemnation upon him? ... [He] knows that there would be a trial and a right good one." In Nova Scotia a "sort of *microscopic* vision [operated] upon the acts of public men" and any House of Assembly which tried to perpetrate "an act of manifest *injustice* upon a Judge of the land, would be inevitably beaten by the all-powerful force of PUBLIC OPINION."

By the third week in March the Reformers were ready with their second bill to adapt the governmental machinery to their purposes, this time through more efficient administration of the Crown lands. Earlier Howe had suggested that John Spry Morris, the surveyor general and commissioner of Crown lands for peninsular Nova Scotia, might be required to give way to a responsible political officer in the assembly. Instead, Morris was to retain his office in a nonpolitical capacity and to assume, in addition, the duties of Henry and Thomas Crawley, respectively the commissioner and surveyor general of crown lands for Cape Breton, who were to be granted retiring allowances.[11] To Howe the bill recommended itself by its appeal to the pocket since it resulted in immediate savings of £700 annually and £1,040 later on; however, he did not rule out making the commissioner a political officer when suitable machinery could be perfected.[12] Surprisingly to him, the bill created little controversy. Perhaps the Tories recognized that the existing organization was hopelessly top-heavy; even the Crawleys may have realized that they were reasonably well treated and perceived the futility of mounting a lobby in their behalf.

So mild a reaction was not to be expected on the Reformers' key measures, the civil list and departmental bills. In November 1846 the colonial secretary, Lord Grey, had insisted on two conditions for the surrender of the casual and territorial revenues of the Crown: the arrears in the salaries of the major public officers, which had developed while the casual revenues that supported them were unproductive, would have to be paid, and the incumbent office holders, although not their successors, were not to have their salaries reduced. Nevertheless, the Reformers' civil list bill of 1848 was almost a carbon copy of the act of 1844 which the colonial secretary had rejected because of special pleading by the officials whose income it reduced. Basically the new bill put the public officers, especially the judges and the provincial secretary, upon the reduced scale of 1844 and paid the full arrears up to that time, but only an amount based upon the reduced scale after that date.[13] The one officer who would have received more than the act of 1844 provided was the incumbent lieutenant-governor, Sir John Harvey, whose salary was to be £3,500 stg rather than £3,000.[14]

Howe wanted desperately to settle a vexed question with which he had been wrestling off and on, as newspaperman and politician, since 1834. He knew that some Reformers were expecting an even lower scale of salaries than the bill provided, but he believed that with persuasion they would accept a compromise. Howe was also hopeful that, although the bill did not fully meet Grey's conditions, the colonial secretary would confirm it because it accorded generous treatment to Harvey. But he and his colleagues miscalculated badly. Johnston, the major defendant of the honour of the Crown, was especially bitter that only the interests of the incumbent governor were to be protected: "a respect for the high position occupied by [Harvey] alone restrains me from a free expression of my opinion, and the use of stronger language."[15] Howe, delighted to have an opportunity to reprimand Johnston for bandying about the governor's name in the assembly, insisted that the bill had been introduced upon the cabinet's responsibility, not the governor's, and "by it we shall stand or fall."[16] In his view a salary of £3,500 was not excessive for someone who had given up his military allowances and would therefore be much less well off than his predecessors. Eventually a disciplined phalanx of Reformers turned down, by majorities ranging from five to fourteen, the amendments of a riddled group of Tories. No less than before 1848, the honour of the Crown and party cohesion gave way, this time in the case of the Tories' country members, to the claims of economical government in which their constituents had an abiding concern.

Not until the closing days of the session were the Reformers ready to proceed with the departmental bill, the very cornerstone of the new system. The bill eliminated the provincial treasurer and in his place introduced two political officers with membership in the Executive Council, a receiver general charged simply with receiving and dispensing public funds, and a financial secretary entrusted with the primary responsibility for determining the government's financial policy. Calling it "the last battle to be fought on a constitutional question, the last of a long line of fights for establishing a great principle," Howe went to extravagant lengths, even for him. In "the noble fabric of her Constitution," he said, Britain had devised the only political system that, so far in the world's history, had been able to preserve liberty by dividing power among several classes; "such is the system which we propose for the government of our Land – and approach in the alterations proposed by this Bill."[17]

This time Johnston objected, not to the creation of the political office of financial secretary, but to the institution of two political finance officers: "the man who stands behind the counter, and receives and pays away the public money [i.e., the receiver general], should not be on the floor of this House."[18] Howe found it difficult to meet this point directly, but when Johnston argued further that the principle of responsibility had nothing to do with the number of executive councillors holding both departmental offices and seats in the legislature, Howe had a ready answer. To have an Executive Council composed largely of unpaid members without office would have made it quite impossible to convene regular meetings throughout the year to determine broad policy matters. "For his own part, he ... knew from his own experience how few here could serve the public without being paid."[19] He found it no less easy to answer Johnston's protest against the removal of S.P. Fairbanks, who had connived with a Tory government to obtain the provincial treasurership during good behaviour. Surely, he said, Fairbanks had been foolhardy to regard it as permanent, "knowing as he did that under a change of government the departmental system would be introduced, and the offices held only on political tenure."[20] Once again a disciplined Reform majority beat back a series of Tory amendments to the departmental bill.

The hurdles in the assembly overcome, Howe looked with fore-boding on the "obstructives" at the other end of Province House. When the Reformers took office, they were outnumbered in the

Legislative Council by twelve to four. They quickly brought it into much better balance by filling the five vacancies with strong, articulate party men, altogether a new breed of councillor. Fortune also intervened in their favour. Illness kept away Tory R.M. Cutler of Guysborough for the entire session, while William Rudolf, formerly a staunch supporter of Johnston's Tory administration, arrived from Lunenburg in mid-March resolved not to oppose the adaptation of the political institutions to responsible government. The Reformers were hurt, however, by the conduct of John Inglis, the lord bishop of Nova Scotia, who had previously meddled only rarely in the temporalities of the province, but who was induced in 1848, at the cost of damaging his credibility, to participate in every division, supposedly to protect the vested rights of the public officers and the honour of the Crown.[21]

In an attempt to water down the judges bill, S.B. Robie, the Tory president of the council, got the upper House to accept amendments which required specific charges to be preferred before the legislature proceeded against a judge and made those charges the only matter that could be considered by the Privy Council on appeal. Thoroughly aroused by this tinkering with "a piece of British machinery," Howe easily defeated the amendments in the assembly. Why, he asked, did Robie and Johnston not show the same sympathy for "the poor man and the humble" as for "the magnates of the land"? Why were they so concerned that a judge might be ruined by having to wait six months for his appeal, yet entirely oblivious of the recent case of a poor man who had been kept in the county prison for months and then discharged without a charge being laid? "But a judge, O! a Judge, do what he may, but don't let him experience any of the sad consequences of the Law's delay."[22]

Despite Robie and the bishop, Rudolf's vote decided, by a margin of ten to nine, that the council would not adhere to its amendments. The division brought in its train a consequence for which Howe had not even dared to hope: the resignation on April 3 of Robie as president and member of the Legislative Council. Apparently "the place became too hot for the old gentleman"[23] when he found the same spirit penetrating the Upper House as pervaded the Lower. For once Howe had not even a twinge of sympathy. His lifelong suspicion of lawyers and the judiciary had begun when, as a stripling, he watched Robie use his position as Speaker and influential assemblyman to foist a highly bloated judiciary upon the province and then become a leading beneficiary of the emoluments. Then, for more than a quarter of a century, he had observed Robie, ensconced in high office, change from a moderate liberal to an extreme Tory, increasingly striving to stymie the Reformers' proposals for institutional change. Now, with no uncommon delight, he joined in recommending his friend Michael Tobin to be president of the Legislative Council. Giving full realization to Robie's fears, the council passed the civil list and departmental bills on the 6th and 7th of April, but it was a very close thing: even with Rudolf's support, Tobin had to cast the deciding votes.[24]

Howe took pleasure in three other acts passed in 1848 with his sponsorship or blessing. One, which he regarded as a device to awaken Dalhousie College from a long slumber and make it the premier Nova Scotia university, permitted the Governor in Council to name a new board of governors. Another gave the government the power to appoint five commissioners to establish an electric telegraph from Halifax to the New Brunswick border. None was more emphatic than Howe that this was the type of undertaking in which "the control ought to be vested in the hands of the Government"[25] and he was delighted to be named one of the commissioners. A third measure which won his unstinting praise, the co-partners bill, permitted partnerships to have a new type of contributor called special partners who would not be liable for the debts of the partnership. He had often wondered why New Englanders were "a great and wealthy people, while we ... are comparatively poor" and, on investigation, attributed it to their system of sleeping partners which made it possible for a young man of character to obtain capital to commence a business; sometimes a chief justice might be "the sleeping partner in a concern for the manufacture of *shoe-maker's lasts.*"[26]

With elation Howe summed up the session for Buller: "Though compelled to form the Administration – carry our Elections and prepare our measures, after the Session commenced the Government introduced and perfected eight important public Bills, more than have been brought in by Administration in five previous Sessions. These are chiefly intended to ... give us, what we really want, the machinery of a working government."[27] The unity of the Reformers on major proposals delighted Howe, but he had anticipated correctly that the Youngs would somehow find means to be a divisive influence, even though William was the Speaker and George an executive councillor without office. William was not above descending from the chair to tell the ministers "he hoped they would not disappoint the high expectations formed of them."[28] Once he insisted that the main arterial roads should be the first concern of the government, while George wanted the responsibility even for the crossroads to be transferred from the county members to the Executive Council. Jokingly, but nonetheless in earnest, Howe read them both a lecture:

William, who had prolonged a debate that ought to have lasted ten minutes, should be made to "put on his wig and sit in the chair till 12 o'clock"; George, who favoured the centralized supervision of roads practised in Canada, should be made to travel its roads, on which Howe "once nearly had his neck broken."[29]

For the moment, however, Howe's main concern was the stream of protests, petitions, and remonstrances that the Tories hoped would lead to the rejection of the Reformers' major bills in Britain. "The mode in which these are dealt with," he told Buller, "will be a decisive indication of Earl Grey's future policy, and if he sweeps them out of his way with a firm hand, he will not be troubled with any further accumulation. I hope to see the day, when Governors' Despatches will be compressed into an occasional 'All's well'."[30] But for the time being it was not to be. In June, after expressing no objection in principle to the reorganization of the Crown Lands Department or to the judges bill,[31] Grey took a position on the Reformers' two major enactments which thoroughly perturbed Howe. Calling the departmental bill "extremely prejudicial to the public interests," Grey insisted that the two financial officers to be appointed "should not both hold their places by a political tenure"; instead, the receiver general, like the comptroller of the exchequer in England, should be a nonpolitical officer, while the financial secretary, like the chancellor of the exchequer, should be political, "the organ of the Administration in all matters of finance." He was equally insistent that S.P. Fairbanks should not be deprived of the provincial treasurership without adequate compensation since it would be "most unjust" to change his tenure to "one of dependance on a Parliamentary majority" without making up the loss of official income.[32]

But Grey's sternest strictures by far were levelled against the civil list bill, and in this he was influenced – Howe thought – by the "mass of papers accumulated ... by ... a party whose last hope is ... to obstruct the steady progress of public affairs here." Insisting to the letter on his two stipulations of November 1846, Grey demanded that the arrears in salaries be met to date and that the existing salaries of the public officers be confirmed unless they were guaranteed only the scale of 1844 at the time of their appointment. Unusually harsh to Governor Harvey, he ordered him to accept a maximum of £3,000 per annum since, if he were the only officer to get more than the bill of 1844 provided, he might be accused of "having unduly courted" the legislature for personal objects. He was even more critical of Harvey for not submitting the bill to the Colonial Office before letting it be introduced in the legislature since it would now have to be submitted to that body for a second time.[33] Altogether shocked, Howe told

Buller that Grey's action "left us powerless to carry on Responsible Government for lack of machinery." Nonetheless, he did not blame the colonial secretary unduly. "Having a Revolution a week upon his hands," he obviously had not the "leisure to attend to us himself" or had "acted under some erroneous impression," created perhaps by dispatches or visitors from Nova Scotia. Could Buller spare time to give Howe advice, if only a line?[34] But he was fated to have no further communication with an ailing Buller, who would not last out the year.

Upon Howe, as the executive councillor most suited to the task, fell the major responsibility of answering Grey's objections. He wanted to assume it in any case. Harvey, a veteran of the colonial service, was in the twilight of his career and his failing faculties left him ill-prepared to cope with complex problems deeply rooted in political history. Highly sceptical of him at the start, Howe quickly became the governor's confidant and friend, and pulled out all the stops in defending him from Grey's criticisms. In the Executive Council's first address on the civil list bill in April, the arguments were the ones Howe had been making for years and the style is often vintage Howe. Especially telling was his point that a Tory majority had passed, and Johnston had advised the governor to accept, the civil list bill of 1844, which gave the public officers "just the salaries they are to receive now, and nothing more"; how, then, did Johnston dare to "assume the right to rebuke [Harvey] ... [and] charge us with violations of justice and honor"?[35]

The Executive Council's second address in July argued that the legislature could always spare money for "any object involving the honor of the Crown," but when asked to provide it for the loss of fees to which the puisne judges were not entitled, it was moved by the same sentiments which "prompt Englishmen ... to question the slightest exaction to which the assent of Parliament had never been obtained." Howe was especially anxious to defend Harvey and the council from the charge of undue precipitancy. Because the Johnston government had insisted on the abstract right to remain in office until voted out, the Reform government had no choice "by our position, and by the natural and perhaps too just expectations of our friends [but] to introduce ... some measures, of which [Grey] might possibly disapprove."[36] Following this explanation, Grey absolved Harvey from blame for permitting his council to introduce the civil list bill and for giving his assent to it, but on the major point he refused to budge, simply stating that "my objections ... are in no degree diminished." Seemingly possessed of the higher wisdom, he was supremely confident that his dictum would "ultimately tend to increase the attachment of the people of Nova Scotia to the Government of

[Britain], by inspiring them with a respect for the justice of its decisions."[37]

In its comments on the departmental bill the Executive Council's address in July exhibited the hand of Howe in its most forceful form. "The inherent vice of old Colonial Governments," it said, "was the absence of adequate control ... over the Departments by which the whole Executive machinery was moved." Nevertheless, the Reformers had demanded only seven offices, "the smallest number ... by the aid of which, it could ever have been sup[p]osed, that Responsible Government could be carried on." In dealing with the smaller offices the Reform council had shown similar restraint. Indeed, Howe was "the only officer friendly to the Administration in the Province Building – within which the chief business of the country is daily transacted." Of 161 civil servants listed in the Blue Book, "but four removals have been pressed, but two or three others are required. We have asked for no office, that is not ... political." Was it reasonable, then, that an administration that had successfully resisted the pressures of its friends for office "should be left for the remainder of the year with no effectual controul over the Land, Finance and Revenue departments, wanting which ... there can be no efficient or satisfactory administration of affairs." Why should Nova Scotia be treated differently than Canada where, since 1840, a receiver general having the precise duties being performed by Fairbanks was the responsible head of a department?[38]

Admittedly in a difficult position, Grey wanted to demonstrate to the Tory office-holders that he was safeguarding their proper interests. Yet he saw that even with two finance officers the council would have only four full-time paid members to give day-to-day consideration to provincial business and act as a policy-determining body. So, although still disliking "the creation of *two* political [finance] officers" and continuing to believe that the "true and permanent interests" of the province would be best served by granting "just and reasonable compensation" to Fairbanks, he agreed, since the honour of the Crown was not pledged in his case and since Nova Scotians ought to determine the principles of their internal government, to accept the departmental bill if the legislature, after reconsideration, passed an address approving it.[39] Howe breathed a sigh of relief: it was another step towards the full realization of his basic objectives.

Talent, experience, and desire had ensured that Howe would play a key, and probably *the* key, role in the adaptation of provincial institutions. In 1860, when he formally took over the government, he would say it was nothing new for him and the evidence suggests that just as J.B. Uniacke had been only the nominal head of the party before 1848, so he was little more than nominal leader of the government after that time. The title "premier" was, of course, rarely used, and the equivalent term, "leader of the government," only occasionally. Uniacke, talented and personable, but always the dilettante in politics, had abandoned his earlier aggressiveness, when as a Tory he used to engage Howe in spectacular oratorical encounters. Though he participated fairly actively in legislative business before suffering a stroke in 1851, he tended to avoid violent political controversy and in Tory eyes Howe was usually the arch-villain behind government measures. Contributing to his pre-eminence in the government was his role as provincial secretary, which made him the chief avenue through which Nova Scotians could communicate with their government, especially in seeking office. No less significantly, the ex-Tory and somewhat aristocratic Uniacke was almost unknown to the Liberal rank-and-file, while Howe was a stranger to none. When W.F. DesBarres left the solicitor-generalship for the bench in the autumn of 1848, he told Howe there were "associations which none of us ... *can or must never forget.*" He and Howe, not Uniacke, decided that his successor should be Alexander McDougall of Antigonish, although they warned him against intemperance: "Our friend Mac has been bending his elbow lately," and if "he has any regard for himself, his family or friends he must *positively* haul up."[40]

In patronage Howe set the general tone for the ministry. Although adamant that any public office which the new order had rendered political must be vacated, he displayed the greatest humanity towards its occupant. Ostensibly it was Harvey, actually it was Howe who explained to Sir Rupert George, the retiring provincial secretary, that a governor could exercise "no influence, which public opinion condemns," but that Harvey had been persuasive enough to get him four-tenths of the provincial secretary's salary as a retiring allowance and to leave him all the perquisites of his second office, as provincial registrar of deeds. Howe also went out of his way to meet George's requests by securing accommodation for him in Province House, by arranging a long leave for him in Britain, and by ensuring that his interest in the Registry was protected in his absence. When George indicated his appreciation, Howe expressed regret that George's fortunes had been "affected by changes which have been pressed [only] from a conviction of their public utility."[41] It was a nice gesture towards one who had once challenged him to a duel and whom he regarded as little more than a good "red-tape" man.

Howe expected greater difficulty with a former virulent foe, John

H. Crosskill, the more so because Harvey had serious doubts about removing a Queen's printer who was not engaging in politics. Grateful for Crosskill's departure without a fuss, Howe thanked him for recognizing that the person who sometimes printed confidential government documents should have "generally sustained, rather than opposed, the views of ... the Provincial Administration."[42] He exulted even more that he could now provide suitably for faithful John Thompson. But his generous impulses sometimes backfired. After putting himself out to find other employment for Fairbanks, he discovered that the latter had made "use of friendly and confidential communication" with him to tell the governor that Howe admitted he had been wronged. Any wrong to Fairbanks, Howe retorted, had been self-inflicted: "If a gentleman, chose to thrust himself on the Track of a Railway the Passengers would not be to blame."[43] A decade later he would write ruefully: "I did my best to serve this man ... and nearly got into bother with my colleagues ... I got but little thanks from the family."[44]

Howe's moderation extended even to his bête noire, Alexander Stewart, probably the most disliked Tory in the province. Somehow or other, Stewart, in his capacity as master of the rolls, had managed to draw £112 10s. more annually than the assembly intended, something that even the staunchest Tories found difficult to stomach. Nonetheless, Howe did not want the House to "act hastily," suggesting that the transaction might wear "a more favourable aspect" if sent to committee.[45] "We think," concluded the *Acadian Recorder*, "we know the Hon. Mr. Howe's weak point ... But the men we have now to deal with neither respect him nor us for such forbearance."[46] In the end the evidence was such that Howe willingly conceded that Stewart had "improperly possessed himself of a large sum of public money." Only in the case of J.W. Johnston was Howe unrelenting. A decade of confrontation between the two men had convinced Howe that his opponent was a pious hypocrite and Johnston's refusal to give up the office of queen's advocate and proctor in the Court of Vice-Admiralty when he resigned the attorney generalship only reinforced that opinion. Reflecting Howe's views, Harvey told Grey that the provincial government could no longer tolerate Johnston's clinging to an office "never before retained by the acknowledged Leader of the Opposition."[47] But it took two letters and a definite order from Grey before Johnston finally relinquished it.

In dealing with the smaller nonpolitical offices, Howe was no less adamant that Nova Scotia should be a model for other colonies to follow. Despite the demands of a Liberal from Bridgetown, he refused to drive his opponents off the School Board: "if you [were] ...

my brother I would not permit your interests to weigh [a] feather against a trust so sacred as I believe our public school system to be."[48] He told another Liberal from Annapolis that he was less frightened of Tories than of Reformers who wanted to make him commit acts of petty tyranny and injustice: "I for one will retire from public life rather than be, to any portion of my country men an instrument of repression. I care not what the Tories did to you ... I will do nothing which I cannot justify as a gentleman and a man of honor. The way to loose [sic] power is to abuse it, & the sooner our friends understand this the better."[49] When an old friend complained that the Liberal members from Digby, the Acadians Bourneuf and Comeau, were "intriguing" on behalf of their compatriots, Howe replied it would not have been surprising if, used to being treated as the conquered and the powerless, they exhibited "some of the vices which that false position is so apt to engender." But members "more honest, fair minded and ... [less] disposed to bargain or intrigue than the French members from Richmond, Argyle and Clare I never met in public life."[50] Howe conceded even less to the Liberal member for Sydney county, W.A. Henry, who, as private member or executive councillor, Liberal or Conservative, would harass all governments with his self-seeking proclivities until he was appointed to the Supreme Court of Canada in 1875. After Henry complained that his nomination as registrar of probate had not been honoured, Howe pointed out that he had recommended no one when first requested and had later proposed a Protestant in a largely Catholic county where Catholics held nothing but a few minor offices.[51]

More regretfully, Howe dealt with Dr Slocumb, his ally in organizing the electoral victory in Lunenburg which had made responsible government possible. When Slocumb complained that he was being treated as if he were a member of "a powerless political minority," Howe replied that the government had done everything he had requested but dismiss one office-holder out of hand. "If you, or anyone else, supposed that responsible government was to mean ... that the *Members responsible to a single County* were to [compel] those who are responsible *to the whole Legislature*, to do acts which they could justify upon no principle recognized in ... British communities, all I can say is that I never so understood it." Did Slocumb not realize the blessings that a Reform government had conferred on the Liberals of Lunenburg: the nomination of road commissioners; a working majority in the Sessions and hence control over municipal affairs; an appeal to a Liberal council in questions of entitlement to Crown lands; and the dismissal of jobbing magistrates who had oppressed the county for years? What good would it do, therefore, to "set an example of distrust and opposition which must certainly be productive of injurious consequences"?[52]

The divisive effects of the power to make appointments were revealed in the disgruntlement of the *Acadian Recorder*, long a supporter of the Reform cause. In April 1848, almost from the blue, it reminded the Uniacke administration that, just as Guizot's government in France had been "humbled and checked, in a moment," so it too might suffer a similar fate for making "such 'a pretty kettle of fish' of the Tariff" and for depriving hundreds of people of their livelihood.[53] Since the only substantive change in the tariff had been to remove the duty on flour and since John English, the editor of the *Recorder*, had never been known as a protectionist, the letter-writer "*Civis*" attributed his dissatisfaction to his not having been made Queen's printer.[54] Although English denied that he objected to Thompson's appointment, he let the cat out of the bag by indicating his dislike of the clandestine arrangements by which Annand (and his partner Howe?) of the *Novascotian* and Nugent and Ritchie of the *Sun* were supposedly sharing in the emoluments of the office.[55] When he continued to snipe at the government, another letter-writer suggested he "wanted office ... thought to bully the Government into giving it – and hence the threatened attitude and subdued thunder of the *Recorder*."[56] No wonder that Howe regarded the appointing power as the least pleasant of his official duties.

The year 1848 having been a poor one economically for Nova Scotia, the Tories were quick to blame an inadequate tariff policy when the session of 1849 opened. For their criticisms Howe had ready answers. "How was it possible that we should not feel the mighty crisis which overthrew thousands of wealthy firms in Europe!" Was it not all to the good that a few young Nova Scotians had sought their fortunes abroad? Would they not "get the rough corners knocked off them, and come back with wiser heads and some money in their pockets – satisfied that the country they had left is one of the most favored in the world."[57] Almost the first order of government business was to meet the colonial secretary's demands for an address to sustain the departmental bill. This year the opposition's attack centred on the lack of checks in the new order that the Reformers were introducing. Scornfully, Howe asked the Tories to name nine men who, with all the powers of executive councillors, would "dare to do acts of gross injustice. I would not require even what Sheridan asked for, the freedom of the Press, to expel them from power." When Johnston called the bill dangerous because it united the executive and legislative powers, Howe showed that they had been united for half a century in such a way as to produce a perpetual struggle between the governing and the governed. But "now we have [a different kind of] union, an Executive acting in harmony with the Legislature – and a Legislature expressing the well understood wishes of the people."[58]

The departmental bill address having been adopted by a straight party vote, the Reformers proceeded with a new version of the civil list bill. In response to Grey's demands, it reduced the governor's salary to £3,000, maintained the salaries of the senior judges, and, with two exceptions,[59] paid the arrears in salaries to date. One thing made Howe very uneasy. He who had always demanded the tabling of the colonial secretary's dispatches in full had no choice but to delete Grey's thinly veiled criticism of Harvey. But the Tories made his task easier by their direct attacks on Harvey and the office of lieutenant-governor. Johnston argued principally that, since the governor had become "the mere mouth piece of his advisers," ready to do the bidding of men desirous only of advancing themselves in office, he need no longer be "a man of high principle and inflexible integrity," and accordingly his salary could be substantially reduced.[60] The slurs, direct and indirect, on Harvey aroused Howe as nothing else during the session of 1849. Johnston, he said, would have paid a previous governor, Sir Colin Campbell, anything for trampling on the people's rights, violating the royal instructions, and ruling through a small minority, "but when we are dealing with a Governor who has given us, and rules by, the principle of Responsible Government – oh! then is the time for retrenchment." Could Johnston really believe that the governor was his own man in the days of irresponsibility when his council could control and even insult him, and that Harvey, who was not in the power of any man, was a servile?[61] But nothing he did or said would arrest the beginnings of a nasty campaign against Harvey and his family.

Successful in the assembly with the civil list and departmental bills, Howe and his colleagues thought they had hurdled their last parliamentary obstacle. Having appointed a Reformer, William McKeen of Inverness County, in place of S.B. Robie, they seemed assured of the support of eleven of the twenty-one legislative councillors. But a snowstorm, "unexampled ... for half a century," prevented McKeen from crossing the Strait of Canso and reaching Halifax on time. Taking advantage of his absence, the Tory councillors proposed an address which, in Grey's very words, declared the departmental bill to be prejudicial to the interests of the province and unjust to Fairbanks. Wednesday, the 14th of February, turned out to be the most exciting day in the entire history of the council. Beating down every attempt to adjourn the debate while refusing to participate in it themselves, the

Tory councillors, "the intellectual and eloquent Bishop, the wily Almon, the fraternal Fairbanks, and half-a-dozen others, determined to carry the question not by force of argument, but by dead weight."[62] In the end, to stave off defeat, the Liberal president, Michael Tobin, followed the practice of the lord chancellor in the House of Lords, never before adopted in Nova Scotia, of voting like other councillors. The result was a tie and the defeat of the Tories' address. Although their outrage knew no bounds, the *Novascotian* gloated that they had got their just desserts, "caught in their own toils – tripped up in the very moment of victory – the laughing stock of the City, the Assembly, and the Government."[63] Howe may, or may not, have devised the tactic, but it was he who decided to wait no longer for McKeen and proposed that a friend of twenty years, Dr William Grigor, take his place. So, after 21 February, the Tory councillors had no hope of blocking the institutionalization of responsible government by the use of the nonelective chamber.

In 1849 the Reformers took only one other step to adapt the governmental machinery to their point of view, a change in the appointment of sheriffs. Hitherto the chief justice had nominated three persons in each county from whom the Executive Council chose one. To Howe it had always seemed that the chief justice's knowledge of suitable nominees was limited to members of local Tory compacts. The new procedure placed the right to nominate three persons in the chief justice, one puisne judge, and two executive councillors, and empowered the entire Executive Council to make the final choice. Johnston, whose political philosophy permitted him to regard the compacts as a natural, gifted, unpolitical elite, argued once again that the change would make sheriffs political and "place the liberties of the people altogether in the power of the Executive."[64] Howe said simply that the matter had been "settled upon in the spirit of mutual compromise of a vexed question – both parties giving way a little; and we had better pass it as it is." Once more he pointed out that the making of appointments, instead of strengthening a government, was "the most unpopular function it can exercise ... If you have one office to bestow, there are sure to be thirty applicants, and while you please one, the twenty-nine others are sure to be down upon your backs."[65]

As usual, Howe participated in a miscellany of debates in 1849, especially in those on legal matters. He spoke with zest on proposals to remedy the inconvenience and costliness of the Chancery Court. Long a Chancery reformer, he found it "a most refreshing thing ... to see one's old opinions again brought forward" and he described the debate as "one of the most delightful days, he ... had ever spent in the house."[66] Likewise he strongly supported a consolidation of the provincial statutes. Since almost every law could be reduced to half its size and made twice as effective, he wondered if the example of the old Italian printers should not be followed and if "some of our laws should [not] be hung up outside the Provincial Building, and a reward offered ... for the best and smallest Act upon the subject that could be procured."[67]

For Howe the session produced near-disaster on an old bugaboo, the public support of sectarian colleges. Intending to put all the denominations on an equal footing, W.A. Henry sought to repeal the longstanding act which made an annual grant of £444 to King's College in perpetuity. Immediately Howe's political friends adopted their stances of earlier years. Herbert Huntington insisted that the claims of public schools and poor children should be put ahead of colleges, while the Youngs regarded the bill as a first step towards establishing a single nondenominational college in Halifax. To all of them Howe the pragmatist read a lecture on the facts of life. The existing colleges, he was certain, could not be swept away by legislative fiat: "withdraw your public money, [and] there will be more socks and mittins knit on the hills of Wilmot – more tubs of butter made – more fat calves killed – and more missionary travellers sent through the country – and Acadia college will stand on the hill side in spite of the withdrawal of our grant."[68] What outraged Huntington and the Youngs most of all was the positive things Howe had to say about denominational colleges. Each of them, he contended, had done at least £200 worth of good annually to the country. If Dalhousie did not get into operation, he would have to send his son to King's or Acadia, but "I am not so afraid of denominational influence – better that he should change his religion rather than that he should grow up in ignorance."[69] Although Howe helped carry Henry's bill in a division largely along party lines, he was not acting inconsistently since he regarded it as only a first step towards putting all the colleges in the same position. He was still adamant that he would "go with no party and man to destroy [the existing colleges], unless some scheme be proposed to give the country a system of education in the higher branches"; further, he could not "see the sense of nailing colours to the mast, and having a fight over the ashes of former debates – and all about nothing."[70]

The vote in the assembly did not end the matter. In the council Rudolf joined his bishop, along with Howe's friend, Dr Grigor, a Liberal but also a churchman, to turn down the bill by twelve to nine. Not unexpectedly, the *British Colonist* perceived a deeply laid plot. Allegedly the leading Reformers, almost relishing the Young's discomfiture, and fearful that Uniacke, a strong supporter of King's, might resign, arranged the bill's defeat. Thus "Uniacke's services are preserved – Howe's consistency is unimpeached, – the Youngs are disappointed, – and Henry may attend the lecture on hydrostatics in the new College, in the capacity of spoon."[71] Partly because of the internal divisions on colleges, partly because of bad times, some Liberal sympathizers worried about the party's prospects. Thinking that the Baptists were beginning to realize that they had been placed in a false position on colleges, Thomas Trotter, the Presbyterian minister in Antigonish, wondered if they might relent if a professorship at Dalhousie was offered to Professor Edmund Crawley of Acadia, who had earlier engaged in bitter controversy with Howe. The latter was noncommittal when Trotter offered to approach Crawley, but agreed that the speeches in the assembly were "droll enough," especially since they seemed designed to "leave the existing Colleges without grants and to *have no other*. This seemed to me to be madness, and I was nearly devoured for saying so." Sadly Howe recognized that many Liberals did not appreciate that patience, forbearance, and prudence were needed to conduct an administration; their "ability to knock things into a mess, is undoubted, but [their] skill to reconstruct, combine, and lead successfully is not quite so apparent."[72]

According to the *British Colonist*, the disagreement on colleges and other matters led to an incident in the assembly on March 16 in which Herbert Huntington, the Robert Baldwin of Nova Scotia and executive councillor without office, applied to Howe "the lowest and most opprobrious of the epithets among the inhabitants of Billingsgate" and struck him sharply across the face.[73] Though the incident was probably exaggerated, it might have had serious consequences if it had led to Huntington's refusal of the financial secretaryship. In April Grey confirmed the departmental bill and made it possible for the Reformers at long last to construct the Executive Council they wanted. Then, in the very blush of victory, came word that, because of impaired health and family considerations, Huntington would not take an office especially suited to his training, experience, and abilities. For Howe the prospect was almost too awful to contemplate. Obviously a financial secretary should sit in the lower House, but a suitable assemblyman was a *rara avis*, to say the least. The Speaker William Young had the required qualifications, but wanted something more to lure him from his lucrative law practice. Both literally and figuratively, the Yarmouth shipbuilder and shipowner Thomas Killam had too many ships at sea. Henry Mott, Samuel Creelman, W.A. Henry, E.L. Brown, and Henry Mignowitz had neither the knowledge nor the experience to explain budgets or the principles of political economy. "Fancy either of the five representing the Government in Committee of Supply and Ways and Means, which occupy half the Session, and in which questions may be started every hour to bother and expose an officer generally understood to be incompetent." So, if Huntington persisted in his refusal, the ministry might have to ask a Tory like James Dewolf Fraser of Windsor or the dismissed provincial treasurer, S.P. Fairbanks, to take the office and thereby risk dissension among its followers. On the other hand, if Huntington changed his mind, "our organization is complete, the offices efficiently filled, the Government strong and secure until 1852, and then, by good management, we can give the Tories another licking."[74] Unable to resist this plea, Huntington became financial secretary in mid-June. In form and membership the Executive Council was finally the instrument Howe wanted it to be.

The Nova Scotia Tory establishment, like entrenched ones elsewhere, did not give up its dominance without violent acrimony. Because the *Times* and the *Post* were collapsing during 1848, the Tories established the *British Colonist* to present their point of view. By March 1849, after only nine months of existence, its circulation had reached 3,000. Typically, it applied Shaftesbury's description of British governments after Charles I to the Reform administration of Nova Scotia: "They all fell to the prey ... endeavored only the enlargement of their own authority, and *grasped at those very powers they had complained of so much.*"[75] Upon Howe, whom the *Colonist* considered its chief opponent, it levelled the very charges that the *Times* and the *Pictou Observer* had made earlier. "The great champion," it said, was practising "the same dirty wit, – the same fondness for creating a school-boy laugh at the expense of decency ... that has ever characterized him."[76] When Johnston complained that Nova Scotia would be ruined by free trade, Howe said he reminded him of "the boarding-school Miss," who returned from a party with her dress soiled. "'Why', said her mistress, 'you'll be ruined.' 'Oh, very well!,' replied the girl, 'I'd like to be ruined that way every night.'"[77] Fancy, lamented the *Colonist*, "a Sir Robert Peel, or Lord John Russell, or a D'Israeli, or a Macaulay, venting such jokes upon the English parliament ... Could [Uniacke] drink at the same foul waters and his mouth remain clean?"[78]

The *Colonist* took greatest umbrage of all at Howe's supposed authorship of the editorials which the *Novascotian* ran following Lord Elgin's signing of the rebellion losses bill and the burning of the Parliament Buildings by the Canadian extremists. "Toryism is

Toryism all the world over," the editorials proclaimed, and the Canadian Tories were simply "disappointed at not being allowed to indulge with impunity in the innocent recreation of arson and murder."[79] Why, replied the *Colonist*, should the English party in Canada not resist Lord Elgin, "the traitorous representative of British majesty"? Why should it "suffer treason to be rewarded as a virtue" or "submit to French domination"? Could any other reaction have been expected from the Liberal press in Nova Scotia whose leader was Howe, "the former friend and correspondent of the rebels?" Perhaps he should send in a claim for indemnification under the rebellion losses bill: "For loss of character on account of having been discovered corresponding with armed rebels – one farthing."[80]

Early in May 1849 Howe addressed a letter to George Moffatt, the president of the British American League and a leading Canadian extremist, which, he said, "set everybody laughing at the league" and was "one of his happiest productions."[81] Could Moffatt not see "something truly original in [the] mode of doing things in Canada?" In England the queen was never pelted; in the United States the president could exercise his veto power without fear of personal outrage; in Nova Scotia even the most unpopular governor "strolled through the streets unattended, at all hours, in periods of the highest political excitement." Surely Moffatt should realize, if he wished Nova Scotians to become part of a British North American confederation, that the Montreal mob ought not to "steal the mace and burn the records." Nor would Nova Scotians be party to a confederation that sought to swamp and anglify the French Canadians by a species of injustice. "We have no desire to form part of a nation, with a helot and inferior race within its bosom ... [We] will never ... consent that a Frenchman on the Richelieu shall have an inferior status to that which is enjoyed by a Frenchman in Arichat or Clare."

In private letters Howe told more moderate Canadians that judicious Nova Scotians of all parties regarded the incendiaries of Montreal as "barbarians" and that "whenever there appears a chance of doing good by rushing into print," he would use his pen to help maintain the British connection.[82] He paid no attention at all to "A Nova Scotian Conservative" who told Moffatt that the writer addressing him was Joseph Howe, "the correspondent and favorer of the French rebels of '37," who knew all the arguments that justified rebellion, or to the *Colonist*, which offered a shilling to anyone who could supply a copy of the "extra" allegedly published by Howe during the Rebellion of 1837 under the heading, "Glorious News – Success of the Patriots!"[83] Why deign to notice anyone so preposterous as to suggest that he sympathized with rebels!

Nearer home his close relations with Sir John Harvey and his family brought him unwanted publicity. A year earlier he had sought unsuccessfully to prevent a brawl involving Harvey's son Frank and later accompanied him to the police station for questioning. Imprudently, out of loyalty to Sir John, he also defended Frank in the *Novascotian*, stating that the worst of his escapades bore but a faint resemblance to those of a wild young sailor, a British prince, "whose social exploits in Halifax, leave Mr. Harvey's quite in the shade!," but who later, as King William iv, "lived ... in the hearts of the people he governed."[84] Not content to rest on his laurels, Frank Harvey later found himself enmeshed in even greater difficulties and with no little delight "A Nova Scotian Conservative" reported him "lying on his bed from the effects of a well merited pounding," and helped by Howe, "busily engaged in imploring an outraged woman not to bring her case before the tribunal of justice."[85]

Other relations of Howe with the governor also invited the bitter comments of those who had never accepted the lessened status that political defeat had brought them. No language, they said, could describe "the tone of breeding at Government House since Mr. Howe and his tail became the principal performers there"; perhaps, when it was "cleared of its present inmates ... society may be purified."[86] Much more significant was the charge that, through Harvey, Howe was being permitted to defile the governmental institutions, especially the magistracy. As was customary every seven or eight years, the Reform administration had issued a new commission of the peace in November 1848 and the immediate reaction, first from former justices of the peace who had been excluded, later from Johnston and the Tories, was violent. In his defence Harvey told Grey that the commission contained much of the "wealth, respectability and intelligence of the province, hitherto systematically excluded," and that most of the persons omitted were either "dead, incompetent, litigious or intemperate."[87] The colonial secretary would have none of it and again adopted an unusually hard line. From the tone of Harvey's dispatches Grey feared that he did not even apprehend that a principal function of a governor was not to let the authority of the Crown be used for party purposes. If, as he suggested, the changes had been politically motivated, he would have to advise the queen to "visit [Harvey's] conduct with her marked disapprobation."[88]

Again Howe was Harvey's chief defendant, but this time he found the role quite uncomfortable. Apparently the provincial secretary's office had had little to do with the preparation of the commission and in private he referred with distaste to the "miserable apology ... [he] was driven to make for the Magisterial lists."[89] In the assembly he contented himself with "a good humored address [that] endeavoured to restore harmony to the debate,"[90] but in defending Harvey he pulled out all the stops in aid of one who was deteriorating in body, energy, and perhaps mind. Certainly Harvey's major dispatch to Grey in his own defence sounds like Howe and is full of the kind of data that Howe would have amassed. Could any governor, it asked, have ensured that Grey's principles were observed in general, much less in detail, in a commission that included more than 500 persons spread along 1,500 miles of by-roads? Even so, in twelve of seventeen counties they were strictly followed in all but a few instances, while in the five others, where the majority of the population had been systematically excluded by "a dominant party that had never been dislodged," action was clearly required to reduce the overwhelming preponderance of Tory magistrates.

The language of Howe is also manifested in Harvey's lament that Grey's instructions were sometimes conveyed in terms "less than grateful to the feelings of an old servant of the crown," and in his hope that he would be acquitted of permitting the authority of the Crown to be abused or of weakly surrendering his authority.[91] Bizarre as it seems, Grey realized only after fourteen months of letter-writing that the justices of the peace performed county business of an administrative nature in addition to their magisterial functions. Relenting a little, he agreed that this business might legitimately be placed in the hands of persons whose political views were those of the majority of the inhabitants. But could it not best be done by transferring the magistrates' administrative duties to representative bodies like the district councils of Upper Canada?[92] Shortly Howe would try his hand at creating such machinery for Halifax county.

For a day or two in June political strife was forgotten on the occasion of Halifax's one hundredth anniversary. Even the *Colonist* agreed that the celebration was "unbroken and unrivalled [with] not a pane of glass ... broken in rudeness or anger"; like others, it delighted in an extraordinary display at Province House, especially "a device of gaslight [which] spun around with amazing velocity and very pleasing effect."[93] Except for this respite, however, the Tories seldom let up in their denunciation of Harvey and Howe for their part in the institutionalization of responsible government. When Harvey amused his parties with "a very pretty toy," the magic lantern, the *Colonist* told him it was "watching the magic lantern of Government" and warned him to act as "master and principal exhibitor, not as the shadow on the wall"; when it was criticized for its attacks on the governor, the paper took aim at Howe, stating that it had never called Harvey a "fusbos" or "fool," written a "song of the shirt," or held up to scorn his private foibles.[94] When the *Novascotian* and the *Chronicle* published editorials, perhaps written by Howe, boasting that the savings under responsible government would in eleven years extinguish the provincial debt, and in thirty-five years build the railway to Windsor, they drove the *Colonist* into a paroxysm of anger. Imagine such nonsense coming from Howe who had earlier seized the collectorship of excise with "all the eagerness and avidity of a vulture" and strained "the law ... to pocket every possible fraction of the people's money."[95]

J.W. Johnston and the *Colonist* had become convinced that the magistrates' affair was simply the last of a series of incidents illustrating how "a corrupt and unscrupulous Government" had defiled "the most sacred interest of society." As a result, Johnston warned that Nova Scotians might be driven to seek "some constitution better balanced and protected" and in the process endanger the connection between themselves and Britain.[96] Warned that the doctrine of resistance might be carried too far, the *Colonist* replied that the real rebels were the Whig government of Britain and Sir John Harvey, who had wantonly violated the royal instructions by dismissing magistrates and by putting a "catspaw" in the Legislative Council when it was full.[97] Johnston was as good as his word. Able to get only a few magistrates reinstated, he began to promote "a well regulated system of democratic institutions" supposedly designed to counteract the ills of an unchecked oligarchy implanted by responsible government. So, like it or not, Howe had no choice during the next seven years but to take stands on Tory initiatives involving such democratic, un-Tory devices as universal suffrage, an elective Legislative Council, and elective municipal institutions.

## CHAPTER TWO

# Above the Muddy Pool
# of Politics

Two years of institutionalizing responsible government were enough for Howe and he was impatient to turn to something more challenging and innovative. For a time in 1850, however, it appeared as if he would be condemned to the pettiness and trials of parochial politics. At long last the Reformers were in a position to make the county registrars of deeds principals in their own right, since Sir Rupert George, wishing to live permanently in England, was prepared to give up the provincial registrarship if he could be satisfied with respect to compensation. Yet, when Howe proposed an annual pension of £300 cy (£240 stg), he could not carry it and had to settle for one of £200 cy which the Liberal backbencher W.A. Henry proposed. Imagine, fumed the outraged Tories, "a member of the Government moving the required sum in the house, and his *majority deserting* him, and refusing to carry out the pledge and promise made by the Government ... There is Responsible Government for you with a vengeance."[1] A chagrined Howe could only say that the government had no responsibility in a question so long debated, nor could it ask its supporters to vote more than their consciences would permit.[2]

That lesson was not enough for Howe who, thoroughly his father's son in this respect, always felt sorry for anyone whom he had helped to deprive of office. But when he moved to grant the deposed provincial treasurer, S.P. Fairbanks, a lump sum of £150 for past services, he had to look on as the ubiquitous Henry, supported largely by Tories, got the House to vote the lesser sum of £100. Even that amount raised the ire of Howe's friend, Richard Nugent of the *Sun*: "Nothing like magnanimity! 'Save your enemies – provide for those who hate you' – that's christian policy, no doubt. We wish that the wisdom of it may *be made apparent*."[3] Howe was learning the hard way that although the government backbenchers would accept without question the major bills effecting responsible government, they could not be counted upon to support less consequential ministerial measures, particularly if they involved a drain on the public purse. Clearly the new order would not erode overnight the deeply ingrained particularism of the Nova Scotia Assembly. It would take another two or three decades before anything like the discipline of the modern House would evolve and until then even a Joseph Howe would have to accept the facts of life.

That he did accept them became clear during debate on a bill which he euphemistically called "an act to aid education," but which did little more than provide for a superintendent of education to administer the educational system. No one complained that it failed to regulate colleges since, in Howe's words, no government could do it "without ... tumbling to pieces in a single hour." He was hard put, however, to defend the absence of provisions for the support of public schools through compulsory taxation, something he had long favoured. All he could say in defence was that "a premature movement" might be "fatal to its ultimate success," that if it were forced on the people before they were ready for it, it might be overturned by the next assembly.[4] Not surprisingly, the *British Colonist* told him that if assessment was the proper course, "it should have been adopted in spite of any consideration whatever ... patriots should have a higher aim [than] to retain office and salary."[5] Johnston, ever obsessed with the supposed evils of an executive oligarchy under responsible government, was mainly concerned with that clause of the bill which permitted the governor in council to appoint school commissioners during pleasure; could these officials, he wondered, be displaced as readily as the magistrates and the road commissioners? These insinuations did not sit well with Howe, who had resisted the introduction of a spoils system for two years. Pointing out that under the existing act the government might have removed school commissioners as it willed, Howe pleaded with Johnston not to make education "the battle ground of party,"[6] but he might as well have saved his breath.

Even more frustrating to Howe was the debate on colleges. Once, he said, there was "a freshness about the ... question – which made it all exciting and interesting ... [now] were we to talk about it for a week, not a single vote would be altered"; should the House therefore not divide upon it at once?[7] But he could not prevent the prolonged wrangling which represented nothing so much as "a swarm of *woolly-headed musquitoes* of a summer evening, buzzing and fluttering – crossing and recrossing – now ascending – now descending."[8] Because long experience in the assembly had led him to "take a practical turn," he again suggested that the existing colleges – certain to defy all attempts to eliminate them – should be encouraged for the convenience of people in their localities. In the end he combined his proposal to place £1,200 at the disposal of the Executive Council for allocation to the colleges with Henry's bill repealing the permanent grant to King's College, so that the Legislative Council would have to "take the Bill, the *whole* Bill, and nothing but the Bill."[9] Not surprisingly, it sacrificed the other institutions to protect the interests of King's College.

In two minor measures at least Howe had his way in 1850. Following Lord Grey's suggestion that Nova Scotia establish institutions similar to the district councils of Canada West, he proposed to divide Halifax county into townships, in each of which five elected officials, a warden and four councillors, would assume both the administrative and the judicial functions of the justices of the peace. Grey was told that, if approved for Halifax county, the measure would likely be extended to the other counties and thereby confer upon all Nova Scotians "the enlarged principles" he intended them to enjoy.[10] Howe was certain that his bill would "train our people to habits of business, and give them a vigilant oversight and control over their own affairs";[11] Johnston, always ready to reduce the power of the provincial executive under the new order, added his blessing; and both Houses quickly approved a measure that did not impose a financial burden. But it was soon to be dealt a mortal blow from an unexpected quarter. Although Grey never explained how one of his predecessors could have approved similar provisions for Halifax city, he objected strongly to the election on a short-term basis of judicial officials who would be "subject to influence from the popular feeling" in performing their magisterial duties.[12] Nova Scotians on the spot, who deemed a system with a dual system of magistrates too cumbersome, declined to go along with him.

Howe's second success, the most eye-catching of the session, was a "free trade in law" bill, which euphemistically authorized Her Majesty's subjects to "plead and reason for themselves or others in all Her Majesty's Courts." Charged with pursuing his long standing dislike of the legal profession, he replied that "all such feeling has long since passed away." Yet in his three speeches he showed an unmistakable suspicion of lawyers, none of whom, he said, had ever gone to jail, although he knew fifty cases where they had kept clients out of their money. More positively, he wanted the bill passed because "all monopolies are bad." When Johnston presented the opposing case for a division of labour in society, Howe denied that there was "somewhat mysterious in the law" which required special training. If there were mysteries, how had they been revealed to Chief Justice Halliburton, who had "stepped out of the ranks of the army [and] devoted but a short time to the study of law," and whose books might have been "carried on a wheelbarrow when he was elevated to the bench"? Had not he himself, after only three weeks of studying the law of libel, had his law "accepted as sound," whereas that of "the bar and of the judges too was voted absurd by the jury." If any blockhead could go into the pulpit and "dispose not of our estates but of our souls," why could ordinary persons not go into court to seek the restitution of a poor widow's rights.[13]

When Johnston argued that only a lawyer could handle complex forms, Howe replied that he knew half a dozen lawyers who were "hardly a grade above the idiot or fit to herd geese upon a common." Being read in the law did not matter most in any case. "It is the grappling and grasping what a man does read that benefits him."[14] Somewhat preposterously, the *British Colonist* called Howe's bill a device to feather his own nest, suggesting that when, like all unjust stewards, he had to give up his office, he would have "something to fall back upon – for dig he cannot, and to beg any more perchance he may be ashamed."[15] Although Howe clearly knew that his arguments were exaggerated and some of his logic unsound, he could not resist taunting the lawyers. Most of all, however, he was determined to make the point that the deprived members of society ought not to be left to the mercies of the legal profession. In the freest of free votes the non-lawyers in the assembly, Tories and Liberals alike, responded positively to his populist demagoguery and passed his bill by twenty-eight to sixteen.

Although annoyed by it, Howe had at least been forewarned of the Conservatives' intention to make a concerted attack on the power of the executive under responsible government. Johnston began in a minor way by lambasting the government for permitting hay to be imported free of duty during a time of shortage; would this infringement of the law, he wondered, set a precedent for more serious violations? Howe replied simply that just "as Nelson destroyed orders when a hostile fleet was before him and ... thus stamped immortality on his name – so the government that would see the cattle of the peasantry starving by the road-side, were not fit to hold the reins of government, if they would not rather suspend a law than evade responsibility." The somewhat humourless Johnston must have seethed inwardly as a jocose Howe went on to suggest that, if the government fell on this action, every half-starved horse, cow, and yearling would "groan with hearty condolences ... just at a moment when they thought they had got into clover."[16]

Johnston continued his attack in more general terms with a long set of resolutions, headed, according to Howe, by a "tiresome preamble; so like a pony led by a halter a hundred yards long."[17] Yet their purport was clear enough: because the colonial secretary and the lieutenant-governor had surrendered their functions to the colonial executive, they could never be looked upon as "legitimate elements" in the colonial constitution, and because the Legislative Council had become a packed body, it had to be either subservient or obstructive to the government of the day. Hence, if the constitution were not adapted to the new situation, the next step might be the direct election of all the chief public functionaries, and failing that, "by irresistible attraction ... absorption into the Great Republic that beside us throws wide its arms."[18]

Once again Howe boasted of the new constitution that "the vigour and intelligence of the British colonists ... wrested ... step by step, against the prejudices and apprehension of various Secretaries from 1837 to 1847." Did Johnston not see that a busy colonial secretary could not possibly "pass upon the dismissal of every drunken or incompetent magistrate, ... every question of salary or appointment to office"? Did he not understand that Sir John Harvey stood in the same relation to his Executive Council as the queen did to the British government? Denying any charge of inconsistency, Howe emphasized he had never wanted both a responsible executive and an elective council. "We asked for either of these; we got the one we preferred ... [one] might as well attempt to stick a dog's tail on a lion's back as engraft an elective Legislative Council on responsible government."[19] Although the Reform majority was adamant against disturbing the province's institutions, Howe was dissatisfied both with his speech and with the debate as a whole. Perhaps he would have agreed with the *Acadian Recorder* that if he and Johnston had given such prolix orations in the Commons, they would have heard "the crowing of cocks – the bleating of lambs – the mowing of cats – a volley of coughs, or a battalion of sneezes."[20] For him it was altogether disheartening to have to maintain the party struggle at a high pitch simply to fight all over again the battles of responsible government.

With undisguised relief he turned to the arranging of new commercial relations with the United States. Even an Anglophile like Johnston was appalled by the repeal of the Navigation Acts and the elimination of the protective system within the empire: without keeping "any lever ... to enforce the admission of our coal, or the production of our fisheries ... Great Britain has swept away the old system and introduced a new [one] ... without enquiring whether or not we should be ruined by the change."[21] To devise a united front for dealing with common difficulties, an intercolonial conference was held at Halifax in September 1849, with Louis-Hippolyte La Fontaine as chairman and Howe as secretary; it asked that the British government negotiate the reciprocal exchange of natural products with the United States and that the colonial legislatures remove all duties on intercolonial trade in these products.[22] The provincial press quickly divided along party lines. To the *Novascotian* "colonial protection has been a curse to the parent country, and not less the bane of her offspring," while the *British Colonist*, certain that protective tariffs had worked well in the United States, expected them to have equally beneficial results in Nova Scotia.[23] Obtaining authorization from the legislature to admit, by proclamation, the natural products of the other colonies free of duty, the government quickly exercised this power except in the case of flour on which, to Howe's regret, a duty needed to be retained for revenue purposes in a time of financial difficulties. He took care to assure one Canadian, however, that "we are here such lovers of free trade that we shall get rid of our own duty the moment it can be spared."[24]

On the need for new trading relations with the United States, Tories and Liberals were agreed, but they differed markedly on the tactics of bargaining. Their highest hopes were that the province's agricultural produce, fish, lumber, coal, iron, and plaster might be admitted free of duty and that its vessels might participate in the American coasting trade and enjoy the privileges of registry in the United States. In return Nova Scotia would offer reciprocal advantages and, more importantly, participation in its coastal fisheries. When Johnston demanded that any concessions by Nova Scotians be matched by the Americans, Howe took strong exception. "I believe ... that a liberal strait forward course of conduct from one people towards another always produces corresponding results."[25] Hence, when Johnston moved that coasting trade privileges should only be granted reciprocally, Howe called for the unconditional opening of Nova Scotia's ports to the Americans: "I have not the least apprehension that American competition will injure us";[26] in all likelihood they would respond to Nova Scotia's overture and open their own coastal trade. Johnston's first proposal being defeated, he next moved that Nova Scotia give up its fisheries only for broad concessions. Again Howe would have none of it. Imagine the effect if someone could rise in Congress and say: "why here is little Nova Scotia ... throwing open ... their fisheries also – and why should we any longer retain those old absurd restrictions." In any case the province would not be ruined by that act of generosity. "Why, hang it, if they only left us the clams and muscles round our shores, they would be found sufficient to maintain our people for years."[27]

Denying that such a course would leave Nova Scotians without the wherewithal to buy the implements needed to dig clams and mussels,[28] Howe got the legislature to adopt his views in exactly the form he wanted. To a Canadian he boasted that Nova Scotia had redeemed all its pledges at the intercolonial conference and, in addition, "thrown our Fisheries into the scale" to strengthen the hands of any negotiators with the Americans.[29] As usual, he denounced those Tories who considered Nova Scotians too impoverished to stand on their own feet. "I would not hesitate to back the rich marsh lands of Kings against [American agricultural land] any day" and "I will venture to affirm that the little City of Halifax will turn out as many well dressed men and women, with money ... to spend ... as any town in the Union."[30]

The most jarring note in Nova Scotia's relations with the United States was injected by William Young who, on a visit to Washington in June 1850, assumed the right to act unofficially for Nova Scotia and brought back word that the United States would grant little of what Nova Scotia wanted in a trade agreement.[31] In council Howe spoke in acerbic terms of the impropriety of Young's conduct, but to prevent the party's dirty linen from being washed in public neither the proceedings nor the conclusions of the meeting were officially recorded. The council agreed, although just barely, to give up the fisheries for the limited type of reciprocity that Young thought was possible; consistently with his former position, Howe voted with the majority.[32]

Starting in 1849, public works had become Howe's primary interest. As one of five commissioners he helped supervise the building of a telegraph line from Halifax to the New Brunswick border at a cost of £31 a mile compared with £37 10s. in the sister province. By November 1849 it was completed at a total cost of £4,248 and Howe was delighted that private speculators had been prevented from establishing a monopoly at the public expense.[33] But it was through the building of railways that he hoped to elevate his countrymen's eyes and minds "from the little pedling muddy pool of politics ... to some thing more enobling, exalting and inspiring."[34] One of two commissioners appointed in 1848 to supervise the survey of a line from Halifax to Windsor, he secured estimates of £330,000 as the total cost of the project, £30,000 as the annual operating expenditures, and £31,865 as the initial annual revenues. With his usual optimism he suggested that by building the line as a government work the interest costs might be reduced to $3\frac{1}{2}$ or 4 per cent and the additional profit used to extend it as far as Granville. In 1849, however, his "little pet railroad" – he also called it "my poor bantling" – took second place to the line from Halifax to the St Lawrence. Early in the year businessmen in Halifax called on the legislature to provide the funds for Nova Scotia's share of the cost and proposed to pay one-fifth by a tax on the city's real estate. Howe took little part in the debate, partly because the matter was in capable hands. Although he realized that anyone who invested "his money in it, with the expectation of profit, would be mad," he voted for the railroad "because it will form a great back bone through these colonies ... a great Roman highway – a military road to bind these governments to each other, and the mother country."[35]

For almost a year no action was forthcoming largely – so the *British Colonist* said – because Earl Grey would "rather transport a cargo of felons to a Colony than do anything to advance its interests."[36] Hence, towards the close of the session of 1850, Howe proposed on his own initiative that the legislature revert to the Windsor line and advance all the funds to make it a reality. To clarify the principle that would guide his future conduct, he announced that he would press any ministry of which he was a member to "take the initiative ... in every noble enterprise; to be in advance of the social, political and industrial energies, which they have undertaken to lead." Ought not the assembly to "use the *credit* as well as the *capital* of Nova Scotia – to build what will make it more valuable in all time to come." He hoped that the day was dawning when candidates at an election would not be asked "to what party do you belong"? but "what great public improvement do you mean to advocate"? Surely men on the public stage ought to "move forward in advance of the times, and not trust too much to the position which they have acquired by past services."[37]

Once again the Youngs demonstrated that with friends like them Howe could not afford to have enemies. When they expressed fears about the cost, Howe wondered how they could have put their names on a prospectus for the same railway in 1845. "If it is speculative and uncertain, and will not pay now, it was ten times more so in 1845." Of what use was "this half friendship for a measure – which cuts its throat – a support which hampers more than it advances any great public work ... For God's sake, do not let us put this project aside now. All of us feel that the old subjects of debate here are worn out, and that we require new subjects on which to act and speak."[38] For all his pleading Howe could get the legislature to provide only half the money, none of it to be advanced until the remainder had been secured through other sources. The *Sun* (and probably Howe) blamed it on "the over-officious intermeddling of the Messrs. Youngs,"[39] but he was buoyed up, nonetheless, by a public meeting in Halifax on the 20th of April which called on the city to issue £100,000 of debentures for the railway, leaving only £65,000 to be secured elsewhere. With his usual enthusiasm he was certain that this sum "will prove as nothing" and that sixty-five men in the Windsor area were in a position to take it all.[40] As it turned out, less than £5,000 was forthcoming.

In July Grey flatly rejected an imperial guarantee for the Quebec railway, but by then the Nova Scotians were off on another tack. Late in the month Uniacke and Johnston attended a railway convention at Portland, Maine, which enthusiastically endorsed a third railway project, the European and North American Railway from Halifax to Portland. Although Howe would say later that he was deliberately denied an invitation, he was inevitably drawn into its aftermath. The Executive Council, aware of an "almost universal excitement" in its favour, concluded that if it took a negative position it might collapse internally. Accordingly Howe devised a resolution which was to be introduced at a public meeting on August 24 if Johnston showed his hand and supported the undertaking.[41] The cautious Johnston having committed himself, Howe had his chance. Pointing out that money for railways could not be secured through private subscription and that Nova Scotia could get no help from Maine or New Brunswick, whose resources were well below their promises at the Portland convention, he argued that the only hope for the project was to "place it in the hands of the government"; accordingly he moved that the meeting request the legislature to construct the portion of the line running through Nova Scotia. While mourning the loss of his dead bantling, the Windsor line, he could say, like the girl charged with bringing a baby into the world, "if a sin at all, it was *a very little one.*" Anticipating difficulties on two counts, he argued it would be madness to let private capitalists build the line when the government could borrow money at $2\frac{1}{2}$ per cent less and thereby save sufficient to pay for it in twenty-five years, and he begged the western county members to treat the question in an enlightened manner and to disregard the fact that Cumberland County, through which the line would pass, had only 18,000 people, while Hants, Kings, Annapolis, and Digby, with 46,000, would receive no direct benefit.[42]

By Howe's own account his speech had an "electrical" effect and "carried the public mind ... with him as if by magic."[43] It only remained for him to apologize to Harvey, recovering from an illness at Martock, for proceeding to such lengths without keeping him informed. But the state of the governor's health had caused him to abdicate much of his authority and his letter to Grey requesting a guarantee for "a thoroughfare of Nations" in times of peace and a work of vast importance in war was obviously written by Howe.[44] When the colonial secretary offered no encouragement, Harvey told him that at the request of his council he was sending a "well qualified" man, Joseph Howe, to arrange a loan of £800,000 stg from London capitalists with or without the British government's guarantee.[45] Howe's message to his constituents before leaving was that no party or government could live on past achievements and that he was responding to a cry in Nova Scotia for "further industrial development; active employment for the people; new and improved facilities for business and social intercourse."[46]

As he set out in the RMS *America* on November 1, he noted that his earlier accomplishments had resulted from "obedience to impulses which I could not control. Knowledge which I never acquired by study, flashed into my mind as if by inspiration ... Something of all this I hope and pray for now. The future is before me without a ray to indicate what it may be – but my trust [is] in Him, whose work in these matters I believe I am called upon to do."[47] By good fortune, when the *America* ran aground between Cork and Cape Clear, it chose a soft beach during a rising tide and it was off in three or four hours. Establishing himself at 5 Sloane Street in London, Howe got into immediate contact with his boon companion of an earlier trip, Major Robert Carmichael-Smyth, who for the next six months worked for him night and day, sympathized in his trials, and exulted in his triumphs, and was indeed, "*the only person I* [trusted] *with my whole plan of operations.*"[48]

During a dinner engagement at the Greys Howe assured the colonial secretary that he would take no unfair advantage of him and would show him draft copies of his official letters before making them public. Meanwhile, instructed by Grey to put his position in an official form, he wrote until his fingers ached. By November 25 he had prepared a letter of "60 foolscap pages," containing – so he thought – material "such as no Nova Scotian before ever ventured to place in the hands of a Cabinet minister."[49] Actually, if it was bold, it was only because it contained the germ of an idea which in a few weeks would dominate his thinking and writing. The North American colonies, he pointed out, lay "between two mighty nations, yet belong[ed] ... to neither." Americans attending the Portland conference could rise in Congress and present their case, while British Americans were shut out from "the national councils of [their] country," unable to raise their voices in the British Parliament and limited to employment in their own provinces. Were they not entitled, therefore, to have their claims dealt with "in a fair and even generous spirit"?[50]

Within three days Grey had described Howe's arguments as "'able and powerful' ... not faint praise, that, from such a quarter ... So far so well."[51] Then, on December 1, there burst upon Howe's mind the idea of making the railroad simply the base upon which to build a vigorous colonial policy which would include representation in Parliament by executive councillors from any colony operating under responsible government. "The idea original (one of the flashes) never heard it suggested at home or here ... Sweeps half the difficulties out of way. Grey & Palmerston jealous of each other. P's policy bold and takes with the Nation. Grey's should be broad, clear and bold, for his and our sakes."[52] Thus, in "chalking out for Grey" a bold new comprehensive policy, Howe was also pointing the way to improving the colonial secretary's competitive position in British domestic politics and at the same time making the loan look "like a small affair, a part only of a commanding National Scheme." For him it was "a great Card" which, "skilfully played, would strengthen ... my game" as well as the position of Grey and the British government.[53] For three days he and Smyth worked almost without stopping and by December 4 a second letter had gone off to the Colonial Office.[54]

After pointing out that a colonial secretary was placed "in worse than Egyptian Bondage" and forced to "make bricks without straw," Howe suggested to Grey that he should enlist "the active aid ... of the finer minds" in the colonies in two ways, one by appointing colonials to his staff and to the colonial governorships, the other by permitting each colony to send two of its executive councillors to the Commons. "This simple expedient" would give Parliament a source of information that was lacking and eliminate "the startling contrast between the two branches of the Great North American family." It would also help to elevate the Colonial Office from a position greatly inferior to that of the Home and Foreign Offices. Seemingly unaware that Britain owned "a magnificent territory in North America," Parliament spent night after night discussing the right of a Jew to sit in the Commons or the affairs of some petty German province. Instead of the colonial secretary being a scapegoat, "ever upon the defensive," he should be a leading member of every ministry "with a Policy as clear as a sunbeam, the broad outlines of which any man could read." Shortly, if Grey did not think it an "impertinent or uncalled for intrusion," Howe would show him how, "link by link, [he might] construct a great National Work through British America," which would also relieve the British poor rate, provide every British emigrant with a freehold, and assure the colonies an efficient means of defence.

Within eight days Grey replied he had read the letter "with the attention which *its great importance* deserves." That, said Howe, was "pretty well from a Minister of State to a poor Bluenose ... supposed to know little or nothing. That 'flash' was 'light from Heaven', ... and the letter is not intrusive or impertinent."[55] But Grey also added the usual objection to colonial representation in Parliament. How could colonials participate in proceedings affecting the financial interests of Britain (and few did not) unless the colonies assumed part of the expenses incurred for the benefit of the whole empire? After four days' work and another letter Howe hoped that this objection would be "swept ... out of [Grey's] path." British Americans, he said, would sooner or later have to contemplate a contribution, but for the moment they might be treated in a generous spirit since the demand was not for representation according to population. Grey should remember that Nova Scotia paid at least £40,000 a year in duties to get its staples into the American market and that its commerce might have been endangered if Britain had become embroiled with France over Don Pacifico, of whom Nova Scotians had never heard. But rather than a question of money, it was one of "honor, strength, national integrity – of prosperous dominion in peace – of imposing attitude in war."[56]

While awaiting Grey's reply, Howe "read a Cartload – [wrote] a Horseload, besides going to some sights, and all manner of parties." He found Countess Grey's soirée noteworthy for the presence of hosts of beautiful ladies and polished men, and for the absence of any refreshments save tea and lemonade; he met with distaste Alexander Campbell who was seeking to make money for himself out of crude, impracticable schemes for the colonies. But mostly he was thinking about the best way to convince the government and public of Britain that it had a deep interest in the improvement of North America. In case of a refusal, "and I am driven to appeal to Parliament or the country, it must not be about a little Nova Scotia Railway, but upon broad National grounds that all comprehend." In any case, "my little country, God bless her snow clad hills, will be better known and more respected over here ... or I am mistaken."[57] On December 28 – "the black Saturday" – Under-secretary Benjamin Hawes "sawed [him] off with a flat refusal." For Howe the timing could not have been worse; sick and "wretched besides ... voice ... gone for a month ... lungs ... dreadfully oppressed," he was "not in good trim to fight an Imperial Government and agitate England." How he longed for a ride through the quiet woods of Nova Scotia where he might think his own thoughts and prepare for the battle. With Smyth, his "one true friend," he discussed his options. Should he demand to be heard before the queen and the Privy Council? Should he appeal to the country by addressing the citizens of London or asking to appear at the bar of the Commons? "These were no light resolves nor did I take them lightly."[58]

Unexpectedly, the first ray of light appeared on December 30, when a delegation from Southampton expressed interest in his mission and asked him to address its citizens. "Will I go down? Won't I, aye, and make Grey and Hawes hear 'a voice from Southampton,' before long." Then, even better, on January 6, after a two-hour session at the Colonial Office, he had the letter of December 28 struck off the file, was told to finish his case prior to the taking of a final decision, and was authorized to test the pulse of the public in any way he pleased. Delightedly, he quoted one of Bacon's maxims: "Viva! 'boldness in civil business'." To celebrate, he and Smyth dined alone at Desbourg's, "wash[ing] the black vomit out of our souls with a bottle of Champaign."[59] With a light heart he turned again to a letter on emigration. At midnight on January 10 he was reading the first draft to Hawes in Downing Street, where he and the London soap boiler ended up by "swearing eternal friendship."[60] The next day brought an invitation to speak in the Guildhall at Southampton on the 14th. "That I should stand, at some time or other, face to face with the people of England, has been for years my firm conviction," and "a wondrous Providence" had brought it about through a series of events over which he had no control. If only his health were better for the occasion![61]

Broadly, his speech[62] proposed "an elevated and enlarged scheme of Colonial policy," including the promotion of major public works through imperial credit, the preparation of Crown lands for settlement, and the encouragement of the emigration of the poor through cheap transportation. "To reproduce England on the other side of the Atlantic; to make the children, in institutions, feelings and civilization, as much like the parent as possible, has been the labour of my past life"; now he wanted to encourage the parent to promote its own interests by demonstrating that across the Atlantic it possessed provinces of inestimable value. Although the British government sympathized with his objectives, the responsibility rested with the people. "Let them assume the desire of Government and act upon it. Let them stimulate the Executive if that is required." As the son of the only male Howe who had gone to British America at the time of the Revolution, "I want when I stand beside his grave to feel that I have done my best to preserve the connection he valued." The reaction to the speech exceeded even his wildest expectations. "Such a triumph as I had at Southampton," he exulted, "I have not had since the old Libel case." Smyth told Susan Ann that no newspaper could "give you any real idea ... how completely your husband electrified his audience."[63] In short order the speech was in pamphlet form and being distributed to MP's, newspaper editors, and anyone else who Howe thought might exercise influence. Besides a favourable press, many of his correspondents were ecstatic. One suggested that "if ever Cobden deserved 70,000 as a testimonial from Englishmen, you deserve the same amount – from us, and an equal sum, from the Nova Scotians"; A.B. Richards was certain that the "future of England lies wrapt in her American Possessions. It will not be your fault, if she do not discover it"; Sir John Harvey prophesied that "wherever the English language is spoken there will your speech at Southampton be read."[64]

Yet Grey and the Colonial Office were the ones whom Howe had to convince. Probably they had never had to deal with anyone quite like him. Although fairly certain he had "got the Colonial Office with me," he sought even more than before to save it from political embarrassment.[65] He also made certain that Grey would have every chance to criticize his draft letter on emigration. Whereas that of November 25 had based his request for a guarantee upon the merits of the railroad itself, the letter of January 16 argued that Britain should facilitate the railway to "provide employment for her surplus capital and labour, to extend her home markets, to relieve her poor-rates, to empty her poor-houses, to reform her convicts, to diminish crime."[66] Replete with statistics about crime and poverty in the United Kingdom, the letter had so much to say about the difficulties in Ireland that Howe admitted it really dealt with "the case of Great Britain and Ireland, not of Nova Scotia and her Railroad." As a result, "no government, I flatter myself, could publish [it] here and confess they had done nothing."[67] "Crotchety" in an interview on the letter, Grey later indicated he would not take kindly to even an implied criticism of the British government's domestic policy. The Irish famines of 1847 and 1848, he told Howe, had resulted from causes altogether beyond the government's control. Dismissing the proposal that the government provide steamboats for emigrants, he contended that "upon every sound principle it should be left to private enterprise." If the colonial governments themselves provided steady employment for the emigrants, cheap conveyance by steam would soon become available.[68]

Disappointed at being unable to return in the packet on February 18, Howe at least had the consolation that his publicity campaign seemed to be paying off. But he refused to accompany Alexander Campbell and members of the Canadian Land and Railway Association when they presented their case to the Tory leader Lord Stanley, even though the latter had requested his presence. Highly suspicious, Howe consulted Grey and was told that Campbell was a swindler who had recently imposed upon the duke of Argyll to the extent of several thousand pounds.[69] Howe did have two interviews with Stanley on a petition relating to New Brunswick railways and found him a "sharp, shrewd fellow. Most courteous and frank." Later, in the Lords, Stanley, Monteagle, and Grey all made complimentary, even flattering, references to him. "If this is not fame and success, what the devil is"? Unfortunately one newspaper omitted Monteagle's remarks and inserted photographs instead. "Hang their pictures. Luckily the Sun has it." At Weir's Howe caught a glimpse for the first time of Cobden, whose views on colonies were the antithesis of his own. "Don't like or dislike – love or fear him. We may measure swords yet."[70]

The 21st of February turned out to be the most eventful of days. First came word of the apparent collapse of the government on the budget. "What now? More delay – perhaps failure." Despondent, he went to see "Belshezer the Mountebank and the extravaganza of Tarantula," only to discover on his return a letter from Grey stating that Lord John Russell, the prime minister, and Gladstone, the chancellor of the exchequer, had agreed in principle to a guarantee. Howe had only a few amendments to suggest to the draft proposals, and then, hopefully, he waited for the political situation to clear up. Clearly Grey's party was bound by the guarantee "if they come back [and] Stanley is pledged to go at least as far." For Grey, who looked as if he had slept very little, Howe felt sorry; although he had fortune and rank, no family to support, and no debts to pay, yet "poor fellow, [he also] has no children to inherit name, or fame, or fortune. Mine were fed, and will soon be able to feed themselves."[71]

Once again he reconciled himself to an anxious period of waiting and fears that his railroad might be "wrecked among the intrigues and conflicts of parties." At his request Grey agreed to have him presented to the queen at a levee on February 26. Smyth showed him how to keep his hat and sword "out of my own and every body else's way with one hand while I raise her Majesty's hand to my lips with the other," but he had other worries, especially that he might get "rheumatism in his legs with these wretched silk stockings and tights." In the event things could not have gone better: "here goes Bluenose – a look – a step, and my knee is before my Sovereign, and her little hand is at my lips." Then Grey seized him and in a minute he was shaking hands with "Johnny" Russell. "Better late than never, but this should have been done before ... [Yet] I am not sorry that the introduction was in such a presence and before the grandees of the Empire."[72] With time on his hands, he whiled some hours away having Debaussy paint the only portrait for which he ever sat, a present for Susan Ann;[73] following a soirée at Lady Palmerston's he addressed some verses to Mrs North with a copy to Thackeray; he sent a copy of a song written by himself to Lady Grey, Alice Lambton, and Miss Stanley, hoping they would put it in their music boxes. Yet almost beside himself during the ministerial crisis, he took care to protect himself no matter what happened: a little brashly he asked Stanley, in case he assumed office, for a short interview before he matured his colonial policy.[74]

Not until March 7 could Howe report Grey back in his department and the guarantee agreed to by cabinet council. Three days later an official letter from Hawes emphasized that the guarantee was being provided only because it was a work of great importance to the empire, that Canada and New Brunswick would be given similar guarantees, but that none would be effective until arrangements were complete for an intercolonial line wholly through British territory. No objection would be taken, Hawes added, if the plan also included "a provision for establishing a communication between the projected railway and the railways of the United States."[75] Although eventually the interpretation placed upon this statement would dash all of Howe's hopes, his first reaction was to thank God "who had crowned all my labours with such success. My solitary thoughts – hopes, fears, toils and trials, he only knows, or can know"; to his deputy in Nova Scotia he reported elatedly that the interest on the loan could not be "higher than four and will probably not exceed three and a half per cent"; otherwise it would have been as high as 6.[76]

Having learned little from his earlier lesson, Howe followed up his success with the draft of a grandiose plan that included the clearing of the land on both sides of the railroad by 1,000 convicts working under Major Smyth and the setting up of a national association, possibly under Prince Albert's patronage, to supervise settling 400,000 of Britain's poor on 80,000 freeholds. But Grey would have none of a scheme supposedly designed to attack crime "at the fountain head ... the Orphanage[s] of Great Britain." Obviously his Whiggism did not include the belief that translation to another environment might change men's attitudes. It took him only a day to tell Howe that people on relief were mainly those whose bad character militated against their employment; that the amount of unemployed labour in Britain was relatively small; and that he could not get labourers for drainage work on his estate in Northumberland even at good wages. Under no conditions would he ask Prince Albert to countenance a national association; instead, let the railroad contractors and the colonial governments see to the sending out of emigrants.[77]

Before Howe left London on April 4 he followed Grey's suggestion and put Hawes's letter in the hands of the reputable contracting firm of Messrs Peto, Betts and Brassey, who offered him two proposals, one based on the railway as a private undertaking, the other as a public work. Aboard ship, as he reflected on the preceding five months, they seemed like a dream. He had gone to secure funds for Nova Scotia's part of the line to Portland; he had returned with a guarantee for a vital intercolonial undertaking. "The very thought of the risk I ran [in] all this makes me quiver. Successful beyond my own, beyond everybody's hopes. But ... will there be union, energy, wisdom, enterprize to realize the vision? We shall see."[78]

Back home, Howe found "politics is a mess, as I expected." The session of 1851, the first he had missed since 1836, had not gone at all well. Devoid of any talent for managing men, Uniacke simply could not keep the discordant elements of the party in line. Perhaps it was just as well that Herbert Huntington, debilitated more and more as his illness spread to his spine, could not attend, opposed as he was to building at public expense railways that could not benefit western Nova Scotia. Knowing "nothing about the passado or the parry" and refusing to compromise with principle even to maintain party unity, he would have found the session frustrating. Had he withheld his resignation as financial secretary for the moment the government might have avoided the suspicion that it was divided, but his colleagues from Yarmouth, the anti-railway Thomas Killam and Stayley Brown, saw that he did not. When the Youngs made an issue out of his replacement, they almost shipwrecked the government before the session opened.[79] As it progressed, the assembly had often appeared rudderless.

Likely Howe was pleased that at long last an act had been passed to withdraw the permanent grant to King's College, though it would later be rejected in England. But he found little else to exult about. Particularly distasteful to him was an act incorporating the Nova Scotia Electric Telegraph Company which, when it completed its lines to Yarmouth and Sydney, was empowered to take over the government line from Halifax to Amherst at cost. It had passed even though the *Chronicle* had called it monstrous to permit a few greedy speculators to convert the "people's line" into a mercantile tyranny. "The people build and manage a line of Telegraph, but the moment ... the stock is remunerative ... a disposition is evinced to hand it over to the tender mercies of a private Company."[80] Howe found the destruction of his own handiwork no less unpalatable but, immersed as he was in a bigger project, he decided he had no choice but to accept a fait accompli.[81]

In his absence the legislature had also dealt with two institutional changes which a conservative Reformer like himself would have opposed. Initiated by his friend Lawrence O'Connor Doyle, one widened the franchise with an additional qualification: the payment of county or local rates. "Away, with the moth-eaten habits of the Saxon settlers," said Doyle; "they are unsuited to our people and our age."[82] For Howe, who thought that anyone worth his salt could easily acquire a 40-shilling freehold in Nova Scotia, it was a retrograde step. He would have reacted even more strongly to Johnston's proposal for an elective Legislative Council, supposedly a key part of a well-regulated scheme of democratic institutions to counteract an executive oligarchy. At a meeting of Liberal assemblymen and councillors the Youngs had pressed for bold action on this measure: "take the thing out of Johnston's hands," they urged, "and make it a Govt. measure." Horrified because "the party was almost to a man in favour," Howe's friend, Legislative Councillor Jonathan McCully, told them it was madness to modify the central governmental machinery at a time when Howe was abroad striving to negotiate a loan. "What person or Govt. in its senses would deal with such an unstable unsettled Government, especially in *money matters*."[83] But it took his best efforts to prevent the Liberals from going further than approving an elective council in principle. Had Howe been present he would surely have cut the Youngs down to size.

Even in his absence Howe remained at the centre of public debate in Nova Scotia. On January 3 hundreds of Haligonians had assembled at dockside, amidst a severe snow storm, to see if RMS *Niagara* had brought a report from him on the railroad. A little later the government was accused of "tinker[ing] up a clause ... likely to provoke hostility" by including in the address in reply to the Speech from the Throne a statement lauding Howe's mission to London. Johnston refused to pronounce on the wisdom of government policy until he knew more about Howe's instructions and the results of his activities; Liberal Thomas Killam went further and criticized the sending of an emissary without prior approval of the legislature. "But that the Eastern fellows were afraid of their Constituents we should surely have been floored," lamented McCully.[84] When Howe's Southampton speech became known in Halifax, the *Colonist* prophesied fearfully that "the fruits of his eloquence" would be "a sudden influx of poor emigrants."[85]

But in the end Howe's opponents thought it would be easier to stymie him, not by writing him down in editorials, but by getting R.M. Dickie of Cumberland to introduce a bill for the incorporation of the European and North American Railroad, the line to Portland. Uniacke argued the folly of opening a fierce debate on railways while negotiations in Britain were still pending, but once again he had difficulty with his backbenchers in caucus. Twice, on January 11 and 12, his government was attacked by W.A. Henry, who was "in very ill humour ... at every body & everything" because members junior to himself had been made queen's counsel or appointed to the Executive Council. Even the governor worried that "Johnston's Partys virulence [might] carry them so far as to throw the Country into such a state of confusion" as to force him to dissolve the assembly.[86] But the government got out of trouble for the time being because only two Liberals joined the Tories in opposing postponement of Dickie's bill. Early in March, however, when the political crisis in Britain made the defeat of Howe's mission not unlikely, Dickie moved that the second reading of his bill be set for March 19. Rising to the occasion, Uniacke "electrified the House" with a speech reminiscent of his earlier orations. "Had [Howe] not worked like a Slave to promote – not his own interest – but the interests of his native Country? ... Was it fair to stab him in the back? You may try it, ... but if you do, the poinard will drop from your hand before you can strike."[87] With difficulty he got the consideration of Dickie's bill postponed until March 27, by which time Hawes's dispatch authorizing the guarantee had arrived in Halifax. Then, delightedly, he proposed that Nova Scotia proceed with railway-building as soon as Canada and New Brunswick concurred.

But again the government proved to be without a strong hand and prone to error. The bombshell fell on March 27 when Executive Councillor George Young, who a little earlier had fallen from his horse on his head on a hard road and had never "been quite right since," complained in public that the British government had been "niggardly" and that it ought to pay half the cost of the line to Quebec.[88] To rescue himself, Uniacke had no choice but to have his own proposal amended and any action postponed until Howe returned. Young insisted he was simply attempting a *ruse de guerre* which, by occupying his opponents' position, would disarm them, but he convinced no one. There matters stood when Howe arrived in Halifax on the night of April 15–16. He was greeted by an editorial in the *Recorder* that "if there have been no resignations it is high time there were," and by a letter in the *Chronicle* that a cancer existed at the council board, "a foul disease nought but the surgeon's knife can cure. ... Take care, Mr. Provincial Secretary, or it will be too late to save the patient."[89] Reluctant to interfere in a matter that had developed in his absence, Howe had no choice when Uniacke made his continuance in office contingent upon Young's leaving it. A little unhappily, but on the governor's instructions, he effected Young's removal in his capacity as provincial secretary. Henceforth Young would have to do his mischief outside the government.[90]

For a few unhurried weeks Howe pondered his next step. Obviously Howe the publicist and propagandist would have to go into action. New Brunswick, with indecent haste he thought, had rejected the railway proposals and Canada was dubious about them. In New Brunswick and in Cumberland, the home of the Dickies, there were fears he had sacrificed the Portland line. By telegraph he quickly arranged a meeting in Toronto to get his proposals back on the rail. But first he had to be sure of his position in his own baliwick, since the *British Colonist* and the *Christian Messenger* were heaping cold water upon them. Highly visionary, his speech at Mason's Hall on May 15 was also one of his most splendid.[91] Many of his audience, he expected, would live to hear the whistle of a railway engine in the Rocky Mountains and journey from Halifax to the Pacific in five or six days. "Will you then, put your hands unitedly ... to the great work? Refuse, and you are recreants to every principle which lies at the base of your country's prosperity and advancement; ... refuse, and Nova Scotia ... should have been thrown back, at least behind the Rocky Mountains ... Aid me in this good work, and ... British North America will rise to [have] ... all the organization and attributes of a nation." Emphatically he rejected the arguments that a government should not engage in public works: "You set up eight or nine men on red cushions or gilded chairs, with nothing to do but pocket their salaries, and call that a government. To such a pageant I have no desire to belong. Those who aspire to govern others should neither be afraid of the saddle by day nor of the lamp by night. In advance of the general intelligence they should lead the way to improvement and prosperity."

Then it was on to Amherst, where he was so convincing that he was asked to stand for Cumberland in the elections to come; to New Brunswick and meetings at Dorchester, Petitcodiac, Saint John, and St Andrews, where he argued that his proposals offered the only hope of building the Portland line and persuaded E.B. Chandler to represent New Brunswick at the meetings to follow; and finally to Canada, where he received enthusiastic hearings at Toronto, Quebec, and Montreal, and helped to fashion a tentative tri-province agreement for building the railroad. His report,[92] issued at Amherst on his return journey, indicated a special effort to accommodate New Brunswick, where the interest in the Portland line dwarfed everything else. The proposal was that New Brunswick would build that line, assisted by the guarantee from the British government, and that the three provinces would share equally the cost of the Quebec line. Since the New Brunswick section of the line was considerably the longest, it stood to gain most from the arrangement.

Howe was back in Halifax on July 21, only five days before the dissolution of the General Assembly. One of his first acts was to tell the electors of Halifax County – his constituents for fifteen years – that he would be running in Cumberland. Partly it was because his new responsibilities made it difficult to "attend to the local affairs of 40,000 people, spread over a [county] 100 miles long"; mostly it was because "a degree of intelligent unanimity" existed on the railway in Halifax. "The Citadel being safe I must take my stand somewhere upon the outworks of the position, that those who are open or concealed enemies, may not gain ... any advantage."[93] The *British Colonist* and the Conservatives apparently believed that Nova Scotia was not big enough to stand another four years of party government and they urged the electors to vote for the best candidates, not for party men. In contrast, Howe, more than ever the de facto leader of the government, boasted of a host of accomplishments under responsible and party government;[94] yet for him the only issue of consequence was the railway. "Providence has blest our labours heretofore, and will again," he declared. "I have never deceived – nor deserted you. You will stand by me now in this last effort to improve our country, elevate these noble Provinces, and form them into a Nation. A noble heart is beating beneath the great ribs of North America now. See that you do not, by apathy or indifference, depress its healthy pulsations."

Earlier Howe had told Grey that "all now depends on our Elections. They cannot, I think go wrong." He had no doubt about Halifax where, he prophesied, an early effect of the railway would be to "cover the peninsula of Halifax with Houses, down to the edge of the North West Arm."[95] In Cumberland, too, he found the project so popular that it was easy to effect an arrangement by which he and Stephen Fulton, a former Tory assemblyman but a strong advocate of railways, were returned unopposed. But in the rural counties, distant from the proposed route, the reaction was markedly different. Disturbed by the situation in Lunenburg, Howe had handbills distributed in English and German, warning its voters not to be misled by stories "about taxation and ruin, and such stuff." To the western counties he gave an assurance that "you'll see the Iron Animal snorting along your Western Valley one of these days."[96]

Because of doubts that were not immediately resolved, both parties claimed victory. Had Stephen Fulton of Cumberland changed his party allegiance? With which party would the members for the newly created county of Victoria associate themselves? Would the victors over former Liberal assemblymen in Cape Breton and Guysborough counties line up with the Conservatives or the Liberals? Almost at once Howe prophesied that all the doubts would be resolved in favour of the Liberals and, with perhaps one exception, he was right. In the end he could count on the general support of thirty or thirty-one of the fifty-three members, but he had nothing like the same approval for his railway proposals even though he told Peto, Betts and Brassey: "a majority to sustain my policy I think secure."[97] Clearly he found it disappointing that his party had elected only ten members of twenty-seven in western Nova Scotia; further, some of the ten, like Thomas Killam of Yarmouth and Dr E.L. Brown of Kings, would support no railway proposals of any kind. Although he called this negativism "the last wretched shift of a beaten and disappointed faction, who ... are envious of every body who tries to do any good,"[98] he knew, or should have known, better. Operating against him was the same widespread fear of heavier direct taxation which had prevented him from getting the educational legislation he wanted and which would take a long time to erode.

Howe was also naïve, if not unfair, in charging the Conservatives with sacrificing provincial to party interests when he found that some of their leaders who had urged him to proceed with his railway proposals had aided Conservative candidates opposing them. But, since Howe and his party were using his railway policy to get themselves elected, he should not have been surprised that his opponents left no stone unturned to defeat him. He had more right to be indignant in September when Johnston, unpledged on the railroad during the election, decided to support an offer to build the railways for grants of land and money from C.D. Archibald, a native Nova Scotian who held a roving commission for British contractors. If, Howe said, Archibald had come forward earlier and fallen in line with terms already granted by the colonial legislatures, "my task would have been simple and my labour light." But all he found then were "lots of embryo companies ... zealous to spend money raised upon our credit, and to speculate in Colonial lands." Now that Nova Scotia had a guarantee, its aim should be to "*make it go as far as possible*" and not embarrass itself with companies who shrank from it in times of need. As for himself, his only interest was in British contractors of eminence who could build a publicly owned line on fair terms.[99] Before Archibald could reply Howe attended a celebration in Boston marking the completion of railway communication with the West; there he voiced the hope that his listeners might soon attend a similar celebration on British soil where, "even if our railroads should not be as long as yours, the festival shall be as long and the welcome as cordial."[100] He returned to find Archibald accusing him of alienating the great capitalists of Britain and thwarting a noble project through "self will." Somewhat mysteriously, perhaps mystically, Howe replied that "the will of a higher power" would be the deciding factor and he would doubt Archibald's infallibility until he showed his "authority from that great power who, to this day, has crowned my toils ... with eminent success."[101]

Meanwhile he was receiving word from London that "things are too rotten here," that "the chief *Jesuits* of Free-trade" were making headway, and that he was badly needed in the British Parliament,[102] but for the moment New Brunswick was his main concern. By August its ministry had been reconstructed and the railway question made the chief item on its agenda. Because of "your magnificent labours," wrote Moses H. Perley, William J. Ritchie, the principal opponent of Howe's proposals, found himself "the leader of an opposition without any followers." Much more realistically, Governor Sir Edmund Head told him that because of "the enormous variety & conflicting character of local interests ... there are always stragglers ready to attract themselves to any one in this matter"; hence the New Brunswick ministry dared not make a false move and he was awaiting action in Nova Scotia before convening the legislature.[103] By this time the omnipresent C.D. Archibald was having considerable success in New Brunswick by freely associating the name of Peto, Betts and Brassey with his own and Perley conceded that his proposals would have to be disposed of before Howe's could be taken up. Somewhat agitatedly Howe wrote to both Grey and Peto, Betts and Brassey, asking them to confirm their tentative arrangements with him.[104]

Local patriotism fairly exuded from Howe when he introduced his railway and allied bills in the assembly on November 8. To obtain the guarantee, "I had but to paint [Nova Scotia] as she is"; surely, then, the legislature should "place her in that position which Nature destined she should occupy." To Thomas Killam, who saw no advantage in Nova Scotia building a railway 1,000 miles into the continent and who feared that the outlay would be greater than all the expenditures on roads in the preceding fifty years, Howe replied simply that the railway was likely to pay its own way. To J.W.

Johnston, who had developed an almost paranoic opposition to the building and ownership of public works by governments and who contended that capitalists like Archibald had been snubbed, Howe had ready answers. How much private capital had been subscribed to build the line to Windsor? In Hants County, £500; in Kings and Annapolis, none. In Britain nothing but crackpot schemes had emerged until the British government offered its guarantee; then all sorts of Archibalds had appeared, fully prepared to spend government money to enrich themselves.[105]

But Howe was in his happiest vein in deriding Dr Brown for suggesting that Nova Scotia was poor and barren. "I would rather live in sight of the sea on two meals a day, than in rich abundance where its endless variety was wanting, or the sound of the surges a tradition." But where in the American Union between Providence and Portland could one find a spot to compare with the country from the Ardoise Hills to Digby Gut, the marshes and uplands of Cumberland, and the green hills and intervales of Pictou? So, "for heaven's sake don't let us undervalue the country we have got [and let us] bend our energies to the development of its resources [rather than be] continually engaged in unnatural depreciation."[106] Only two Liberals, Killam and Dr Brown, joined some of the Tories in opposing Howe's major proposals. On a resolution to permit borrowing up to £1,000,000, Johnston sought, first, to keep the Nova Scotia line independent of the others and, later, to let the province assume responsibility for only its section of the line and not, as he calculated, an additional twenty-two miles of the New Brunswick line and sixty-five miles of the Canadian. In neither case could he muster more than ten votes.

Two bills to promote emigration and colonization completed Howe's somewhat grandiose plan of provincial development. One consolidated the existing Land Departments under a commissioner of Crown lands and, in effect, made him the head of an expanded immigration program; the second permitted the formation of land companies in cases where groups of emigrants wanted to settle together. Howe denied the unavailability of large blocks of land: "Why take [Halifax] county alone. On the new Guysborough Road, you may travel 30 miles through an unbroken forest, and not find a house except Becky Langley's, and one or two others." Against criticism that the proposal would fill the province with misfits, Howe defended the poor of England. Of a hundred unfortunate girls seen every mile or two on the streets of London, thirty might betray "the brazen look of shameless vice," but the others were "as pure in heart as our wives and daughters." Similar people of both sexes who emigrated to the United States twenty or thirty years ago with scarcely a rag on their backs were now worth up to £25,000. Why could the example not be repeated to "reduce the pauperism of England" and "add to the wealth and power of the Colonies"?[107]

By the end of November Howe had got everything he wanted. Calling it "one of the most gratifying sessions ever held in Nova Scotia," he boasted that the voice of faction had manifested itself only in "faint and indistinct murmurings." He had carried measures involving heavy expenditures with the support of at least half the Tories and all the Liberals but two. His native province, in consenting to make eighty miles of railway beyond her border, had "done an act of generous enterprize which no poor State or Province ever did since the world began."[108] In New Brunswick, too, everything seemed to be unfolding as he wanted, even though Governor Head still warned him that its people had "no enlarged view of the interests of New Brunswick as a part of British North America."[109] One development in England was likely to be helpful in that province. Caught in a breach of trust suit from which he escaped only on a legal quibble and with a severe castigation from the lord chief justice, C.D. Archibald had lost his capacity to engage in mischief-making in the colonies. As the session ended in Nova Scotia, Howe still marvelled that he, a colonial, had been able to convince opinion makers in both British parties that an intercolonial railway should be made an imperial undertaking and that the Russell government had agreed to reverse itself and provide a guarantee. All of it had resulted from that "flash" in December which showed him that much more than a railroad was in question. Now that the year 1851 was almost over he willingly admitted it was "the first that ever was long in my life ... [it] *seems like three.*"[110]

## CHAPTER THREE

# The Bantling Revived

For Howe the closing weeks of 1851 were even longer than the earlier ones since they brought news that would destroy one of his greatest visions. The 28th of December 1850 had been "the black Saturday"; if anything, the 11th of December 1851 was even blacker. On that day RMS *Niagara* arrived with Grey's dispatch of November 27 which insisted that the railway guarantee had been intended only for the intercolonial line and not for the interconnecting line with the United States.[1] For the moment neither Howe nor anyone else hinted that the British government was seeking a way out of its railway commitment in order to serve powerful financial interests in Britain. Rather the questions were of another kind: Had Howe, in his exuberance, read into Hawes's letter of March 10 something he wanted to believe which was not there at all? Had the Colonial Office itself slipped up in permitting an alleged misinterpretation to be continued for months even though it had had ample opportunity to correct it? Grey took the position that the guarantee was "so explicit and unambiguous" that he was in no way responsible for "the error, into which [Howe] has been betrayed, most probably, by the natural eagerness with which he pursued an object of such deep importance to the whole of British North America." Howe, he added, appeared to rely as much "on the language which he has himself [used] since his return to America" as on Hawes's letter.[2] But was that letter as "explicit and unambiguous" as Grey suggested it was? Peto, Betts and Brassey, to whom Howe referred the correspondence, had reached the same conclusion as he;[3] so had the cabinets of Nova Scotia, New Brunswick, and Canada.

Howe could also demonstrate that Grey and the Colonial Office were guilty, at least, of the fault of inattention. For, in reporting to the Executive Council of Nova Scotia from Britain, he had stated explicitly that the guarantee included the Portland line within its ambit and that report had "passed under the inspection of the authorities in Downing Street."[4] Again, in his speech at Mason's Hall in May, he had explicitly pointed out that, because of the guarantee, New Brunswick would get "two most important lines at $3\frac{1}{2}$ per cent, the other provinces but one," and Grey, to whom he sent a copy of the speech, had acknowledged it personally. Anxious, however, to maintain good relations with the Colonial Office, Howe refused to enter into a debating match with Grey. So when the latter wrote to him solicitously, he replied that he had thrown himself frankly upon "the fair consideration and good feeling of my countrymen," and Grey "need not have any anxieties on my account."[5]

Nevertheless Howe felt terribly chagrined that he had raised the hopes of British North America so high only to have them dashed so completely. Nova Scotians learned about the turn of circumstances in early January 1852 through the Canadian newspapers, but the *British Colonist* did not take aim at Howe until the latter part of the month. Then, quickly working itself into a fury, it heaped scorn on the "magician who worked ... a spell over the minds of a too credulous people." But was it not to be expected of one whose talents were not suited to negotiations of this kind and should it be surprising that his "want of accuracy and precision" had thrown into complete disarray the well-conceived plans for the European and North American Railway to Portland?[6]

For the moment Howe was adamant that Nova Scotia should not "move a step, till she knows what all parties wish *and what they are at*"; above all, it should not appear to be exercising unfair influence, nor he to be motivated by "wounded vanity."[7] But he feared the worst. He knew that his scheme, envisaging as it did a line to Quebec along the east coast of New Brunswick, had little attraction for that province and the only chance to get its acceptance had been to couple it with a guarantee for the Portland line. Left to itself, New Brunswick would certainly choose a route far less favourable to Nova Scotia. Accordingly Howe declined an invitation to meet the delegates of the other provinces in Fredericton, simply saying he did not care which line was chosen so long as it could be defended by argument. By January 26 Hincks, Taché, and Young of Canada and Chandler of New Brunswick had concluded their deliberations and arrived in Halifax. Their first proposal, to route the railway by the valley of the Saint John and have each province pay one-third of the cost, met with instant rejection in Nova Scotia. Why should it pay for eighty-eight miles beyond its borders of a line which would not let Halifax participate in the carrying trade of the Gulf of St Lawrence and Canada and seriously reduce the amount of land to be thrown into the common pool? A second proposal, which reduced Nova Scotia's contribution to one-quarter of the total, meant that it would have to build only 159 miles rather than 212. Almost beseechingly, Hincks warned Howe about "getting into a wrong position" since, if he adopted a negative stance, neither he nor Nova Scotia would be "elevated in the estimation of the world & *all the* responsibility of failure falls on you."[8]

With a heavy heart Howe threw his support behind the proposal, although he did not like it as a North American measure. He would have to use quite different arguments to justify it in Nova Scotia since the plans for emigration and the sale of lands in the centre of New Brunswick would have to be abandoned and Saint John and St Andrews, not Halifax, would become the principal Atlantic shipping ports. Yet "if St. John grows larger than Halifax, we can thank God it is a British City and be proud of its prosperity." For Howe the question was not "what we would like to do, but what we can do," and since he was definitely for a railroad, he had no choice but to go along with the only proposal likely to be practicable.[9] Because he was one of "the old stock actors" in Halifax, he let Hincks play the major role at a railway meeting in Temperance Hall on February 4, saying simply that, although he would do all a Nova Scotian should to further the scheme, he would not assume the same single-handed responsibility as in 1851.[10]

He did not have to wait long for criticism to develop. As usual, he did not mince words with Johnston, who feared that New Brunswick would gain at Nova Scotia's expense: "in God's name what is New Brunswick? A Foreign nation, under a foreign Crown with hostile interests and feelings to our own? No, but a Province under the same sceptre, and descended from the same stock." Would the day not come sooner or later "when all these British North American Provinces shall be confederated, when there shall be no necessity for these delegations we being one family and one people"?[11] He gave equally short shrift to Killam, who had contended that Anglo-Saxon people depended upon themselves, not upon governments, for public improvements. Had not all the great public works of Britain from Westminster Abbey downward been constructed by high-minded, energetic, enterprising tyrants? Was it not true that until recently English people had not even been permitted to manufacture leather breeches without the intervention of the government? Imagine the dire condition of Nova Scotia's roads and bridges if they had been left to the people.[12] All but fourteen assemblymen – nine Conservatives, and five Liberals from the western counties – agreed with Howe that he had put forward the only practicable proposal.

Other than railways, the session of 1852 was marked by the continuing efforts of Johnston to emphasize the evils in the working of responsible government. For one thing he demanded that the assembly be accorded the right to be shown dispatches except under the most exceptional circumstances. It followed the reluctant tabling of a dispatch from Harvey to Grey, undoubtedly written by Howe, which castigated "the recklessness of the opposition" and the "entire want of knowledge on their part and that of their leader, of the system of government now happily established in this province."[13] Having complied with Johnston's demand in this specific instance, Howe was unwilling to recognize it as a general principle, even though he intended generally to follow it. Jokingly, he quoted *Romeo and Juliet* to the effect that in the first case the Conservative leader had been "biting his thumb at us," but that in the second "we are disposed to let him bite his thumb off."[14] Yet in managing to have Johnston's demand turned down by only two votes he unintentionally showed up the precarious position of the government. By this time Killam and Dr Brown were giving scant support to the ministry and the *Chronicle* might well ask, "What say the Liberals of Yarmouth and Horton to the course pursued by their members"?[15]

Continuing his campaign for a well-regulated system of democratic institutions, Johnston introduced a bill for the municipal government of counties, only to have Howe go him one better by suggesting that, despite Grey's opinion, even the judicial officials of the municipal corporations should be elected. That may explain Johnston's abandonment of the measure and his pressing of another for an elected Legislative Council. When, because of the support given him by Killam and Dr Brown, he failed by only one vote, opposition members and newspapers began to demand the reconstruction of the government. Departing markedly from its usual line, the *Colonist* declared that Howe was the one man in the ministry who "possesses any claim to talent and energy"; of Uniacke it spoke sadly: "Think of him as he was, and lament over him as he is."[16] In this situation Howe feared the worst during his enforced absence from the legislature for more than a month after February 24. Unknown to himself, he had been a party to breaking a provision in the election law. The two candidates who retired to permit Fulton and himself to be elected by acclamation had not done it before 4 p.m. on nomination day, the time at which the sheriff was required by law to close his court. Although the fault was purely technical, the four Tories who, by the luck of the draw, comprised a majority on the controverted election committee nevertheless vacated the Cumberland seats. "Mr. Howe had outwitted himself," gloated the *Colonist*, "and is now reaping the fruits of one of [his] artful contrivances."[17] As Howe left for Cumberland, he at least had the consolation that Tories James Fraser and John Clarke Hall, and Stewart Campbell of Guysborough, who was in the process of becoming a Liberal, had promised not to let the government be pressed unfairly in his absence. "If they keep their words, and I think they will, no great harm can be done, even *should Killam and Brown do their worst.*"[18]

It was a nasty election, especially since the Tories acted as if a victory for them would mean the fall of the government. Howe himself argued that his defeat would throw the railway negotiations into disarray but, more than was his wont, he also tried to show that he had not neglected his constituents. Had he not taken action to rebuild the bridge at Advocate Harbour, construct a pier at Parrsboro, and throw a bridge over the River Philip?[19] Countering him, he said, was a host of Tory handbills and *Colonist* extras filled with "the most outrageous falsehoods."[20] Following the line of the *Acadian Recorder* six weeks earlier, the *Colonist* pictured "a neat little [Howe] Family Compact of *five*, costing the Province some two or three thousand pounds a year, and in possession of the most profitable offices within the gift of the Government."[21] Even if exaggerated, the *Colonist's* complaints had some foundation. Although Susan Ann's cousin, James McNab, had clearly become receiver general on his own merits, and a distant relative, Ross, held a minor office, perhaps without Howe's intervention, there was no denying that Joseph Austen, the half-brother who had backed Howe's notes in the trying days of the thirties, had been made a warehouse keeper through Howe's influence at a time when he was down on his luck. Most suspect of all, however, was the case of the youthful Joseph Howe, Jr, who was being paid £150 for acting as general factotum to his father. Once again Howe appeared to think that because of his great contributions and sacrifices he need not be as circumspect as other men.

The election led to Howe's first direct contact with a thirty-year-old doctor from Amherst, Charles Tupper, who delayed the nomination proceedings until he was given half an hour to "tear the railroad from Mr. Howe's flag, [and] smash responsible government into smithreens." In return, said one observer, Howe treated him as "a naturalist would an insect of extraordinary size or color, sticking a pin through it ... for study at a suitable time." Having taken "the length, breadth, and weight of the little man" and shown up "his utter ignorance of ... constitutional principles," Howe told him that if his "physic was no better than his politics his patients were very much to be pitied."[22] That ended the first of what would be many bitter encounters.

Although pleased with his majority of about 200, Howe found his equanimity thoroughly disturbed on Declaration Day when one of his opponents demanded an investigation of the voting in some districts. Giving vent to his pent-up exasperation, he held up a long list of political opponents to "mockery and blighting ridicule, in a manner peculiarly his own."[23] Seaman of Minudie was alleged to have manufactured votes as he manufactured grindstones, and Ratchford and Dewolf of Parrsboro to have kept voters "drunk for a whole week"; then, when "they were *required to be used*," they were "rubbed and chafed with snow." It was another instance of his being able to endure only so much before he gave his tongue free rein. He would have done better to hold himself in check, for "Timothy Tickle" of Amherst immediately went him one better. Adverting to the gossip of the day, he suggested that "every man hereafter who becomes the reputed father of a black bastard, either on Hammond's Plains or in the city of Halifax, being also an Executive Councillor and a married man," should pay £100 for each offence and be expelled from the council.[24] Apparently the charge was not refuted; whether it was simply an instance of the vituperative politics of the day is not ascertainable, but it appears to have been limited to the one letter-writer.

Back in Halifax Howe got quick approval for the Executive Council to borrow £800,000 for the Halifax–Quebec Railway and to arrange for the construction of a quarter of the total mileage, even though Dr Brown would have preferred to "have five hundred barrels of gun powder under the Province Building, & blow all in the air than have the Railroad go on!"[25] Otherwise a highly unproductive session, it at least gave Howe time to consider his next step. Tentatively, he had assured Hincks that, after the by-election and the session, he would join him and Chandler in London to seek a guarantee for the line by the Saint John.[26] His friend Dr Grigor kept telling him that the British government would find it hard to resist their united demands, but by the end of April he had found "difficulties ... almost insuperable" that prevented him from going. His throat was still as "raw as a beefsteak from travelling in the open air, and making speeches in hot meeting-houses," but he stressed even more the death on March 22 of Sir John Harvey – "my personal friend and father ... for as a father he ever behaved to me" – and the delay in naming his successor.[27] So he told Hincks to manage without him and act as if Nova Scotia would go along with any proposals that the other two provinces could accept: "If you [Hincks and Chandler] can finish all – so much the better. Share the honor and glory between you."[28]

Howe had still other reasons for not joining Hincks. The Russell ministry having finally fallen and been succeeded by the Tories under the earl of Derby (the former Lord Stanley), he was convinced that the new government would take no action until after the forthcoming British election. But this combination of reasons only cloaked his primary motivation. In confidence he told Derby that Harvey's death had simply furnished him with "a very good excuse for staying here." Grey's letter of November 27, he said, had destroyed Nova Scotia's moral influence and left it powerless; New Brunswick, if driven to make one line, would choose the wrong one. So his heart was not in the matter, and he preferred not to go to England "at the risk of thwarting the other colonies if I told all I felt and doing violence to my nature if I did not."[29] Time would show that Howe gratified his personal feelings at a cost, since Hincks never forgave his "desertion" of a common cause.

Meanwhile Howe did his best to retain good will in both camps in Britain. He told Grey, now out of office, that he would always be highly regarded in Nova Scotia; he assured Derby that, if the latter won the British election, he would show him how to "retrieve the errors of the past."[30] But he still yearned to enter British politics directly. If only he could "throw himself into the electoral fray with an *address to the people of England*," he wrote Carmichael-Smyth. How much more important it was to send men of intellect to Britain from the colonies than to have "old fogies or rough sworders *sent to them*" as governors.[31] He even thought of asking Mayor Richard Andrews of Southampton to help get him elected to Parliament, "for upon my soul I very much fear, that without ... some more thorough means of communicating our ideas and interests to each other, we old and new Britons will bye and bye turn our backs upon each other ... The *big loaf* and the *little loaf* are important questions but the reorganization of the Empire is even more important."[32]

When Hincks and Chandler failed to secure a guarantee for the line by the Saint John, the *Colonist* could not resist gloating and launching another attack on Howe. Would private contractors not have the Portland line under construction if he had not led the public meeting in Temperance Hall completely astray? This was only the beginning of a concerted campaign which the paper pursued, week in and week out, against every facet of Howe's life, past and present, personal and political. Piously its editor pointed out that he had never received as much public money as Howe nor embezzled any; he was not, after years of denouncing red tape, living at the public expense or making the people pay for his trips to England and elsewhere; he had "not a suckling of a boy of sixteen, who cannot write good

English, ... foisted on the public at £150 a year, besides relatives to the hundredth degree"; he also knew how to behave in society and to "speak decently and respectfully of and to ladies."[33] As Howe's friend Hugh Bell put it, the *Colonist* was at its "chosen ... avocation, of misrepresentation, defamation and scurrility, in which as usual you [Howe] are honored with a large show of attention."[34]

Howe's one reply – a letter in Nugent's *Sun* explaining that his railway bills were not passed until April 8, at about the time Hincks and Chandler were preparing to return home – did not satisfy the *Colonist*, which called it a "shallow, shuffling" excuse for not joining them. It also blamed Howe for causing the *Chronicle* to spread the rumour that Grey had been persuaded to interpret Howe's dispatch as he did by William Jackson, now a partner in Peto, Betts, Jackson and Brassey, and a prime mover in getting the railways of Canada built as private undertakings. "Ah Joseph, every one knows [the reason for the rumour]. Mr. Jackson ... made you look and feel as foolish and small as man ever looked."[35] To another critic Howe needed to pay little attention. George Young had begun to publish letters in the *British North American* which fastened every imaginable sin on the government and told Howe he could never "reach the heaven of political virtue ... till he ... felt the purifying influences of a fresher and holier faith."[36] Young's acquaintances suspected that his lucid moments were becoming less frequent.

Behind the scenes the Executive Council was doing what it could to further the railroad. Following the arrival of the new governor, Sir Gaspard le Marchant, in August, it passed a minute of council pledging a start on the work after the next session of the legislature; it received proposals to construct the line from William Jackson on behalf of Peto, Brassey, Jackson and Betts, and from the firm of Sykes, Brookfield and King; and it persuaded the latter to survey a line from Windsor to Victoria Beach in Annapolis County. Then, almost like a thunderbolt, came the news on October 30 that Howe had left for Europe. Working itself into a new paroxysm of anger against him, the *Colonist* dug more deeply than ever before into its bag of invective: "dishonest, treacherous, malignant, a tyrant yet a slave, ... an incapable financier, a superficial statesman, a grasping nepotis[t], ungentlemanly in mind and manners ... A man so blown in character that he was compelled to steal away by night on his self-constituted delegation."[37] This time Hugh Bell wondered if Howe's critics would even forgo any benefit to the province if they could only prevent his making an arrangement creditable to himself.[38]

Howe needed answers to three questions. What were the credentials of Sykes, Brookfield and King, who had made a more favourable offer than Jackson but who were relatively unknown? On what terms could Nova Scotia borrow money without the British government's guarantee? Would the Derby government, in office at least temporarily following the elections, agree to renew negotiations for the Halifax–Quebec line? Anxious to avoid charges either that he was going with the powers of an ambassador or that he was having a pleasure trip at public expense, Howe took leave of absence, paid his own way, and left it to the legislature to reimburse him only if it wished.[39] His decision was a sudden one – he had hardly a chance to chat with his family before leaving – and it resulted from another of his "flashes." Would good come of it? "God only knows – He says 'go', plainly and distinctly – thats enough." But he had none of his former enthusiasm. "I go with the energy of a messenger not the zeal of a missionary."[40]

Aboard the RMS *America*, much to his disgust, he found William Jackson, who through Hincks's efforts had just got the contract to build the Grand Trunk and who, in seeking to be provocative, could not have chosen a better subject than the denigration of Nova Scotia and Nova Scotians. "Canada and New Brunswick every thing. Nova Scotia nothing ... Blue Noses dreadful fellows. No faith – no credit – no knowledge – no anything." Yet Howe did not lose his temper: "we get on, like fencers, trying each others powers" – and later Jackson told him he had borne the banter well. Little did he know that Howe's inward reaction bode him no good for the future: "An ugly customer ... Shrewd, fluent, daring, unscrupulous ... Canada and New Brunswick at his feet. God help poor Nova Scotia if she submits, or quarrels with such a man and such a combination."[41]

In Glasgow Howe sought information from James Forman, a young Nova Scotian engineer with whom he would soon be closely associated; in Sheffield he tried to establish the bona fides of the Sykes company. As usual, he missed no chance to see new sights, such as York Minster, and Skiddaw and Lake Windermere in the Lake District; as usual, they brought to mind a score of incidents from his encyclopedic knowledge of British history. In London he busied himself with financial houses, his head "too full for sights," although he did observe the duke of Wellington's funeral: "blackness and gloom over all. Too much of a show for solemnity – and too solemn for a show."[42] But he found the greatest gloom of all in a dejected Carmichael-Smyth, who wrote: "my day dream is gone ... We have no statesmen here, ... The Nova Scotia railway nothing – The Colonial question, nothing ... I have learnt to worship Louis Napoleon – as the only man in the present day that has any energy, that can think and dare at all events."[43]

Not nearly so despondent, Howe directed his ideas of empire at a new target, the earl of Derby. As usual, he sought to demonstrate the inferior position of British North Americans to Americans, both economically and politically. Recent changes in the commercial policy of the empire had been arranged with little concern for colonial interests; a New Hampshire lawyer, Franklin Pierce, had just been elected president of the United States, whereas his equal in the British American bar had no "National field of competition" open to him. Now Derby had an opportunity to "recover the Ground lost – to restore a better state of feeling, and to give to the Empire the advantage of a great highway from the Atlantic to the Western frontier upon British soil." All it required was a Treasury minute offering a grant or guarantee for the Halifax to Quebec line. Cobden and others like him would object, but surely the advocates of dismemberment "ought not to be deferred to by those who seek to maintain the integrity of the Empire."

Howe's conclusion was a warning (James Roy calls it a "Parthian shot"): if the colonies built their railways without help they would end up owing "a good deal of money, but not much gratitude" and would feel as Samuel Johnson had done towards the patron who let him struggle through a work of great magnitude, "the weight of which a little judicious aid would so materially have lightened."[44] By Christmas Howe was back in Nova Scotia and shortly afterwards writing to all the Liberal assemblymen – even Dr Brown – offering them the choice of one expensive road or three cheap ones, the main line to New Brunswick and branches to Windsor and Pictou. "What say you? ... With a railway to Pictou, and a Steamer on the Gulf [of St Lawrence] we may reach Cape Breton in a day. With a road to Digby we can reach Yarmouth in a day." At all costs Nova Scotia needed ports on the Gulf or New Brunswick would tap all its trade by a line to Shediac.[45] Publicly Howe took pleasure that the agony would soon be over: "I would not go through the same thing again for all that I could accumulate in public life, although it is true the work was self-imposed."[46]

On January 22, only two days after the session of 1853 opened, he tabled a mass of papers from which he concluded that the offer of Sykes, Brookfield and King was immeasurably superior to that of Jackson; that Baring Bros would lend the money on favourable terms; and that the Derby government was quite prepared to consider new proposals for a guarantee. Five days later he was ready with his four railway bills. One permitting an additional £100,000 to be deposited in the Provincial Savings Bank was designed to encourage "less affluent" Nova Scotians to be "frugal, industrious, and prudent" and at the same time let the government obtain funds at 4 rather than 6 per cent. The second, a strange one for the former chief apostle of a sound currency, authorized the issue of a further £100,000 of provincial Treasury notes. "God forbid that I should be a party to any measure ... which would ... depreciate the value of our paper issue ... but I believe ... we can issue £100,000 ... under due guards and checks ... without in any way injuring the Country." The third and fourth bills authorized a loan up to £800,000 for the railroads and bound the contractor to take one-third of the stock and to complete the main line to New Brunswick first. But Howe insisted he was not downplaying the branch lines; the day was past, he said, when members east and west could be expected to support only a main line which ran across no more than one or two counties. Still of special concern to him was "my first love," "my poor bantling," the line to Windsor.[47]

When Johnston charged that in proposing 320 miles of railway instead of 120, he had inoculated "the public mind with extravagant and unrestrained ideas," he pleaded guilty:

I have endeavoured to give my countrymen enlarged views and conceptions on these subjects, ... I have striven to elevate their eyes and minds from the little pedling muddy pool of politics beneath their feet to some thing more enobling, exalting and inspiring ... I have dealt with great questions since my advent to political life ... I have taught [my Countrymen] to discard their little jealousies and intrigues ... if ... we do sometimes expand our wings a little too broadly and soar somewhat too near the sun, we are at least refreshed by the contrast it affords to those mud puddles which render public life so nauseous.[48]

Mainly Howe had to counter arguments against public works being built and owned by government. To give a company of speculators entire control over the railroads, he maintained, would produce a monopoly that would dominate the assemblymen and "wrest from them every particle of power, and leave them but little of liberty"; in contrast, his own proposals would result in "a mighty piece of reproductive property within [Nova Scotia's] own bosom; belonging to herself – led by her own Legislature, and it operated upon by the people."[49]

Behind the scenes Howe had also to convince Sir Gaspard le Marchant, who for six months had been exposed to other Nova

Scotians telling him that "*private* individuals only should expend *public* money on a Railway." To him Howe conceded that governments ought normally not to embark on enterprises that private capital would undertake, but when the province provided more than half a million pounds its legislature and government ought to retain substantial oversight. It was folly to expect Jackson to keep the costs down. Had Archibald, his agent in North America, not become "notorious as one of the most reckless adventurers in bubble Railway shares in England" and had Jackson himself not "distinguished himself in the same line"? Over the last century millions of pounds had been collected and disbursed by the public men of Nova Scotia without three cases of fraud or defalcation; in fact, more fraud had been committed by a single notary or bankrupt trader than had "ever appeared in all the Branches of the Public Service since the Province was settled." Surely le Marchant could not expect him to abandon his own convictions if it meant sacrificing the public interest and his own reputation at the same time.[50]

Howe soon discovered that the Tories would present a united phalanx against him and that Johnston had him at the same disadvantage that "the Philistines had Samson when they seduced his wife." Hoping to make some converts, he addressed an open letter to the assemblymen on February 7, pointing out that Jackson's proposals were beyond the province's resources, while those of Sykes were readily manageable.[51] But three days later he could carry his proposals by only two votes. Joining Killam and Dr Brown in opposition was John Munro of Victoria, moving ever closer to the Tory camp. An excited gallery – the most unruly some newspapermen had ever seen – booed Johnston's reply to Howe and let him leave the House only with difficulty: "After ... receiving many kicks on my ancles and legs, I with the assistance of the Sergeant-at-Arms forced my way out."[52] Howe joined Johnston in insisting that the mayor of Halifax appear at the bar of the House to be questioned on the adequacy of the city's police force, but he did not satisfy the *Colonist*, which was certain that under his governance Halifax was reaching such a state that every honest man would have to go armed. "How inviting for English and foreign capitalists!"[53]

Not wishing to carry the railroad as a party measure, Howe agreed reluctantly to the appointment of a select committee, chaired by himself, to consider the best method of constructing it. Its majority, all Liberals, reported that Sykes, Brookfield and King would construct all the lines at £4,500 stg a mile, the trunk line for £5,200, while Jackson et al., who had no interest in the feeder lines, would build the trunk line at rates varying from £6,500 to £7,000 a mile. Because the offer of the Sykes company would apparently permit savings of about £700,000 on the trunk line and £2,000,000 on all three, the majority recommended that it be authorized to complete the main line in three years and the branch line in seven, but that the executive, if conditions made it desirable, might postpone the feeder lines at specified stages.[54] To Howe's surprise he found himself outvoted on February 23 by twenty-seven to twenty-five on a resolution extolling the benefits of building railways as government works. Two Acadian Liberals, François Bourneuf by mistake, and Anselm Comeau by design, cast negative votes though Howe was imploring Comeau even as he voted. The next day, through the reversal of Bourneuf, Howe got the previous vote rescinded and the resolution adopted by the deciding vote of the Speaker.[55] In effect, the railway question was deadlocked. A numerically small group of western county Liberals, which tended to oppose all railways, was, like "the Irish brigade" in the British House of Commons, checkmating both the Liberal majority and the Tories. Partisanship, sectionalism, and parochialism had prevented Howe from raising his countrymen above "the little pedling muddy pool of politics."

Deciding it was both undesirable and impracticable to carry important bills on the casting vote of the Speaker, he announced reluctantly on March 9 – "I yield to compulsion not conviction" – that the Executive Council would accept the principle of building railways as company rather than government works.[56] But he also insisted on "guarding the interests of the public by every fair means" and he took steps to ensure it by nominating four Liberals who thought on railways as he did to be members of the select committee of seven which was to draft the new railway bills. Prolonged jockeying occurred at every turn. Johnston demanded, but did not get, a majority of advocates of company railways on the committee; later he complained that the committee had dealt with English capitalists "in a contemptible huxtering spirit" and frustrated him on almost every point of detail.[57] Indignantly Howe replied that he had "receded from every point we could reasonably be asked to relinquish – but [Johnston] will not be satisfied unless we yield him *everything*"; so much had he and his friends been abused that "I begin to lose confidence in the Government myself."[58]

In the final version of the bills Howe's supporters took care that no speculator would make a killing out of Nova Scotia's railways. By including the branch lines and requiring their completion by 1860 they had made almost certain that Jackson would build no railways in Nova Scotia. By allowing a government loan or guarantee of only one-half the cost of work actually completed, they had made it necessary for the company to inject substantial capital of its own. If that was not enough to scare off speculators, they had required that half the railway's directors be government watchdogs. Finally, to ensure that the work go forward without delay, they had insisted on a second bill which authorized the government to construct it should a company not be organized within six months.[59]

A little surprisingly, both the *Chronicle* and the *Sun* seemed certain that a company would be formed. "Who," asked the latter, "fancies that British capitalists will hesitate ... to ... seize upon so promising an opportunity of making themselves masters of ... a whole province, reducing the people thereof to the condition of 'hewers of wood and drawers of water'"?[60] But they were not nearly as knowledgeable about the facts of railway building in Nova Scotia as was Howe. From the beginning he was "not sanguine" about a company being formed "as the terms are rather hard"; a little later he told an audience at Amherst that it was only a matter of time before his alternative bill came into effect.[61] The presumption is that he had deliberately made sure that private companies would not build and operate railways in Nova Scotia.

Though the session of 1853 was dominated by the railway issue, Howe played his usual prominent role in the continuing debate on the perfecting of responsible government. He was especially active in tidying up the anomaly which permitted his old opponent of Baptist quarrels, J.W. Nutting, to draw his salary as prothonotary and clerk of the Crown for the province and pocket a third of his county deputies' fees as well. As usual, the proposal was to let him retain his office for Halifax county but to let his deputies be principals in their own right. Moderation itself, Howe was even willing to give him £600 annually as compensation, but he "drew a wide distinction between the man who sat quietly in his office with no elections to run, ... and those office-holders which under the responsible system, were dependent upon the people's will."[62] In the end Nutting got a third of the county deputies' fees up to a maximum of £500 and the opposition's only complaint was that the government had added the county prothonotaries to an already too extensive patronage list.

In response to Johnston's continuing pursuit of well-regulated democratic institutions, Howe again lambasted a bill to institute an elective council and it died on the order paper. He did support the Conservative leader's attempt to introduce elective municipal corporations, but was adamant against leaving incorporation optional with the counties. That would be like a father buying a box or two of Morrison's Pills and telling his children, sick with scarlet fever, that although the medicine was not very nice, they might help themselves if they wished. "Is the bill good? Is the country prepared for it? If not, let us not waste time. Leaving the adoption to the option of the counties will only herald its failure."[63] Although he did not convince his fellow members, the committee perfecting the bill had insufficient time to report.

Almost unprecedentedly, the assembly witnessed the spectacle of Howe joining Johnston a second time in condemning the rate-paying franchise that had been introduced in his absence: "If the assessors are political partisans ... or you can find a man to run away with the Poll book, an Election is defeated." The only choices were to revert to the 40-shilling freehold or adopt universal suffrage, and he called "wise and salutary" Johnston's bill which, while it retained the freehold qualification, practically introduced universal suffrage by granting the vote to anyone who had resided in a county or township for one year. But why not take "two steps in advance" and introduce the secret ballot as well?[64] An astonishingly liberal Legislative Council added it as an amendment, but too late to have it considered by the assembly.

It was not the congenial Howe, however, who drew the most attention in 1853. For months he had been accused of defrauding the public by using the government telegraph line for his own and his party's advantage; allegedly he had sent his personal messages free, put the line at the disposal of his "cullies" at election time, and obtained news items without charge for Liberal newspapers. That was the situation when the directors of the private company which had taken over the public line petitioned to the assembly against Hartley Gisborne, its former superintendent, charging him with fraud. Linking these charges to the ones against himself, Howe proceeded to give James Stewart and G.E. Morton, two officers of the company who were also his political enemies, "such a lesson as they shall not soon forget." Should either repeat the charges to his face, "my word [is] for naught, if I don't [take action] which will not improve the complexion of his countenance." Yet, perhaps not, since "physically I would be ashamed to set a dog at them." It might be best to follow the course of the Aberdeen Scotchman of Musquodoboit who, when the blackflies got into his ears, eyes, and mouth, "just wrapped [his] breeks around [his] face and let them have fair play at [his] duff ... So I ... have just turned my 'duff' to these gad flies."[65] Seldom had Howe been so excited and the Speaker's "but be calm" did nothing to restrain him. Again it was a case of his tolerating abuse for months and then, impetuously, losing control of himself. This time he did not escape charges of doing harm to the right of petition. Nova Scotia, said

Martin Wilkins, was supposed to have a responsible government in which the people were the masters, "but now we find ... that when the people come here with a petition they are to be kicked out of doors."[66]

As far away as Hamilton newspapers called Howe "the most vulgar and morally incompetent Provincial Secretary in all British North America ... The pugnacious man is represented as a scientific pugilist, and takes considerable pains to keep the 'Bluenoses' in mind of it."[67] Nearer home the *Colonist* pictured Howe as having the characteristics of a prize-fighter, "broad shoulders, bull neck, bony brows, strong flanks, sinewy calves, and wide heels ... But the courage is wanting." The disclosure that the legislature had voted £250 for his "runaway trip" to Britain roused it to new heights of polemic. No matter where it turned, Howe "invariably comes out as a dishonest man"; his unfailing motto was: "Let others speculate. Let me peculate."[68] In June, at a public dinner in Amherst, Howe spent three hours answering the "regular manufacturer of defamation ... in Halifax," calling Alpin Grant, the publisher of the *Colonist*, "a poor cadaverous creature, who drinks like a fish, who is not worth six-pence in the world, but who has a white liver, a red head, and is awfully pitted with the small-pox." To one charge he pleaded guilty, that he liked the ladies and kissed the girls as he rambled about. "But who can ride over this county of Cumberland, and not have almost an invincible inclination to commit such small trespasses as these? ... There may be an ugly one found, occasionally, on the Tory side of politics, but if there is, I do not regard myself bound, by any extreme views of political obligation, to kiss her."[69] As usual, his jocose remarks amused the public while his opponents seethed in frustration.

During the session of 1853 Howe continued to worry about the state of the government. Aware that it was largely lacking in energy, he knew that the remedy could never come from Uniacke, whose deteriorating health was causing him to recede further into the background. Nevertheless, he would be no party to pushing him out. Delighted that the close of the session brought him a respite after months of exacting labour, he awaited the dénouement of the railway question which would be determined largely without him.[70] Meanwhile the *Chronicle* and the *Colonist* continued to jockey with each other on railways for another six months. Even as the former condemned the unseemly conduct of Jackson's associates in the building of the Quebec and Richmond Railway, the latter congratulated the province on its "miraculous escape" from a government line "thanks to the energy and patriotism of Mr. Johnston." Howe, it said, could not have raised a shilling on the British market: "we have it from undoubted authority ... that his character at the Colonial Office is blown. A pickpocket might as well apply there as Mr. Howe."[71] When the *Chronicle* complained that nothing was happening, the *Colonist* repeated *ad nauseam*: "Mr. Jackson wants Nova Scotia in his grand scheme ... if Mr. Jackson does not undertake our Railroads no one else can."[72]

Its "bubble burst" on October 14 with the publication of letters in which Jackson told Hincks and le Marchant that his surveys had found the Nova Scotia works to be "heavy and expensive ... unconnected with a through route" and the traffic insufficient to "support even a very cheap line." Similarly the European and North American line to Portland was not feasible because Maine could "give no state aid and her cities and citizens are too poor." Hence the one hope of making Halifax "the great mart of the east" was to extend the Grand Trunk from Canada to Halifax, a possibility only if Nova Scotia and New Brunswick each contributed annually £20,000 stg and Canada £30,000, for a period long enough to purchase 3¼ per cent terminable annuities.[73]

Delightedly the *Chronicle* applied the needle to Johnston and the *Colonist* for their misplaced faith in Jackson. Was it not apparent that, with an Atlantic terminus connecting Montreal with Portland in his hands, he believed he could get along without Nova Scotia and New Brunswick, but they not without him. "Were ever people so duped and insulted as we have been"? Johnston, who admitted to being Jackson's pecuniary and legal agent in Nova Scotia, had found his master at last: "he has been used – sucked dry – and then thrown away like a dry orange." Yet he should not take it too hard. "The man who is said to have 'boasted that he bought up a majority of the Spanish legislature in a day' ... would not, we presume, very much mind taking a quiet rise out of a conceited Blue Nose Lawyer if it was only for the fun of the thing."[74] Johnston and the *Colonist* expostulated, but were more and more on the defensive against the *Chronicle, Sun,* and *Recorder.* The heat was off Howe and for a short time at least he enjoyed not being the central issue in Nova Scotia politics.

As the session of 1854 began the stage was at last set for Howe to realize his aim of having Nova Scotia build its own railways. The hard terms he had set, the difficult state of the European money market, and the growing danger of war with Russia had combined to ensure that no British money would be available for a joint intercolonial enterprise. He knew, of course, that he would have trouble with the legislature. No sooner had he introduced his railway resolutions when Killam moved to spend £100,000 on roads and bridges. "Mr. Killam's new born zeal for mud roads," growled the *Novascotian,* "is only equalled by his antagonism to those of a more permanent character."[75] It was no less indignant that Johnston had introduced a resolution on union of the colonies and bills relating to an elective council, municipal corporations, and franchise bills, all instruments of delay in its eyes.

This criticism was not altogether fair to Johnston, since the bills were his customary ones and he defended them perhaps better than ever before: "The system of government most debased and debasing in itself," he reiterated, is "that sustained by a clique and an oligarchy operated upon by the corrupting influence of bitter party feeling ... true Conservatism must hereafter consist of a well adjusted, well regulated system of Democratic Institutions."[76] Again his elective council bill got nowhere, and although a municipal corporations bill, optional in character, passed the assembly, it died in the council on a technicality. He was completely successful, however, with a measure effectually introducing universal suffrage, even though Howe, backtracking from the previous session, thought it went too far and wanted "some middle course" which would make the "universal education of our people" a prerequisite "before we force on them privileges and powers, of which they may not know the nature, and of which they should not deprive the freeholders of soil."[77] But he could not think of a middle ground and a majority of both the assembly and the council, determined to get rid of the evils of the rate-paying franchise, went for universal suffrage.

Howe welcomed Johnston's other digression, a resolution favouring the union of the colonies, "as something clearer, more elevated, more exciting ... than some of the discussions in which we have been engaged,"[78] even as he rejected outright the idea of union or any other "new modes of political organization ... until we have tested [our present] expansive powers" and demanded "the full rights of citizenship in this great empire."[79] If Nova Scotia had had representatives in the British Parliament, would one company have continued to monopolize most of the province's minerals; would a railway guarantee have been withdrawn and a pledge violated for the pecuniary advantage of a few British MPs;[80] or would anyone have even suggested that Nova Scotia's greatest birthright, its fisheries, should be sacrified in the interests of Britain?

The sons of the rebels are men full-grown; the sons of the loyalists are not ... How long is this state of pupilage to last? ... I will live under no flag, with a brand of inferiority to the other British races stamped upon my brow. ... How long are we to have this play of 'Hamlet' with Hamlet himself omitted? .. Talk of annexation, sir! what we want is annexation to our mother country. Talk of a union of the Provinces, which, if unaccompanied with other provisions, would lead to separation! What we require is union with the empire, an investiture with the rights and dignity of British citizenship ... what might not this empire become, if its intellectual resources were combined for its government and preservation? If the whole population were united by common interests, no power on earth ever wielded means so vast or influence so irresistible.

Surely, then, British statesmen would not let themselves be deluded by economists who scorned colonists, or fanatics who preached peace with foreign despots whatever the cost; surely they would not let the other half of North America be lost and invite trouble in the old homestead itself.[81]

Widely circulated as usual, Howe's speech brought replies that must have elated him, extravagant though they often were. Many were like that of Moses Perley who said it was "the best you ever made" and lamented that the New Brunswick legislature, instead of dealing with great themes, seemed content with "squabbling over the revised laws."[82] But bringing him back to reality was the *Acadian Recorder*, which told him bluntly that, because of current thinking in Britain, it would be easier for Nova Scotia to "secure representation in some future Parliament of the 'Celestial Empire'" than in the British.[83]

Digressions or not, the session of 1854 was a railway session and Howe's course was determined for him by the new Tory member for Windsor, L.M. Wilkins, Jr, an old opponent whom Howe had "battled from School-House to School-House and from Barn to Barn." When Wilkins indicated that he was prepared to sacrifice sectional, local, and party differences to get on with the railroad, Howe replied he had no desire to have the rest of his career embittered by party strife and only the railway question could "detain me in public life a single day ... Let Nova Scotia be but covered with railways, and ... some other more youthful, more aspiring, more ambitious, is welcome to fill [my office] as soon as he may."[84] Accordingly he proceeded to test "the right feeling and good sense" of the House with six resolutions which, he emphasized, were his own proposals. To Johnston's complaint that under responsible government a minister should be introducing such a scheme only in the name of the government, Howe simply replied that no one political party could by itself make a start in railway construction. Basically the resolutions provided that six commissioners appointed by the Governor in Council and limited to an annual expenditure of £200,000 should direct the building of a government-owned line, starting with the section common to both the trunk line and the branches to Pictou and Windsor. Howe made no attempt either to be provocative or to engage in fine talk, but that did not prevent Johnston from prophesying the impairment of the provincial credit, additional taxation, an increase in the public debt, and a reduction in the road and educational services. Because he considered the resolutions imprecise, he also accused Howe of proposing "a Railway to begin anywhere – to be constructed any way and to go anywhere"; Howe retorted that Johnston's motto was to "begin at no time – build nowhere and construct nohow."[85]

Most of all, Howe minimized the risk. To complete a few miles in the heart of the province, "will not hurt us very much; and there will be an end to any doubt about the cost."[86] Surely Nova Scotia, which rivalled in prosperity any area of comparable size, could afford some risk to make its people better acquainted with each other by means of "this labour-machine." In turn, according to their critics, Johnston, Killam, and Dr Brown used "every argument that sophistry could devise" to defeat Howe,[87] proposing at one time or another a province-wide referendum on the project, a reduction in the £200,000, and a requirement that each county through which the railway passed take £30,000 of stock. Howe stood it all with equanimity until Johnston moved to exclude the commissioners and their employees from the legislature. Knowing himself to be the target, he insisted he could not have been "mean enough" to treat Johnston in the same way; besides, "the principle was not right – not English. It would exclude the ablest men from public office, and if such a principle were adopted, a very different and inferior set of men would take their places here."[88]

The closing days of the debate brought utter mortification to Johnston when it became known that, because of the likelihood of war in Europe and the difficulties of financing, Jackson could no longer "keep up any expectation ... to prosecute the work for some time to come."[89] Nonetheless, Howe could carry his bills by no more than a margin of one in the council and three in the assembly, and, allegedly, only by "forcing one sick man from his home, at the risk of his life – bribing another by giving him his salary in winter, as a first instalment – and paying the full price demanded by a third *honorable* member for his adherence."[90] Howe was particularly chagrined by the defection of the two Acadian Liberals, Bourneuf and Comeau, whose constituents in western Nova Scotia saw no benefits for themselves in the railway, and by the necessity of relying upon Wilkins and three other Tories from Hants County at the end of the branch line to Windsor.

Naturally Johnston and the *Colonist* were indignant at Howe's ill-concealed attempt to "catch the flies" from Hants,[91] for although it was not explicitly stated, the Windsor branch would clearly have priority. "Everyone ... perfectly understands," wrote one correspondent, "that the Railway, if it ever leaves Bedford Basin is to stop at Windsor, and yet Mr. Howe coolly tells you he is building the Trunk line to Amherst!"[92] Almost as if in confirmation, Howe pointed out that Jackson's own engineer had considered the Windsor line a paying proposition; a little poignantly he suggested a more personal reason for proceeding with it: "I have at this moment a daughter – the last, perhaps, that may be left to me – dear to me as the apple of my eye – residing 70 miles distant [in Cornwallis] and whom I have not seen for 6 months. Why? Because I have no means of going there rapidly and returning to attend to the public business which daily presses on me."[93] Thus Howe's vision of an intercolonial line had evaporated and after four years of almost unending activity he had ended up with nothing more than the "poor bantling" he had first proposed in 1835. But he had at least some consolation: he would finally be able to make a start on the provincial railways and he would have another kind of vocation for the next three years.

## CHAPTER FOUR

# Railway Builder and
# Army Recruiter

Howe began his new duties on April 4, 1854, the day the government underwent a major face-lift. The changes, he said, "provided for all our men who were worn or wearing out, reconstructed a Cabinet with solid, good material," and established "a Capital [Railway] Board, all men of character."[1] Among those leaving the ministry were Provincial Secretary Joseph Howe, who became chief railway commissioner, and the attorney general and leader of the government, J.B. Uniacke, who, "poor fellow," one Liberal assemblyman wrote, "appears to be fairly used up and wholly unfit for public business."[2] Criticism followed within hours. The financially straitened Uniacke escaped most of it, even though he was made commissioner of Crown lands and burdened with duties that failing health made him incompetent to perform. Instead the attack was centred on the government for being so brazen as to create a vacancy for him by superseding John Spry Morris, on temporary leave of absence in Britain.

Succeeding Uniacke in his two capacities was William Young, who, it was said, had been "a complete political weather-cock, but one which has always pointed office-ward."[3] Canny Scot that he was, he had bided his time in building up his fortune while waiting for the office that led naturally to the chief justiceship. How, it was asked, could he be on fraternal terms with Joseph Howe, who had termed his brother George an imbecile and a madman, and might almost be called his murderer?[4] Almost scotfree from criticism was the ever complaining W.A. Henry, who became solicitor general allegedly because he threatened periodically to go into opposition; perhaps those responsible for appointing him thought him less dangerous inside, than outside, the Executive Council. In the end the full fury of the attack fell upon the three Tory defectors who accepted office. Stephen Fulton, a new minister without departmental duties, got off most easily, possibly because his defection was now ancient history. Stewart Campbell, who succeeded Young as Speaker, became the "Guysborough rat," while L.M. Wilkins, who had made it possible for Howe to implement his railway policy and took over from him as provincial secretary, was described as "a man who can be bought and sold," who "bartered reputation, friendship and self-respect" for office, and who would therefore "feel very much at home in the society of the great patriot and embezzler," Joseph Howe.[5]

In the defections the *Acadian Recorder* saw further evidence of the decay of the party system which it had long been lamenting. "The principles upon which the two parties avowedly started in opposition to each other have long ceased to be matters of consideration. The struggle, for many years, has been merely for place, power, and the lucre of office."[6] Howe dismissed the moanings of the editor John English as frustration at his failure to become Queen's printer, but he had much greater difficulty with his old friend, Richard Nugent of the *Sun*, who stood by principle even if it meant offending his bishop or his old political allies. Horrified when Wilkins told the electors of Windsor that "in a change of place in the House of Assembly *no change of principles is necessarily involved*," Nugent demanded assurance of "the completeness of his supposed conversion." Some of his correspondents also wondered how Wilkins, who one day was "a high Churchman ... an unwavering support of Toryism – the aide-de-camp of Johnston," could the next day be "a Liberal! – the associate of Howe!! – the friend and colleague of Bill Young!!! – the supporter of a party composed principally of Catholics and Dissenters! – the *very dear friend* of the reviled mob!!"[7]

This was too much for the *Chronicle* (and Howe?) to take, and it accused the *Sun* of supplying the texts in advance for the attacks of the *Colonist.*[8] Within the day Nugent replied that his paper was "too liberal, ... and certainly too independent ... to meet the approbation of Mr. Howe and the bevy of flunkies with whom he cares to surround himself." Although he knew his opposition to Wilkins would "anger the Dictator," he simply could not accept Howe's prattle "about party distinctions fading away."[9] While conceding that the agenda of provincial politics was subject to continual change, he insisted nonetheless that the differences along the conservative-liberal spectrum remained as they were. In contrast, Howe held that only the railway mattered and, because of the assembly's particularism, he willingly accepted any of its advocates into the party whatever his previous political stance. Though annoyed by Nugent, he looked forward to "the grand rows between the new Cabinet and the old opposition," now that he was free of ministerial duties. "My eyes, if the wool won't fly when Young and Wilkins and Johnston get at it. Fancy me, with grave face, looking on, and occasionally imploring them, for the welfare of the State, to keep the peace."[10]

Within twenty-four hours Howe had vacated the provincial secretaryship (while retaining his assembly seat) and had established the railway office in the former "President's Room" in Province House. The same day he convened the first meeting of the board and was delighted with the representativeness and the credentials of its members. He had taken special care that his pledge of equal party representation was honoured. Besides himself, the Liberal members were his long-time political ally Jonathan McCully and Thomas S. Tobin, a wealthy Catholic merchant of Halifax. The Conservatives were John H. Anderson, a Halifax business man worth £40,000 and a leading Methodist; William Prior, member of a large Halifax mercantile concern; and Perez M. Cunningham of Windsor, perhaps the wealthiest and ablest business man in Hants County. The board's accountant was John Morrow, who, Howe prophesied, would "keep a set of books that we can chain to the Town Pump, as they used to do the Bibles in old time."[11] He was no less pleased that its engineer would be his nominee, James R. Forman, the native Nova Scotian who had had extensive experience in building railways in Britain.

By May 3 the board had invited tenders for grading six and a half miles, beginning at the Halifax terminus in the city's outskirts at Richmond and extending to the Nine Mile River. In a month the tenders were in and the contract awarded to a Pictou group, who broke the first sod nine days later. According to Howe, le Marchant was so amazed at the speedy action that he "swears that I would undertake the building of a Line of Battle Ship, and lay the keel in 24 hours."[12] By the end of the year the board had awarded contracts for a further two sections, in all more than ten miles, extending from the terminus to the head of Bedford Basin. Perhaps anxious to assuage Howe a little, Nugent congratulated him on the success of his railway policy to date, even as the *Recorder* condemned "the peddling, niggardly system of dividing the job of making the road into small, paltry parcels," which, it contended, was well devised for "filling the maws of parasites, and pampering favorites."[13] But if it had been really serious about preventing large-scale jobbery, it might have seen that the board's procedures were especially designed to avoid it.

Using a New Brunswick source, the *Recorder* and *Colonist* also complained about the number and sharpness of the curves on the first section of the line. In his reply Howe reported only one curve with a radius under twenty chains, that at Birch Cove, where the terrain was very difficult. Instead of being "botched," the line would be superior in many respects to William Jackson's in New Brunswick; for one thing the Nova Scotian sleepers, ten feet long instead of eight or nine, would provide "that much more bearing."[14] Admittedly the initial costs were heavy because of the rocky terrain leading out of Halifax and the "heavy embankments [that] had to be formed across coves and arms of the basin," but once "the river beds and fertile lands of the interior" were reached, the cost would be materially reduced.[15] When the *Recorder* questioned the board's dealings with such picayune matters as the purchase of sleepers and wheelbarrows, it needed only to say in reply that it was making sure that no materials were supplied at excessive prices. Day after day it considered tenders for rails of various weights, spikes, switches, picks, dobbin-carts, and T-chairs. It also made a host of other decisions: not to use juniper sleepers; to buy its first locomotive in New England; to subsidize the bringing in of Newfoundland labour. Periodically its critics would doubt its bona fides. Who, they asked, would question aught that Howe decided? But although he was the only full-time member of the board and received a salary of £700 to the others' £200, the evidence is that its decisions were corporate, not individual, ones.

Even while immersed in railway building, Howe let no opportunity pass to demonstrate both his concept and support of empire. In March 1854, as the Crimean War approached and British forces were being moved to the Baltic and Black seas, he demanded that Nova Scotia "not detain a single [British] Regiment here that may be wanted in the Mediterranean ... there is but one feeling in Nova Scotia, when the Flag of England is unfurled."[16] Later in the year he denied John Robert Godley's contention that the separation of British America from the Mother Country was inevitable and suggested that his picture of "John Bull ... blowing off colonies ... would make a good frontispiece for Punch." Was Godley not naïve to believe that, in case of separation, the former colonies would come to Britain's aid with fleets and armies? Did he not realize that there was "a powerful suction towards the [American] Republic while you apply no counteracting forces"? Was it not sad that a man of his talents thought it impossible to devise some means by which "the national aspirations and honorable ambitions of these high spirited [colonial] people can be gratified without offence to British prejudices"?[17]

Still intent on securing colonial representation in the British Commons, Howe lamented the lack of a common arena in which to discuss colonial matters. If it had existed in the 1770s, he told C.B. Adderley,[18] the opponents might have "buffeted each other into mutual respect" and the American Revolution might not have occurred. Washington would have been "selected to command a

Brigade in Flanders. Jefferson would probably have been a Secretary of State and the Declaration of Independence might have been indefinitely postponed." Like his father before him Howe wanted, above all else, to preserve the British connection and hence his share of the British heritage.

> Whether you allow it or not we feel we have a common right to inheritance in much that our ancestors have bequeathed. ... I walk into Westminster Abbey and the Howe banner hangs as high as any other in Henry the 7ths Chapel. I walk into Greenwich Hospital and there stands Black Dick, in white marble, but with the broad chest and ample forehead which the Howes 'of this ilk' have never wanted. Now I feel that I have a property in these two noble piles which our common ancestors built and bequeathed, quite equal to that of any gentleman in London.

A few months earlier Howe had been given clear-cut evidence of Nova Scotia's inequality within the empire. Shortly after assuming office, William Young agreed to join the governor general, Lord Elgin, at a convention in the United States on reciprocity and the fisheries.[19] Later, after Hincks requested a preliminary meeting with the Nova Scotia and New Brunswick delegates in New York, the lower provinces were told to await further instructions from either Lord Elgin or John Crampton, the British ambassador in Washington. Word came to Chandler of New Brunswick, but not to Young, and the arrangements for a reciprocity treaty were eventually concluded at Washington without Nova Scotia's participation. Although Young found "something mysterious" about it, he was by no means unhappy: "Now we are free as a Govmt from the responsibility of the Treaty which is highly unacceptable to a large body of our people and will be resisted I believe à l'outrance by Johnston."[20] Hincks, however, was bitterly disappointed; his relations with Howe having cooled noticeably after the latter had failed to join him in Britain in early 1853 and then had criticized his use of Jackson and private companies to build railways in Canada, he had been hoping to establish a better rapport with Young.[21] Whatever the cause of the slip up, not all Nova Scotians were convinced of his innocence in the failure to let Nova Scotia know about the timing of the convention.

Because Young disavowed responsibility for the Reciprocity Treaty when the legislature met late in 1854 to pass legislation for its implementation, Howe could speak uninhibitedly.[22] In its fisheries, he said, Nova Scotia had the only thing the Americans valued and hence it "was not wanted to send delegates to Washington." Canada, without fisheries of its own and frozen up for half the year, willingly gave up Nova Scotia's for the reciprocity it had wanted for years and it could not have cared less if, "after having robbed us ... Nova Scotia had been submerged in the waters which surround her!" Equally guilty were the British statesmen who "pandered to the blustering of American diplomatists" in order to induce the United States not to act against Britain in the Crimean War. If the province's most valuable rights could be swept away by the dash of any colonial secretary's pen, "the time is rapidly approaching when we should have to appoint here a Committee on Foreign Relations – these Foreign Relations to include the Realm of England."

That night, the 5th of December, Howe read the documents relating to the negotiations and the next day he expressed himself even more strongly.[23] Was there "a man here who is of opinion I would shrink from the performance of a duty, however unpleasant"? What had the loyal colony of Nova Scotia ever done to merit such treatment? Though it had no more interest in the Crimean War than in "disputes between the King of the Musquitoes and the Government of Central America," it would still give Britain its full support. How, then, without the province's consent, could anyone even contemplate giving American fishermen permission to land on the Nova Scotian coast to cure their fish and dry their nets? "Would any Englishman, Scotchman, or Irishman, submit to such a humiliation; the barriers guarding their sacred soil broken down, and a footing given to the alien and foreigner upon it ... thus have we been sacrificed to British necessity and American pressure."

Although Howe gave wholehearted support to Johnston's resolutions denouncing the failure to consult Nova Scotia, only fifteen assemblymen – three Liberals and twelve Conservatives – joined him. He had no greater success with resolutions of his own condemning the granting to foreigners of privileges along the Nova Scotian coast which Britons had never conceded even in the darkest period of their history.[24] Young had been right that, although the zealots would find the method of effecting the treaty and some of its provisions obnoxious, most assemblymen would not consider them unpalatable. To Howe the proceedings constituted only one more reason for machinery that would permit colonial participation in the decisions of empire.

Howe's railway duties prevented him from playing an active part in a session which carried over into early 1855 and, even when present, he tended to assume the role of a nonpartisan senior statesman. Once he warned that the distance of Nova Scotia from the Crimea did not necessarily shield the province from attack: "money was all powerful and the Emperor of Russia could purchase the fleet of the United

States – bombard our seaport towns and perhaps overrun the Country."[25] He called it "a move in the right direction" when the British government made one naval cadetship available annually to a Nova Scotian and was delighted that, because of his own advocacy of provincial claims to imperial patronage, his son Sydenham secured the first nomination. Although he did not expect him to contribute much to the reduction of Cronstadt or Sebastopol, he hoped he would do his duty and remember the example of his great namesake, "Black Dick."[26]

Two matters which had always interested him came up late in the session when he could not be present. Although pleased that the Court of Chancery had at long last been abolished, he would later comment bitterly on the generous retiring provisions for his old *bête noire*, Alexander Stewart, master of the rolls. He also disliked the Act for the Municipal Government of Counties, since its elective provisions were limited to four counties and then only on their own volition. Despite other preoccupations, he took pains to be present to resist Johnston's attempt to impose the Maine Liquor Law, which prohibited the importation, manufacture, and sale of alcohol, and by implication sought to regulate morals.[27]

Who will venture to argue that because mischief is done by many of God's gifts, they should on that account be circumscribed or prohibited by human laws? ... Woman is God's best gift to man ... Yet, when even love is indulged in to excess, when reason is overpowered, when passion hurries on to folly – how numerous the victims ... Who denies that law is the safeguard of our lives and property; ... But has not even law been abused? How many pettifoggers defile the courts, ensnare the ignorant, waste men's estates and embitter their lives?

Had not everything valuable in the past, in heroism, architecture, oratory, sculpture, and painting, been handed down along with the juice of the grape and had any country been long without it or drunk nothing but cold water? Had Maine yet turned out a statue that anyone would look at or a picture that anyone would buy? "I resist this bill ... because it is defended by the old arguments by which fanatics and persecutors in all ages have sought to propagate religious opinions ... The right of one man to coerce others into belief ... has been tried a thousand times, and has failed, as this attempt will fail." Fearful that the assembly would succumb to a wave of temperance, he proposed that a commission should first examine the "character, working and effects"[28] of similar acts in the United States, but got little support. The Legislative Council came to his aid, however, when, by requiring publicity for the bill, it prevented its enactment. That was

Howe's last major intervention in the session; perhaps he was glad to miss six weeks of proceedings which one colleague described as "altogether annoying if not disgusting,"[29] and to be engaged in another mission, little knowing that it would drain his energy, endanger his liberty, and perhaps injure his later career.

Alarmed by the serious losses sustained by its army in the Crimea, the tottering Aberdeen government in Britain was attempting remedial action. Because Britons showed no great enthusiasm to be recruited, it resorted to the old practice of encouraging foreigners to enlist through the Foreign Enlistment Act of December 1854. The act took special cognizance of the economic recession and seasonal unemployment in the United States, which were inducing scores of revolutionary emigrés to offer their services to the British army. Though at first reluctant, the British minister in Washington, John F. Crampton, bowed to pressure from the foreign secretary, Lord Clarendon, and sought the permission of Governor General Sir Edmund Head to send to Canada emigrants who might wish to enlist there. He got nowhere, however, when Gen. William Rowan, commanding British troops in North America, raised all sorts of objections, including the absence of depots and the inability to transport the recruits down a frozen river.

Howe became involved when the war secretary, Sidney Herbert, asked Sir Gaspard le Marchant to communicate with Crampton on the practicability of sending "volunteers" from the United States to Halifax. The letter requested le Marchant only to investigate and report, and when Clarendon sent a copy to Crampton, he emphasized that the domestic laws of the United States were to be scrupulously respected.[30] That was the catch, since the American neutrality laws made it an offence to "hire or retain" any person to go beyond the jurisdiction of the United States "with intent to be enlisted." The trip to Halifax "even from the seaboard cities was expensive and the potential recruits were 'out-of-works'. Merely to get them off to Halifax on the chance that they *might* enlist was a poor gamble. To contract with them to enlist was a breach of the ... laws. The stage was set for some impatient and active person to cut the Gordian knot."[31] Consulting Joseph Howe, the most active person he knew, le Marchant was advised to send an executive councillor to expedite matters with Crampton; none being willing, Howe himself agreed to go at le Marchant's "most earnest request." Even in the preliminary discussions J. Bartlet Brebner sees "the predominance of Howe's vigorous and inventive mind,"[32] but throughout the complex web of events which followed Crampton seems to have been more conspirator than dupe and le Marchant himself was not entirely innocent since he agreed that it would be a useful and harmless deception for Howe to act as an employer of railway labourers – "being commissioner for Provincial Railways, [he] *might require for carrying on the works such persons as are in requisition for her Majesty's service.* His movements would, in this respect, be sufficiently masked."[33] The governor insisted, however, that Howe confine himself to inquiries and investigation unless Crampton had received additional instructions from Britain.

One critic has suggested that Howe should have "stood with Bright and Cobden" in the Crimean War and refused to have his hands stained with blood, instead of going along with "weak Aberdeen, bellicose Palmerston, and ... inept Raglan."[34] But to say this is to fail to understand Howe. It never occurred to him that he needed to probe deeply into the background of the war; for him it was enough that it was a British war and British troops needed reinforcements. So, at the beginning of March 1855, with barely an hour's notice, he was making a dash to board the brigantine *Africa* for Boston, with "everybody helping me and requiring everybody's help." He spent much of March 8 in New York talking to British consul Anthony Barclay and labourers in all parts of the city. That was long enough to make him doubt Barclay's optimistic prophecy of a plentiful supply of volunteers in the area: "my own impression was *that the most favorable moment had passed.*"[35]

In keeping with the clandestine nature of his visit Howe arrived in Washington after dark on the 9th and spent the night mapping out strategy with Crampton in the absence of further instructions from Britain. Shown General Rowan's objections to establishing a depot in Canada, Howe called them "perfectly 'Balaclava'" and made it his first duty to "get rid of this General and his Report." Arguing that none of Rowan's objections applied to Halifax, he quickly convinced Crampton that it should be the rendezvous for volunteers and that, aided by the British consuls, he "should have full powers to act according to my own discretion in carrying out the views of Her Majesty's Government."[36] It was also agreed that Crampton would on no account be allowed to become identified with the recruiting process and later Howe could say that he "acted invariably upon the principle that whoever was to be compromized or sacrificed, the Queen's Representative at Washington ought to be protected."[37] Finally the two concluded that, in addition to paying the costs of the operation out of the military chest or the Provincial Treasury until authorized to use secret service funds, le Marchant should also assume the full responsibility for advertising, and for receiving, maintaining, and training the recruits, but should do nothing beyond Nova Scotia to which the Americans might object.

From Howe's report of the meeting Brebner has deduced a reversal of the roles of the two men: "one can imagine Crampton's relief as this lively stranger proposed to take on his broad shoulders the responsibilities which had so worried him and the consuls. Now the officials need not soil the hems of their garments."[38] It is going much too far to suggest, however, that Crampton had largely abandoned his role to Howe. By his own account of March 12 he was "hard at work on the subject of the recruitment," and making it very clear to Clarendon that he could not await instructions, "for if anything is to be done it must be done *now*." But his hope to stay legally within the hiring or retaining provision of the neutrality laws received a setback when the embassy counsel, the distinguished J. Mandeville Carlisle, told him the words were to be given a very broad interpretation and that they prohibited "every case of payment, expenditure, or other valuable consideration (however ingeniously devised)" to a prospective recruit.[39] Forwarded as a warning, this opinion did not daunt Howe. "The ground is indeed narrow ... I shall treat it circumspectly," he observed. "[But] it is better that I should run some risk rather than that our Government should be without men."[40]

Howe quickly concluded that for reasons both of economy and of practicality the limits of his recruiting would be Philadelphia in the south and Boston in the east and north: "between these two points (New York lying between) I shall vibrate until my work is done."[41] Between March 11 and 14 he was in Philadelphia establishing contact with the British consul, George Mathew, and seeking out persons who had offered their services. Misery, he said, made one acquainted with strange bedfellows: "I have dived into Oyster cellars, and lounged through Lager Beer houses, until I have imagined myself qualified for any Club of conspirators in Christendom." At any moment he feared he might be "in some precious mess, requiring great coolness and dexterity to carry me through," but he relied on his superiors for a "generous construction of my acts"; otherwise, "I would go home tomorrow."[42] The unprepossessing lot of fellows whom he interviewed included "Schleswick Holstein officers, Scotch Military enthusiasts, German Jew Crimps and God knows how many more strange animals." Most he could quickly dismiss on grounds of age, attitude, or general unsuitability, and he was left with Henry Hertz, "an infernal Jew Crimp, one of the greatest rascals I ever met ... I think he is a lineal descendant of the Jew who sold his Saviour for 30 pieces of silver, and for 30 pieces of gold this rascal would sell the whole British Army."[43] Nevertheless, in the absence of better material, he let Hertz have $300 of his limited private funds and authorized him to raise 1,000 men from Pennsylvania and Maryland at $8.00 a man delivered in Nova Scotia. Time would amply confirm his initial judgment of Hertz.

On March 14 Howe put up at Delmonico's in New York and spent half the night "cabbing" about the city, contacting many who had written to Crampton. On first appearance they appeared a much better lot than those in Philadelphia. He was especially taken with "a respectable merchant," Angus McDonald, and agreed that for landing 1,000 men in Nova Scotia he would receive a lieutenant-colonelcy, £250 for his equipment, and $1.00 a head from the bounty money as a gratuity. Lewis Grant also promised to raise 1,000 men and Andrew Lutz 436. As his man of all work, Howe engaged Thomas S. Bucknall, an unemployed but "sharp and active" civil engineer. Wherever possible, he decided to make the bounty of $8.00 a head cover the expense of getting a man to Halifax. "Where I cannot I shall exercise my discretion my rule being, to get the men, *cheap if I can*, but at any price, *to get them*."[44] He also devised a system of forwarding recruits which, he hoped, would offer the least chance of offence to the Americans. A person raising men would be given cards marked "N.S.R." When presented to a shipping agent, a card would entitle the prospective recruit to free passage to Halifax and also act as a voucher assuring payment to the carrier. "N.S.R." could, of course, mean Nova Scotia Railway or Nova Scotia Regiment.[45]

The fertile mind of Howe could not be expected to content itself with the mundane, if dangerous, chore of recruiting and refrain from intruding into weightier matters at a higher level. A new stock of ideas followed his meeting with Ward B. Burnett, a senior officer at the Brooklyn dockyard, who offered to arrange the sale of surplus rifles for the recruits. Accordingly, on March 15, Howe approached Lord John Russell, several times before the target of his ideas, with a proposal to improve the fire-power of the soldiers. British rifles, he pointed out, still used the ramrod, a "clumsy contrivance"; in contrast, American forces were equipped with Sharp's carbines and rifles, which were primed by cocking and loaded at the breech, and which could fire fifteen shots a minute to the British five. "The Coldstreams, at Inkerman, armed with the weapon would have annihilated the Russian columns with small comparitive loss." Yet, though important, he expected little to come from his suggestion: "No doubt shall get 5 cold lines expressing 'Johnny's regret'."[46] But a day's visit to Sharp's factory at Hartford convinced him he should continue to press the matter. On March 21, during Russell's absence at a congress in Vienna, he had the temerity to approach Lord

Palmerston, who had become prime minister a month or two earlier. This time, not content with mere verbal description, he forwarded him a rifle and carbine through his agent, E. Sanford, a bookseller in Charing Cross Road, and told him he had only to give the word to get enough of the weapons for all the new regiments.[47] If Howe had not reminded him, Palmerston would perhaps not have remembered that this was the colonial upstart whom he had entertained during the railway mission of 1852.

Howe had still another idea for his superiors. Why not send the British regiment in Nova Scotia and the two in Canada to the Black Sea immediately? "To have a British force of [only] 11,000 men in the Crimea, opposed to such a power as Russia, renders us ridiculous."[48] Until the war was over the militia could easily defend the North American colonies. Only a few drill sergeants needed to be left behind to whip into shape the recruits who, as his first days in New York indicated, were available in abundance; optimistically he thought in terms of 1,000 men in a week, 3,000 to 4,000 in a month, and 10,000 before the first of June. But that bubble of enthusiasm burst almost as he wrote.

Shortly after arriving in New York he had circulated handbills announcing that anyone presenting himself to le Marchant in Halifax would, on enlistment, receive a bounty of $30 and $8 a month, together with food, clothing, and quarters. By making it purport to provide information only he may not have infringed the "hiring and retaining" provisions of the neutrality laws, but Angus McDonald, not nearly so circumspect, actually connected the British government with the contents of his signed handbills. Horrified, Crampton told the British consul in New York to deny it and warned Howe of the "mischief [that] might be done by proceedings of this sort." Equally worried, le Marchant also cautioned Howe: "for God's sake do not exceed your authority. Look to Mr. C. in everything – for I am really without powers or instruction from the Home govt to order anything."[49] In reply, Howe willingly admitted he had trouble in restraining both McDonald and Lewis Grant: "I have repeatedly cautioned them *to do nothing which was unlawful.* You are quite right in disclaiming responsibility for any thing they do, or any thing I do either."[50]

To add to his difficulties, his private funds were soon exhausted and he did not receive additional money drawn on the Bank of Commerce until March 21. Even then he had to use a distant cousin living in New York, "Tommy" Tilestone, for purposes of identification. It annoyed him no end that on each of the four times he had left home on public business "it never once occurred to any body that I might want money, and that to provide it is one of the first duties of those who send me."[51] Although not long in disbursing the funds to keep the machinery of recruiting in operation, he was realizing more and more the difficulties of meeting his objectives. Clearly most of his agents were interested in little but personal gain and it "proved impossible to impress upon them, and upon the remoter figures at the fringes of the organization, the technical delicacy of [his] devices for keeping within the law." Worse still, American opinion was decidedly anti-British and the American authorities "would not passively accept evasion of neutrality, nor would Russian officials and indignant Irishmen allow them to ignore it."[52] By the 24th Howe's agents had attracted so much attention that he reported the "Heather on fire. Newspapers blazing away, and every body frightened." Not fearful of himself, he did "fancy that there is always a Policeman at Delmonico's Corner."[53]

Summoned by a worried Crampton, Howe spent the 25th in Washington explaining his circulation of handbills and distribution of tickets. Mandeville Carlisle discussed the legal aspects of recruiting with him and instructed him in the precautions he should take if he were detained. Perhaps with intent to deceive, perhaps self-deceived, Howe wrote that he "soon put all right, [Crampton] approving of all that I had done"[54] in the previous ten days. As Brebner indicates,[55] these assurances and the actual facts are difficult to reconcile, but they do become understandable in light of the inarticulate major premises of Crampton and Howe. The former naturally wanted to avoid any appearance of illegalities, especially at a time when he was assuring the American secretary of state, William L. Marcy, that he would not infringe the American domestic laws and Marcy was concurring in the correctness of his position.[56] Yet, no less than Howe, he wanted to provide the troops badly needed by Britain and he likely gave his sanction to Howe's activities "in the only mode that he as a Minister ... dare give, or [Howe] as a gentleman could ask it."[57] He could hardly have been so naïve as to believe that Howe might accomplish his mission by staying within the strict letter of the law.

In contrast, Howe's position was more open, that of a man who said he never shrank from responsibility when the path of duty was clear. "Being convinced that the Queen's Minister – the Ambassador – and [le Marchant] wished this work done, and nobody else being here to do it I did not hesitate to put my hand to it."[58] From Philadelphia, the day after he left Washington, he outlined,[59] perhaps for the only time in detail, a conception of the role he was playing that was markedly different from his public thesis on recruiting. From his first meeting with Crampton, he said, the basic assumption was that, by operating from Nova Scotia, the neutrality law need not be breached and publicly he still adhered to it. Hence he continued to write and say he had done no more than provide information about le Marchant's recruitment of a foreign legion. But almost from the start he knew that this approach would yield few recruits and that "agents must be employed, vessels hired, passages by ship or Rail secured and paid for, officers talked to and poor men aided, to pay their debts and get away."

Now I mean to do *what the British Government want done,* and what Your Excellency [le Marchant] sent me here to do, without expecting what the nature of the service precludes, "orders or detailed instructions *from any quarter"* ... My purpose is, to ... get 7000 men or more into the Crimea *at all hazards.* That I can do this without violating the neutrality laws I do not believe – that I can do it, in a Country where Russian feeling and hatred of England, are almost universal, without personal risk I can hardly hope, but I am prepared at all points, and all that I must stipulate for is, *room to move.*

Howe was certain that, although the British government did not provide detailed instructions, it would "approve his actions, as it, in effect, did."[60] It was this conviction that led him to persist in his recruiting mission.

For Howe the days that followed were nothing short of hectic.[61] In Philadelphia, after "a tremendous battle to choke off and bring the Jew [Hertz] to reason," he attended the circus with some newfound friends and then "drank them all drunk" at the Philadelphia Club. Late at night a telegram from Bucknall announced everything to be in a state of collapse and he was off to New York immediately: "half a night's sleep in three nights." Daylight of the 27th found him and Bucknall clearing decks and then he was off to less dangerous quarters in the Napoleon Hotel on the Jersey side, where he quickly rid his box of all "combustible materials." His position could hardly have been worse: his agents scattered and frightened out of their wits; Bucknall arrested and carried off to Philadelphia; a bill of indictment before the grand jury of New York charging Howe himself with a misdemeanour. For almost three weeks he kept no diary and inevitably he made mistakes when he sought to recall the lost days.

Those days were, in fact, unlike any others he would ever experience. For the only time in his life he was forced into concealment and a change of name, first to Mr Vail, later to Mr Cumberland. The arrest which he expected hourly was not pleasant to contemplate. "To be in the rude hands of a Yankee marshal and of his Myrmidons even for an hour would be no joke. To be consigned to the Tombs in the absence of or failure to procure Bail would not be pleasant." Should his superiors not have thought of the contingency of his arrest since "bail in such a service as this is as necessary as bullets at Sebastopool"? If he were released on bail, what ought he to do: forfeit it and add substantially to the cost of the operation or stand trial under the most unfavourable circumstances? Every Irishman and almost every native American was pro-Russian and they would constitute a majority of any jury. Besides, he had talked to 300 or 400 persons since he had come to the United States. "How many of these may be Russian spies who will swear to any thing, or Secret Police"? Even if they were all honest, who would answer for their discretion? "Can a man touch filth and not be defiled"? Finally, could a court operate in the midst of an excited anti-British population and not be hostile to him? Such were the matters he meditated in his little parlor at Hoboken. His conclusions were to use every fair means to avoid arrest and, if arrested, to give bail and carry on his work until his trial, and then to follow instructions from home either to forfeit bail or to trust to one of his own appeals to the jury. As was usual when he had determined his future course his spirits rose. "I am in the Queen's service, and am bound to serve her. The interests of my own country and not the Laws of this must govern my actions, – and shall. My duty is, to accomplish my mission with as little risk as possible, but to accomplish it at all hazards."

Meanwhile the movement against the recruiters was developing into what was almost a crusade. The American attorney general, Caleb Cushing, not only ordered the seizure of vessels, but spurred the district attorneys and marshals into greater enforcement activities. The result was to paralyse the work of Howe's agents. McDonald, who proved to have neither nerve nor discretion, gave up altogether; so did Grant who, after sending sixty or seventy Irish to Windsor, was betrayed by his associates. Lutz, whom Howe respected, was arrested, as was Hertz who, even after his arrest, continued to make almost daily demands. Although Howe regretted that Hertz had been given about $700, he congratulated himself on his foresight in ensuring that the agent had not "a line with [his] name to it, or receive[d] a dollar in any body's presence."[62]

Because of the excited state of public opinion, Howe decided to suspend operations temporarily and simply to avoid arrest, if at all possible. First, he moved to another hotel in Jersey City and then, because it was inconvenient for his friends, he put up at Holridge's Hotel under an alias. "Wonder if her Majesty or any of her ministers would run this risk for me."[63] Within a day he was off to private lodgings at Boudin's, taking care to disguise his trail by stopping the cab short of the place and carrying his baggage to it. He also made sure that few knew his whereabouts, not even Crampton or le Marchant, and that nothing in his handwriting should get into anybody's hands. These steps, he told Crampton, were intended to fulfil his first duty: "to baffle McKeon [the New York district attorney] in finding his Bill" against him.[64] Nevertheless, within a day or two, "two villainous looking rascals" appeared at his lodgings. "Thought the game was up ... Kept cool. In search of Englishman with whiskers ... Was not me .. All puzzled. I strangely perplexed." Later, during dinner at the Tilestones', "those infernal fellows' hard faces are present to me all the time." So, taking greater precautions than ever before, he "never travelled the same route ... rarely slept twice in the same bed. Walked the street by day and night."[65] It worked, since, by cutting off McKeon from any source of accurate information, his bill of indictment against Howe failed for want of evidence.

On April 9, while still in the midst of the crisis, Howe received a telegram in cipher requesting his return to Halifax to "concert measures" with le Marchant, who had been left in the dark on some material points about the mission and who was worried by reports of police action against Howe's agents and rumours of his arrest. Thunderstruck, Howe replied that to return would be to "treat [Crampton] with great disrespect ... violate other obligations ... and cover us all with ridicule."[66] Attempting to play one off against the other, he asked Crampton to confirm his view of things, adding that if he went to Halifax he was not likely to return. To a third party he confided that "the difficulties, and perils and impediments were here, *to be met and overcome here*, if they could at all."[67] His pleas were successful and by the 13th he was told it was "all right" to remain.

Almost from the outset Howe had concluded that the chief impediment to his "sending goods in large quantities" was the fact that the United States was "*as much a Russian stronghold as Sebastopol.*" While Russia had "her spies – her writers – her gold, freely at work there," England had not a man "with the head, the nerve and the ability to counteract her influence."[68] He looked in vain for a generous sentiment towards England in the American newspapers; instead he found the "harassing details" which the English radical John Arthur Roebuck had furnished about the mismanagement of the war. As a publicist, he found the situation intolerable and he decided to fire in return a temperate, plain letter "which, his friends tell him, will do good."[69] Because his name had not yet been mentioned in any editorial, he decided it would be bad taste to issue the letter in his name; instead he called it the "Letter of a British American addressed to the People of the United States." Should a

British American, it asked, not have the right to return home without having to declare he did not intend to enlist? Should an Englishman who wanted to fill a place in the Coldstream Guards be prevented from leaving or an Irishman who saw a vacant saddle in the Inniskillings? Why should French, German, Holstein, Polish, or Hungarian gentlemen, whom the convulsions of Europe had displaced, be condemned to music, fencing, or dancing, when they had the chance of honorable service in their own profession? Surely Americans with their intelligence, common sense, and "reliance upon the free spirit which pervades their institutions" would not stand in the way of any such person. "State it fairly to the Democracy of any large city of the union, in their wildest moment of excitement, and the people would say, 'Let him go!'"

The letter did not point out that purely voluntary activities of the kind it described would not run foul of the American neutrality laws. Yet Howe was characteristically delighted that, just as earlier he had been brought into direct contact with the Nova Scotian and British publics, so now he would have a similar relationship with the American. He thought he was successful too. After the *New York Times* printed his letter on April 5 he, if no one else, noted a change of tone in many of the papers: "Tribune civil. Journal of Commerce favourable. All the others silent or more moderate ... Breathe more freely."[70] Having had the letter translated and published in the leading German, Italian, and French papers in the United States he again reported that "the effect was all that I had hoped." But undoubtedly he exaggerated its influence. By the time of its publication the public outcry was already subsiding; moreover, as he would soon discover, it made recruiting no easier. The almost irrepressible publicist tried his hand again when McKeon boarded a steamer leaving for Boston and without warrant ordered ashore persons whom he believed destined for Halifax. Writing as "A Foreigner,"[71] Howe argued that an attorney general of England who so abused his office would "not hold up his head in the House of Commons for an hour" and that none in the smallest British American province would similarly degrade himself and "*go and serve the process himself.*" But the New York *Herald* chose not to print the letter and it was a wasted effort.

Undeterred by his setbacks Howe started to reorganize his "shattered machinery," choosing, as a successor to Bucknall, John Turnbull, the best of all his agents, and, as messenger, a young German named Parkus. On April 2 he expressed an intention to employ only "men of higher capacity, standing and experience," to "get hold of officers of rank and talent and raise the levies if possible, through them."[72] Again he relied on Crampton and the consuls for names of foreign officers, the most promising being Col. Gabriel de Korponay, a Hungarian nobleman recommended by Charles Rowcroft, the consul in Cincinnati, and considered by Howe to be one of the most gifted men he had ever met. Not only had he served with distinction in the Mexican War, but he was supposed to have "an *organized, & officered* corps of 600 Riflemen [in Kentucky] – his former corps – ready for the parade or field – in 30 days."[73] Apparently he was all the more anxious to serve in the hope that the British government might use its good offices to secure the release of his brother, a former minister of war, imprisoned in a Hungarian fortress.

Howe used de Korponay to communicate with the leaders of the foreign population and sift out the most reputable officers. Many he recommended were interviewed by le Marchant in Halifax before being commissioned and offered a rank dependent upon the number of recruits they might obtain in the United States. Although le Marchant was generally impressed by their quality, inevitably there were mistakes. Thus M.F.O. Strobel turned out to be in the pay of Attorney General Cushing and later testified against Hertz in a test case on recruiting. Most of them, however, returned to the United States and used their prestige among the foreign population to secure recruits, while Turnbull discreetly supervised the operation, assisting financially when necessary. Nonetheless, the difficulties were immense, since the ports were still being closely watched and desertions were numerous.[74]

To these troubles new ones were added on April 11 when Wilkins sent word to Howe that the sixty-six Irish sent by Lewis Grant to Windsor had all refused to enlist; a little later fifty others did the same at Halifax. Not unexpectedly, the *Colonist* wondered if they were recruited for the foreign legion or the railroad; could not Howe, a man "capable of anything that might serve his purposes," be "guilty of deceiving the poor Irish"?[75] So perturbed was Howe that he made a special trip to Boston on the 14th to see if Grant had, in fact, been guilty of deception. Finding that these men were intended to constitute his own company, he acquitted him of blame. "What I hear and what I suspect is that they were tampered with from the moment they got to Windsor, and were well schooled before they got to Halifax. If I am not misinformed *even officers of the Government have been at this work.*"[76] Little did he know that this alleged intervention would lead to politico-religious conflict which would materially affect his own career and the politics of the province. He did know, after le

Marchant gave orders to stop sending the Irish, that half the prospective recruits had been cut off. But he still had one card left to play.

For some time he had been told that the best materials for a foreign legion were to be found in the west. From Cincinnati the British consul, Charles Rowcroft, reported the possibility of raising 1,000 men in that area, and there was, of course, de Korponay's corps in Kentucky. Recruiting there was all the more desirable since it appeared easy to move the men across the border into Canada. As early as March 21 Howe had asked Crampton to approach Governor General Sir Edmund Head on the setting up of recruiting depots in Canada and New Brunswick. Receiving no reply, Howe put his request to the Canadian premier, Sir Allan MacNab, on April 4, only to be told that no authority existed to receive troops. Ready to proceed westward, he asked Head on the 14th to wire "yes" or "no" on his willingness to provide depots.[77] When he reached Niagara Falls four days later and found no reply, he put the question to General Rowan. Roused finally into activity, Head told him bluntly: "Cannot authorize what you ask. Must decline correspondence by telegraph on this subject." He did send his civil secretary to Niagara, where he found "many traces of Howe's enthusiasm, but ... no recruits.[78] Howe's indignation knew no bounds. To have borne the trials he had, and then to have the Canadian garrisons closed against recruits and "the Governor General, secure in the Citadel of Quebec, unwilling even to receive a Telegraphic communication,"[79] was almost too much to bear. He first thought of taking the steamer to Halifax, but in the end returned to New York and there, between April 25 and 27, he took stock of his situation.

Susan Ann had always been concerned about his mission. "I do not like what you are engaged in, but suppose you are all wiser & I *should feel satisfied*." Naturally she became even more anxious as rumours of his adventures spread throughout Halifax.[80] In April Liberal politicians added their pleas for his return on other grounds. "We cant spare you at all," wrote Benjamin Wier, "... our Railway wants you. Our coming Elections wants you."[81] James McNab warned him that, unless he returned for the May elections, the party would be "shipwrecked." Indignantly Howe retorted that he could not be expected to abandon his duty and disgrace himself to "save a party which cannot, having all the honors, influence and organization of government, take care of itself." As he saw it, "the party had dug its own grave and ... burnt brandy would not save it"; giving a pension to Alexander Stewart was "the greatest job on record" and would "weigh like lead" upon them in the elections.[82]

But towards the end of April he began to wonder if he still had a useful role to play in the United States. The Canadian authorities' refusal to cooperate meant he could have little success with recruiting in the west. On the seaboard the efficient John Turnbull could do anything he might do himself in supervising the activities of the foreign officers and in disbursing the remaining funds as they were earned. So, on April 26, believing he had "covered the whole field of operations," he told Crampton of his intention to leave. Brebner is not correct, however, in intimating that he was recalled or that he needed to be restrained from further recruiting activities;[83] he went on his own volition and did not intend to return. By May 2 he had completed his business in New York and Boston, although not without one original touch. With Turnbull he devised a $30 promissory note engraved to look like a banknote and payable as a bounty to a recruit when he was actually enlisted in Halifax. Before leaving for home, he also authorized de Korponay, purportedly on instructions from le Marchant, to recruit a regiment of 600 Kentucky riflemen and to command it; in Boston he empowered Counts Smolinski and Lanckoronski to raise a second regiment on similar terms. Although these last steps do not seem as remarkable as Brebner suggests, they were unwise since they led to quarrelling among the foreign officers and in turn to the disclosure of evidence that the American authorities would later use for their own purposes. But Howe had been circumspect in at least one thing: except for the letters to his superiors, only those he issued as he was departing bore his signature. Publicist to the end, he fired one last shot as he left Boston by land for New Brunswick, a second letter from "A British American," addressed this time to the New York *Tribune*. From Saint John, on May 4, again within the queen's dominions, he admitted to being "relieved from great anxiety."

In Halifax his first major activity was to give a detailed estimate of the mission to le Marchant.[84] Its gist was that, despite the difficulties with the Irish and his inability to recruit in the west, he was still optimistic that the foreign officers spread throughout the United States were sufficiently motivated to raise three or four regiments, or about 3,000 men. In transmitting the report to Lord John Russell, le Marchant suggested, a little prematurely, that Howe had conducted a delicate mission "without having, in the slightest degree committed himself or Her Majesty's Government, in any of the proceedings" and, at Howe's request, expressed the hope that his services would be "duly appreciated and acknowledged by Her Majesty's Government."[85] For the members of the informal recruiting organization Howe's departure was nothing but a disaster. George B. Mathew, the consul in Philadelphia, was especially fearful that it "would 'tell' most detrimentally" on future operations.[86] Crampton, however, took the position that Howe had lent "an air of mystery and intrigue to what can only be done with any effect publicly and loyally"; hence he was not sorry he had left since "his movements have lately been so erratic and obscure that I have had difficulty in following or understanding them much less controlling them."[87] In assessing the relations between Crampton and Howe, Richard W. Van Alstyne concludes, seemingly with validity, that the ambassador, although never a "dupe," permitted "himself to be imposed upon to some extent by Howe."[88]

J. Bartlet Brebner agrees that Howe's difficulties led him to injudicious actions. But rather than make harsh judgments he tries to explain Howe's conduct by putting it in a larger context. From his account emerges a picture of Howe's strongly felt sympathy for the suffering of British troops in the Crimea and his striving to find means to relieve it – "*primarily*, his sympathy and patriotism were involved, and when the chance came for him to act, he leaped at it."[89] Did Howe himself not write: "if I could have taken five Regiments out of Tartarus to back the gallant fellows who at the time had crowded the heroism of the Iliad into a single year I would have done it"?[90] But Brebner might have added that these words were addressed to an American district attorney in public defence of his own conduct and, though true, they tell only part of the story. "Patriotism" with Howe is not simply to be coupled with "sympathy," but has to be understood in an even wider context. Though the British authorities had spurned his ideas for the organization of the empire and eventually rejected his proposals for railway guarantees, he was still "the noblest Briton of them all." Always a man of action, he wrote and spoke as if he would have liked to serve in the Crimea himself and he came close to saying that, if he had to lose a son, the end would be glorious if it came while fighting beside British troops in that conflict. So, not surprisingly, he was prepared to take whatever action was needed when above-board measures were not enough, something that Crampton would soon discover for himself.

Deciding to take matters into his own hands, the latter journeyed to Quebec, where he had inconclusive talks with Head and Rowan, and then to Halifax, where he saw a trickle of recruits arriving and interviewed foreign officers who told him of large numbers of Germans across the border from Canada wanting to enlist. The plan he came up with was, in effect, Howe's "public thesis" on recruiting. It apparently involved Howe's writing to de Korponay and Smolinski, albeit very reluctantly, cancelling their authority to raise whole regiments,[91] and Crampton's taking to Quebec five officers who were to station themselves across the border and do nothing more than provide information about the facilities in Canada for enlistment. According to Van Alstyne, the British minister, like Howe, thought of the enterprise in relation to American domestic law rather than international law; unlike Howe, he naïvely believed he could stay within the letter of the neutrality laws, if not their spirit, and still have success in recruiting.[92] It took him only a fortnight to discover that his plan would not bring results proportionate to the cost and he ordered its abandonment.

For Howe it must have been a bitter pill to receive letters from Turnbull indicating that he was inactive through lack of funds and from de Korponay complaining that he was in desperate straits,[93] and not be able to do anything about it. For a few weeks the frenzied activities of a difficult general election would distract him from the foreign enlistment question. But it would return to haunt him and affect his fortunes for months, even years, to come.

## CHAPTER FIVE

# The Seeds of Racial-
# Religious Conflict

Badly in need of a rest, Howe found himself immersed almost at once in a general election. Young, agreeing with his caucus that the time was propitious, had had the assembly dissolved on April 25 while Howe was on his way home. Although the *Chronicle* contended that the election had been delayed a week to permit him to wind up his American mission, the *Colonist* insisted that its timing had been designed to embarrass him.[1] It would have been more accurate to say that Young was trying to catch the opposition off guard. Through the connivance of William Annand, the newly appointed Queen's printer, he deliberately held up the publication of the *Royal Gazette* announcing the dissolution until Johnston was engaged in a complicated land case at Windsor and hence cut deeply into his chief opponent's time for campaigning.[2]

For Howe it was the unhappiest election of his career. Despite the leaders' arguments to the contrary, he might almost have agreed with the *Recorder* that "no cogent reason [now existed] for the division of the Representatives of Nova Scotia into two parties, regularly organised for the annihilation of each other."[3] Young argued mainly that a Conservative victory would extinguish any "hopes of a Railway either to Windsor, or to Pictou," while a Liberal success would mean its extension to Amherst and Victoria Beach. Had not Killam, "The Lord of the West," stated that railway building should be halted at once to "save Nova Scotia from bankruptcy before it be too late."[4] Though Johnston, in his turn, contended that the Conservatives, through their advocacy of an elective Legislative Council and elective municipal institutions, had become the true liberal party, he laboured mainly to prove the government guilty of serious misconduct. "Two weeks," wrote the *Recorder*, appearing at long last in full Tory garb, are "insufficient for showing up all their evil deeds to the country."[5]

Clearly these were not questions on which Howe could campaign in the grand style and almost inevitably the election became a series of constituency contests in which he was confined to Cumberland.

Personally he experienced several adverse factors: the lack of time to campaign; the desertion of the Methodists and temperance men, partly because of his stand on the Maine Liquor Law; and the collapse of the Liberal organization – he had not been in the county three hours, he said, before he knew it alone would beat him. He did not acknowledge, however, the greatest obstacle to his success, Dr Charles Tupper, the man whom he had earlier put under microscopic examination and found wanting, but who was already well on the way to establishing his hegemony over Cumberland. Personal defeat was especially bitter to Howe, coming as it did when the Liberals appeared to have won thirty-three of fifty-three seats,[6] largely as a result of the Conservatives' negative stance. Naturally the *Chronicle* was indignant that the county would choose "a third rate lawyer," and "a very fair judge of lotions and potions" but of little else, in preference to Fulton, an executive councillor, and Howe, "one of the ablest of Colonial Statesmen, ... whose connection with the Railway Board gave him more than ordinary claims upon that county at the present time."[7] Altogether ungracious in defeat, Howe told his successful opponents they would have neither influence nor patronage in the county, indeed, not even "the power to appoint a hogreave."[8] Outraged, the *Colonist* wondered if the late Emperor Nicholas could "play the despot more grandly than does the late M.P. for the border county"; perhaps he would say next that the railway would not go to Cumberland because the chief commissioner was under no "*particular obligations to take it there*."[9]

Not until May 28, after an absence of almost three months, did Howe return to the Railway Board. So far, construction had proceeded on schedule. In January the first four miles had been completed and on February 1 much of the province's officialdom had celebrated the establishment of public railways in Nova Scotia by proceeding to William Davey's Four Mile House in a train drawn by the Nova Scotia Railway's only locomotive, "The Mayflower," built in New England by Elias Woodworth, a native Nova Scotian. There Howe had been at his convivial best in presiding over a bounteous dinner marked by a multitude of toasts. Unrelenting in its criticism, the *Colonist* marvelled that everyone had escaped injury considering the "rickety" state of the tracks; it was sure that the event could have produced "great delight and gratification [only] among the boys who pay no taxes ... [But] like the Iron Horse we must pause to let off the steam."[10]

On June 8, a year to the day after ground was first broken, the railway accepted passengers for a further four miles to Sackville and Nine Mile House for a total fare of 1s.3d. Howe was not there to mark the occasion, for he was just setting out on his fourth trip to Britain, accompanied by objections from the *Recorder* to his accepting all sorts of roving commissions from the lieutenant-governor. "What sort of a conscience must he have to demand his salary, at the rate of £700 per year, for periods when he applies his time and talents to totally different employment"?[11] But at least on this occasion his essential work was related to the railway, since he had been chosen by the Executive Council, not the governor, as especially suited to negotiate railway debentures and to secure permission to run the line through naval and ordnance property and thus complete the two miles from the governor's farm at Richmond to Halifax harbour.

To date, £112,000 had been secured for the railway through a loan from the savings bank and the use of Treasury notes. It was Howe's mission to borrow £150,000 to cover expenditures for the rest of the year and £450,000 to £650,000 for the next two to three years. The case he presented to Baring Bros was a good one: free of external debt, Nova Scotia levied ad valorem duties of only 6¼ per cent compared with Canada's 12¼ per cent and could therefore increase its revenues with ease; its line to Windsor would be connected with Portland by steamboat and hence provide daily service to the United States and Canada, while the line to Pictou would secure for Halifax the trade of the Gulf of St Lawrence; both lines were certain to promote provincial development.[12] Barings agreed to purchase £150,000 of debentures themselves and to negotiate the larger sum for an appropriate commission, but would make no offer until he was empowered to accept or reject it without reference to Halifax. That authority was forthcoming in early August, accompanied by Wilkins's expectation that Nova Scotia's 6 per cent bonds would sell at a premium.

Howe found it "most distasteful," therefore, when Barings offered to buy the bonds only at par even though Canadian 6 per cents commanded a premium of 12 to 15 per cent. When he demurred, Barings educated him in the facts of life about colonial bonds. Because Nova Scotia was borrowing for the first time, no market existed for its securities. To attempt to sell them all at once could not succeed and might damage future sales, "for we can only look to time and good management to introduce them gradually into favourable notice."[13] If the bond certificates had been available, Howe would have tried to place the issue elsewhere, but he feared that all sorts of contingencies might disturb an unstable bond market if he waited;

besides, unofficial inquiries led him to believe that no reputable company would offer better terms. So, because he knew the Nova Scotia government wanted no delay in having "its credit placed beyond a doubt," he accepted Barings' offer on August 16.[14] His political superiors proved not to be hard taskmasters, for Wilkins and McNab gave their blessing at once and Susan Ann reported general satisfaction in Halifax.

Unexpectedly, Howe found it infinitely more difficult to facilitate bringing the railway from Richmond to Cunard's wharf, the terminus for Europe. The Halifax City Council strongly supported his efforts by resolution; le Marchant told him "it is so very essential to us, that I do not see how it can be well refused"; the Catholic archbishop of Halifax even suggested that earlier annexationist sentiment had its roots partly in "the enormous proportion of the Halifax side of the Harbour [being] absorbed by the Government, to the great detriment of commerce and of public improvement."[15] Because the line would run through the powder magazine and naval hospital grounds, Howe had to negotiate with both the Board of Ordnance and the Admiralty, using the Colonial Office as an intermediary. By August 7 he had made generous offers and was prepared to "do battle with the two Boards." On seeing that their reply was certain to be protracted, he was off to Paris and the Exposition on August 18.

The trip produced four remarkable letters to Susan Ann, three of them from Calais, and all the product of a guilty conscience for being absent most of the year while she grappled with varied family problems such as securing another house and arranging for Sydenham to enter the navy. One letter on the Palace of Industry resorted to the imperative mood in telling her what she was to imagine: "But my dearest wife, what grieves me is, that you can not fancy any or all of these things ... and that with all the pains I have taken to give you a faint idea of them," she would remain largely in the dark.[16] The letters are full of vignettes in Howe's characteristic vein. Parisian women were just as plain as they were in 1838; besides two out of every three had beards. "In a pretty woman this takes the form of a slight moustache, and sometimes is not disagreeable, but it adds too much to the deformity of an ugly face." Another peculiarity of Paris was even more disagreeable: "you are never out of the smell of urine. Every tree in every park smells of it, or is perhaps surrounded by a puddle." Whether the light wine Frenchmen drank led them to "this gentle exercise oftener than we British who drink pale ale and stout I cannot tell, but the ... over flow every where is most disgusting."[17] A few of the vignettes related to Howe himself. In Notre Dame Cathedral, where a priest was saying mass before some of the faithful, he "knelt beside them, and there, in my solitude, with the noble old pile above my head, thanked God for all his mercies." Later, in the Bois de Boulogne, he was "rewarded by a most gracious bow" from Queen Victoria, also a visitor in Paris, "in return for three most glorious cheers which I gave her as she came along." The five days in Paris led Howe to heights of lyricism extraordinary even for him:

It was like a roll in the fleecy clouds of a summer sunset – or among the leaves of Vallambrosa ... It was like wandering through Solomon's Temple and taking tea in his Harem at night. It was like what Byron's kiss would have been had all the pretty lips in creation been so arranged that he could have "kissed them all from north to south." It was like the phosphorescent ocean – the creations of poetry – the dreams of prophets – Cleopatra's voyage – the roar of battle – a Roman triumph – a stampede of wild buffaloes – or any other rare or multitudinous combination of the sublime and beautiful which produces delirious and sustained emotion.[18]

In one letter,[19] largely a testimonial of gratitude to "the Giver of all Good," Howe expressed special thanks for the opportunities afforded him to overcome the deficiencies in his education. Books had done much for him even though Susan Ann sometimes thought he "was moping over them too much." No less important was the deep insight he had gained in human nature through "the actual collisions of public and social life," for although the Nova Scotia theatre was "so narrow that every muscle and flash of eye could be observed," it was wide enough to prevent the mind being "contracted by the dimensions of the actual scene itself." Especially valuable, too, was the information he had gleaned from "all sorts of chance occasions, that could not have been planned or foreseen by any management or skill in divination:" the coronation in 1838, the Crystal Palace (without its contents) in 1851, Wellington's funeral in 1852, the celebration of the 4th of July in the United States, and the inauguration of a lord mayor in London. Writing especially for his children, he wanted them to appreciate how much pleasure and instruction "lye along the paths in which we merely perform our duty."

Back in London on August 27 Howe gave up philosophizing and devoted his full energies to "bringing the road into town."[20] Lord Panmure, the secretary of war, and the Board of Ordnance indicated their willingness, but at a cost that appalled Howe. The Railway Board would have to acquire another site, build new magazines, transport the powder, and ensure free access to the harbour.[21] Presented with the alternative of taking or leaving the offer, he had no choice but to accept. The Navy was even more difficult to budge and finally Howe told Susan Ann he would "*go out by the Next Boat for certain.* Nothing shall stop me, as I know how much I am wanted."[22] Though he secured an informal assurance from the Admiralty, he was much too optimistic in recording the complete success of his mission as he entered Halifax harbour on September 27.[23] For, in exacting their full pound of flesh, British officialdom had effectually guaranteed the status quo. The Nova Scotia government, already under criticism for the mounting cost of the railway, declined to spend an altogether disproportionate amount on a mere two miles and it was another twenty years before the first train would arrive at North Station on the waterfront.

Neither official business nor his trip to Paris prevented Howe from pursuing two interrelated objects, the organization of the empire and an office for himself within it. Totally unsympathetic, James A. Roy calls it the beginning of "one of the most humiliating and self-abasing dunnings of Downing Street on record,"[24] altogether oblivious to the fact that Howe always fitted his claims into a consistent concept of empire. Other students also appear to have magnified the intensity of his quest out of all proportion. As I have noted elsewhere, "fifteen letters to the English officialdom over a six-year period hardly constituted a highly concentrated campaign of self-aggrandizement," particularly when they are scattered among hundreds of others in which Howe addressed himself to a host of problems. Long experience had convinced him that "the Colonial Office moved only under persistent urging; moreover, it required special efforts to keep one's claims under active consideration when three ministries and six Colonial Secretaries held office in five years."[25] Also off the mark is Donald Creighton, who suggests that "poverty drove [Howe] into an unseemly hunt for jobs";[26] in fact, at the time he was owed more than he owed and enjoyed a comfortable salary of £700.

   The quest for office began in March 1855 during Howe's mission in the United States, when word arrived that Lord John Russell had become colonial secretary and the under-secretaryships had not yet been filled. Because Howe had been addressing Russell on public questions since 1839, he approached him without diffidence and requested one of the appointments as evidence of "the announcement of a new policy by which the highest Civil employments of the Crown were to be thrown open to the Queen's Colonial subjects." Russell could do nothing for him at the time because the vacancies no longer existed, but he did agree on the advantage of "holding out to men of capacity and character [in the colonies] the promise of an honorable ambition in the Imperial service."[27] Howe renewed his quest in London in July, but preceded it with the publication of a pamphlet on "The Organization of the Empire," a reproduction, with slight editorial changes, of his speech in the legislature the previous year.[28] As usual, he sent it to a score of recipients, one of whom he told that the speech was "delivered without a paragraph being written. With good models before me here, and stores of information all around me, I know that I could make much better ones."[29] The pamphlet was sent to Russell with a letter[30] stating that, although he would not refuse a governorship, "to win a position here, in the heart of my fatherland, is my highest ambition." Eventually he might win his way into Parliament and distinguish himself by the intelligent dispatch of business entrusted to his care. Throughout the letter Howe presented his claim to office as a means of improving the government of the empire. "His long experience, he felt, could be put to use in devising colonial institutions and generally improving colonial organization. His talents as a public writer might be 'turned to account in the controversies which perpetually arise' in government."[31]

Howe could hardly have chosen a worse time to press his claims on Russell. A few months earlier, at a congress in Vienna, Lord John had accepted a compromise for solving the problems of the Black Sea and the Middle East, and it was producing a storm even as Howe was approaching him. For although Russell now rejected his own compromise, he could not assuage the public fear that the sacrifices of the war would end in a dishonourable peace.[32] Indignant because nobody had defended him in Parliament or the press, Howe dashed off a "fair statement" of his case, hoping it would do some good if published in a government paper. But Russell declined, doubting "whether the noise of the present clamour [would] allow the voice of justice to be heard."[33] That same day he resigned; no worse blow could have befallen Howe's aspirations, for the statesman most cognizant of his services and ability had lost his position of power and influence.

Howe's pamphlet drew all sorts of reactions. One admirer supported its major points, but feared that "the English Aristocracy, still more the English bureaucracy will never *originate* Colonial representation" unless pressed by public opinion.[34] Captain Bigg, possessed of the same morality as Howe's newspaper foes in Nova Scotia, turned dour eyes on the sentence: "Large, vigorous, healthy families spring from feather beds in which Jack Frost compels people to be close," and feared that such "remarks ... prevent your notions being placed before female eyes."[35] But the main reply came from Francis Hincks who, chancing to be in England at the time, dissected almost every paragraph of the pamphlet in one of his own. Apparently Howe's charge that a vast scheme of jobbery and corruption in railway construction in Canada had overthrown a vital British American scheme touched the Upper Canadian to the quick. In his rejoinder[36] Howe lambasted Hincks for minimizing the ills resulting from the General Mining Association's monopoly over the mines and minerals of Nova Scotia. "You used to strain at a gnat, and now you can scarcely see a camel"? What would Canadians do in like circumstances? "They would burn down a Parliament house and pelt a Governor-General." To meet Hincks's charge that he had thrown British American railway building into complete disarray by misreading a letter on railway guarantees, Howe simply made public Grey's dispatch of June 12, 1851, commending one of his speeches which made reference to a guarantee for the Portland line. Would representation in the Commons not provide the most effective means of redressing the ills of the Mining Association monopoly? Would it not have been the best means to protest against Grey's shattering of "the noblest scheme of colonial policy ever devised"? How, then, could Hincks write that "the present colonial system is all that can be reasonably desired"?

Likewise Howe dismissed Hincks's contention that a colonist was not deprived of appropriate distinctions within the empire. Did not a colonist's career practically stop when he became a provincial minister? "... having reached that point, he is hedged in by barriers he cannot overleap, ... he had got into a cul-de-sac; ... he finds John Bull, looking very like a beadle, guarding the rich scenery beyond and saying ... 'No thoroughfare here'." Howe also disagreed with Hincks on the willingness of the colonies to share in the cost of defending the empire. If they were to participate in its government and distinctions, almost all would send a regiment to assist the Mother Country in time of need. The result would be to make British statesmen feel independent of treacherous allies and the British people more certain of the safety of their soil, institutions, and civilization. "To realize this great conception there is nothing wanting but to draw into the Councils of this Empire the ripened intellects and noble spirits that lead this population. Talk not to me of difficulties."

The Hincks-Howe exchange had an unexpected sequel. Having given Russell's successor, Sir William Molesworth, time to settle down, Howe renewed his quest for office on September 4. But seeing that the possibilities of employment at the Colonial Office were limited, he suggested this time that a governorship would be almost as acceptable as an undersecretaryship.[37] Only three days later Molesworth reported his satisfaction at being able to establish "a precedent for seeking occupants for Imperial posts among distinguished men of the colonies."[38] Francis Hincks was to become governor-in-chief of Barbados and the Windward Islands and it was to be hoped that Howe's wishes might be met when a suitable vacancy occurred although there were no immediate prospects at home or abroad. The Montreal *Pilot* called it "the most practical comment which can possibly be offered upon the solemn and sorrowful complaints of Mr. Howe ... Perhaps his turn may not be too far distant."[39]

The irony of the development was not lost upon Howe. When the principle he had sought to establish was at last accepted, it was for the benefit of a politician who had allegedly used his public position to further his private interest,[40] while he, whose abilities were not inferior and whose public conduct was irreproachable, remained unrecognized. He realized, of course, that he was unknown to Molesworth, that powerful interests might have intervened in Hincks's favour, and that the latter's unequivocal support of the status quo in empire relations might have stood him in good stead. But he made the best of it, observing that if the appointment of colonials was to become a regular practice, a new spirit would be infused into the colonies; if not, Hincks's appointment would be regarded as merely an indication of the strength of the English combinations he served and others refused to conciliate.[41] Following his general thesis, Roy pictures Howe returning to Nova Scotia "sorely troubled in spirit" and oppressed by a "sickening sense of failure,"[42] but the lack of supporting evidence would suggest that he is here indulging in imaginative licence rather than in the writing of serious biography.

As usual, Susan Ann had managed affairs well in her husband's absence, although the problem of what to do with Joseph, Jr, remained unsolved. Sydenham had finally become a midshipman, with a reminder from his father that "gold and anchor buttons" did not in themselves bring glory and happiness, and the advice to improve his writing: "A ready pen and a good hand writing will often ... help you along while others lag behind."[43] While he was away, le Marchant had been very solicitous about Susan Ann, calling several times to see if he might be of assistance. Apparently a relationship was developing between Howe and himself similar to that which had existed with Harvey, as the governor learned to appreciate Howe's capabilities and usefulness.

The day after his return Howe was at the Railway Board, where he found almost everything in good order. McCully, deputizing in his absence, had reported to him that all the Windsor branch and several sections of the line to Truro were under contract and that it was hoped to have the former completed by June 1857. He did find the line temporarily inoperative, however, since its only locomotive had struck a horse six days earlier and been severely damaged; resumption of service therefore awaited the arrival, shortly expected, of two locomotives from Greenock. There were other annoyances, too, especially the discovery that an engine house was forty feet too short. "Nobody can tell who is to blame. We eat our leek and pay the money." Until the end of the year most of Howe's work was routine, but he did receive instructions from the Executive Council on December 29 to proceed further with the location of the line from Truro to Pictou.[44]

During 1855 the New Brunswick railways caused Howe almost as much concern as the Nova Scotian. Early in the year Perley told him that Jackson had suddenly abandoned the Shediac line without constructing a single mile and leaving several hundred navvies destitute. Could Howe use any of them?[45] Later Howe warned the New Brunswickers not to give Jackson better terms, but to construct by themselves the lines which they wanted and would pay best. "Limit your obligations to a million. I will ensure you money, and contractors and labour enough ... I know the ropes pretty well now."[46] Personally he was even more interested in the Quebec and St Andrews Railroad because its contractors were Sykes, Brookfield and King who, with his blessing, had surveyed and bid on some of the Nova Scotian lines. The company having suspended construction, the contractors strove for some years to have their claims against it recognized by the Chancery Court of New Brunswick, while their personal fortunes went from bad to worse and they were forced to sell their plant at a third of its value. Because Howe was their only friend in a strange country, Brookfield, King, and Mrs King wrote him scores of letters between 1854 and 1856 beseeching his assistance.[47] First, it was to secure funds for their survey work in Nova Scotia for which they had no claim in law; later it was for money to meet the ordinary necessities of life. Never able to resist pleas of this kind, Howe apparently assisted them from his own resources. Meanwhile he was helping Mrs King's father, John Shortridge of Sheffield, to determine if their legal case was strong enough to warrant his financial support. Naturally these experiences served to reinforce Howe's views that railways ought to be built only under government auspices.

Much more worrisome to him were the repercussions of his American mission. Late in June, Russell had ordered that recruiting be "stayed and the project definitely abandoned,"[48] but its consequences could not be turned off so readily. Already Howe had warned that all the adventurers whose promises had misled the consuls were likely to present extravagant claims for their services.[49]

Never was prophet more correct. He dismissed at once those of Angus McDonald and Lewis Grant as altogether inadmissible and, except perhaps for Andrew Lutz, "the best of a bad lot," he adopted a harder line than either Crampton or the British government towards the other claimants. Because Smolinski had been denied nothing he had been promised and had accomplished little, Howe described as ridiculous his demands for a colonelcy in the British army. But he reserved his greatest indignation for Bucknall who, returning to England, recounted a tale of woe to Lord Clarendon himself about his loss of a salaried position of £500 in Texas and £800 in legal expenses to secure his release. It was "all moonshine," said Howe; his sufferings were not great and £90 had more than compensated him for his fortnight's work. "I can forgive the poor Foreigners, for wanting to fool the Treasury, but really it is too bad to feel that Her Majesty's Subjects are even yet more rapacious."[50] He may have been all the harder on his associates because of the treatment accorded himself. In 1858, when making his final accounting of $8,000 entrusted to his care, he reported keeping the small balance to meet, in part, the cost of publishing pamphlets in defence of the mission and a deduction of £27 4s. from his salary for his absence. At the same time he told John Turnbull: "If it will be any comfort to you ... I have never yet received a sixpence for my own services."[51] Highly indignant over this nonrecognition, he contrasted his treatment with that of others: "Mr. Crampton has been appointed to Hanover, Mr. Mathew to Odessa and Mr. Barclay ... has received a handsome pension."[52]

Howe's capacity as publicist drew him even more directly into the wake of the recruiting controversy. In Britain the papers were full of comments on the subject, and he feared that, because of American clamour, the British government might abandon a source of supply that could provide two or three regiments a year. Accordingly he directed a letter to the London *Globe* (published on August 31 1855), which again put forward his "public thesis" on recruiting. Its fruits, he pointed out, were the 350 men for the Foreign Legion recently arrived at Portsmouth and the 200 men preparing to embark at Halifax. "Here, then, are the materials for a regiment collected in a few months, in spite of clamour, ignorance, and Russian spies, and devilish agencies of all sorts. What is to prevent us from collecting a fine regiment every few months?"[53]

Later in 1855 Howe noted a growing clamour for the recall of Crampton and some of the consuls, as American politicians pandered more and more to popular feeling. Trying to divert a little of this "superfluous indignation" to his own head, he found a pretext in the use of his name (incidentally as Sir Joseph Howe) in court proceedings in Philadelphia, where James C. Van Dyke, district attorney for the Eastern District of Pennsylvania, was pressing the prosecution of Hertz and Perkins, and had secured the former's confession. In two letters to Van Dyke[54] Howe summoned him before another tribunal, "where your official garb will invest you with no advantage ... where scoundrels cannot fabricate with impunity"; that tribunal was "the civilized world, the centres of which are London and Paris, and not Philadelphia." The first letter sought to demolish Van Dyke's view of the United States as a home ordained by Providence for the oppressed of all nations. What was the actual condition of the foreign population with which he had allegedly tampered? Thousands were sweeping the streets, living in soup kitchens, or supported by public charity. Because the Know-Nothing organization was relentlessly proscribing Irish Catholics, even "Paddy" was beginning to believe that Brother Jonathan was no better than Brother John Bull. What was better: to "grace the dead cart [and] sweep the streets" or "wear the uniform of a nation of which you are too meanly jealous ever to harbour a generous impression"? The more factual second letter put the entire blame for any infringement of the neutrality laws on secondary figures like Hertz who, when caught, turned state's evidence and perjured themselves: "are such persons as these to slander away the character of officers high in the confidence of their Sovereign ... to interrupt diplomatic relations, and to disturb the public peace"?

Crampton, allowed by Howe to decide the disposition of the letters, was altogether horrified at the thought of publicizing the first since, by pointing out "unwelcome truths of a ... general national character," it might provide "a certain substratum of public indignation" for which his enemies had long been looking.[55] But the second raised no such objection and on December 1 he had it printed in a Boston paper, the *Anglo-Saxon*, which a Dr Bartlett had established to publicize the British viewpoint in the United States. Because Bartlett lacked "the nerve, humour and deviltry, to grapple with ... blatant bullies," Howe doubted if it would do much good. So, as usual, he circulated the letters privately to a wide audience, including Lord Clarendon, hoping they might provide ammunition for resisting attempts to remove Crampton.[56] All to no avail: on May 28, 1856 President Pierce dismissed him and revoked the exequaturs of three British consuls.

John Arthur Roebuck also felt the wrath of Howe's pen after le Marchant suggested that his parliamentary speech of February 15 afforded "a good opening to fire a shot at ... a vastly mischievous little fellow full of *venom* to the back bone." In a letter sent to the London

*Times* late in March Howe singled out a paragraph which stated that "Sir Joseph Howe" had been employed to break the American neutrality laws, that he had personally paid agents who did so, and that, after spending $100,000, he had collected only 200 men. "I have rarely seen in the same number of lines," wrote Howe, "more ignorance, or reckless misstatement displayed before a deliberative Assembly. John Arthur Roebuck ... shall take no such liberties with me."[57] Howe also took on William Ewart Gladstone who, in the Commons on July 1, condemned Crampton and his agents for breaking the American domestic law. If, replied Howe,[58] he had been told to violate it, he would cheerfully have spent five years in the most loathsome of prisons to "give the gallant fellows in the Crimea effective succour," but he was given no such instructions. Nevertheless, he was not prepared to give up the right to "use all legitimate means" to recruit men in the United States and would resist "truckling to menace" that was intended to bring about its abandonment. Although Gladstone replied that he could not subscribe to the doctrine that foreign laws might be breached "under certain circumstances of public emergency," he also denied any intention to include Howe in his censure since he had always thought it unjust to lay the blame upon secondary agents for a policy approved by ministers of the Crown.[59] That satisfied Howe and his public defence of the recruiting mission was finished.

Not a member of the legislature, when it opened in February 1856, Howe was in the gallery so often that except "for the absence of that old tin box, it might almost be supposed he was still one of the 53."[60] To him, as to other observers, it quickly became apparent that William Young simply could not manage men. While still in England, he had learned from McCully about the dissatisfaction with "the statesmanship of the Premier. A good many People begin to think he is not a witch."[61] By March 1856 the *Acadian Recorder* was picturing Young as "once, twice, or thrice, every day, piteously calling his 'followers' together in 'caucus,' that he may count them once more, and see if all are there." Compounding his woes was Charles Tupper, who was making his mark in his first session, helped by the opinion that it must be an extraordinary man who could defeat Howe. According to one observer, he believed, like Howe, that "all other men were alike as to their gullible susceptibilities, whilst he alone was an inscrutable genius capable of duping everybody or moulding them to his own purpose." In 1856 he made up for his lack of political experience by extraordinary energy. Although the details are obscure, he was accused by Young and the opposition press of participating in "a series of [the] most unscrupulous & singular intrigues ever heard of," the object being to depose Johnston and make himself the leader of a third party.[62] Later he provoked a major constitutional debate when Young refused either to confirm or deny the proposition that "to the victors belong the spoils" of politics. Because it was obvious that, unlike Howe, Young was not resisting the full introduction of the patronage system, his government was put even more on the defensive.

Fraught with the gravest consequences for Howe was the beginning of his party's rift with the Catholics. During the session James McLeod, one of the two Catholic ministers, resigned because of "disingenuous conduct, and want of candour, ... towards me" in the making of appointments. His spokesman, James C. McKeagney, denounced the "scandalous proscription" of Roman Catholics who, though constituting a third of the population, had been "shamefully insulted and deprived of ... honorable distinctions [despite] ... their political services to the Liberal party? ... Is there to be no limitation to human endurance – no end to degradation and insult"?[63] Meanwhile John Tobin of Halifax was almost as critical in his complaints that he could not serve his fellow Catholics and his political leaders faithfully at the same time.[64]

Although Young survived Tupper's motions of censure by six and seven votes, le Marchant warned him he had by no means "brought [his] ship into smooth water."[65] He was quickly to be proved right. Having introduced a bill to support common schools by compulsory assessment, Young bowed to pressure from his Catholic members and promised to add a clause providing for separate schools. That action produced an instant hostile reaction. "What right," asked the *Presbyterian Witness*, "has the Catholic minority ... to tax the whole country that the dogmas of the Romish faith may be taught to their children"?[66] Indignantly Young put over to the next session a bill that had "cost [him] an infinite deal of trouble." He was even more bitter when, despite his attempt to accommodate the Catholics, his second Catholic minister, Michael Tobin, resigned on April 6. Fearful that McKeagney might "still further inflame" his coreligionists, he was relieved when the government closed the session "firm as a rock with a good working majority."[67] But, as he well knew, his government rested on a shaky foundation, dependent as it was on his Catholic backbenchers. Howe watched all of this with foreboding but did not intervene, even though he suspected he could have prevented the resignation of McLeod, "my loved, respected and devoted personal friend."[68] Only one event of the session pleased him very much, the more so because nine of the nineteen Tories supported it despite their leaders' objections: his being voted a gratuity of £500 stg for arranging the railway debentures, a delicate mission he was declared to have concluded on highly satisfactory terms, even though it was not part of his normal duties.

As chief railway commissioner he kept driving Forman and the contractors without let up to meet two deadlines: the completion of the main line to Schultz's by September 1, 1856 and of the entire Windsor branch by June 8, 1857. Most worrisome was contract no. 2 on the line to Windsor, the Long Lake and Mount Uniacke section, which, he told the contractors, needed a doubling of the effort to have it completed on time. "The whole expenditure at the two extremities of the line will be comparatively useless if any portion is not complete."[69] Causing him concern of another kind was the death at Three Mile House on March 3 of Elias Woodworth, the principal locomotive engineer of the line and builder of its first locomotive, who had been proceeding without proper caution, unaware that three inches of snow concealed a mass of ice beneath it. His locomotive, the "Joseph Howe," toppled over an embankment and landed, wheels up, in several feet of water. For Howe it was "a day of sorrow and gloom. Breaking bad news to widow & boy in the morning ... Poor fellow – zealous, fearless, but I fear rash."[70]

During these months his relations with Young and the cabinet as a whole were anything but to his liking. Perhaps thinking the time opportune, Young dunned him for £200 owing to him and his brother's estate, with interest going back to 1850 and 1853.[71] To Howe it was another reminder that he was beholden to someone he did not like. To the cabinet collectively he expressed indignation for its failure, supposedly because of the financial burden, to approve his recommendation of George Wightman as resident engineer on the Shubenacadie section of the main line. Expostulating that the other engineers had "more than enough to do in traversing about 50 miles of contracts," he threatened to pay Wightman out of his own pocket rather than "leave so important a portion of the work without efficient superintendence."[72]

Dwarfing all events of these days, however, was the Gourlay shanty incident. Some months earlier a dismissed Irish navvy named Whalen had disturbed law and order along the line, but his actions were as nothing compared with the events of May 26, when eighty to a hundred Irish navvies working on contracts no. 1 and 2 on the Windsor branch joined in a preconcerted attack on Gourlay's shanty, beating fifteen to twenty Scottish Presbyterians from the eastern counties with pick handles and leaving it to look, in the words of one Supreme Court judge, like a "slaughter house." Rising from a sick bed, Howe accompanied a contingent of the 76th Foot to view the scene of the riot for himself. While there, he learned that Irishmen led by John Lovett and Patrick Fitzgerald were terrorizing the workers on the main line near Elmsdale. Finding no one else prepared to intervene, he went unaccompanied to remonstrate with the gangs although "I could not but feel that my life at the moment was at the mercy of each gang that I addressed."[73]

Matters might have developed no further but for a complicating factor which Howe learned about at Elmsdale, the prospective arrival in Halifax on June 5 of the dismissed John Crampton. Determined that he would be received with honour on "the first British soil" after he left the United States, Howe hurried home, where his resolve was strengthened by the *British Colonist*, which attributed Crampton's downfall to the "incompetency ... of the Nova Scotia officials ... for the service which they undertook to perform" and advised Haligonians not to attend a meeting in his honour in Temperance Hall. After Howe had moved an address praising Crampton's services, the Irishman Thomas Cunningham told the meeting that the minister had deserved dismissal, an opinion echoed by his compatriots Condon and Carten. At that Howe's pent-up indignation erupted against men who, he believed, had sought to thwart his recruiting campaign and were now causing disturbances on the railroad; according to the *Colonist*, he launched "one of the most cutting merciless attacks against the Irish," charging them with "every species of disloyalty" and with being "promoters of turbulence and insubordination."[74]

According to Howe himself,[75] his attack was primarily on the Irish priests who, in 1854, had inspired the founding of the Halifax *Catholic* and were directing its campaign, in support of Irish causes and against Protestantism and Britain, to extremes unprecedented in Nova Scotia. Hitherto silent, he now condemned those "who seek to foster in this peaceful community a war of races and creeds – who remind us they are Celts and howl eternally at the Saxons ... [and] who would have intercepted reinforcements, and left [the British troops] to perish before the walls of Sebastopol." Yet he also made it clear that neither his speech nor his letter was aimed "*at the Irish Nation* – their liberties, or their creed"; if it had been, he would have been giving the lie to a long life "devoted to the establishment, in Nova Scotia, of political, religious and social equality." Rather he was attacking a small faction which chuckled at every reverse of British arms in the Crimea and sought, through its friends, to have him arrested or his brains knocked out during his recruiting mission. Because Irishmen had supported him when he was right, did he have to support them when they were wrong? Should he let a handful of them drive all the other classes of people off the public works? Should he let sympathizers with his country's enemies denounce the queen's ministers without rebuke? Of the Irish nation he had never breathed an ungenerous sentiment. But no people suffered more from gross misleading: "there is scarcely a city on this continent where [Irishmen] with some fluency, and little judgment, have not embroiled the immigrant with the resident population. So it shall not be here, if I can help it."

Howe was not done yet. When a correspondent in the *Catholic* called the ten arrested Irish navvies "unoffending martyrs" and the *Acadian Recorder* glossed over the riots as "grossly misrepresented and exaggerated,"[76] he pulled out all the stops in the *Chronicle* of June 17, describing the Gourlay shanty affair as "the foulest transaction that has ever stained the records of this Province ... in devilish forethought – in disproportion of numbers – in cowardly and reckless brutality." Yet in another way he considered the actions of Lovett and Fitzgerald at Elmsdale to be no less nefarious. After getting their men excited in Adams's grog shop, they had used them to drive the workers from Colchester, Pictou, and Cape Breton off the line, hoping thereby to create a monopoly and get the wages of 3s. 6d. a day they had been demanding. To tolerate this conduct would be to put the contractors at the mercy of the rioters, raise the price of labour, and cost the province heavy additional expenditures. This letter brought into the fray William Condon, president of the Charitable Irish Society and one of the interrupters in Temperance Hall. Though vulnerable as a civil servant, he insisted on following "the dictates of my own conscience." In denouncing Howe in the *Chronicle* of June 19 he was at times unjust, even outrageous. To suggest that Howe was proposing to organize lodges like those of the xenophobic Know-Nothing party in the United States, in order to keep the Nova Scotia Irish in their place, was altogether ludicrous; to state that Howe had disgraced himself by trying to prejudice the case of the prisoners in advance was unfair since Howe had emphasized his intention to do no more than point out the gravity of the riots when others were minimizing them.

Basically, however, Condon was making an honest presentation of a case which clashed fundamentally with that of Howe because their premises stood at opposite poles. From the early thirties no one had done more than Howe to assist the Irish of Halifax politically, socially, and economically. But the Crimean War pitted him against Irish leaders like Condon who regarded the British government as the perpetrator of major wrongs against the Irish people. Naturally they took under their protection Irish navvies who, they contended, had been inveigled into coming into Nova Scotia under false pretenses. To Condon the loyalty "mania" in Halifax that was venting itself in "addresses, bunkum speeches, and 'God Save the Queen' ejaculations" was decidedly amusing and in itself not harmful. But surely Howe could not expect the Irish leaders to be diverted from their duty for fear of being called disloyal. Knowing nothing about Howe's "*honorable* scheme" until the "entrapped Railway laborers" arrived in Nova Scotia, he then reacted, as the president of the Charitable Irish Society should have done, and sent two telegrams and accompanying letters to Boston and New York in an attempt to put these "unfortunate men" on their guard. Why was Howe frightened of this publicity unless he was breaking the law?

For the moment Howe let the press carry on the battle of words with a myriad of voices. On the Tory side the *Colonist* occupied itself mostly with Crampton and the legality of recruiting, while the *Acadian Recorder*, edited by Catholic John English, supported the Irish Catholics of Nova Scotia to the hilt. The Liberal *Sun*, organ of Catholic Richard Nugent, said simply: "*Judge not hastily – prejudge not,*" and Annand's *Chronicle*, fearful that the issue might damage the government, avoided it as much as possible. Consequently Howe's major support came from the Protestant weeklies, especially the *Presbyterian Witness*, which became the self-appointed protector of Presbyterian railway workers from eastern Nova Scotia and for weeks on end lauded Howe's "manly and characteristic attempt to put down treason and civil dissension." Laughing at the contention that the Irish had "made *him*," it warned Howe to be "aware of the real character of the foe ... the cunning and selfish spirit of priest-craft" which had always sought to separate the Irish of Nova Scotia from their fellow citizens.[77]

Behind the scenes Young, his cabinet, and the Liberal assemblymen looked on in gloomy anticipation. One backbencher, John Locke, was worried because Condon, a subordinate officer of government, seemed to be setting everybody at defiance: "no doubt the opposition will spare no pains to make as much out of it as possible."[78] Young was no less fearful that Howe's "violent rupture with a portion of the Catholic Body might operate however unjustly against the Govt."[79] So far, however, the quarrel was confined to the Irish. Writing to Howe in July, the Liberal assemblyman John McKinnon hoped that "the Irish *howl* has not frightened you, the Scotch and French of the Diozies [Diocese] of Arichat are your friends."[80] A little later his brother, Bishop Colin F. MacKinnon (the brothers spelt their surname differently), told Howe that his recent letter denouncing the editors of the *Catholic* had given "great satisfaction in this quarter. I can assure you ... that 'Watchman' and writers of his class are far from being exponents of politico-catholic views in the Diocese."[81]

Ever anxious to return to the assembly, Howe had his chance in July when a committee asked him to stand for Cape Breton county in the place of his friend James McLeod. But when he made it a condition that he not have to engage in personal canvassing, the invitation was withdrawn.[82] For Howe it was fortuitous since L.M. Wilkins's appointment to the bench in August left a vacancy in the township of Windsor to which he was anything but a stranger. On nomination day he made no bones about his preference.[83] Had he been twenty years younger, he would not have minded spending "a month in the saddle" learning about the people and wants of Cape Breton county; in contrast, he could ride around the township of Windsor in a single day and he already knew most of its people. In addition, the General Mining Association had vast power in Cape Breton and he expected an issue to rise shortly in which he would have to oppose it or be suspected of losing his independence. Correctly forecasting the events to come, he also pointed out that Cape Breton county was heavily Catholic, a religious body with which he might be compelled to differ upon an important public question. "As your Representative I shall at least be independent."

Howe made it clear that, as an assemblyman, he did not want to be considered just another party man. Pointing out that for two years he had not meddled in politics "except to laugh at what was going on occasionally," he insisted that "from the mere party politics of the country I wish to stand comparatively free." Perhaps he emphasized it all the more because the group which requisitioned him included Liberals and Conservatives, and standing by him as he spoke were Liberal Edward O'Brien and Tory Dr B.DeW. Fraser. Because the only issue of substance in Windsor was the railway, he told his listeners what they all wanted to hear, that although rock fillings near Mount Uniacke would prevent the 1857 deadline from being met, "before the snows of 1857 descend upon us, we shall be travelling by Railroad between Windsor and Halifax." Launched on the railroad, Howe pointed out that the small section in operation was already paying working expenses and 2½ per cent on the capital invested. Although the lines to Windsor, Pictou, and Amherst would cost £1,200,000, he hoped they would pay operating expenses and interest charges from the start; if not, they would do it shortly by the natural increase in traffic. "We shall then have self-sustaining and productive property worth a million of money in our midst." Ecstatic when he was declared elected by acclamation, he promised to lead

Windsor "into the path of public improvement." Because it had something royal Windsor did not have, "a great ship ready to be launched, along side of a Railroad Station, ... you require all the energies you possess in full vigor" to prepare for the traffic of the future.

The Liberal caucus looked with no ordinary interest on the return of Howe to the assembly. Young hoped he might "rely on him out and out as a supporter of the Government" rather than as an armchair critic; William McKeen had greater hopes of Howe "in the House than I would have [if] he was out of it," especially since he would be attending caucus meetings and hence would appreciate the government's difficulties; G.W. McLelan of Colchester thought Howe would be "usefull for somethings and not much for others as he is very little of an oeconomist."[84] For the time being Howe went back to the Railway Commission, where the only incident of note resulted from his own rashness. Late in the summer, accompanied by his wife and son, he was foolhardy enough to drive his carriage, drawn by two horses in tandem, down the railroad track near Sackville station. Frightened, the leading horse wheeled round and threw the shaft horse and the carriage down a ravine. Although the only injuries were bruises, le Marchant scolded Howe: "What could have induced you to drive Tandem? It is always a most difficult affair & on *our* Rail I would say a most imprudent one."[85]

Another change at the Colonial Office led Howe to apply again for imperial office in October, this time through Henry Labouchere, Molesworth's successor. Reminded that there were many claimants to the patronage of the Crown, Howe again stated he would be content with a governorship, but for the first time he also expressed his determination not to serve again under a lieutenant-governor. Having earned and held all the provincial offices, he would not descend, if he could not rise; rather he would resume his former profession and be "content with the influence I can command, and the rank which British America, fairly estimating my services, may accord."[86] But for one drawn to political life like iron filings to a magnet threats of this kind meant nothing. Had he been unable to secure promotion to a wider sphere, Howe would still have remained in Nova Scotia politics and at its very centre.

In the midst of relative calm neither Young nor Howe could have realized how precariously the government rested on a time bomb of sorts. That only became clear during the trial of nine alleged railway rioters which opened in the Supreme Court at Halifax on December 8 with all the appearances of a state trial. For the accused the Charitable Irish Society had not only provided bail but also engaged the best of counsel, J.W. Johnston; prosecuting them in his capacity as attorney general was William Young. James O'Brien, the only accused against whom there was evidence of using a weapon to inflict injury, was tried alone and the case really became that of Robert Gaston versus Patrick Lyons. Who was to be believed, Gaston, who testified to seeing O'Brien, stick in hand, beating his victims, or Lyons, who provided him with an alibi? Although Young sought to show that Lyons was "unworthy of credit," the jury divided evenly on the guilt of the accused. Unlike Johnston, Young had not used his challenges in the selection of the jury and thereby drew the ire of the *Presbyterian Witness*; if he persisted, it said, all the cases would "end in moonshine" without convictions.[87]

The other eight accused were, in effect, collectively tried on charges of conspiring to commit crimes, and there was clear-cut evidence that four were present while the victims of Gourlay's shanty were being assailed. Nevertheless, four of the jurors refused to convict. On investigation, the *Presbyterian Witness* discovered that, except for one Protestant juror in the O'Brien case, the juries had divided completely on religious lines. The one side immediately denounced Irishmen high and low for regarding any accusation against a member of their race as "an insult to the national honor" and for sticking to him so determinedly "that all the law and evidence under Heaven would not convict him";[88] their opponents attributed the outcome to a belief that the government and the railway commissioners had pounced upon some innocent people, who were to "be made to expiate the sins of all their countrymen."[89]

Howe might have accepted the latter analysis without comment had it not been for the Halifax *Catholic*. One of its writers, "A Lover of Fair Play," held that his denunciation of the accused in Temperance Hall had roused sympathy for them and "saved these poor men [the] ignominy" of fine and imprisonment. Even more horrendous to him was the editorial "Railway Rioting," which for the first time revealed "the causes and provocation which led to this unhappy event." Protestants, it said, had no right to make fun of Catholic religious practices, "knowing how sensitive the Irish people are to every thing which affects their religion."[90] That defence of the riots had an explosive effect upon the slow-burning fuse of Howe's temper.

## CHAPTER SIX

# Sectarian Politics Prevails

For Howe the die in the religious-racial conflict was cast on December 27, 1856.[1] Convinced by the *Catholic*'s editorials that the Gourlay Shanty "outrage" had not resulted from bad rum but had been perpetrated "*in the name of religion*" and was designed to "*trample out freedom of religious opinion in the woods and solitary places of Nova Scotia,*" he let his feelings get "the better of him for a time"[2] and vented them emphatically in a public outburst:

*The right to discuss all questions or doctrines involving our worldly interests or our eternal salvation* – to maintain what we believe to be free and *to laugh at what we believe to be absurd, is the common right of every Novascotian*; and all the 'mercurial' people that can be mustered will not trample it out of our hearts, or of our homesteads. This right the peasantry of our eastern Counties enjoy when at home. *They brought it with them upon the public works of their country.* It was or should have been as sacred in Gourlay's shantie as it is in any Church or Dwelling in the Metropolis.

Catholics were, of course, appalled by the suggestion that Protestants had the right to scorn their most cherished beliefs to their faces, nor did they like being told that they were seeking to propagate their religion by the bludgeon. Howe, no less horrified when the *Catholic* glorified God for bringing about the failures of Britain in the Crimea and circumscribing its power to do evil, appeared again in print in the *Chronicle* on January 6, 1857. Gloating over British reverses was about the worst in his category of crimes. "Halifax is a British community ... Nova Scotia is a British Province; and ... the glory and integrity of the British Empire are not myths." To the *Catholic*'s demands that its fellow religionists oppose any government that kept him in office, he simply replied that he was paying the penalty "for speaking out what every British subject feels, what every Protestant ... thanks me for speaking."

Howe's third letter, which was directed against the "Irish Brigade" in Halifax on January 15, opened with a general defence of his conduct towards Irish Catholics. As a struggling editor in the early 1830s he had been one of four or five Halifax Protestants to join an association formed to cooperate with Daniel O'Connell, even though all who had "patronage to give or power to injure, were on the other side." But in 1841, when every Catholic Irishman became a Repealer, he refused to support an impracticable and impolitic movement. In 1857 no more than in 1841 would he let himself be coerced, this time into approving the breaking of men's heads in the wilderness or the writing of sedition in Halifax. The high point of the letter, however, was his commentary on an editorial he had just discovered in the Irish weekly, the New York *Citizen*, published by John Mitchell, who had earlier been banished to Australia after conviction of treason in Ireland. On July 15, 1856 the editor had stated that Condon's exposure of Howe's recruiting plans was "*mainly instrumental in defeating the scheme.*" Swift and trenchant, Howe's reaction was calculated to make every executive councillor fearful of what would come next. If, he said, Condon was permitted to retain his appointment under the Crown, "the British lion has lost not only his teeth, but his mane and tail too."

Condon, in his turn, used the *Chronicle* of December 29 to argue that the accused rioters had escaped conviction, not because of a want of integrity in the jurors, but simply because of a lack of evidence. Later, on January 21, he again defended his intervention in Howe's American mission: after two batches of Irishmen avowed they had been recruited as railway workers, not as members of a foreign legion, had he not a duty, as president of the Charitable Irish Society, to prevent more of the unwary from being entrapped? But to hold him responsible for all the comments and interpretations of a New York editor was "ludicrous in the extreme." Howe, who had previously ignored Condon, would have none of this and forthwith convicted him on three counts.[3] First, he had done his utmost to turn back Irish volunteers en route to the Crimea. From his personal investigations in Boston Howe was convinced that the Irish knew they were recruits for the British army and that they had been tampered with there and in Windsor. Next, Condon had stigmatized an imperial officer at a meeting called to honour him in which the provincial government itself participated. Finally, he had made a "beautiful exhibition" of himself by appearing in court day after day as part of "an organised conspiracy to defeat criminal prosecutions." As a subordinate officer who opposed government policy, he was therefore subject to dismissal by the British rule of administration.[4]

Though powerless to do anything about the deepening imbroglio, William Young continued to receive disturbing reports from Liberal assemblymen. Stephen Fulton of Cumberland feared that the outcome would be new political combinations; Hiram Blanchard of Inverness warned that the Catholics of his county were prophesying the general secession of their coreligionists from the government.[5] Despairingly, Young asked his solicitor general, Adams G. Archibald, if the government should yield to Protestant Liberal demands and dismiss Condon for "gross impudence." Indignant at Condon's behaviour, Archibald replied that the government could not keep him in office "without defending his conduct and identifying themselves with his principles"; would Catholic Liberals not see that unless he was let go the government was certain to lose much of its Protestant support?[6] But forces had already been set in motion which neither Young nor Archibald could halt.

Great excitement prevailed at the opening of the assembly on February 5, especially when the "B'hoys in the Gallery" booed Howe, their long-time favourite, and greeted Johnston's motion of nonconfidence with a round of applause. The next day, following a caucus of government members, Condon was dismissed and the fat was in the fire. Because Howe made his support of the government dependent upon the dismissal, the *Catholic* outdid itself in denouncing "the besotted bigotry of that modern Babylon, 'Great Liberalism'," and castigating Howe, its foremost champion, for being enveloped in No-popery virulence.[7] Two Irish Catholic assemblymen, John Tobin and Peter Smyth, deserted the Liberals forthwith and joined James McKeagney on the other side of the House. Nevertheless, Howe believed that the government would survive, if just barely, through the continuing support of its French and Scottish Catholic members. He was much more dubious about its position in the Legislative Council, where his friend Edward Kenny, unable to resist his coreligionists' pressures, resigned the presidency on February 7. Hearing that the Tory councillor William Black was outraged by the behaviour of the Irish, Howe invited him, through an intermediary, to join other Protestants in resisting their pretensions. Black, he added, might even take a seat on the Executive Council and thus give representation to the Methodists.[8] But, recognizing the handwriting on the wall, Black resisted all overtures.

Although Young and Johnston studiously avoided the religious issue in debating the nonconfidence motion, the speakers who followed made it the centre-piece of attention. Howe spoke three times, always evoking coughing, hissing, booing, and even yelling from the gallery, a new experience for him. It was clearly traumatic for him to have to confront a racial-religious group with which he had always enjoyed a complete rapport. "... did Joseph Howe come forward," he asked, "and attack Catholics as a body – assail Irishmen as a people, or as members of a church? He did not ... no lure however tempting, could provoke me to persecute any man or body of men on account of religion." Let anyone turn to the journals, reports, and public prints of the past thirty years, "you will everywhere see my foot-prints" in the advocacy of Catholic claims and interests.[9]

In his second speech[10] he wondered if his letters were being made an excuse for the break-up of the government which some Catholics had sought to effect a year earlier. But he also made a special plea to the Acadian members whose vote in the crucial division was assuming an ever greater importance. Could any but a madman believe he had charged his old friend Mathurin Robicheau from Clare with rebellion, disaffection, and crime? "A more inoffensive gentleman, distinguished for his religion and piety, for his attachment to his church, and for his manly deportment, there is not in this House." Had not the Acadian members worked with him to give Nova Scotia a free constitution? How, then, could they possibly join men who had always reviled the new governmental system as worse than that of the aborigines. Altogether unrepentant, Howe used his third speech[11] to tell the Catholics that even if they brought down the government, "no sentiment I have ever uttered – no line I have ever written – no act I have ever done, will I retract or feel shame for."

To Howe's opponents his speeches were simply special pleading, intended to save him from the natural consequences of his misbehaviour. "No street mendicant," wrote the *Recorder*, "ever begged more earnestly and abjectly for his bread than Mr. Howe."[12] But if begging it was, he was to be shown no mercy. Insisting that all the Catholic members must do their duty, the *Catholic* came out with an extra threatening to "hold up to public execration and scorn, any wretch who would be base enough to betray us now."[13] Protestant Liberals complained openly that William Walsh, the archbishop of Halifax, was manipulating the Catholic members as he willed and more obscurely William Young lamented the presence in the legislature of influences hitherto unknown to the constitution acting palpably and fearfully behind the scenes. But all in vain; although Howe still clung to the hope that the Scottish Catholic John McKinnon and the Acadians François Bourneuf and Mathurin Robicheau would hold firm and let the government survive on the Speaker's vote, the pressure was too much for them. In the division of February 18 the defection of eight Catholic members, all elected as Liberals, and two Protestant Liberals brought about the government's defeat by twenty-eight to twenty-two.[14]

Young resigned at once and Howe followed forthwith, for, although chairman of a bipartisan board, he had indicated earlier that he would go out with the government. Almost boasting that he had resigned an office in 1843 when ten children depended upon him for support, he declared he could do nothing less in more affluent circumstances, especially when a government had been forced out on an issue he had done most to create.[15] Later he would tell his half-sister that, required either to "bow my soul to the Priests and rowdies I despised" or to "take my stand at the cost of my income," he had done what he "believed to be right."[16] Left without employment except as an assemblyman, he pondered his next move. His correspondents left him in no doubt where they stood. From Sherbrooke Hugh McDonald wrote that all the Protestants except the Baptists would unite and "then we can manage the Catholics, that they will not at the beck of their Bishop, change the Government when he pleases." Howe's old friend in Musquodoboit, the Rev. John Sprott, reported an unparalleled "burst of indignation ... levelled at the heads of our new Cabinet." But what else could be expected of "those misguided men who profess to sail in the Bark of St Peter ... Romanism is a masterpiece of Satanic policy ... [It] never changes and its priests never slumber."[17]

Howe's intentions became clear on March 3 when he sent Hibbert Binney, the Anglican bishop of Nova Scotia, a copy of a platform calling on Protestants to form an organization that would "ensure a Government independent of Roman Catholic Support" and asked him to nominate two or three leading Anglican laymen whom Howe might consult in all "future movements that may be necessary."[18] Whether the platform was the one contained in the *Chronicle*'s editorial addressed to the people of Nova Scotia or the version in a similarly addressed letter signed by Howe himself makes no difference since the gist of each was the same.[19] Declaring that it was "no light thing to turn out a government," the editorial went on to ask: "Shall we pass under the yoke and bend the knee to the Catholic Archbishop, now our political master and ruler"? and concluded with an appeal to all who distrusted the insidious and rapid advance of Catholic power to join an organization, the nucleus of which was a large committee drawn from both branches of the legislature.

The signed letter sought more specifically to demonstrate that Archbishop Walsh was the chief villain of the troubles. As Howe saw it, the French and Scottish Catholic members had agreed to Condon's dismissal at a meeting of caucus and left the party reluctantly only because "the Catholic Archbishop so willed it." Because the incident exemplified the new aggressive policy that the papal power was pursuing in the United States and British North America, he and his friends had decided to take the higher ground, recognize that the Liberal and Conservative parties had fulfilled their missions, and work towards an independent Protestant majority which would vindicate the public honour; otherwise, the Catholic members, by shifting from side to side, would continue to rule the province.

In the assembly Young, Munro, Archibald, Locke, Annand, and Wier – all Protestant Liberals – joined Howe in expressing support for some kind of Protestant alliance. "It is high time," said Young, "that the distinctions between liberals and conservatives should be forgotten, and a new standard erected, beneath whose folds men should unite to restore to this house ... independence of action."[20] As it turned out, Howe had already done almost everything he would do towards establishing a Protestant alliance. For him to expect Bishop Binney to respond favourably to a politician who, by himself or through his party, had never shown the slightest sympathy for the Church of England was nothing less than naïve. Not unexpectedly, the bishop gave him short shrift for a variety of reasons:[21] he made it his invariable rule to play no part in politics; the leading Anglican laymen supported Johnston; Catholic influence presently constituted no danger and was, in fact, no greater than under the Liberals, who had helped to augment it; and, above all, the Liberals never missed the opportunity of "attacking and robbing us whenever they could do so with advantage to themselves." Offhandedly, Howe replied that "the Past is behind us" and that Binney's proper "position is at the head of the Protestants of this Country,"[22] but this time he drew no response.

If it ever existed, Howe's large committee of legislative members seems to have evaporated overnight. Coincidentally, ministers of the province's three Presbyterian synods met on March 4 and agreed on the need of some vehicle to express openly their views on the claims and power of Popery in Nova Scotia. Following an adjournment of two days to permit clergymen of other denominations to attend, they decided to set up "the Protestant Association of Nova Scotia" and to seek affiliation with the London Protestant Alliance, even though the Wesleyans and apparently some Anglicans pleaded off for a time until religious and party animosity had subsided. Deriding these "manifestations of frantic imbecility" as designed to drive Nova Scotia into a religious war, the Tory press took special aim at the Rev. Peter G. McGregor of Popular Grove Presbyterian Church in Halifax, the driving force in the efforts to organize the clergy. "This coxcomb ... acts the part of 'Peter the Hermit,' whilst Mr. Howe is shortly to appear terrible as a Blue Nose Godfrey de Bouillon."[23]

Nicholas Meagher, hardly a reputable historian, describes Howe's appeals to Protestants to unite as "a device to detach Conservatives from their party" and through their help to "regain official place, pay, and power."[24] Disagreeing, the more respected Chester Martin suggests that "Howe's own savage wrath in itself would absolve him from a cold, sly, calculated 'device' which was indeed foreign to his nature."[25] But neither diagnoses the situation correctly. Perhaps Howe did write the letter of December 27 impetuously and unthinkingly (he denied it, of course), but his proposals to form a Protestant combination resulted neither from a fit of uncontrollable anger nor primarily from a determination to regain office. To him it was "no light thing" to turn out a government, monstrous to turn it out because of the dismissal of an officer who had interfered with the recruiting of troops and prevented the successful prosecution of rioters, and nothing less than outrageous to have it done with the sanction, perhaps on the orders, of an archbishop. Several of his basic convictions – including his immense loyalty to Britain and his profound distrust of organized religion – came into play in the working out of a genuinely traumatic situation. Of one thing he was certain, "that what had been done in the House of Assembly must never occur again.[26] But for Meagher and others to accuse him of proscribing Catholics and renouncing his lifetime advocacy of equal rights for citizens of every race or creed was to misinterpret completely both his motives and actions. Misguided though he may have been, he honestly believed he was following the tenets of a liberalism that upheld the right of anyone to criticize the political and religious views of others.

Thinking that most Protestants were equally indignant about the manner of the government's defeat, Howe and his political friends went out personally to wage battle in the ministerial elections that followed the change in government, Howe against Attorney General Johnston in Annapolis, Young against Provincial Secretary Charles Tupper in Cumberland, and Adams Archibald against Financial Secretary J.J. Marshall in Guysborough. Apparently the largely Presbyterian population of Pictou was to give Solicitor General Martin Wilkins his quietus on its own. Even as the *Chronicle* was hailing Howe's meetings in Annapolis as one triumph after another, the *Colonist* scorned the exhibits he had taken with him; a navvy who had been injured at Gourlay's Shanty and a four-pound weight supposedly dropped from the gallery to frighten a Protestant witness during the rioters' trial. It had the last laugh, for when Johnston actually increased his majority, it painted a jocose picture of Howe trudging back to Halifax, singing a melancholy ditty, "followed by his 'horrible example,' the Gourlay subject, with the *four pound weight* slung over his shoulder."[27] Of the four ministers only Tupper had his majority reduced, allegedly because of an outpouring of money by Young: a Cumberland Conservative thanked him for adding very considerably to the circulating medium of the county.[28] Howe could not understand how Pictou county with its 30,000 Presbyterians had returned Martin Wilkins, who had justified an Irish faction's breaking of their own people's heads; to him it was "a reflection on Presbyterian intelligence which will not readily be wiped out." But although he had grossly overestimated the indignation evoked by recent events and thought better about pressing personally for a union of Protestants, he remained confident that the latter "will do their work yet."[29]

Acknowledging that the Johnston administration was firmly in the saddle, Howe and his colleagues let it finish out the session without obstructive tactics. Sparks flew in abundance only on railways, following Tupper's tabling of papers which purported to show that the lines to Windsor and Pictou would cost £9,000 a mile, not £5,000 to £6,000, as Howe had calculated. Indignantly the latter stood by his previous estimates that the two roads would be completed for £1,050,000, not £1,242,000.[30] The controversy was revived in September in a lengthy exchange of letters between Howe and James McNab[31] and later between Howe and Provincial Secretary Tupper, which provided more in the way of heat than light.[32] "Is it true," asked Tupper, "that the man who has essayed to wield the destinies of our country and mortgage our revenues in a gigantic commercial speculation" could so deceive the public on costs? Although refusing to be "responsible for Dr. Tupper's calculations," Howe maintained that even if the railways cost £9,000 a mile, it would be £1,179 less than New England's seventeen lines and still less than Canada's Grand Trunk. When Tupper said he expected all sorts of insinuations to be made against his veracity by the author of the *Letters of a Constitutionalist*, Howe wondered how those letters were germane to the controversy; in any case, just "as Actaeon was devoured by his hounds because he viewed Diana naked, [so] the Doctor has a horror of the naked truth." Thus the conflict between the two ended as it often did, in nasty irrelevancy.

For Howe the rest of 1857 was largely uneventful. He thoroughly enjoyed proposing a toast to the officers of the *Circassian*, a steamer which completely dwarfed those of twenty years earlier. As in the case of the old man who, when he looked into his telescope, thought he could see an old church and hear its organ play five miles away, so these leviathans made Howe fancy "he heard the rumbling of the carriages in the Strand."[33] Not so pleasant was to have to act for another year as the intermediary between John Shortridge and his daughter Sarah King, the former enjoining him to "keep [the Kings] well in hand in the money matters," the latter always expecting to have her drafts honoured.[34] Hardest of all to bear was the death of William Grigor, a confidant of thirty years, whose loss he "felt more than any ... since our brothers died."[35] All in all it had been "a year of trial" with "a great deal of vexation" still to come, but he was confident that "all will come right some of these days."[36]

The year 1858 started with Howe being enveloped in controversy of another kind. Invited to address the students' Lyceum of Acadia College and denied the use of its buildings by a board of governors which still nursed bitter memories, he found himself relegated to the basement of a factory-like structure. Speaking to an overflow audience, he told the Baptist theological students, perhaps tongue in cheek, that they ought to examine the pulpit oratory of France and especially the magnificent orations of Bishop Bossuet. Having advised all his listeners to "get knowledge – get understanding," and having been asked how it might be got in Wolfville, he replied, "it was to be got anywhere."[37]

From February to May, Howe was engaged in one of the longest and, by consent of both parties, most time-wasting assembly sessions in provincial history. "Poor Bluenose, whether he likes it or not," lamented the *Chronicle*, must "pay the piper" to the tune of £100 a day in legislative expenses, all because the government had failed to present proposals of a practical and useful nature.[38] No less derogatory, the *Recorder* stated unequivocally that even "a gathering of scandal-loving, old women, at a tea-drinking, anywhere in the Province, ... would ... blush to know themselves overheard giving utterance to such malicious malignity ... such silly gossip, and such unmitigated twaddle." In its view the ill was due partly to the two human conglomerations calling themselves political parties, but which had no right to any names more definite than "Ins" and "Outs," and partly to Howe and Young for factiously opposing every proposal of the Johnston government.[39] For its part, the *Colonist* put the blame squarely on the shoulders of Howe, who had "no occupation, save office-hunting, – no business save agitation – no vocation, save misrepresentation." Clearly an office or an annuity had to be provided for him: "*date obolum Belisario*, and let him be contemptible and content."[40]

Early in the session Howe was outraged by the government's refusal on the grounds of economy to present a sword to Maj. Gen. Sir John Inglis, the hero of Lucknow. Although long a political foe of his father, Bishop John Inglis, he nonetheless recounted at length the exploits of the son, hoping to persuade a government which, he thought, should have needed no persuading; for him it was a question of the provincial honour and Nova Scotians had better "pull up stakes" if they could not afford it. When Johnston proposed to deduct the cost of the sword from the members' indemnities, the Liberals insisted that all Nova Scotians would want to honour Inglis. In the end Johnston consented to a vote of 150 guineas, but not before the assembly, by Howe's estimate, had spent (or wasted) enough time to defray the cost of two or three ceremonial swords.[41]

Howe's three speeches on Johnston's "pet project," an elective Legislative Council, could not be considered factious, since he genuinely believed that the proposal constituted an insidious attempt to destroy responsible government and would do about as much good as sticking "the tail of a dog on the back of a lion." Did not the present system work well and was not the British constitution the "safest and best model" to follow? While "continental thrones [were being] shattered, [and] systems of government ... scattered to the four winds of heaven," had not Britain "gone steadily onward in the development of its constitution," preserving the lives, property, and freedom of its people in the process.[42] Johnston quickly discovered that he could not always count on two of his newly won supporters, Henry and McKeagney, and when he carried the bill's first clause by only one vote, he gave up on it, accompanied by Howe's taunts that a government which abandoned the only major proposal in the Speech from the Throne should bow to necessities and get out.

Howe's opposition to the government's mines and minerals bills also rested on strong grounds. On being granted a lease of almost all the province's minerals for sixty years by an act of the prerogative in 1826, the duke of York had quickly transferred them to his creditors, who established the General Mining Association. By getting control of the mines at Sydney and Pictou two years later, the association enjoyed a virtual monopoly, but because of its failure to promote the industry the province's return in rentals and royalties, until very recently, had been pitiful. For two decades William Young had led the fight against the improvident arrangement and in 1856, as premier, he had got the legislature to indicate the terms it would accept for the elimination of the monopoly. But when the time came in 1857 to send one person to Britain from each party to negotiate a settlement, the Conservatives were in office and Johnston asked Adams G. Archibald, not Young, to accompany him. Although they made the best arrangements they could for the remaining twenty-six years of the lease, they were frustrated because the association knew full well that the British government would not modify vested rights without its consent.

Even before the assembly met in 1858, Johnston and Archibald had argued strongly that the arrangements came close to meeting the assembly's conditions of two years earlier, but Young disagreed, contending that there were substantial deviations which were highly disadvantageous to the province. The differences between Liberals Young and Archibald were bothersome to Howe, who had begun to think of the next election and the health of the party. Although he wanted at all costs not to alienate Archibald, he found that the case which Young – sorely aggrieved at not having participated in the negotiations – had amassed against the proposed settlement was unanswerable. Hence, in a far cry from his usual practice of making his own case, he largely repeated Young's arguments that, in allowing the coal deposits at Springhill and large areas at Pictou, Joggins, and Sydney to be left in the hands of the association, the government's bill ensured the continuance of the monopoly for another quarter of a century and, in giving up existing royalties to the extent of £6,000 per annum the government was paying too heavy a price for the meagre amount it was likely to receive from the opening of new mines in the immediate future.[43] But despite Young and Howe, the government had its way with relatively little delay and neither was guilty of the obstructive tactics with which he was charged.

On railway matters, however, both parties sought at great lengths to make political capital or save face. Always critical of the cost and quality of the railway, Johnston had earlier secured the assembly's authorization to resolve any doubts about the permanence of the work and during the session he presented with satisfaction the report of James Laurie which, the *Sun* estimated, cost $65 a page, contrasted with the £5 that Milton had received for all of *Paradise Lost*. "What a pity Milton did not write a blue book full of twaddle and figures instead!"[44] Among other things, the report dealt with the claims of three railway contractors for extras amounting to the enormous total of £70,000. According to the Tories, the railway's chief engineer, J.R. Forman, had taken a reasonable attitude towards extras until the change of government; then, allegedly to save his reputation, he would not recommend their payment to the board even though the fill in the Grand Lake area so far exceeded the estimates that it was doubtful if soundings had ever been taken.

Of the new claims Howe was highly suspicious. Although the chief engineer's certificate was needed before the contractors could proceed with extras, none had been issued before he left office and certificates were not presented until six or seven months later when Tupper's letters in the *British Colonist* almost invited the contractors to inflate the costs to make the previous chairman and government look bad. The matter became the subject of controversy in February 1858 when Johnston moved for a committee to report on the claims. "Are you to say," he argued, "in a civilized land, governed by law, and by principles of integrity, [that] those who complained should be denied enquiry?"[45] But neither Howe nor any other Liberal would serve on the committee or agree in any way to remove the question from the proper authorities, the board and the government. Why, asked Howe, "give these contractors an opportunity, which would not be given to a poor man, of pressing for enormous sums"? Like Benjamin Wier, he believed that "something remains behind the curtain" and that the contractors, recognizing a sympathetic government, had formed a combination against the public interest.[46]

For thirty days, three to four hours a day, seven backbench Tories heard evidence and Howe did not like what he saw. Johnston, supposedly representing the chairman and the board, scarcely intervened in the questioning of witnesses, while two Tory lawyers acting for the contractors, J.W. Ritchie and Johnston's nephew, R.G. Haliburton, treated Forman like a criminal at the bar. Eventually, on the pleas of the committee member Thomas Killam, Howe did some cross-examining and introduced a degree of balance into the proceedings. With not a little relish, he showed that the greatest error occurred at Grand Lake, where the board's engineer was J.R. Mosse, another nephew of Johnston. He also demonstrated that the 10 per cent deductions, intended to secure the quick completion of the contracts, had not been withheld from the contractors' payments and wondered if that was why the Windsor branch, supposed to be finished before the end of 1857, was still not in operation. Although the committee's recommendation, to pay for the extras at scheduled prices after the quantities of fill had been determined by actual measurement, was in accord with Laurie's report and quite unexceptionable, Howe feared that the province's interests would be sacrificed in determining the quantities. Reluctantly he pointed out that his successor as chairman, James McNab, "as worthy a man as ever lived," was about "as fit to deal with such a 'complication,' as he was to command the channel fleet." Fearfully he prophesied that disputes which he could have settled for £7,000 to £8,000 would cost the province dearly.[47]

Because the railway had become an object of partisan recrimination, the completion of the Windsor branch on June 3, 1858 passed almost unnoticed. "Perhaps in no other country in the world," complained the *Sun*, "would a new line of Railway, and a *first* line, have been opened without some demonstration. A funeral procession would not have been observed more quietly."[48] But Howe's friends saw to it that he did have recognition. On June 8, the 109th anniversary of the founding of Halifax, many of them journeyed by rail to Windsor, where, in the presence of his constituents, they presented him with a testimonial address and a gift of £1,000 for his services to the province and the empire. "Gifts, such as those which Grattan, Cobden and Webster have felt themselves honored by accepting," he stated, "I have neither the false pride nor morbid sensitiveness to decline."[49]

Longer and more violent than the debate on railways was that on appointments and dismissals, which strayed on from irrelevancy to irrelevancy between March 19 and April 9. Although the Uniacke administration had been highly circumspect in not removing subordinate officials for partisan reasons, Young's opened the door substantially in this direction, Johnston's even more so, and Nova Scotia was well on its way to the wholesale adoption of the spoils system. Much of the Liberal attack, however, was focused on two specific appointments, those of the Catholic William Condon as superintendent under the Board of Works, which was labelled an insult to the feeling of attachment to Britain, and the Catholic James McKeagney as inspector of mines, an office not recognized by law and one for which he allegedly had no qualifications whatever. From that point the debate proceeded irrelevantly to angry confrontation over the Protestant Alliance of Nova Scotia, which, in affiliation with the London Protestant Alliance, had finally come to life without the inclusion of any prominent politicians in its ranks. Howe rejected outright Tupper's charges that its prospectus was a "fraud and a forgery" or that it had acted precipitately. Had not a body of Catholic prelates met in Halifax during the summer of 1857 and issued a synodical letter condemning as reprobate the Protestant version of the Scriptures? "How long [was the Alliance] to be silent? ... Were they to wait till Popery had seized upon all the vantage grounds of social and public life"?[50]

Tupper's unprovoked attack on this occasion was one of the nastiest Howe had ever to endure in the assembly. After raking up every instance of Howe's alleged dereliction of duty starting with the excise incident of 1843, Tupper suggested that any Englishman in similar circumstances would "never more venture to hold up his head." Scorning the idea that "we owe our present institutions to

Howe," he went on to say that "his efforts have ever run parallel with his interests" and he regretted Howe was not the richer for his efforts, "for I do not think that Nova Scotia is much richer for his exertions."[51] Howe's reply was briefer, but no less offensive. Referring to a recent innuendo relating to Tupper, he pointed out that no one on the list of the Protestant Alliance had "gained his education by a fraud of the basest character," a comment that almost led to a "general 'set to'."[52] Still unawed, Howe later responded to the Catholic synod's criticism of the Protestant Scriptures by moving that no school receive a government grant unless the Old and New Testaments were read in it daily. Naturally his enemies were scornful that a man of his character would be brash enough to take charge of Protestant interests in the province.[53]

For all his vigorous participation in the session of 1858 Howe still found time to use his pen elsewhere. More than once the Tory press insinuated that the *Sun* had come under his direction, a charge that its publisher A.J. Ritchie said was "absurd and unworthy of refutation."[54] Nevertheless, Howe did publish anonymously a number of editorial-like articles in the *Sun*, on topics ranging from old-time theatricals in Nova Scotia to the naval power and designs of France. One of them gave a new twist to imperial relations. Britain, he said, was driving the provinces into union because of its incompetent colonial policy. Especially disgraceful was the case of J.W. Johnston who, "with his gray locks floating in the air, working for his bread amidst the stifling atmosphere of a Colonial Court House," had no prize before him but a seat on the bench, "while some Lord's son, or Member of Parliament's brother, without a tithe of his talent, ... is sent to reign over him, in his own country."[55]

On June 28 Howe was off to the United States, mainly to bring to publication the volumes of speeches and letters on which he had been working for some months. As usual, he complemented his work by an unrelenting round of social activities, much given to the consumption of oysters to which he had always been partial. All of it was interrupted by the death of Ichabod Dimock, a Liberal member for Hants, and the calling of a by-election for July 29. Prevented from engaging Tupper in the nomination proceedings by missing his connection at Portland, Howe later engaged him head-on at Maitland and thought no better of him for it: "an ichor of falsehood ... oozes from every pore of his skin, a flavor of unveracity and disingenuousness ... offends the sense whenever he opens his mouth.[56] Howe was, of course, elated when the Liberals increased their majority from 91 to 250 even though the few Catholics in Hants voted solidly against them: if only the Protestants of Nova Scotia behaved as the Protestants of Hants, the Liberals would win a solid victory at the next general election. If the issue in that election was not already clear, the *Novascotian* made it doubly so in a long poem in four cantos:

> Hants has spoken out in thunder,
> Hants has done her duty nobly.
> . . . . . . . . . . . . . . .
> By the blood of Gourlay's Shanty,
> By the green graves of our fathers,
> Catholics shall rule us, NEVER.[57]

Because he "could do little good at home," Howe was back in the United States in early August, by his own account making an examination of the social, political, and industrial conditions of the country from Maine to Texas, investigating every railway route across the continent, and delving also into the affairs of Central America, including prospective canal routes across the Isthmus. All this information, he was certain, would be useful to him in the future.[58] By November he was receiving the first copies of the two-volume *Speeches and Public Letters of the Hon. Joseph Howe* from his publishers, Messrs. Jewett and Company of Boston. Howe had done all the work although ostensibly Annand was the editor, a device which enabled him to say flattering things about himself in the connecting pages without appearing immodest. In the introduction he suggested that the books would attract little attention beyond British America; nonetheless, he would shortly make them a major exhibit in Britain in the renewal of his quest for imperial office.

Feeling himself increasingly restrained by the pettiness of provincial politics, he had made another start in June after the installation of the second Derby government. Because he did not know the new colonial secretary, Bulwer-Lytton, "the best course seemed to be the bold one – an approach to the man at the top."[59] Derby, the former Lord Stanley, might recall his interviews with Howe during the railway negotiations of 1851 and 1852. Abandoning any hope of an under-secretaryship, he concentrated on British Oregon, his name for the future colony of British Columbia. There, if appointed governor, he would lay the foundations of a "noble colony"; instead of letting it drift into the United States, he would make it "a commercial emporium, from which lines of steam communication might soon radiate, and through which [Britain] might hereafter exercise a powerful influence in all that part of the world."[60] Since no reply from Derby was forthcoming, at the end of November he forwarded the volumes of his speeches and public letters to anyone who might help him to get office. Although W.L. Grant suggests that "in none of his [accompanying] letters do we find the real tone of the office-seeker," they differ from the earlier ones in exhibiting irritation at having to wait so long for what he considered a right. To William Bridges of Mitre General Life Assurance he complained about the promotion of "all sorts of simples and blockheads" in preference to himself. Not quite so outspoken to Derby, Bulwer-Lytton, and Under-Secretary Herman Merivale, he asked them to imagine his feelings "when men of no Colonial experience, who have done no service to British America, ... who are intellectually ... not [his] superiors, are sent to rule our Provinces, whose resources, mental and industrial, [he has] illustrated and developed by the labours of half a life."[61]

He should have known better than to ask Lord John Russell to plead his case with a ministry to which he was politically opposed. Although Russell found the two volumes "mark'd with the talent & patriotism which distinguish you," he could only state his inability to interfere in the patronage of the Derby government. To call this reply "an unmistakeable snub," as James A. Roy does, is incomprehensible;[62] he may be more correct in saying that Derby threw out only "a meagre crumb of comfort," though Howe considered his letter a "very handsome one."[63] Eventually Bulwer-Lytton told him that, because of the limited number of offices at his disposal, he would be unable to serve him in the immediate future.[64] Apparently the clamour for office by Britons themselves was preventing colonials from being appointed to the colonial administration on a regular basis. Again Howe vowed, this time to Sir Gaspard le Marchant, recently retired as governor, not to serve again in any capacity under any lieutenant-governor; yet for a political animal like himself it was a vow he could never hope to keep.

Meanwhile the Tory press had been exhibiting an almost morbid curiosity about Howe's long absence. Laughingly, the *Novascotian* mocked them: "What can the man be about? It is most provoking that neither he, nor his friends, will inform the Government."[65] Howe, in contrast, knew very well what the government was doing, especially in its dismissal in August 1858 of J.R. Forman, the Nova Scotia Railway's chief engineer, allegedly for the injudicious and inefficient performance of his duties. Liberal circles guessed, however, that the real cause was his membership of the executive of the Protestant Alliance, since under him railway construction in Nova Scotia had proceeded without a hint of scandal or corruption. Both Howe and the *Novascotian* prophesied the results to follow. "Thousands and tens of thousands of pounds will probably pass now into Contractors pockets,

– money never earned ... and Roman malice will be abundantly gratified.[66]

Howe would have been back in Halifax much earlier had he not become interested in an enterprise that left even him awe-struck. For the promise of $1,000 he agreed for three months starting on October 16 to provide advice and assistance in promoting an organization for completing a canal between the Atlantic and Pacific oceans. Although he concluded the agreement with Edward W. Serrell, the latter was acting for Frederick M. Kelley, who was sometimes identified as "a prominent Wall Street Banker" but may be more accurately described as a high-grade adventurer with good connections and little money. By his own account Kelley had sponsored two exploratory trips to New Granada (now Columbia) in 1851 and 1853, which had determined that a ship canal could be built without locks. Its key was a river flowing into the Pacific, the Atrato; by following it and its tributary, the Truando, and in turn the latter's tributary, the Nerqua, ships might be taken as far as the Andean Cordillera, where a tunnel $3\frac{1}{4}$ miles long, 100 feet wide, and 120 feet high through solid rock would provide a short access to Kelley's Inlet on the Atlantic side. At $75,000,000 the estimated cost was far less than that of the Panamanian or any other alternative. Supposedly Kelley had referred the engineering reports to Baron Humboldt, the Emperor Napoleon, and the Royal Geographical Society, and supposedly they were awaiting some information that President James Buchanan was to provide before commenting on the validity of the project.[67]

Howe had little to do under the first agreement, but in a second signed in January, it became apparent he had been singled out for his experience in public relations and securing railway guarantees, since his main task was to get backing from the British, French, and American governments for the canal. In return he was to receive fourteen scrip certificates of $1,000 each and one of $40 which, by the mysteries of high finance, would entitle him to $99,995 of the company's stock.[68] Howe attributed his enthusiasm partly to the nature of the project – the "noblest" enterprise to which a man could devote his energies – and partly to his appreciation of Kelley's "modest and manly character." That was the gist of his message to Baring Brothers and a spate of private individuals before he returned to Nova Scotia on 28 January.[69] Obviously he had refused to put the fascination of a project with uncertain financial rewards ahead of his political prospects in Nova Scotia and perhaps the empire. With scarcely a day of rest at home he was on his way to Truro on February 1, there to receive its tributes for denouncing the Irish mob which had committed an outrage upon a citizen of Colchester County and for promoting the county's development through the railway to Truro which was to open six weeks later. Characteristically, he started his reply by reminiscing about his first sight of the vale of Truro and the Salmon River twenty-nine years earlier and concluded with comments on his recent examination of the United States and its institutions: "You will ever find me in the right place at the right time; and none the less prepared, I trust, for the performance of my duties because I prefer to enlarge my intellectual range by travel and observation."[70]

Two days later the General Assembly began its 1859 session amidst prophecies that it would be a wasted session, partly because it preceded a general election, and partly because the political climate prevented anything else. Accordingly the *Acadian Recorder* told the government to "*attempt nothing, and get through the attempt as quickly as possible.*" It expected to see reenacted the "ridiculous farce" of the last session, in which Young had posed as leader of the opposition, but was actually the "unconscious puppet" of Howe.[71] Allegedly Young was altogether mortified when, later in the session, Howe suggested that "his government would have fallen to pieces like a barrel without hoops three several times [in 1856], had I not exerted myself to sustain them." Naturally the Tories could not resist making gibes at "Howe the cooper."[72]

Setting the tone of the session with his speech in the debate on the address, Howe declared that Protestants needed to show the Catholic population they were "not the omnipotent dictators they assume themselves to be" and that eight or nine members of their religious faith, "dragooned by a foreign ecclesiastic" should not be able to "make or unmake an administration in an hour." Forman, he asserted, would still be chief engineer, no matter how incompetent, if he had belonged to "the right church and ... the right party." Even more outrageous to him was the profanation of the country's flag during the previous summer, when it was lowered at Government House to mark the funeral of Archbishop Walsh, an ecclesiastic who gave that flag no support when it was "sore beset" during the Crimean War.[73]

Howe's second speech, six days later, was distinguished for almost turning the assembly into a bear-garden. As he spoke, John Tobin, in what the *Novascotian* called "a manifestation of the spirit of the Catholic Priesthood,"[74] banged the clerk's table with his fist and, to the accompaniment of hurrahs from the people's gallery, declared "they were not going to be put down by the Opposition." In a moment, to cheers from the Speaker's gallery, he was confronted by the Protestant champion, Benjamin Wier, twice his size, with fists clenched, and prepared for battle. The next day Howe was interrupted by boos and yells, and forced to state that he "observed strangers in the House," the usual signal for clearing the galleries. Enraged at being excluded, the crowd knocked and kicked at the doors, drowning out the members' voices. To prevent a recurrence, the House spent the day drawing up new regulations which permitted access to the galleries by ticket only. Such was the state to which religious warfare had reduced the House of Assembly.

To the *Acadian Recorder* the disorder was largely contrived, the outcome of a "provocation game" in which Joseph Howe was the chief provocateur. For years, it said, he had used the largely Irish Halifax mob for his own purposes. Demagogue that he was, he would "half turn his back ... to the [Speaker's] chair, throw his coat collar back and his face up to the eastward, and harangue the people's gallery by the hour."[75] But in 1859, in an effort to turn the populace against the Irish Catholics of Halifax, he was deliberately seeking to provoke the spectators in the people's gallery and the Liberal press was abetting him by exaggerating the disorder he had purposely created. Whether contrived or not, the acts of Howe and his supporters were clearly producing the results the *Recorder* feared.

Religious confrontation dominated the two weeks' debate on the address; it would be no less prominent in the discussions on the government's major proposal, the representation bill. A year earlier Johnston had introduced a measure to equalize representation, both within and between counties, but had met opposition within his own party; in 1859 he was back with a much less comprehensive bill concentrating on equalizing representation within the counties.[76] From the outset the Liberal opposition hailed it as the "Roman Catholic Representation bill," Young going so far as to prophesy that through the "crafty and subtle division of Counties," sixteen Catholics would be elected to the assembly. But he was mildness itself compared with the Liberal newspapers. "Pass this Bill, and old Jacob's posterity were not more surely the bond-slaves of Egyptian Pharaohs ... than will Nova Scotians ... be priest-ridden and downtrodden by a power ... proverbial for its hatred of ... liberty and true religion."[77]

In perspective, this extreme reaction seems incomprehensible and can be explained only by the political atmosphere of the day. Arguably Hants County's loss of a seat and the addition of one to both Inverness and the western district of Halifax might have been designed to strengthen Catholic influence, and the merging of Catholic Clare with the rest of Digby county might have been intended to let Catholic voters determine the county's three members, but exactly the opposite could have happened if Clare had been swamped by the overall Protestant majority. Although Howe agreed that the bill was designed to strengthen the Catholics, he adopted, at least outwardly, "a more cheerful tone" than his colleagues: "there were only so many plums in the pudding, and you could not make more of them by cutting it in any particular method."[78] Actually so much of the speech was unpalatable to the Liberal newspapers that they did not report it in detail and the modern student is dependent upon the summary which the *Colonist* provided with relish.[79] Dissociating himself from the extremism of his colleagues, he went out of his way to criticize Young for his unkind treatment of James McLeod and his unnecessary reference to a conflict between Bishop Connolly and Judge Wilmot in New Brunswick. Clearly Howe was unwilling to take the Catholic fight to lengths that his reason rejected on grounds of credibility.

Only once during the session did he have a chance to wax eloquent on a project clearly to his liking, the extension of the railroad from Truro to Pictou. Could not a goodly part of the needed expenditure be secured by economy in managing the existing railways? Surely the new chief engineer, James Laurie, need not be paid the enormous salary of £1,500, nor were 284 persons required, at a total cost of £30,000 a year, to work 100 miles of line. Imagine the value to the Halifax consumer of bringing coal from Pictou by train; imagine how useful the line would be in tapping the trade of the St Lawrence. Would it not be a lasting disgrace to Nova Scotia if, having got a head start, it was beaten in the race by New Brunswick?[80] But the government refused to add to the public debt at a time when the province's finances were in poor shape and before the earning capacity of the existing lines was known.[81]

Dissolution occurred the very day of prorogation, with the election set for May 12. Unique in provincial history, it was fought almost everywhere on religious grounds. Johnston did his best to divert the voters' attention to the delinquencies of the Young government and the Liberal assemblymen: waste in building the railways and the Hospital for the Insane, maladministration of the Land Office, and factious opposition to proposals dealing with mines and minerals,[82] temperance, and the equalization of representation, but without success. Later Howe would heap scorn on the man whose government and nephews were helping the railway contractors secure "extras" not rightfully theirs; who, by an improvident mines and minerals bill, had "locked up more coal ... than would keep all Nova Scotia warm for a hundred years"; who had worked zealously for an elective Legislative

Council only until he had filled the upper House with Conservatives; who had left unfilled "the promises of half a life" by not pressing a prohibitory law measure; and who, to make political capital, had exposed the foundations of the Lunatic Asylum for weeks, hoping it would tumble down, and then built a chimney higher than the gallows on which Haman was hanged.[83]

But this review of Johnston's manifesto took place some weeks after the election, not during the campaign itself. So, whether they liked it or not, the Conservatives had no choice but to argue in the main that the Catholics had neither received nor sought privileges and power beyond what was enjoyed by others and that the Liberals were sanctifying the principle of proscription to serve their political ends. In this light the two parties' labels for each other, Romo-Johnstonites and Proscriptionists, become understandable. Aiding the Liberals was a flood of publications emanating from religious sources, some virtually invoking the wrath of God upon anyone voting for a government connected with the Church of Rome. One pamphlet, the work of ministers embracing Free Church Presbyterianism, drew fire for stating: "You cannot serve Christ in your closet or in your Church and deny him at the Hustings. Take heed. God is not to be mocked."[84] All the opposition papers accused Howe of outright bigotry. The *Recorder* told him that his attempt to ride into office on the cry of Protestantism was "the most disgusting ... that was ever put into practice" in Nova Scotia.[85] In one of its wildest concoctions the *Evening Express* (successor to the Halifax *Catholic*) pictured him having a field day among the "simple-minded and uninformed peasantry of Lunenburg," telling them that Catholic soldiers in the British East Indian service had perpetrated the massacre of Cawnpore and that the same fate awaited them if they voted Conservative: "their Bibles would be burnt, their churches destroyed, and their own and their wives and children's *throats cut*."[86]

Even before prorogation Howe had made it known that he had no desire to be considered "a Champion of Protestantism"; he did, however, expect Protestant clergymen to help the Liberals, since if "large Counties, full of Protestants, return those who justify outrage and disloyalty, we may [as well] quit the field, and long years will go by before there is the same chance to control the Papists in this country."[87] Substantially the aid he wanted was forthcoming, especially from the Free Church ministers. So, except for a few days organizing the county of Lunenburg, he devoted his energies to getting to know his own constituency, extended by redistribution to include half of Hants County. At one juncture he told Susan Ann he had "kissed about 500 women since I left, but shall be glad to find myself in your arms again." Although, as usual, he solicited not a single vote, it was an easy personal victory on May 12, Susan Ann's birthday, "a lucky day for me in all the concerns of life."[88] By the time he left Windsor, suffering from a chest cold of the kind that would bother him for the rest of his life, he had learned that the Liberals had won twenty-nine of the fifty-five seats and the *Chronicle* was proclaiming that "Nova Scotia is herself again. Her big heart once more beats healthily. She has thrown off the yoke of tyranny ... Nova Scotia, Protestant Nova Scotia, is free."[89]

Generally the vote had gone as he expected: almost solid Catholic support for the Conservatives and an even larger numerical switch of Protestants to the Liberals. In Digby and Yarmouth the Acadian vote had enabled the Conservatives to win all six seats. In Cape Breton county the Liberals were easily beaten, again because of the Catholic vote, and they did not even bother to contest Catholic Sydney County. They also lost the three seats in the western district of Halifax, even though only 470 of about 2,500 Protestants voted against them. In largely Protestant seats, however, the Conservatives were almost always hard pressed or beaten. Free Church ministers campaigned vigorously to defeat C.J. Campbell, an executive councillor, by 500 votes in Victoria county. Charles Tupper barely retained his seat in Cumberland, where William Young, who had deserted strongly Catholic Inverness, led the poll. Most surprising of all was Annapolis, where so many Baptists deserted Johnston that he won by a scant seventeen votes. Later, at Bridgetown, Howe gloated that time had done him justice and that hundreds of Baptists were returning to "solid connections." He could not resist adding that Acadia College had lost £2,910 in government grants in fifteen years because of the "unnatural quarrel with her best friends," and if the £4,000 or more which his old enemy Dr Crawley had unwisely invested in a salt mine was added, "any shrewd Baptist may count the cost of the sublime operations of these political intriguers" to Acadia College.[90]

Some of the egotistical Howe emerged in letters to his correspondents, in which he took full credit for the electoral victory and boasted that "the issues decided were chiefly of my raising."[91] Perhaps he should have asked himself if he had done all he could to prevent questions of this kind from convulsing the province, but he had little time to ponder anything before Serrell was pleading with him to return to "the great Atrato conflict," offering him one of five trusteeships if that number was established.[92] Howe did publicize the work in Nova Scotia through five articles entitled "Union of the Oceans," which appeared in the *Morning Chronicle* and the *Novascotian*."[93] But Kelley had upstaged him, since the articles consisted mostly of excerpts from Kelley's pamphlet extolling the project. Or perhaps Howe had upstaged himself if he had contributed sentences like this to the pamphlet: "Franklin was not more delighted when he drew the lightning from the clouds, or Columbus when he discovered America, than I was when it was demonstrated, by instrumental measurements, that the two oceans could be united."

But Serrell could not induce Howe to return to the United States and the Atrato project. "I am not mercenary, and perhaps care less for money than most people," but "as a man of ordinary prudence, I cannot afford to throw away places of Colonial distinction and £800 a year without seeing my way clear to a certain provision for my family at least equal to what I abandon."[94] Roy, in his usual manner, intimates that Howe was practising a form of deceit since his occasional contributions to the *Novascotian* could hardly have brought him so large an income.[95] Howe was thinking, however, in terms of his sessional indemnity and the salary of an executive councillor with office that he would soon enjoy; clearly his financial prospects were not nearly as bleak as Roy had suggested. By this time, too, he had learned that the Atrato project had not attracted sufficient funds even to permit the launching of a share-selling campaign; so, by making his demands equal to his immediate prospects, he ensured that Kelley could not meet them.[96] That ended Howe's connection with the Atrato Ship Canal project, fated never to get off the ground. Perhaps the project did have possibilities but failed to attract private capital because of its risky nature. More likely it was an instance of Howe's too-gullible acceptance of a grandiose undertaking.

## CHAPTER SEVEN

# The Premiership:
# Ambition Unfulfilled

The election over and Atrato abandoned, Howe was at loose ends. In mid-June 1859, deciding to pay his respects to the Baptist counties which were returning to the Liberal fold, he found himself in a procession of 200 waggons proceeding from Middleton to Bridgetown, "blue flower in his button hole," celebrating the near-emancipation of Annapolis county from "the political yoke of Mr. Johnston." A series of receptions, dinners, and speeches throughout the county greatly exhilarated him, although he did note some hard-shelled Johnstonite houses "with the blinds down ... looking as melancholy as the Glebe House did at the fall of Sebastopol."[1] He also managed to spend a few days in Digby with his half-sister Jane, just recovering from a stroke which fortunately had not disfigured her or impaired her speech.[2] Then, in late June, he revelled in a monster political picnic at Sheffield Mills in Kings county, where "lines of tables literally groaned beneath the choicest viands ... served up after a fashion which would have reflected infinite credit on a Metropolitan Stewart, a Nichols, or a Waterfield."[3]

Back in Halifax, he took stock of his own situation. In June Palmerston had again become prime minister of Britain with Lord John Russell as his foreign secretary and the duke of Newcastle as colonial secretary. Howe had never met Newcastle and, besides, had "spoken too plainly ... to be much of a favourite" at the Colonial Office.[4] He did know Palmerston and Russell, however, and even more to the point, he had made great personal sacrifices carrying out and defending their policy during the Crimean War. Yet although he approached Russell for employment at the Foreign Office, the reply came from Newcastle, who feared that Howe's early prospects were bleak because so many unemployed governors were "eagerly applying for any [vacancy] that chance [might] bring." An outraged Howe promptly read him a stern lecture on the principles that should operate in the appointment of colonial governors. Were not the ones being sent out much like those who had lost the thirteen colonies by their lack of understanding? To maintain the empire, did it not need to be "organised and its energies called forth and directed by men of a different stamp"?[5]

Baulked in one direction, Howe turned his attention to provincial office where only the timing was uncertain. Under Liberal pressure the governor, Lord Mulgrave, was grappling with the first of a series of constitutional issues which were to trouble him for the rest of his governorship. Ought he to insist on an early summoning of the legislature to determine who should govern the province? Not satisfied that enough pressure had been applied, Howe sent him a memorandum in August,[6] partly to secure an "in" with a governor whom he scarcely knew despite Mulgrave's eighteen months in the province, but mostly to show that his strong personal claims and his loss of office and £2,000 of official salary entitled him to demand that the General Assembly be convened forthwith. "*I do think that when I have gone down into the arena, and beaten these people*, in my own country, with constitutional weapons, that it would be a singular spectacle, *if, by a stretch of the prerogative I was to be punished for ... upholding ... the honour of the Crown.*" What conclusions should he draw if Condon was kept in office and he was kept out?

Proceeding to the length of implied threats, Howe asked if he or his friends could be blamed if they had the question raised in Parliament and the British press, lost their faith in the honour of the Crown, and even became the governor's enemies. Prudently Mulgrave maintained in reply that the interposition of the prerogative was unwise except in the most extreme cases and that in this instance the Johnston government was simply following the normal practice of not convening the legislature until January or February. But even while this question was being decided, Mulgrave had the first glimmering of an even more contentious one. Should he acquiesce in the defeat of the Johnston government by the votes of assemblymen who appeared to be holding their seats contrary to law?[7] The genesis of this problem lay in the recriminatory politics of the period. In 1858 the Conservatives, taking special aim at Jonathan McCully, pushed through a measure to ban judges of probate and prothonotaries from both branches of the legislature; not to be outdone, William Annand replied with a measure based on the Canadian practice which applied the same prohibition to any office-holder. But while the major officers were to forfeit £10 for every day's violation of the law, no pecuniary penalties of any kind were to be incurred by the minor ones. Shortly the Liberals would almost be hoist on their own petard for initiating "Annand's Law" and a Conservative attorney general would rue his failure to insist upon adequate means of enforcing it.

Told by Johnston that at least half a dozen Liberal members had held office of some kind while running for election, Mulgrave had a stated case referred to both the provincial and English law officers, none of whom doubted that even the most minor office-holders were subject to Annand's Law. They also agreed that an assembly which resorted to a majority dependent upon supposedly disqualified members to give them an *ex post facto* eligibility ought to be dissolved forthwith. But the English law officers, in contrast to their Nova Scotian counterparts, held that the oath of qualification which any assemblyman might be required to take applied exclusively to the matter of a property qualification and not to the holding of an office; hence the members supposedly infringing Annand's Law could not be restrained from taking their seats, at least temporarily. In effect, this was the death-knell of the Johnston administration since there was no way to prevent them from voting it out. As Howe put it, "Young and I must be rather unapt scholars if we did not know how to lead [our] troops now ... we have [only] to be cautious that we commit no great mistake. Like men walking on rather thin ice, we must not press too heavily."[8]

As soon as the legislature convened, late in January 1860, Johnston proposed that the assembly itself take evidence in the case of the six Liberals who he thought were ineligible. To Howe he was like a boy playing at toss penny who said, "heads I win, tails you lose"; in effect, Johnston was asking the Liberals to join him in turning out six of their members, while the dozen Conservatives being petitioned against were to escape unscathed.[9] Howe and his colleagues simply argued that, since the adoption of the Nova Scotia version of the British Grenville Act in 1820, the assembly had never interfered with the functioning of the committees which tried election petitions. Rejecting the Conservatives' contention that because of the special circumstances the assembly as a whole needed to take action to protect its independence and dignity, they carried their nonconfidence vote on February 18. When Johnston requested a dissolution, Mulgrave declined on the ground that, although the Liberals might have "pressed matters somewhat to extremes," they had done nothing unconstitutional in insisting that the trial of election petitions be left to committees whose exclusive function it had been for forty years. To the Tory press his refusal reduced him to "a cipher, a puppet with the semblance of power, and of no use whatever."[10]

The Conservatives' sense of outrage intensified when Young, in forming his government, assumed the hitherto nonexistent and unpaid office of president of the council to avoid a ministerial election in Cumberland. Unusually frank about it, Howe pointed out that Young wanted only one office, the chief justiceship, and it would be his if his party held office when it was vacated. "What is to prevent him, meantime, from folding his arms as regards offices of emolument, and giving the country the benefits of his talents without pecuniary remuneration."[11] Because the new government would lose its majority if the House continued in session while Howe, Archibald, and Annand, the new executive councillors holding office, were seeking reelection, Young secured an adjournment for a month. By running candidates against them the Conservatives made a tactical error, for all three increased their majorities and helped create the impression that the government was firmly established. "The Romo-Johnsonite domination has ceased forever," exulted the *Novascotian.*[12]

Howe's success was dampened by his son Edward's death on February 28, when the by-election was still in progress. In 1850 Edward had married Elizabeth McDougall of Musquodoboit, whom he had met while the Howe family was occupying the Annand farm, and they had taken up residence at Maitland, Hants county. Because Edward was long incapacitated by the serious rheumatic condition which resulted in his death, Joseph had been providing financial aid to the family. The vituperative politics of the day led almost as a matter of course to an attempt to make capital out of the death. Although the obituary columns of the Liberal newspapers did not disclose Edward's parentage, the Conservative newspapers paraded the fact that he was the son of the Hon. Joseph Howe. Edward left four children ranging in age from one to eight; to them their grandfather showed the greatest affection and helpfulness to the end of his life.

During the adjournment Howe explained how he thought the election committees would and should act. The English version of Annand's Law, he pointed out, was intended to prevent the independence of the Commons from being impaired by the presence of members appointed to high-salaried offices by the Crown. "But who ever heard or thought that a Nova Scotian [like coroner A.M. Cochran of Hants] could be corrupted by an office worth forty shillings a year?" Technically, perhaps, the language of the law might be applied to such members, but Howe was certain that the committees would "take a broad view of the law."[13] After the recess neither party missed a trick in seeking to gain an advantage, although the Liberals made sure they could not be accused of breaking either law or custom. Since a member petitioned against could not serve on a committee, both parties challenged the election of any opponent against whom there was the slightest scintilla of evidence, or even none at all, to improve their chances in the draw. Because he was petitioned against, Howe was ineligible to sit on any committee.

As it turned out, both the draw and the striking-off process[14] favoured the Liberals. But their greatest fortune was to let Conservative John Hatfield of Argyle serve on all seven committees on which he was drawn. A genial retired master mariner, he simply did not have it in him to vacate the seats of members who came within Annand's Law by a mere technicality. Like Howe, he believed that the committees should take a broad view of these cases; like Young, he insisted that no member should be unseated unless it was clearly shown he had been legally appointed to his office and held it under all the requirements and sanctions of the law. Indeed, he set the style for the committees to follow in the case of Liberal Dr W.B. Webster of South Kings; there, as chairman, he aligned himself with three Liberals against three Conservatives to find that no evidence had been adduced to prove that Webster had ever received a commission as a health officer, or performed the functions of the office, or received fees for his services. Another Conservative, Colin Campbell of Digby, adopted much the same stance and both he and Hatfield were, in effect, read out of their party.

The outcome was that no election was invalidated because of a violation of Annand's Law. The only member to be unseated was a Conservative unlucky enough to be tried by a committee containing five Liberals, which found that his majority was created by nineteen unqualified voters. Later a committee containing six Conservatives adjudged Attorney General Archibald guilty of bribery, but fortunately for him the law did not permit it to vacate a seat on that ground. So the Liberal majority in the assembly simply declared the charge to be unproven, despite the *Acadian Recorder*'s moans about "whitewashing the Briber General."[15] Thus an atmosphere already poisoned by religious strife was further embittered by what the *Colonist* called the "shameless conduct" of the election committees. With alacrity it accepted Tupper's description of the Conservatives as "Constitutionalists" and called the Liberals "Usurpers."[16] Aggravating the bitterness was the disposition of the chief justiceship, likely to become vacant shortly. "For the first time in provincial history the Colonial Secretary would certainly accept without question the nominee of the Executive Council. Both Young and Johnston wanted the [office] to crown their long careers in public life, while their heirs-apparent, Howe and Tupper, ... aspired to the premiership,"[17] Howe if for no other reason than to possess it in name as well as in fact. Thus all the party leaders had more than the usual reasons for wanting their own party to be in control of the government.

Back in his old office as provincial secretary, Howe played an even more dominant role than before as Young receded into the background while awaiting a call to the bench. In taking over the government in the course of the session, the Liberals could do little more than implement the proposals, largely noncontroversial, in their opponents' Speech from the Throne. Howe, delighted at being able to adopt their plan to give the initiation of money votes exclusively to the Executive Council, something he had been advocating since the 1840s, promised to use the new power "with courtesy and kindness, and with a due regard to those in opposition."[18] He also sponsored a bill for the organization of a volunteer militia force as a complement to the volunteer companies which Mulgrave had been establishing throughout the province. Was this step not necessary, he asked, when Boston alone could send out enough armed men to "give us a great deal of trouble" in case of war?[19]

Otherwise the session of 1860 was largely sterile, marked especially by continued recrimination over the dismissal of office-holders as the province took another step towards the wholesale adoption of the spoils system. Naturally William Condon was the first to go and none protested. But a mighty howl went up when P.S. Hamilton, the editor of the *Acadian Recorder*, was removed as registrar of deeds for Halifax county. In justification, a committee of Howe and Annand later reported that Hamilton had not only displayed "unmitigated hostility" to the Liberals, but had also made the *Recorder* "conspicuous for the insertion of personal defamation unrelieved by the delicate wit and gentlemanly sarcasm which lend a grace even to political warfare.[20] Howe also dismissed Amos Black, the steward of the Lunatic Asylum, which became, as usual, the plaything of the politicians; "the lunatics," Howe said, "seemed to be the only sane people about the establishment."[21]

The chief sparks flew, however, over appointments and dismissals relating to the railway. "No act of my political life," said Howe, "gave me so much pain" as the dismissal of the chief railway commissioner, James McNab, with whom he had "lived as brothers" for three decades. Apparently thinking that "his old friends were shipwrecked for 20 years to come,"[22] McNab had been unwise enough to desert to the Conservatives. His successor, Jonathan McCully, introduced a cost-paring scheme which reduced railway expenditures by £4,000 annually and involved the dismissal (and nonreplacement) of Johnston's nephew, J.R. Mosse, as chief engineer. Perhaps to annoy Johnston, Howe described Mosse as "a good second rate engineer" at best; "any one looking at the conformation of his face will see that he was never intended to control large operations."[23]

James Laurie, who had finished his calculations of the extras just before the Liberals took office, escaped dismissal only by resigning. After he had lambasted the leading Liberals in the newspapers, Howe went him one better by laying bare "the miserable mismanagement and craven corruption of Ministers and Contractors" who had combined with Laurie against the best interests of the people. "The destroying angel must have flapped his raven wings, and croaked hoarse notes of triumph, when Laurie signed his last certificate that swelled these extras to their final exorbitant amount."[24] They may not have totalled the £162,000 that Howe calculated, but obviously Laurie had given the contractors almost all they had asked. In denouncing him, Howe also took aim at Tupper for his "splenetic and petulant harangues ... He is always abusing somebody, ... and is becoming as tiresome as that termagant lady 'renowned in Padua for her scolding tongue'." He had his greatest fun, however, with Tupper's peroration, which impeached McCully in the style employed by Edmund Burke in the impeachment of Warren Hastings. Unfortunately for Tupper, "the counterfeit oratory did not produce the same effect as the true." None of the ladies in the gallery exhibited "any very 'uncontrollable emotion.' We saw no 'handkerchiefs or smelling bottles handed around' ... and strange to say, ... not one of them could be got ... 'to be carried out in a fit'."[25]

As Provincial Secretary Howe coordinated the plans for the visit to Nova Scotia on July 30 of Albert Edward, Prince of Wales, and Newcastle, the colonial secretary. The state of provincial politics ensured that there was sniping at every detail that could possibly lend itself to criticism. Disregarding all of it, Howe was at his most effusive, particularly at Windsor where, in proposing and responding to toasts, he brought both his Nova Scotia-ness and his concept of empire fully into play. Undoubtedly, he said, the prince had seen ampler halls and heard finer music, but perhaps "he had never seen prettier girls" or been more fascinated by a scene "where the graces of civilization seem to be reproduced, as it were, on the borders of the wilderness." Perhaps, too, the prince's visit would turn the attention of Britons to the resources of North America and they might decide to "continue the Strand through Halifax to Vancouver's Island, ... to pour the surplus population and capital of the mother country into the North American Provinces, ... that a home market would be secured in time of peace, and gallant defenders in time of war."[26]

The visit had stilled, though only for a moment, a new controversy which inevitably arose following the death of Chief Justice Sir Brenton Halliburton on July 16. Two days before the prince's arrival the *Acadian Recorder* came out in mourning to protest the likely succession of William Young, a man who, it said, had outraged all the proprieties of public life in his management of the election committees.[27] Nevertheless, the Executive Council recommended it and Mulgrave approved it provisionally on August 3. Although the *Chronicle* scoffed at the idea of keeping up political agitation during the "hot weather ... the season of the year for ice-creams, for strawberries, for pleasure-parties and picnics,"[28] addresses and counter-addresses flowed in a steady stream to Newcastle, opposing and supporting the confirmation of the appointment. Such was the state of politics when Howe became leader of the government or premier for the first time. Yet to him it brought little exhilaration since the politics of the day was "deficient in the great themes upon which the Tribune of the People liked to expound eloquently to the Freeholders of Nova Scotia."[29] For him the premiership was but a stop-gap while he awaited other employment. Thinking it improper to approach Newcastle during his short stay in Nova Scotia, he forwarded a letter to him in Canada, again expressing a desire to "reproduce Nova Scotia ... in some region [particularly British Oregon] where the vital energy which free Institutions bring with them is most required."[30] In office or out of it, impoverished or comparatively well off, Howe steadily pursued the quest for an imperial appointment.

Barely installed as premier, Howe was off to Prince Edward Island for six weeks to deal with that province's land question. In granting most of the Island to a relatively small number of proprietors in 1767, the British government had imposed conditions that were honoured more in the breach than in the observance. As the political consciousness of the tenants increased, they demanded more and more vociferously the confiscation of the estates or at least the right to purchase their land at reasonable prices. Only after much prompting did the colonial secretary agree in 1860 to appoint a commission of investigation, consisting of three persons: a chairman, John Hamilton Gray, nominated by the British authorities; J.W. Ritchie representing the proprietors; and Joseph Howe representing the tenants. The Islander Edward Whelan was convinced that Howe would not serve on a commission whose majority was likely to defeat his exertions on behalf of the tenants and whose findings the tenants and the Island Assembly, but not the proprietors, were, in effect, bound to accept.[31] But he reckoned without Howe's inability to resist the urge to embark on new ventures, especially between sessions when the Nova Scotian government normally ran itself with little direction from the political executive.

So for most of September Howe was in the shire towns of the three Island counties, listening to reams of evidence from proprietors, tenants, and their attorneys. The commissioners soon discovered, in language likely Howe's, that they were dealing with "a controversy unexampled, perhaps, for length and virulence, in the history of colonization." At the outset they hoped that the application of a few general principles would permit the rights of all parties to be adjusted quickly and equitably. But they soon found that every estate had a history and complications of its own which made equitable consideration difficult; besides, the question had "collateral branches" like escheats, quit rents, fishery reserves, Loyalist lands, and treatment of the French and Indians, which could not be cut off from the main inquiry. Hence they decided to hear everything that the witnesses had to say and adjourn for some months to digest "the documentary history of the question, scattered through the files of nearly half a century."[32]

Hardly back in Halifax, Howe was off on the first of several trips to Cumberland to participate in the by-election caused by Young's appointment to the bench. The government's majority, only three after the election, had been increased to nine following the unseating of a Conservative and the defection of John Hatfield and Colin Campbell to the Liberals. To Howe, who wanted at all costs to maintain it at that level, the 31st of December brought near-disaster, since his party lost seats it had formerly held in Cumberland and Victoria. He informed Mulgrave he could likely carry on with a majority of five, but in case he could not, he would attempt a reconstruction, and that failing, advise a dissolution.[33] In turn Mulgrave wrote to Newcastle, in words that he would shortly regret, that "any further diminution of ... strength would necessitate either a reconstruction of the Government, or an appeal to the country."[34] That did not satisfy Johnston, who told Newcastle that the leading government newspapers had agreed to accept the results of the by-elections as either a ratification or condemnation of the way in which the Liberals had attained and exercised power. But to his demands that the governor should insist on the retirement of the Executive Council, the council simply replied that Mulgrave would have been in grave error if he had interfered with the privilege of the assembly to act as sole judge of the qualifications of members whose election had been disputed.[35]

On January 31, 1861, Howe began the most laborious of all his sessions. "I rarely left the House at the Lunchhour but kept up my Correspondence from 1 to 3, and then often sat to 8 or 9 with no food but a few figs and crackers and a glass of Water."[36] To the opposition press his speeches were of the "laboured, halting, tedious [character] ... so common with him of late years," generally "a tissue of incomprehensible inanities" with "the usual seasoning of stale yarns and smutty jokes."[37] But if the synoptic debates reflect the facts, he was still dealing seriatim with a host of arguments as logically as ever and using his elephantine memory to recall the pointed anecdotes that made his opponents writhe in frustration and the galleries dissolve in gales of laughter. As usual, he tried to make Tupper understand that to "blast the reputation of a human being is not a political virtue, nor in nine cases out of ten a political necessity." Could not Tupper himself realize that he would have little influence until he displayed "more of Christian charity in dealing with his fellow-men."[38] Howe was fortunate that the opposition, taking its cue from the legalistic Johnston, spent much of the session reviving the issue of the supposedly disqualified members. He had his innings when Johnston, strangely and unwisely, accused Hatfield and Colin Campbell of altogether outraging constitutional propriety by turning against the party they had been elected to support. Did not Johnston realize how many Liberal members he had "stolen" from him. "Brown, McNab, Killam, [Michael] Tobin, Kenny, Henry, Wade, John Tobin, Martell, McKeagney, P. Smyth, Townsend, ... are all my disciples ... If I don't begrudge them to him, don't let him, with such a hetacomb piled up for himself, envy me the two *pet* lambs I have got."[39]

Howe also laughed off criticism that his government had broken the law in two instances. Admittedly it had taken the management of the Lunatic Asylum away from nine commissioners as the law provided and given it to the Board of Works. But, as he saw it, the government had no other choice when it discovered the extravagance of the institution and the internecine war between its superintendent, matron, and steward: "Balaclava was nothing to it!" Why, he asked, should the government not save £1,000 by ignoring a bad law that it intended to repeal?[40] Similarly he justified McCully's carrying on singlehandedly the work of a Railway Board which legally could consist of no fewer than three members. Under McCully, he pointed out, the cost of maintaining the road during the previous three months had been reduced from $404 a mile to $64.32 and earnings increased sufficiently to pay not only the operating expenses but also

£6,000 of interest. In both cases his facts were so compelling that simply by bringing the law into accord with the new practice[41] he effectively muzzled all complaints.

But other aspects of railways caused him infinitely more trouble. In the previous November, exuberant over the state of the province's finances, he had asked Premier Tilley of New Brunswick if he had "any scheme to hitch us on to Canada or the States," promising that it would "go hard with my progressive spirit if I do not scare up the means to meet you." Ten miles of the line to New Brunswick would be common to the Pictou branch and even the additional thirty miles to Pictou "will not frighten us much."[42] By the time the House met, however, the province's financial prospects were gloomy, for the American Civil War was already causing a derangement of trade and a lessening in customs receipts, the main source of provincial revenues. Nevertheless, Howe's Pictou supporters were insistent that an immediate start be made on the Pictou branch; why, they asked, should they have to bear the costs of the lines already built without benefit in return? Howe replied candidly that no party could carry the Pictou branch as a government measure, but that later, as a private member, he would move that the ten miles common to the trunk and branch lines be built during the summer of 1861.[43] His resolution to that end, however, was rendered so complicated by the introduction of amendments that it remained on the order paper unpassed. His Pictou members were not pleased, to say the least.

Much more satisfying was the efficient handling of the money votes in the first session in which their initiation had been exclusively entrusted to the government. Howe had taken special care to ensure that the estimates were fair to the opposition members and the voting of supply took only two days. The substantive business of the session completed, he let loose his supporters, "hitherto held in with a strong hand, ... upon the Opposition and Morrison, Annand, S. Campbell & Mosely [sic] particularly distinguished themselves."[44] He and they had their chance when Johnston once again raised the constitutional issue and called for a dissolution after the close of the session. In a speech stretching over two days,[45] Howe pointed out that the Tories were concentrating their abuse on three persons not in a position to defend themselves, Newcastle, Mulgrave, and Young. Scoffingly he ridiculed Johnston, of all people, for charging the representative of the Crown with sanctioning "open and flagrant violations of law and honor" and the *Acadian Recorder* and *British Colonist* for picturing him as being entrapped "in the toils of Mr. Howe, Mr. Young, and their myrmidons."

The Tory arguments had a new twist, following a series of

meetings held by Tupper between January 10 and 21 in Argyle and Digby, the seats of Hatfield and Colin Campbell. The outcome was a number of resolutions and addresses condemning the conduct of the two members and calling for a dissolution. The pressure increased when the Tories learned of Mulgrave's dispatch of January 8 suggesting that any further diminution of the government's strength would necessitate either a reconstruction or a dissolution. They reacted with further petitions pointing out the growing weakness of the government and demanding an immediate election. Howe made the obvious reply that diminution of strength meant a reduction in the government's parliamentary majority and that little attention should be given to "a cartload of Petitions manufactured in a single town by disappointed politicians, beaten in manly conflict in all the avenues known to the Constitution, ... and signed chiefly by their own partizans throughout the country." To give them recognition would mean "no steadiness in Government – no independence in Parliament ... annual instead of quadrennial elections and perpetual agitation."[46]

In mid-April Howe, in his capacity as provincial secretary or, in effect, "minister of the residuum," turned his attention to gold. A year earlier hundreds of persons rushed to the headwaters of the Tangier River in Halifax county where the province's first gold-bearing deposits had been discovered. Following "a toilsome march of ten miles through the wilderness," Howe had the lands laid off in lots of twenty by thirty feet. But all the gold he saw "put together would scarcely fill a lady's thimble,"[47] and he quickly published a report which he hoped would avert a mad rush to diggings that appeared worthless. In March 1861 further deposits were discovered near the mouth of the Tangier River, within half a mile of navigation, and again Howe was there in short order, this time in the sloop HMS *Daring*. Although still dubious of the deposits' value, he arranged to have law and order preserved and to have appropriately sized lots offered for rental at $40.

Then, early in June, he was off to Yarmouth for its hundredth anniversary celebrations. On the way he learned that his party had lost the South Kings by-election, chiefly because its candidate was disliked by the Methodists, but that it had regained the Victoria seat and its majority still stood at five. Strangely Howe knew less about Yarmouth county than almost any other; he had not been in it for sixteen years and had never spoken there. Earlier he had lost the county, once solidly Liberal, over the railway question; more recently the Acadians over the religious issue. His tactics were "not to say a word in self-defence or to touch upon politics at all." Instead he told his listeners that their festivities had gratified him no less than those of the "Three Days of July in Paris," that their enterprise contrasted markedly with its absence in Halifax, and that the beauty of their ladies was second to none. Naturally those comments brought "one universal burst of applause from the whole audience."[48]

He found the going a little more difficult when he called on the Acadians of Argyle:[49] "Treading upon eggs. The Tories hardly reconciled and Catholics very suspicious." Nevertheless, Father Quinan of Eel Brook treated him to fruit and wine, someone else to pressed peaches and quinces, and the surfeit was such that it led him, James A. Roy suggests, to abandon "the path of strict sanity" and indulge in some "amazing rigamarole": "Always hurrying over the face of the earth and never getting time for enjoyment but as the bird lies. But she can see the sky and the clouds, and the stormy hosts, the sun and moon, and their rising and setting and the comets and the rainbows and so can I, thank God. And she can see the beautiful earth with its forest trees, loaded with foliage in spring and masquerading in ten thousand colours in the autumn, and so can I, thank God." But was it rigamarole or an exceedingly apt description of the incredibly restless spirit that was Howe? Almost as if to demonstrate his own picture of himself, he was off to Meteghan; then by sloop to Westport on Brier Island to lecture on the province's resources; then, fed on fish and potatoes, in some young fellows' schooner to Sandy Cove for another lecture; and finally up Digby Neck with the courier on Sunday morning to Digby town where he saw the bishop confirm some girls at the Anglican church. The rest of the day he spent with his half-sister Jane, charmed by her granddaughter, also called Jane, "who was to die within the year, the pet of the family, everybody's plaything, the single stream of light, that illumined the family picture."

By Tuesday he was at Rothesay, New Brunswick, to bring the work of the Prince Edward Island commission to a close. For Howe those three weeks in late June and early July were sheer pleasure.[50] He found it "most refreshing" to "rest from the eternal buzz of House politics," the more so because he was lodged in "the best kept Hotel in British America." Equally delightful were the evening parties arranged by Mrs Gray and Mrs Ritchie, although they had one drawback: because the girls they brought from Saint John were "passionately fond of dancing [and] Beaux were scarce," he found himself "nearly danced to death." His relations with Gray and Ritchie remained excellent: "we never had an unkind word." While he drafted the material clauses of the report, the others looked after the historical narrative and legal sections. Usually rising at 4 a.m., he often went on little trips of his own later in the day, including a visit to Saint John to see his one-time apprentice George Fenety, publisher of the *Commercial News*, the first penny newspaper in the Maritimes.

Despite the gloomy prophecies the commissioners reached their conclusions without "deciding any thing by a vote. We were in fact unanimous throughout." Although the report[51] was decidedly unfavourable to the proprietors, it also blamed the British government for treating them "with an excessive indulgence." It proposed two simple principles to get rid of a vicious system: to let a tenant "purchase the land on which he lives" and to give both landlord and tenant "the security of a fair valuation of the land in case of difference." In words that may have been Howe's it suggested that Prince Edward Island, "enfranchised ... from the poisoned garments that enfold her, ... will yet become ... the Barbadoes of the St. Lawrence." But Edward Whalen's second prophecy, if not the first, turned out to be correct when Newcastle took the position that the findings were not binding on the proprietors. So once again "Her Majesty's unofficial advisers in London had won over her constitutional advisers in Charlottetown."[52] For Howe his labours on the commission served him personally, for within the week he was using them to press his claims before another shift in North American governors occurred. Although still believing he might do most good in British Columbia, he told Newcastle he could also be useful in Newfoundland, "where some tact and common sense appear to be much wanted."[53]

Back in Halifax he discovered that the city was getting more excited by the day about new gold discoveries. By this time the metal had been extracted in sufficient quantities at Tangier to attract visits from Mulgrave, Rear Admiral Milne, Prince Napoleon and Princess Clotilde, and Leonard Tilley. To Howe's delight, the industry was developing, like everything else in Nova Scotia, "in an orderly and law-abiding spirit ... There has not been an act of violence, or a life lost, hardly a blow struck."[54] In June the centre of interest became the Ovens, near Lunenburg, and Howe hastened there by naval sloop shortly after returning from New Brunswick. Originally discovered in the cliffs, gold was later found in the sands upon the sea coast below. So "every body rushed from their upland claims, and began to scramble for the treasure over [beaches, from] which, strange to say, the farmers in the neighbourhood had gathered sea manure for more than a century, without dreaming of its existence." The quarrels over disputed claims almost degenerated into violence until Howe restored a measure of tranquillity. When further finds were made shortly afterwards in Lawrencetown and Waverley in Halifax county, and at Wine Harbour and Isaac's Harbour on the eastern shore, he began to believe for the first time that they might contribute substantially to the province's development. For even if the gold fields were disappointing, the newcomers would not lose because of "other pursuits which are presented on every side." In a land where an emigrant could get 100 acres of good land for £10 stg, he might make himself independent in three years.[55] Nova Scotia's greatest booster, he painted the same idyllic picture of the province in 1861 as he had in the *Acadian* of 1827.

Scarcely returned from the Ovens, Howe was off with Susan Ann, daughter Ellen, and grandson Johnny to Cape Breton, where he renewed old acquaintances and attended a score of receptions. On the way back he took a side trip to Prince Edward Island to "make the rascals pay us our £200" to cover the expenses of the land commission. The last day he rode all night from Pictou to Truro, "smoking Cigars and humming all the songs I knew [with] Cold Lamb & Whiskey at 2 in the morning."[56] Then, for the rest of the summer, he was attending to the gold discoveries, entertaining Prince Napoleon, and enjoying concerts at the Horticultural Gardens.

These social activities were to be interrupted, however, by another plunge into matters intercolonial. In the previous summer the Canadian John Ross had requested his help in promoting colonial union. Howe replied noncommittally that he wanted to provide a wider field for British Americans, but whether it should be done through a Maritime Province union or a wider union was "a question floating in my mind, which our conference perhaps might solve."[57] During the session of 1861, at John Tobin's urging and with Tupper's agreement, he had got the assembly to adopt a resolution which invited Mulgrave to determine the attitudes of the colonial secretary and the other colonies towards union, the aim being to secure "an enlightened consideration" of the question which would put "the public mind ... at rest."[58] At the request of a British member of parliament, Joseph Nelson, he had also secured a second resolution favouring an intercolonial railroad, although he renounced the idea of personal participation in further delegations to Britain. When the British government held out no hope of financial aid, he dismissed the project from his mind. Even after Nelson came back with detailed plans he was not impressed. "To go again and break my back hammering thoughts into people's heads who know nothing of British America and care less is an elegant recreation that has for me but few attractions."[59]

Yet, when Nelson and Edward W. Watkin of the Grand Trunk called on him later in the summer, he found himself unable to resist being drawn into a great venture, and so, on September 26, 1861, accompanied by Archibald, McCully, and his son Sydenham (discharged from the Royal Navy for lack of physical stamina), he set out for Quebec City. After two nights of partying – the first night "all the Delegates and Members of Government [except for Tilley and Watkin were] half seas over"[60] – the conference got down to work and by September 30 it had concurred in an earlier proposal that £60,000 per annum be provided for the railroad, equally divided between the provinces. It was hoped that this amount would lead to a parliamentary grant of equal size and the renewed interest of English capitalists.[61]

Wanting to inspect the lines with which their own were to be connected, the Nova Scotians travelled the Grand Trunk from Rivière du Loup to Sarnia, entertained lavishly along the way by Watkin.[62] As usual, Howe missed nothing. At Montreal he saw La Fontaine in action in a court room and felt sorry for the parties in an abortion case. Out of curiosity he took the railway from Prescott to Ottawa to see the Parliament Buildings being constructed in the capital-to-be of the province of Canada: "Florid Gothic ... Don't like the style ... situation for seat of Government a mistake. Will be abandoned I think." At Ottawa he met Anthony Trollope gathering material for a book, "a brute in his manners." In Detroit he and Archibald marvelled at the grain elevators and the machinery for loading flour into ships; then "feeling an invincible desire to see Chicago," they were off to the city "which stands in the same relation to the boundless and rich prairie country round it, that Halifax does to the sea ... What it is destined to grow to God only knows." Later they took the Chicago, Burlington, and Quincy Railroad to Mendota for a sight of the prairies and travelled by the Great Western from Windsor to Niagara and Hamilton before returning to Montreal and Portland by the Grand Trunk. So ended, Howe wrote, "one of the most delightful excursions that I ever made." Yet he came back to Nova Scotia "abundantly satisfied with what we have and enjoy [even when compared] with the richest Prairie Country ... The sea is our Province, and the riches are inexhaustible."

"Reading the future by the past," he was still not very sanguine about the railroad.[63] Yet if proposals were to be placed before the spring sessions of the legislatures, the British government would have to make a decision soon. So, on November 1, he found himself aboard RMS *Arabia* with Leonard Tilley, bound for another round of railway negotiations. Although Roy pictures 1861 as a period of almost unrelieved gloom, Howe himself said it was "crowded with labor and yet diversified by as much variety & enlivened by as much rational pleasure and excitement as almost any previous year of life."[64] Now it was to be crowned by an event for which he had long hoped: Susan Ann was to accompany him. As usual, the rising of his hopes provided the energy to meet the new challenge. Much to their delight, Tilley and he found Newcastle forthcoming to the point of telling them that it was his cabinet colleagues, not he, whom they needed to convince. Like Grey in 1851, he gave them an entirely free hand in their choice of tactics, including the means best calculated to create a favourable public opinion.

Once Philip Vankoughnet of Canada had arrived, the three presented their case in turn to Prime Minister Palmerston and the leading members of his cabinet, and also began to prepare a paper for the cabinet's consideration. The proposal was that Britain guarantee half the interest upon a borrowing of £3,000,000 stg at 4 per cent, the three provinces to guarantee the rest. It was hoped that the British outlay of £60,000 per year would gradually diminish as the work became productive. Then fate and the Americans took a hand. When the Union navy's removal of the Southern commissioners, Slidell and Mason, from the British mail steamer *Trent* almost brought Britain and the United States to war, Howe made it unmistakably known where he stood: "God send that Jonathan may have sense enough to eat his leek, but if he does not we must go at him in good style." To Mulgrave he suggested that the navy and the militia, if suitably disposed, could easily defend the province; besides, "our privateers will give the Eastern States enough to do." So, if the Northerners attacked New Brunswick and Canada, there should be no question about sending the two British regiments in Halifax to their defence.[65]

These events also led the delegates to adopt a new tack. In forwarding their unfinished memorandum to Newcastle, they told him that recent events had rendered its completion supererogatory. Their frontiers, which might readily have been defended by rapid communication, remained unprotected, and, with winter approaching, the enemy could throw 100,000 men upon the border "with more ease ... than a single barrel of flour can be brought down to the seaboard Provinces." To rectify this situation not an hour should be lost in deciding "a question which lies at the very basis of national defence."[66] Hoping to get the decision he wanted by adopting the role of publicist, Howe, accompanied by Tilley and Watkin, went to Lancashire for ten days. It was particularly important, he thought, to "change the current of public opinion in that very influential county," because the government needed its support to retain its precarious majority and because the Manchester school of politicians was either hostile or indifferent to colonial interests. In short order they persuaded the mayor and the corporation of Manchester to memorialize in support of the railroad. Then, on December 3 and 6, Howe gave speeches at Ashton-under-Lyne and Oldham which were notable mainly for his advocacy of Nova Scotia's interests and his condemnation of the North's conduct in the Civil War.[67]

Nova Scotia, he said, was "most like England of any country on the face of the earth"; yet even when he brought samples of gold nuggets which savants in England told him were as important as the early discoveries in Australia and California, Englishmen were still being sent to the far ends of the earth. Why, instead, should they not take a cheap and easy journey to a province whose people had "shown that the constitution of England could be transplanted, consolidated, and confirmed, wherever the Anglo-Saxon was to be found"? In dealing with the Civil War, Howe may have been influenced by his old friend Carmichael-Smyth, who wanted belligerent action unless the United States acted more reasonably and who was outraged by that "little mind," Richard Cobden, for suggesting that Britain had little leverage in the case of Slidell and Mason.[68] Howe, though an out-and-out opponent of slavery, argued that Britain could do no more than indicate its dislike of that institution to the South and reserved his strongest criticism for Lincoln and the Northerners.

As he saw it, they had adopted an equivocal position on slavery, seemed willing to let the South have slaves to raise cotton for the North to use, and sought to put the Southerners in thraldom by crippling their trade with Britain and forcing them to consume Northern goods under the high Morrill tariff. By "sitting upon five or six million bales of cotton which they could not eat or manufacture," and which the factories of Lancashire needed, they were behaving like nothing so much as the dog in the manger. From British factory workers Howe's speech won rapturous applause; from the *British Colonist* nothing but contempt. How delightful it would be, it said, when the North's representative in Halifax met Lord Mulgrave's first minister, the man who prophesied that the North could never overrun the South; who suggested that the Southerners were simply doing what they were most practised in, the only difference being that, "instead of shooting squirrels, deer and racoons, they were shooting Yankees"; and who compared Southerners to "the boy's nose that had been wiped over and over again [but] would not stay wiped."[69]

His speech-making interrupted by the death of Prince Albert, Howe went back to London, where, with Vankoughnet, he answered all sorts of questions about the state of defence in British North America. The lack of knowledge of this subject being even more abysmal than he had thought possible, he revived an idea he had long entertained: that British Americans should have a permanent association in London which would collect and diffuse information about themselves and through which, when in Britain, they might appeal for "fair consideration" either to the government or people. Australia had a similar association and "for one person that you meet who knows anything accurately of North America, there are ten who have either returned from or read something about Australia."[70] Accordingly he drew up the prospectus for a British North American Association, which held its first general meeting on February 28, 1862, approved a constitution, and established temporary offices – Howe called it a home – for British Americans in London.

Meanwhile the lack of attention he and his associates were receiving, socially and otherwise, was making him more indignant by the day. Adding to his irritation was his failure to get answers to his own questions even while being asked to provide other information for the British ministries. Finally, an evasive reply on the matter of compensation to the members of the Prince Edward Island Land Commission, coming at a time when he was afflicted with another of his chest colds, led him to write a "tickler" to Under-secretary J.F. Elliot with the request that it be shown to Newcastle. No reply was forthcoming, and knowing that Newcastle had received a letter on the railroad from Gladstone, he sought and got an interview with the colonial secretary early in January. Using the prerogative of a senior politician of the empire he took two hours to speak his mind plainly on all the matters that concerned him. The duke said little, but showed no annoyance.[71]

Earlier Howe had told Elliot that because of the magnitude of the responsibility assumed by the Land Commission each commissioner should receive at least £500 stg. But at the interview Newcastle informed him that since "the proprietors were very savage at the manner in which we had handled them," the most he could recommend to Gladstone was £400 stg. "The whole affair," Howe told John Hamilton Gray, "has been managed in a shabby spirit. One expected nothing better from old Palmer [in Prince Edward Island] but they ought to be a touch above that in England."[72] Because Howe warned Gray not to show his letter to "anybody who writes, gossips, or can make mischief," Roy draws the inference that Howe had not genuinely pressed the case for compensation in London for fear it might disturb other claims he was pressing for himself.[73] But actually Howe wanted no more than to prevent his criticism from reaching the ears of Governor Arthur Gordon of New Brunswick, an appointee and favourite of Newcastle. In fact, it was on the urging of Gray, who had told him that colonials should be able to look to "the [once] proud distinction − 'Civis Romanus sum',"[74] that he outlined to Newcastle the general case for the appointment of colonials to imperial office while he was presenting his own. Any suggestion that he acted evasively to sacrifice the other commissioners' interest is without substance.

In pointing out the failure of the Colonial Office to grant the delegates and their wives the usual official recognition and courtesies, Howe embarrassed Newcastle most of all. "Not a soul in the department had called upon or invited one of us" and "not a lady upon whom we had *official* claims" had called upon Mrs Howe or Mrs Vankoughnet. Imagine, said Howe, how he felt while dining by himself at the Athenaeum to have Newcastle pass him by and eat alone. "I thought Punch might make a sketch of the two Secretaries [using] the motto, 'No connection with the concern over the way'," as an appropriate caption. All apologies, Newcastle said he had not seen Howe on this occasion and explained that only the death of the Prince Consort had prevented the delegates and their wives from being invited to the palace. Newcastle pressed Howe to stay a few days at Clumber Park, his country seat, and on his way to embarkation Howe spent a few hours there and was entertained royally. After dinner, to Susan Ann's delight, Newcastle took a candle and spent an hour showing them his collection of paintings.

At the interview Newcastle also promised Howe an informal paper outlining Gladstone's comments on the railroad. In the meantime Howe and Joseph Nelson were off to Bristol where, after Howe's speech, the city pledged its support. "In another month," Howe told Tilley, "... we could have carried all the large cities in the Kingdom."[75] Back in London, and anxious to return home to get ready for the legislative session, he, with Vankoughnet, Nelson, and Watkin, prepared answers to Gladstone's points in a day. At Clumber he gave them to Newcastle, who seemed delighted that "Gladstone's slate" could be so easily "rubbed out." Although he left London in mid-January 1862 with the railway business unfinished, he had put it in the best possible shape. Unable to address meetings at Liverpool, Chester, and other major cities, he had enlisted Nelson's services in seeking memorials from those cities in support of his cause.

Even before leaving England he had arranged for the General Assembly to meet on February 13. But the prospect of the session of 1862 brought him no sense of exhilaration. The utter derangement of commerce by the American Civil War had reduced revenues to the point that it would be difficult to maintain even the existing services. Basically it would be a housekeeping session and the Speech from the

Throne proposed no legislation other than to regulate the gold mining industry and revise the militia law. Though Howe participated in debates less than usual, he could always be counted upon to refute the opposition's criticism. When Johnston complained that the rentals to be charged to gold miners were excessive, Howe replied that "this matter ... *grew* upon us, step by step"[76] and as the industry developed the rentals were steadily reduced and were now about right. To objections to the failure to renew the appointment of John Hill as sheriff of Cape Breton county he gave short shrift. Any officer who "could, from ignorance or stupidity, refuse to deliver to the weeping relatives, for examination and burial, the body of a man who had died [while incarcerated for debt], should hold the office of sheriff no longer than the government were restrained by law, from turning him out."[77]

In the absence of other eye-catching issues, the Tories so belaboured the "financial degeneracy" of the province that Howe expressed horror at their denigration of "this poor little country of ours ... I have heard the cry of her going to ruin a dozen times."[78] An extraordinarily large budgetary deficit of $125,000 was almost entirely traceable to the decrease in import duties and the increased expenditures on the militia and the Volunteers in a period of international insecurity. In the time-honoured, Nova Scotian way the government sought to make up the deficiency through temporary increases in the general tariff from 10 to $12\frac{1}{2}$ per cent and in duties on luxuries like coffee, tea, leather, tobacco, brandy, gin, and rum, an action all the less burdensome since Nova Scotia was easily the most lightly taxed province in British America: no direct taxes at the provincial level and customs duties amounting to $2.37 per head per annum, compared to $3.74 in New Brunswick and something much higher in Canada. But Tupper, capitalizing on the provincial hostility to increased taxation, caught the public eye with retrenchment proposals designed to effect savings of $79,648. Since most of the cuts were to be in the salaries of the lieutenant-governor, judges, and principal officers of government and would therefore have breached the bargain for the surrender of the casual revenues, Howe suggested scornfully that Nova Scotia, "now that we have become older and wiser, and now that our revenue is doubled," was to go on its knees to the British government and ask permission to "violate this bargain ... to suit the great necessities of the year 1862."[79] Offhandedly, Tupper brushed aside these objections, stating that Britain would willingly concede anything the Nova Scotia legislature considered necessary in straitened circumstances and the lieutenant-governor would lend his cooperation.

Retrenchment might have died a natural death had not Colin

Campbell of Digby, a recent convert to the Liberals, but trammelled by some previously expressed views on retrenchment, retired from the Executive Council and, in effect, from the party. The outcome was that the ministry defeated Tupper's proposals by a mere two votes, a diminution in strength which, as Mulgrave's dispatch of January had indicated, would require either a reconstruction of the government or a dissolution. Taken completely aback, Howe made it known on March 24 that he would first try to pass the revenue bills that were about to expire; then attempt a reconstruction of the government by "honorable proposals"; and in the event of failure take appropriate action.[80] Two days later Johnston stated categorically that no Conservative member would "entertain any overtures whatever for a reconstruction of the Government"; obviously he was reacting to Howe's proposals to Tupper and himself, and to offers of preferment to individual Conservative members who would switch their allegiance. Again Howe replied that he was "not the man to conduct a government ... resting upon a majority of two,"[81] a statement which the opposition regarded as equivalent to a pledge to dissolve the assembly.

The Conservatives should have let well enough alone, but the energetic Tupper could not resist moving, in committee of supply, for a reduction in the indemnities of assemblymen and for the elimination of the lieutenant-governor's private secretary. On March 28 the proposals were rejected by three and four votes respectively, the increased majorities being produced by the abstention, on the second division, of Colin Campbell and, on both, of Moses Shaw, Johnston's Conservative colleague for the county of Annapolis. The result was to restore the confidence of the badly shaken Liberals. Although Shaw said only that he could support no motion which might be "construed into a belief that members were overpaid," the *Chronicle* presumed that the government no longer "need ... trouble itself about resignation, reconstruction, or dissolution" and Howe told Mulgrave that Johnston was no longer "in a position to reduce his majority below that by which he has been supported for the last year."[82]

Thus the exponent of great causes was being reduced to behind-the-scenes cajolery merely to keep his government alive. In Moses Shaw he had found the opposition's weakest link. Almost cast aside as a candidate in 1859, Shaw was being treated with little respect by the Tory leadership and feared being discarded at the next election. On April 4 Howe offered him a seat in the Executive Council; however, if he considered it unwise to take that step at once, Howe would, in return for his support, consult him on appointments in Annapolis county and assist him at the next election. In turn Shaw assured Howe that for the time being he would protect the government, either by his vote or abstention, and at the next session give it full support whether or not he accepted a seat in the council.[83]

None of this was revealed publicly and as prorogation approached the opposition insisted more and more vehemently on a dissolution forthwith. Hence Howe's major pronouncement of April 10 reduced it to absolute fury. "No rule of the constitution ...," he said, "names any certain number as the majority which a government must have to carry on." Admittedly in this instance the government's position was "a little varied" by a governor's dispatch "which I accepted when I brought it down ... and accept now that it is in the Journals." But since he had put himself in a position to meet its terms, he intended to take no advice from Johnston or Tupper on the matter: "I shall hereafter ... take my own steps, and my own time, and do my work in my own way." Why, he asked, did the Tories, instead of insisting on a dissolution, not test the government's strength with a vote of non-confidence?[84] But they did not respond and when prorogation came without dissolution, the *Acadian Recorder* declared it had lost all "faith in the integrity of an English nobleman's word." In the months that followed the Tory press made even more unflattering references to the "unfortunate imbecile called a Lieutenant Governor."[85] Meanwhile Mulgrave was telling Newcastle that the province was suffering severely from the bitterness of party feuds, even though "no great political question ... divides them" and "the matter in dispute is now simply one of men, not measures." Since an election would only exacerbate matters, he had decided to use "every constitutional influence" he possessed to bring about party amalgamation; Howe, he knew, would meet the opposition" on fair and honorable terms."[86] It is nothing short of incomprehensible, however, that Mulgrave could have imagined that Johnston and Tupper might even consider a union of the parties.

Actually Howe was hoping to strengthen his government in a way that would have meant more than the defection of half a dozen Moses Shaws. A year earlier he had said jocularly that the Catholics had "left me foolishly and without cause; and like little Bo-peep ... I let them alone till they choose to come home, wagging their tails behind them."[87] Nonetheless, he continued to "do them justice" and when Bishop MacKinnon of Arichat requested a favour for an unfortunate member of his flock, Howe obliged him at once and asked to be shown how he might serve others similarly situated. Obviously he was hoping that, since the Scottish Catholics had left him reluctantly, reconciliation with them would be all the easier. To that end, in May he offered a legislative councillorship to the bishop's brother, John McKinnon, and, more importantly, the solicitor generalship and membership in the Executive Council to Catholic Hugh McDonald, hoping in this way to "strengthen the administration" and "re-establish the kindly relations out of which so much of public advantage resulted in times past." But it was not to be. How, asked McDonald, could a lifelong Conservative like himself abandon his party "*without any change – in the persons or the public policy of the Govt.* to which I was so long opposed – without any pressing public necessity or grievance which might be remedied by my joining the Government."[88]

McKinnon would have gladly accepted the legislative councillorship, although only as an independent, since most Catholics would have regarded his joining the Liberals as "the next thing to the changing of his religion." But for Howe it was the double arrangement or nothing at all. "A half measure," he said, would still leave the Catholics without representation or influence in the government and without any inducement to support it.[89] For all his dickering he had not been able to restore to politics the normality that he wanted; the most he had done was to persuade one nondescript Conservative to give him the support he needed to retain office. And for his overtures to the Catholics he would later have to pay the price of being charged with brazen impudence. "We know not who should consider themselves most insulted – the Roman Catholics, or Mr. Howe's zealous supporters of last election."[90]

In mid-April Howe was back in a role he found much more congenial. Newcastle's letter of thanks for his work on the Prince Edward Island Land Commission gave him the opening he needed to approach the duke on a variety of concerns.[91] The railway negotiations, he surmised, had fallen through, but of even greater concern to him was the tone of the recent debate in Parliament on colonial defence. "If we are driven to shape our future without regard to England's honour and interest (which appears to be the advice given by some of these wise acres) we can make a Nation sooner than they think." Surely it was madness to wound the susceptibilities of a loyal people and to "set them thinking of separation for no greater advantage than to leave England without a Harbour, a spar or a ton of Coal on the Continent of America." Could not Newcastle settle the "war question" by sending him to the other provinces to work out some intelligible principle for determining the strength of garrisons in time of peace and the proportion of the burden that each would assume in time of war. Would this not be a better course than to have "speeches flung to and fro across the sea which only create irritation."

Unexpectedly word arrived in early May of some support for the railway. But Gladstone had turned down the colonies' proposals and offered instead to guarantee the interest on provincial loans in much the same way the British government had done for Canada in 1842. The extent of the guarantee would be determined by the particulars of the scheme and the kind of security offered.[92] Although Howe told Newcastle that Nova Scotia would be hard pressed to raise the additional £10,000 per annum that would be required, he promised to explore all the possibilities and in June he and Tilley had informal discussions with the Canadians which led Lord Monck, the governor general, to convene a conference at Quebec on September 10. Before then the *Acadian Recorder* had told its readers, "we are a bankrupt people," and the *British Colonist* warned Mulgrave not to send delegates to Canada and to "shut his ears to the false counsels which drag him to personal dishonour."[93] At Quebec Howe and Tilley argued that Canada, because of its extent, resources, and need of the line for its defence, should assume half rather than a third of the railway's cost, but in the end they had to accept a Canadian "ultimatum" offering to meet only five-twelfths. At the same time they all agreed to postpone any discussion of colonial union to "a more convenient season, after public opinion has been prepared by the intercourse over the Road."[94]

While a guest of the John Sandfield Macdonald-Sicotte government, which had succeeded the John A. Macdonald-Cartier ministry following its defeat on the militia bill, Howe defended Canada against Lords Ellenborough and Grey, and Professor Goldwin Smith of Oxford University, in a speech at Port Robinson in the Niagara Peninsula.[95] To charges that Canada had become "corrupt and politically demoralized" he replied that its public men had escaped "the taint of corruption" until the British MP William Jackson, "with the power and influence ... of a combined body of contractors at his back, began to operate on the Legislature." Surely Lord Grey was the last man to condemn the Canadians, since his failure to carry out the policy adopted in 1851 had "led to all the corruption, if corruption there has been, and all the waste ... from that hour, down to the present hour." To British criticisms that Canada was unwilling to spend enough to defend itself, he replied that the Parliament of Canada, and it alone, had the right to determine the outlay upon defence. "Suppose a war to break out with the States ... Would Lord Grey's estate be in danger? Would Lord Ellenborough's country seat be destroyed?"

Naturally Howe treated with scorn Goldwin Smith's suggestion that the connection between Britain and Canada should be severed at once. But if the day came on which England told the colonists to go, he had no fear for the destinies of provinces whose people would still possess the blessings of the British heritage. Not unexpectedly, the Canadian papers opposed to the J.S. Macdonald-Sicotte ministry discovered all sorts of faults in the speech. The Montreal *Herald* found it too full of triumph over the faults of the mother country; the Quebec *Morning Chronicle* called it "an impudent and indelicate calumny ... a gross violation of the privileges accorded by a generous hospitality"; and the Montreal *Commercial Advertiser* outraged all common sense by declaring that Howe wanted "access ... to the Canadian purse, and he thinks our people are fools enough to give it to him in exchange for the abuse of the mother country."[96] When Nova Scotia's Tory press began to take the same line, the *Chronicle* reminded it that Howe's remarks were directed at a few Englishmen only, not at the English people generally. But it could not halt the references to "the insane folly of [Howe's] speech in Canada, in which he slandered and insulted everybody whose assistance we require."[97]

By the end of October Howe and Tilley were in London, awaiting the arrival of L.V. Sicotte and William Howland, who were delayed for more than two weeks by the continuing political difficulties in Canada. Howe's intelligence had not been encouraging. Sandfield Macdonald had told him that the Halifax-Quebec railway was "anything but palatable" in Canada, except in Quebec city and its environs, and "unless we can manage to galvanize it a little by assurances from the Colonial office – of a move toward its Western Extension – I do *not think we can float it* in the Assembly"; his hope was that Newcastle might be persuaded to "put up" the project as indispensable for defence and offer liberal terms, "which should go far in lieu of the outlay expected of us for militia organization."[98] This year Howe could not complain of his treatment socially or otherwise. Though unwell, Newcastle accorded the delegates several interviews, cheerfully acquiesced in their proposals, and advised them how best to adjust their differences with the Treasury.[99] The Treasury officials generally met their wishes in "a liberal spirit": they agreed that the British government would borrow the money and pay it over to the provinces without any brokerage charges and they arranged the provisions for repayment to suit the capacity of the provinces. Only in the matter of a sinking fund did the delegates raise objections and seek an interview with the chancellor of the exchequer himself. Gladstone, the previous year so grim and foreboding, "received [them] graciously, and discussed ... the whole subject in a spirit at once frank and conciliatory." But "with his characteristic moral fervour,"[100] he insisted that a guaranteed loan without a sinking fund was contrary to his own principles and would not be accepted by Parliament.

Accordingly the delegates sought to have the sinking fund rendered only "lightly burdensome" by delaying its coming into effect for ten years during which the work would have been built and, they hoped, would have become productive. They also asked that the sinking funds be invested, not in the three per cents, but in colonial or other bonds which might earn as much as six per cent. Because the points were new to him, Gladstone asked time to decide, and, thinking that his decision would be long in coming and likely unfavourable, Howland and Sicotte went off to Paris. But Howe and Tilley warned Newcastle bluntly that "the whole negociation hung upon these two points," and within a day he replied that Gladstone had conceded both. Although Howe feared that the sinking fund would still cause trouble and lead the colonies to lose "some interest however skilfully managed," he was convinced that the lower provinces could cope with it.[101] Not so Sicotte and Howland, who returned on December 18 and entered their dissent five days later.[102] Canada's experience with a sinking fund, they pointed out, was that it "made the rate of interest higher than she would have paid by borrowing on her unassisted credit." Further, although the work was not popular in Canada and would be undertaken only because it was "conducive to the greatness and defence of the Empire at large," the British government's proposals were in a form that acknowledged no obligation on its part to make a contribution. If, instead, it provided the funds at $3\frac{1}{2}$ per cent in the manner requested, it would be giving genuine support to "a work of national concern and a measure of public defence."

As usual, Howe filled his time in England with a host of other activities. At the British North American Association's "splendid Dinner" he gave the managers of businesses connected with North America "a couple of half serious and half playful staves."[103] At Birmingham, where he went to inaugurate the Colonial Emigration Association, he spoke from the same platform that John Bright often used and his audience, he thought, "did not suffer by the Comparison."[104] He had another exchange with C.B. Adderley, but since the latter believed that the empire had its uses and should be kept together, he addressed him in moderate, persuasive, and not belligerent tones. Why, Adderley had asked, should not the five colonies of British North America provide for their own defence through standing armies and a militia much as the old thirteen colonies had done?

For Howe this conjured up the picture of "half a hundred little armies, scattered all around the globe, ... with uniforms as various as were the colours in Joseph's coat – with ... no provision for mutual succour and support." As he saw it, a nucleus of British soldiers ought to be retained which could incorporate as much of the colonial militias as the circumstances required, and when "so incorporated, they should be moved, paid and treated as an imperial force." But if the British troops were withdrawn and the colonies "left to drift into new experiments, 'shadows, clouds and darkness' will rest upon the scene, and of the glories of this empire we shall chance to see the beginning of the end."[105] Again Howe was linking his views on defence to his larger ones on the organization of the empire. Unlike him, his old friend, the thoroughly dispirited Carmichael-Smyth, had abandoned his earlier vision. Because he knew "by what tricks and dishonesty England & her most valuable colonies have been governed ... I tell you candidly that if I was now a North American colonist I should wish to shake off the poor old country. My opinion is that she has done for herself ... & I think that we [are] going [down hill] fast."[106]

Late in November Tilley wrote Susan Ann that her husband had gone to Torquay "for no other purpose in the world except to see a middle aged maiden Lady, of great wealth, if not of great beauty. What think you of that."[107] By accident Howe had met the British philanthropist Angela Burdett-Coutts at the Nova Scotian section of the London Exhibition of 1862 and later, in an effusive letter, had told her that she could win as much immortality as Florence Nightingale by organizing the women of London to reduce the misery in the British Isles and strengthen the queen's dominions at the same time. "Let us hope that God, in making us acquainted, has some work for us to do."[108] Accordingly he drew up a plan of emigration which, at her request, he showed to her adviser, the bishop of London, and to herself at her country estate at Torquay. He also promised to have legislation passed in 1863 which would provide for the care and distribution of immigrants who came to Nova Scotia. For once he would find a Briton who needed no extra urging.

Howe's social invitations were almost too numerous. Regretfully he declined to spend a week with Lord Shaftesbury, the son-in-law of Palmerston. "They say that [he] makes all the bishops. I would have gone if there had been any prospect of his making one of me." He did spend two days at Clumber Park as Newcastle's only guest, "revelling in Pictures, Statuary, old Trees, flower gardens, and all that can give pleasure and convey instruction to say nothing of unrestrained converse ... with one, to whom all these things are as familiar as I was with the trees at the North West Arm." But most memorable of all was his visit over Christmas to Wroxton Abbey in Oxfordshire, home of the Norths, relatives of Howe's friend, Gen. Hastings Doyle, commander-in-chief in Halifax. As often happened, Howe was awed by his sense of history. "You walk through corridors and ascend and descend staircases with Warriors and Statesmen and beautiful Women almost speaking to you from the canvas. I slept in a room that had scarcely been disturbed since it was occupied by Lady Jane Grey. The Rooms where James the First, George the 3rd and 4th slept are there, bed, furniture, Arras tapestry, untouched and perfect as they were left." What elated Howe most was to prove wrong those who had held that his rough treatment of some noble lords and other Englishmen on the Niagara Peninsula would prevent his going to Britain or securing an official position. They "do not know glorious old England as I know it."

Some months earlier he had learned of the death of Moses H. Perley, fisheries commissioner under the Reciprocity Treaty, and although the vacancy was one for Lord Russell, the foreign secretary, to fill, he wrote to both Newcastle and Russell, pointing out that since the deaths of Sir Allan MacNab and Hamilton Merritt he was "perhaps the oldest man in the Provinces who has done any thing for them"; hence he would not like to be passed over "if a selection is made from this side of the water."[109] Having raised the matter again in London and being asked if he had made himself *persona non grata* with the Americans, he pointed out that the commissioner did not live in the United States and hence stood in a different position from an ambassador who might be dismissed. If objection was taken because of his participation in the enlistment of foreigners during the Crimean War, his answer was that he was simply carrying out British policy and that he had visited the United States many times since then without incident. If exception was taken to his opinions on the Civil War, he was merely expressing sentiments that few British Americans did not share.[110] To his elation he received the appointment shortly afterwards. Although it was not the position he would have preferred, his long quest for imperial office had achieved a modicum of success. Aboard ship, thinking that he had also "placed the Intercolonial Railroad once more within the grasp of the Colonial Legislatures," he called his seventh visit to Europe "one of the most gratifying and triumphant I have ever had."[111] But his hopes were to be dashed almost as he exulted in them.

## CHAPTER EIGHT

# "A Sabbath of Rest"

Howe might have escaped vexation had he assumed the duties of fishery commissioner at once. But feeling duty-bound not to desert his colleagues, he got Russell's permission to postpone taking over the position formally until the end of the spring session of 1863 and the calling of a general election. His annoyances began on his way back to Halifax. Aboard RMS *Africa* were Howland and Sicotte, who showed him their letter to Newcastle. To Howe it was the very kind he would have written if he had been trying to persuade the government and Parliament of Canada not to build the railroad.[1] Accordingly one of his first acts in Halifax was to tax John Sandfield Macdonald with sending delegates who would find some excuse for not submitting the railway question to their Parliament: "if the Lower Provinces are to be a second time sacrificed by Canada after faith solemnly pledged," it would be a long time before it had another chance; "with old England on one side of us and homogeneous New England on the other, our own wit will make our own fortune pretty secure whatever may happen in Canada."[2] This growing distrust of Canadian politicians would reach its zenith in the Confederation debate.

From the day Howe landed in Halifax he met criticism, both for increasing Nova Scotia's commitment to the Intercolonial Railway (ICR), and for accepting imperial office while still holding the provincial secretaryship. His conduct, wrote the *British Colonist*, was "sufficient to arouse the burning indignation of every freeman in the Colony."[3] Tupper could hardly wait for the opening of the session to castigate the appointment as fishery commissioner of one who had earlier broken the recruiting laws of the United States and more recently held up the Northerners to contempt and ridicule. Would Howe dare to occupy two offices at once and thereby violate the principles of responsible government; was he, who boasted about being its father, "resolved to become its executioner"?[4] To both charges Howe replied with questions. Could a Nova Scotian "not go abroad and make remarks in public without having ... the whole rehashed and served up" in a legislative session? Were offices of this kind so plentiful that "colonists could afford to hurl them back into [Britain's] teeth"?[5]

When Tupper continued without let up, Howe told him not to worry because he was drawing two salaries. Although he had earned a good deal of money in his life, he had never spent it extravagantly. "Where is it? Back, as everybody knows, in the hands of my countrymen, from whom it was received ... if my pockets are filled, it will be all the better for those whose pockets are empty."[6] Later he declared that, even if it had cost him his right hand, he would not have raked up events of many years ago to "peril" his opponent's appointment to office. Tupper's conduct had been neither fair nor generous; "it was not what one Nova Scotian had a right to expect from another under the circumstances." He also made it clear that, in leaving provincial office, he would not be abandoning politics altogether. Many of his evenings, it was true, would be given to books, since "literature still has attractions for me which I trust it will continue to have to my dying day." But important questions would surely arise in which his voice might help to "calm the virulence of party strife" and in which he might "atone for having given perhaps too much animation to our debates in my earlier days."[7] Meanwhile could Tupper not change his style? Instead of "little, perpetual, peddling, snarling assaults on all subjects, and on all occasions," why did he not confine himself to facts and exhibit discretion in the choice of his weapons and time of attack? "Did he name a day – give notice of his intention – and get up a good rattling party attack, once a fortnight, or once a month," the interests both of himself and the public would be better served.[8]

Though Archibald took over more of the leadership than before, Howe played his usual active part in three minor bills and all the major ones. He accepted the opposition contention that the existing laws put too much of a burden on gold prospectors and agreed that henceforth they should pay royalties only and not rentals as well. As a result, he was charged with designing measures to benefit the Nova Scotia Land and Gold Crushing and Amalgamating Company, of which Executive Councillors William Annand and Benjamin Wier were directors. When his critics went on to argue the low state of Nova Scotia politics, he angrily asserted that other legislatures had shown more self-seeking and corruption in a few years than the Nova Scotian in its entire history. "The politics of Nova Scotia are her life-blood. Look at the time when we had no politics, when everything relating to the interest of the country was directed by a clique in conclave."[9] Howe also participated in a move which he hoped would fulfil his long-held wish to make still slumbering Dalhousie College the provincial university. Pressed strongly by two of the college's major benefactors, George Munro and William Young, he got his chief opponents' consent to a bill which reconstituted the board of governors so as to include himself, Young, and Tupper.[10] Although the changes did not appear to be of a substantive nature, it is a matter of record that under the new order Dalhousie finally did begin a genuine era of development. The third minor bill – Howe called it his "last legacy to the Province" – dealt with the more mundane matter of cattle shows and horticultural exhibitions, and provided for two exhibitions annually in each of six districts.

In major bills Howe was sponsor and chief defendant of the one dealing with representation. "This measure," he said, "has been framed on the principle, if you can't do all the good you wish, do all you can."[11] Although it did nothing to equalize the representation between counties other than to add a seat to Halifax and Cape Breton, it did equalize the voting strength within all the counties except Lunenburg and Annapolis. It also enabled Howe to provide the people of Clare with a member of their own: "They are a body of men who never unwarrantably pressed on the Government for anything, whose requirements were always reasonable."[12] Finally, the bill readjusted the districts in those counties which, in his view, had been "cut up most unfairly" before the last election. Although the *British Colonist* described its villainy as "too palpable,"[13] it would have passed except for H.G. Pineo, who brought about its defeat in the Legislative Council by a single vote. Great was Howe's indignation against the man who, though once a Conservative, had "voted with us for four or five years, ... promised to support [the bill], failed us at the last moment and went over to the enemy."[14]

Much more consequential was the franchise bill, which Howe defended at least three times as a device for rescuing Nova Scotia from its downward tendency towards democracy and republicanism. Never friendly towards the universal suffrage adopted in 1854, he lamented that it rendered "the sterling men of the country" ineffective, while a small minority "who make a trade of their franchise, who can be and are bought up ... carry the election."[15] Tupper might represent Cumberland for twenty years and still be "a gray-headed man with but little money in his pocket" because a rich man could "beat him out of his seat at any time."[16] The solution was to tell the youth that the right to vote depended upon their industry and frugality. "The one is industrious, he is frugal [and] saves and appropriates [his earnings] to the acquisition of property; the other says, 'I will not work – will not save; what little I earn I will squander recklessly in dissipation.' Would it be right ... that both these should enjoy the same rights"?[17] It sounded like the Howe of the 1830s over again and the remedy was still an incentive to industry: to confine the franchise to those who had managed to acquire real estate worth $150 or personal property worth $300.

An aroused opposition called it the Garrotter's Bill, a diabolical attempt to "swindle a free people out of their rights. Had not the government "spent the last year in secretly cooking the Assessment rolls through wily agents in the country ... to give effect to the fraud they have just practiced"?[18] Even Howe conceded that it might seem ungenerous, even unfair, at the close of his long political life to "contract the privileges of a single human being in Nova Scotia." He admitted, too, that the measure would likely prove advantageous to his party. Did the Tory party not consist of the very rich who operated on the very poor? Were the Liberals not supported by most of the people between these extremes, especially the most intelligent and, in the aggregate, the most substantial part of the population, and clearly a majority? But even if he was charged with lack of generosity and promotion of party, the bill was still a necessity. "We have the power ... to relieve ourselves from the charge of being the only British Colony, save Australia, governed through universal suffrage, to purge our constitution and purify our electoral system."[19] Once again, however, H.G. Pineo provided the vote which prevented the bill from becoming operative until after the next election.[20] For the Liberals its only good was to furnish an explanation for their defeat a few weeks later.

Fortunately, for his equanimity, Howe set much greater store by his railway bill. After their return from Britain, he and Tilley engaged in a continuing correspondence on the ICR, both agreeing that if the Canadians backed out of their commitment because of the sinking fund, they would be taking "a most disreputable course."[21] To gauge attitudes in Canada at first hand Tilley went there in January 1863 and discovered that the machinations of its politicians were beyond unravelling. Although convinced that the government had not "done all [it] might have done to carry out in good faith [its] engagement," he could get nothing from it but a promise to meet five-twelfths of the cost of the survey and to go further only if it increased its parliamentary strength. Yet Tilley was not completely disheartened, for should the tottering Sicotte-Macdonald ministry fall, its successor could not possibly be more difficult to deal with. So, following the advice of friends of the railway in Canada, he suggested to Howe that

Nova Scotia and New Brunswick pass their railway bills and thus give an impetus to the work in the upper province.[22]

Yet, because of the Canadians' foot-dragging, Tilley met unexpected opposition, while Howe found himself in one of his stiffest fights. From the start of the year the Tory press had kept up the refrain that if he had not been so anxious to get "a snug Imperial retreat for himself," he would not have been "content to swallow the most extravagant terms"; that the Whig government in Britain was acting over again the story of the Sybilline leaves and offering terms which not only contained less but would cost more. Who then could blame the Canadians, a practical, business-minded people, for withdrawing?[23] In answer, the *Chronicle* resorted to the patriotic cry: "Turn our backs now upon the old flag and upon the mother country ... and you do much to sever the strong link that has ... made us part and parcel of the Great Empire upon which the sun is said never to set."[24]

Almost at the session's end Howe finally proceeded with a resolution authorizing the government to borrow money on the British government's terms and to build the eleven miles from Truro to Walls Mills that was common to both the ICR and the Pictou branch. Even if Canada did no more than provide for the survey in 1863, he insisted that the Maritimes needed to do something. Otherwise the offer would never be made again. In any case the Pictou line was feasible in itself since the coal traffic would make it valuable almost at once and the £80,000 it would cost could be got without going to foreign capitalists.[25] Johnston, objecting to doing anything as "a piece of mere etiquette," was especially indignant that the British government had treated Nova Scotia so illiberally as to force her to build sixty miles of the ICR beyond the province because of its failure to recognize a great national enterprise.[26] Nevertheless, Howe carried his proposals by four in the assembly and by nine in the council, where the Tories were badly split. Boastfully he told Newcastle that the Canadians' intemperate action had been rejected in his province and that they were now isolated and put in the position of having either to accept or reject British aid.[27]

Early in the session Howe's tranquillity had been somewhat disturbed by a letter from Miss Burdett-Coutts, telling him that 120 immigrants were on their way. James A. Roy suggests that if she had known him better she would have insisted upon going into the practical details, which, "as usual, the enthusiastic Howe had failed to supply."[28] But actually Howe had told her that operations could not begin until he had got a bill through the legislature appointing an agent who would be authorized to distribute funds to poor immigrants. Still, he knew that, living in the south of England as she did, she could not realize that February was Nova Scotia's coldest month and that agricultural operations could not start until April. Seemingly his old foe Sir Samuel Cunard was participating in "a wretched Job, for the benefit of the steamboat proprietors." Not only had he let the immigrants go out at a season that he knew was unpropitious, but he had had them sent by steamer at double the cost of sailing ships. Always solicitous of Miss Coutts's feelings, Howe told her not to grieve, that all these troubles would disappear when the arrangements he was devising were put into operation.[29]

Not surprisingly, Roy distorts Howe's reaction and suggests that the news of the imminent arrival of the immigrants led him to "panic." But, although annoyed, Howe took it all in stride. Within half an hour of their landing, a committee headed by the gold commissioner, Samuel Creelman, had placed the new arrivals in Mason's Hall, Sailors' Home, and a vacant hall, where fires, food, and beds awaited them; in short order all but the Irish had secured employment. So, by early March, Howe was once more his effusive self. Providence, he told Miss Coutts, was with them in this good work and within a month he would be ready to receive another 100 immigrants.[30] A little later he announced delightedly that he had got his legislative arrangements accepted and had appointed as immigration agent his old friend, Thomas Morrison, "energetic, and of sterling integrity and great kindness of heart." Only two things clouded the venture: the Irish, who would not take employment as long as the government maintained them, and Jaques, Miss Coutts's agent, who was "too much intoxicated to be of any service ... when most needed." But these were only trifles and Miss Coutts must make up her mind to "be loved and honored over here as you are on the other side of the Atlantic."[31]

Dissolution followed prorogation, the election being set for May 28. Almost at once it was apparent that the direction of Nova Scotian politics was falling into new hands. For reasons of health Johnston did not want to offer for Annapolis and did it only on condition that he would not have to engage in a personal canvass. It was therefore left to Tupper to issue a series of letters which sought to show that "the tales of Munchausen are not more fabulous than the writings and speeches of Mr. Howe"; the *Chronicle* replied in kind that Tupper was "like a bayou, stagnant and full of crocodiles, alligators, lizards, and creeping, slimy reptiles, burying themselves in oozy mud, breathing nephritic gases, fatal to all living creatures."[32] Because Howe was proposing to retire and his assembly colleagues were busy with their own campaigns, Legislative Councillor Jonathan McCully assumed a leading role for the Liberals and attempted to answer the "misrepresentation" of the *Colonist, Express, Reporter,* and *Recorder* in a "Letter to the People of Nova Scotia." But the party "wheels" in Halifax did induce Howe to contest Lunenburg, hoping he would get himself elected and pull in two Liberals with him. He may not have needed much urging; political animal that he was, he was clearly reluctant to abandon the assembly where, except for one session, he had sat since 1837.

His decision could hardly have had unhappier results. It was bad enough that the opposition asked who was to be cheated: the British government out of his salary as fishery commissioner or his constituents out of the time he should spend attending to their interests?[33] It was worse that, after spending ten days in New Brunswick arranging with Perley's son to assume the duties of fishery commissioner, he arrived in Lunenburg late in the campaign to find hardly the semblance of an organization. To McCully he confided that the situation was "hopeless" and that without extensive financial support he would suffer "the disgrace of defeat."[34] Although he did what he could, he lost by about 500 votes, running only second among the Liberal candidates. Even then the annoyances of the campaign were not over. Asked to defray its expenses, he replied indignantly that he had been assured they were not his responsibility. Having "cheerfully paid out a good many other expenses forced upon me by the utter absence of all arrangements," he would go no further.[35]

Overall it was a crushing defeat for the Liberals, who won only fourteen out of fifty-five seats. Many of them, including Howe, blamed it on the failure to put the franchise bill into effect immediately. "This was a fatal blow to the Government. My retirement it was known, would weaken it a good deal, but of course all the rascals who would have been disfranchised had the bills passed voted against their authors."[36] Actually there was much more to it than that. After winning every election since 1848, the Liberal party was in a pronounced state of disarray. Its credibility had been gradually eroded by the never-ending attacks of Tupper; it went into the election without even letting the public know who was to lead it; it could not attract candidates and let nine Conservatives win by acclamation. For Howe the results meant that he could give his undivided attention to the fishery commissionership.

To some his new office may have seemed an inglorious anticlimax to his campaign for imperial office. Probably Newcastle or Russell would not have offered it for fear of demeaning him. Certainly its duties appeared modest enough. The Reciprocity Treaty of 1854 had opened the inshore fisheries of British North America and the United States to both countries as far south as 36° latitude. But it did not include the salmon and shad fisheries, nor those in the rivers and mouths of rivers. One British and one American commissioner were to determine what were, in fact, rivers and then draw lines defining their mouths and hence the limits of the reserved rights. Though lacking the prestige of a governorship, the office carried with it a salary of £750 stg and expenses, considerably better than the perquisites of any provincial office. It also removed Howe from parochial provincial politics which, as he said, turned trivialities into mountains and gave him, in the words of his old friend, the Rev. John Sprott, a "safe berth ... out of hearing the noisey debates and unchristian bickerings in the House of Assembly."[37] But those who expected Howe to take a limited view of his new duties would soon be disappointed. He saw the office not only as an instrument for his own education and development, but also as a roving commission to safeguard British interests anywhere in North America, something that would have horrified Russell.

In his earlier trip to New Brunswick Howe had invited George Perley, son of Moses, to continue to act as surveyor to the commission. Apparently Moses had never kept a regular set of books, but George promised to do his best to meet the Foreign Office's request for a statement of his father's expenditures since 1855 with vouchers. Howe also discovered that his predecessor had surveyed all the American rivers except fourteen southern ones including the Potomac and Delaware, and all the British North American ones except those in Newfoundland and Labrador. The former, he concluded, could not be examined until the end of the Civil War, while many of the latter would be blocked by ice until July.

Early in June he was on his way to consult Lord Lyons, the British minister in Washington, on the whole a pleasant trip except for "the usual stupid night ride" from New York, "sleeping on a jumping board ... and dreaming hideous dreams."[38] Lyons, "affable, frank, intelligent [but] very guarded," introduced him to W.H. Seward, the secretary of state, who in turn arranged that he meet the president. Howe found Lincoln to be "taller than I thought, something of the Jackson cut about him – 'good man struggling with the storms of fate'." To "the wretched sneaks at home" who had prophesied that he would be *persona non grata* in Washington he could now say, "go to grass." His official business completed, he had a first-hand look at the havoc of war. South of the Jerseys, he told Lady North, "you can almost sniff the carnage or imagine you can from bloody fields not

[too] far off." It might be pleasant, he noted in his diary, to read the record of battles not seen, but "to be shot down by thousands, by persons you never saw and cannot personally hate ... to be left on the battlefield till the ravens pluck out eyes and wild beasts tear the flesh – to be wounded and left upon the field ... till heat and thirst ... aggravate what the bullet or the bayonet [did] ... All these things ... show ... what war really is." Sometimes the ludicrous was so mixed up with the poignant that he laughed in spite of himself. There was the Kentucky rifleman who eyed a sentinel from a distance and exclaimed, "About my size. I think his boots will fit"; shortly "'pop goes the rifle' and the boots are transferred."[39] An epitaph to a federal soldier in a Virginian churchyard also caught his eye:

> The northern hordes with sullied hands
> Came southward, to invade our lands
> This narrow and contracted spot
> Was all that *that* poor Yankee got.[40]

On his way to Baltimore his purse was stolen – "the first time I have been robbed though travelling about the world for 30 years" – but fortunately it contained only three New Brunswick dollars. In Baltimore he had a "kind offer" to be taken to Miss Mary's. "Who is she"? In Bangor, Maine, he met his fellow commissioner, Elijah Hamlin, "a fine old gentleman" with whom he established an instant rapport. Then, anxious to see the Aroostook country, the centre of disputes that had disturbed the even tenor of Maritime ways, he went up the Penobscot in a small steam paddler and came down by the St Andrews railroad to the coast. But for once his propensity to explore new places resulted in disappointment: mosquitoes almost devoured him on the Penobscot; most of his fellow passengers were "stupid"; and the only exciting thing he saw was a cockfight.

In Halifax he waited impatiently for six weeks until August 7, when Vice-Admiral Milne finally placed the steam corvette *Greyhound* at his disposal for his trip to Newfoundland and Labrador. Because of the lateness of the season, he decided to concentrate on the more northern areas that might soon be blocked by ice. Before he returned early in October, he had examined the Bay of Exploits, Gander, Green and Hall's bays, and the French centres of Croc and Quirpon on the east coast of Newfoundland; Chateau, Red, Black, and Fortune bays and the anchorage of Blanc Sablon on the Labrador coast; and St George and Bonne bays and the Great and Little Codroy rivers on the west coast of Newfoundland. Where appropriate, Perley would survey and mark the mouths of rivers and thus put Howe in a position to compare notes and negotiate with Hamlin. All this was in the official report,[41] but it conveyed little of what the trip really meant to him: "such a blessed sabbath of rest ... as I have not enjoyed for a quarter of a Century."[42]

Willingly he admitted that his trip was one he could not have given himself if he had had his own yacht and £10,000 a year.[43] Adding to his pleasure were scenery "more grand and varied" than anything to be found in Nova Scotia and the most attractive field sports into the bargain." Up the Humber his party shot three deer and fed the whole ship's company on venison for two days; by his own account he himself caught 180 trout ranging from one to four pounds in two hours. But no delicacy he had eaten from the western prairies to the Rhine could compare with the Newfoundland curlew. "We had it roasted and broiled and fried and made into pastries, but still 'increase of appetite but grew with what it fed on'." His greatest delight, however, was to "be for two months where there were neither Railroads, Telegraphs, Post Offices or Newspapers. Where politics were never mentioned and where communication with the outer world was so rare and so uncertain that you lost all interest in it and would not throw down your gun or rod to read the London Times fresh from the Press." How much better it was than "a life of sedentary drudgery with 350,000 masters and £700 a year," half of which he spent in elections or gave away. But even to him it must have seemed rather extravagant to maintain a man-o'war with a crew of 180 for months on end to permit two men to mark the mouths of rivers.

Back in Halifax, Howe enjoyed the freest three months he had spent since youth or would ever spend again. For a time he helped Susan Ann put their new house in order. Since the sale of the *Novascotian* office in 1842 (its upstairs had served as a residence) he had lived in various rented houses throughout the city and in 1857, by one account, he had sold his household goods and gone into furnished quarters.[44] Seeking to establish more normal living and put himself in a position to entertain, he now leased Fairfield, "a pretty place" fitted out by an "eccentric Yorkshireman" on the Dartmouth side, across the harbour from the dockyard. For £50 stg a year he got a three-storey house with five bedrooms and all sorts of conveniences. A verandah, "covered in like a Hotbed," ran the whole length of the house and enabled the Howe family to hear the band music from the ships and Wellington Barracks. His father's "fine face once more look[ed] down upon [his] dining table"; indeed, it was "the old North West Arm over again with a livelier outlook by night and day." On most mornings Howe, in grey suit and grey beaver hat, walked downtown to the post office, picking up the morning mail and asking the postmaster, Luther Sterns, to hold back his little dog until he boarded the ferry for Halifax.

During these months he also got to know his family better. Mary, perhaps his favourite, had died in 1853 just as she approached twenty-one; John three years later at the age of ten. Thus, of ten children born to him and Susan Ann, only five survived. Ellen, the eldest, had by this time several children, in whose company Howe revelled; Joseph, Jr, had taken to the sea and was always coming and going; Fred, serving the cause of the North in the 23rd Ohio Regiment, had escaped unscathed from some of the bloodiest battles of the Civil War and had been warned by his father not to interfere in American politics, since he knew no more about them than would an Ohio man know about Nova Scotian politics if he dropped from the clouds; Sydenham, having left the navy, was training to be a merchant at Stairs'; and Bill had entered a counting house. Leisure also made Howe nostalgic. Now that he had a house over his head again, he decided to have "all my friends together." So he wrote to the governors under whom he had served and requested photographs of themselves and their wives; in response, Lady le Marchant sent him the only remaining ones she possessed. Leisure also gave Howe a chance to render little favours and compliments. Lady North got baskets of Nova Scotia vegetation, including fern leaves entirely new to her; Miss Burdett-Coutts was assured that the happily settled immigrants sent her the "blessing of those who [had been] ready to perish";[45] but to an Anglican minister who assumed that, because he was a politician, he must also be an infidel, and who presumed to express concern for his soul, he gave short shrift. "All the great truths of Christianity my Father taught me when I was ten years of age and continued to enforce till I was 30. I do not think that even you can add any thing to the simple eloquence with which they were illustrated in his life and conversation."[46]

Throughout 1863 Howe's disillusionment with Canadian public men grew steadily. The exception was D'Arcy McGee, who lectured in Halifax on July 21 and whom Howe declared to be the ideal man to take the lead in the intercolonial railroad and union questions, although he told McGee that "the road ought to be first built, and union come after."[47] In November he conceded that the ICR was "fairly 'up the spout'" and that he might attend the next session of the Canadian Parliament to study "the modern Canadian" a little closer; certainly he could not "make him out" if John Sandfield Macdonald represented "either his brains or his sense of honour." Still later in the year he described the ICR as "dead and buried" and Canadian politicians as "shuffling humbugs."[48] Strangely, he who had got nowhere with the Pictou Railway showed no sympathy at all for the difficulties of Canadian politicians confronted with problems of far greater magnitude.

Early in January 1864 Howe was off on a two-month jaunt to the United States in which he transacted business with Hamlin, wrote letters on the Reciprocity Treaty, and read American poetry. Hamlin and he agreed to do nothing concerning the Fishery Commission for the moment. The American had completed all his surveys; Howe would dispose of Newfoundland that summer; and the two could then dispose of everything at one sitting. In New York Howe had his usual frenzied round of activities, including a visit to Barnum's exhibition, the writing of comic verses on the giantess, and dinner with his relative, "Tommy" Tilestone, and his old friend Lawrence O'Connor Doyle, both of whom would die within a few months. In Boston he experienced almost a satiety of things which delighted him: he established a lasting friendship with some of the non-Loyalist Howes; he heard Edward Everett, the president of Harvard, speak and Edwin Percy Whipple deliver a lecture on Thackeray; he observed Oliver Wendell Holmes lecture to his class and then dined with him at the Literary Club, where he met Emerson and other literary notabilities.

But something else kept Howe weeks longer in the United States than he had intended. To his consternation and horror, steps had been initiated in Congress for the termination of the Reciprocity Treaty. The policy of the Palmerston administration, he told British officialdom, had turned Northern opinion against Great Britain almost from the start of the Civil War, and the irritation had been strengthened by the widespread sympathy for the South in Parliament and much of the British press, and the depredation inflicted on Northern commerce by such raiders as the *Alabama* and the *Florida*. Hoping to dispel the ignorance and prejudice surrounding the treaty, he published three letters under the signature "Saxon" in the New York *Albion* on January 30, and February 6 and 13, 1864. The first was already in print when he sought approval for their publication. To Lord Lyons he gave assurances that he would not interfere with matters beyond the range of his instructions, although, as he conceived them, they were highly elastic. Later, indeed too late for the warning to be effective, the Foreign Office told him that the letters should not give offence and should be written "with no presumption of an official character."[49]

The first two[50] sought to demonstrate that the treaty did not give

British North America a disproportionate share of the advantages; actually "the very reverse of the proposition [could] easily be proved." Further, had the Northerners not continued to enjoy all the trading privileges of the treaty during the Civil War, while British Americans were excluded from ports from the Potomac to the Rio Grande? Did the Northerners not know that hundreds of young colonists had "fought and bled, and died in all the great battles [on the Northern side];" while almost none served in the armies of the Southern Confederacy? Could Northerners not understand that British Americans had been angered by the Trent affair and by threats to whip the colonies and England which had been flung across the border for months by sensationalist newspapers? Howe's third letter dealt with the suggestion of the governor of Maine that, if Americans refused to trade with British Americans, the latter might be compelled to seek annexation and adopt American political institutions. Why, he wondered, should British Americans want to change their constitution when they had institutions "modelled after those of the mother country ... They have but to open Hatsell or the Journals of Parliament, and the most intricate question is solved by the record." But surely, he concluded, the continuance of the treaty should be governed by a "logical examination of the statistical returns, by which alone its value can be determined."

Then he was ready for home, not too soon, for he was making altogether inordinate demands on a constitution which simply could not take such punishment. In New York he had suffered from a heavy cold with a stiff neck and neuralgia; he had not taken care of himself in Boston and the cold worsened on the way home, first on the steamer and then on the open boat which took him across Halifax harbour at three in the morning. The result was "an obstinate attack of neuralgia" which he only worked off in the spring by "sweating in the open air ... as he cleared and planted [his] kitchen garden ... made compost ... and dressed the fields."[51] For three months he was little in evidence. But he did note with satisfaction that, with returning prosperity, the Tories "hardly know what to do with the money" and that those who had said his railroad would bankrupt the country were proceeding with the Pictou branch.[52] And he did make a public appearance of note on April 23, when he delivered the oration at the tercentenary celebration of Shakespeare's birth and drew acclaim, sometimes a little too extravagant, in the Nova Scotian and American newspapers. Only the *Acadian Recorder* had a few reservations, wondering if Howe had accorded Shakespeare "so lofty and dignified and heroic a place among the great princes of literature" as some contemporary thinkers had done. But Roy is convinced that Howe was "thoroughly conversant with the latest Shakespearian criticism of the day."[53]

By the time Howe returned to the United States on June 1 he had put his financial house in order and could write elatedly: "my family [was] once more in comfort with a house over their heads and the comforts of life around them – my business was arranged – a great many old debts paid."[54] Only his relations with Annand disturbed him. Although the *Novascotian* had been Annand's for more than twenty years, he had paid Howe little of the purchase price even though he had enjoyed a salary as financial secretary for some years and both the *Novascotian* and *Chronicle* had prospered. Worse still, Annand kept maintaining that the *Chronicle*, which had been established after his purchase of the *Novascotian*, could not be regarded as part of Howe's security for the loan. Angrily Howe replied that he would not have been "such an Idiot as to lend the aid of [his] own purse for many years to build up the *Chronicle*" if he had thought this was so; "... in asking you to pay £700 out of nearly £2400 ... I am only doing justice to my family which for nearly five years have left you and yours in full enjoyment of the earnings of the entire establishment."[55]

Other than marking a few of the rivers in Maryland and Delaware, Howe's six weeks in the United States were largely devoted to his own pleasure and gratification.[56] Worried about not hearing from Fred, he finally learned from the War Department that he was with General Hunter in West Virginia. Much of the time he rambled about Maryland, Delaware, New Jersey, and Pennsylvania as the spirit moved him, noting all sorts of minutiae that fascinated him. Going south, he found a gold sovereign to be worth $8 at Eastport, $9.25 at Boston, and $10 at New York; on the way back it was $11 at Baltimore and $12 at New York. Salem, although a dead old place, did have its linden-perfumed streets and a wonderful old oak in the Quaker burying ground. A debate in Congress was paralysingly dull, but he found much to interest him at the fair in Philadelphia, including Washington's state coach and Stephen Girard's "One Horse Shay." It was typical of Howe that he concluded the American part of his trip by taking up a subscription at Portland for a poor factory girl who had been robbed. But nothing delighted him so much about his trip as its conclusion, when he persuaded his half-sister Jane and her daughter Sarah to accompany him back to Dartmouth. By July 9 he had got her safely to Fairfield and there, for a month, he was all attention. "We gave a dinner to all her old friends – a lunch to the General and the Governor of New Brunswick – a *Fête-Champêtre* to the Squadron and Garrison, and had our house full of young and old in whom Jane took an interest." Because it would be her last visit, he was thankful he had been able to "associate her with the highest in rank, intelligence and influence as well as to surround her with every relic of the past."

Not until August 1 could Admiral Sir James Hope let him have the HMS *Lily*, a sloop of light draft, for his trip to Newfoundland. Although at first life aboard her was not as congenial as on the *Greyhound*, "the 'Lilies' improve upon acquaintance and I have been very happy among them." Still, the exhilaration of the previous year was absent for a number of reasons, especially the weather, the worst in the history of Newfoundland. "They have in fact had no summer ... [even] with clothing as heavy as I should wear at home in February, I have found it difficult at times to keep myself warm."[57] Almost as uncongenial were his relations with George Perley. The previous summer he had cautioned him about his "habit of drinking spirits at all hours from eleven o'clock in the forenoon till bedtime." He also suggested that Perley's long delay in compiling a statement of his father's expenditures was due to intemperance. When Perley behaved no differently aboard the *Lily* than in 1863, Howe addressed him in severe terms: to prevent the character of the commission from being lowered, he was either to mend his ways or suffer "an abrupt termination" of employment.[58] The late start and bad weather limited Howe to an examination of Bonavista, Trinity, and Conception bays and the beginning of work on Placentia and Fortune bays; it would require another summer, he feared, to complete the rest of the south coast to Port aux Basques.

Meanwhile some steps towards intercolonial union had been taken. Since the autumn of 1863 Nova Scotian newspapers of both parties had been suggesting off and on that, inasmuch as the Canadian politicians had so alienated Maritimers as to preclude a larger union, perhaps Maritime union might be a "very possible, nay, a very hopeful expedient."[59] To these views Tupper was responding when, in the spring of 1864, he got the assembly to agree to the appointment of five delegates to discuss a more limited union with the other Maritime Provinces. Because he had intimated, in a chance street meeting with Howe, that he hoped he would be one of two Liberal delegates at Charlottetown, the latter sought permission from Russell on July 25 to act in that capacity. But he did not receive Tupper's formal invitation until August 16, when he was already aboard the *Lily*, and he replied that his "summer's work would be so seriously deranged" that he could not go without permission.[60] Those who have suggested it was a clear case of his refusal to play "second fiddle to that damn'd Tupper" are perhaps not acquainted with the subsequent stern injunction of Russell that he undertake no other duties until the commission had completed its work and that he also let the Reciprocity Treaty "alone unless the American Government seeks to disturb it."[61]

If Howe had gone to Charlottetown, he might have been infected with the prospects of nation-building. As it was, he had been a little infected when, just as he left for Newfoundland, ninety-seven Canadians arrived in Halifax on August 10 on a get-acquainted visit. After attending the Hodge Podge and Chowder party of the Halifax Yacht Club, they spent much of the next day at Prince's Lodge in "feasting, and song, eloquence and good fellow-ship." There they did "not scruple to bend themselves to leap frog with the more frolicsome of the Blue Nose Commoners." After supper the French Canadians sang French songs in capital style; D'Arcy McGee entranced everyone with a speech half-serious and half-humorous; and Joseph Howe followed with one "chiefly in praise of the beautiful women of our Colonies who were not represented."[62]

But for Howe his major effort was at the grand dinner on Saturday, August 13, in the drill-room of the Halifax Volunteers, when he replied to McGee's toast to "Nova Scotia's Distinguished Sons." Starting at ten minutes to midnight after hours of conviviality, he, who had always hedged his support of the larger union with all sorts of reservations, expressed pleasure that "the day was rapidly approaching when the Provinces would be united." He had always regarded himself as a British American as well as a Nova Scotian and he wanted "every now and again to see the seething falls of Montmorenci, to see the Indians of Loretto dancing about the silver stream." But he also wanted the western men to come down to the ocean "when they had got the fever and ague, and bathe themselves here. The pool of Bethesda was nothing to the ocean." Would not Canada and the Maritimes complement one another? "With the territory of Canada, ... with the inexhaustible fisheries [of Nova Scotia], what a country to live in! And why should union not be brought about? Was it because we wish to live and die in our insignificance?" The outcome would be to "make a new England here; not a new England with republican institutions, but a new England with monarchical institutions."[63] This was his only utterance on intercolonial union which would later cause him trouble and he would simply say: "Who ever heard of a public man being bound by a speech delivered on such an occasion as that?"[64]

When Howe arrived back in Halifax on November 2, the Quebec Conference was just over and the debate on its resolutions had not yet begun. Indeed, they did not see the light of day until November 10, when they were published by the Charlottetown *Monitor*, "the littlest paper in the littlest island in the world."[65] For Nova Scotians the debate began nine days later when both the *Halifax Citizen* and the *Morning Chronicle* editorialized on them. The *Citizen*, published by E.M. McDonald and William Garvie, contended that the proposals would bring "sectional interests not into combination but constant collision"; history, it said, "proved that legislative Union is the only lasting Union." The immensely more prestigious *Morning Chronicle*, owned by William Annand but edited by Jonathan McCully, took the opposite view. In August it had warned against a federal union as a "doubtful expediency adapted to the exigencies of Canadian necessities."[66] But that was before McCully had become a delegate to Charlottetown and Quebec, and been "transmogrified" in the process. Later Howe would say that St Paul was converted by a flood of light; Danaë was changed from a virgin into a strumpet by a shower of gold; "you, who know the man, can judge whether McCully was converted after the fashion of Danaë or St. Paul."[67]

At first the Confederates had all the advantages: the most fluent speakers; the support of all the Halifax newspapers except the *Citizen* and the inconsequential *Bullfrog*; and, through Tupper, the control of provincial patronage. Clearly Tupper thought he had the clinching argument when on December 23 he published a *Royal Gazette Extraordinary* which contained a confidential dispatch from the colonial secretary endorsing the scheme. No wonder the *Evening Express* inquired in mock puzzlement about the opponents of union: "Who are they?"[68] Nevertheless, a genuine grass-roots movement against union had developed without benefit of leaders of prominence. It was reflected in the *Yarmouth Herald* of December 1 which warned against placing Nova Scotia "at the mercy of Canada. Surely, if we accept such a scheme, we shall 'pay dearly for the whistle'." Throughout western Nova Scotia, and eventually through the entire province, the attitude was much the same. Of all the country newspapers, only the Pictou *Colonial Standard* supported union. Coastal areas prospering under the Reciprocity Treaty could see no benefit from closer ties with the backwoods of Canada. If for no other reason, a political culture that had already congealed militated against the acceptance of substantial change.

For once Howe found himself handcuffed: as an imperial officer, he could not participate openly in a debate of consequence to Nova Scotia. He must have gritted his teeth when, starting on November 21, his old friend and ally, McCully, began to use his name and utterances to bolster the case for union he was making in the *Chronicle*. Indeed, "given a little more time, he might have made Howe an honorary Father of Confederation."[69] Howe, who was absent in Wolfville addressing the Acadia Athenaeum on "Reminiscences of Great Men," did not attend the first public meeting in Halifax – a Confederate one – on December 9. But at the subsequent meetings of December 19, 23, 30, and 31 – some Confederate, some anti-Confederate, and some mixed – he sat on the platform, always silent except on one occasion. He said nothing on December 23 when the anti-Confederate A.M. Uniacke noted that Howe had never advocated a federal union, "nor do I believe that gentleman to be favourable to the proposed Constitution." But he did say something when his former ally, Benjamin Wier, pointed out that, although both Johnston and Howe had earlier opposed propositions similar to the Quebec scheme, they might have changed their minds. Had they not also opposed reciprocity and later admitted its benefits? Immediately Howe was on his feet to deny that he had objected to the treaty *per se*, but only the manner of effecting it.[70] For George Johnson, himself in attendance, the effect was electric. Every man in the meeting, he says, knew at once that Howe opposed Confederation even though he had not referred to union in any way. At that moment, he suggested, "the Anti-confederate Party ... sprung into existence, like Minerva from the brain of Jupiter, full-armed, full-blooded, full-statured."[71] Yet he was going much too far. No newspaper of the day and no other writer accorded Howe's statement the same significance. Likely the knowledgeable inferred from its tone and content that Howe did not like the Quebec scheme. That, perhaps, is all that can be said of it.

Howe also refused to intervene directly in the management of the *Chronicle*. Annand had returned from Britain late in 1864 to discover that McCully had committed his paper to Confederation. Since Annand wore his principles upon his sleeve, he would not have minded if the stance had been popular. But the merchants upon whom he relied for advertising had come out against it and the paper's country subscribers were even more hostile.[72] Facing financial loss, Annand asked Howe if he should get rid of McCully and, having been refused an answer, intimated that McCully must go. Laughingly, Howe told him he was "very like a woman. You make up your mind first and ask counsel afterwards."[73] Told that the *Chronicle* must reflect Annand's views on Confederation, McCully – puffed up, Howe said, in his new role as nation-builder[74] – reluctantly got out. Offered a handsome inducement to write for the *Chronicle*, Howe declined, but over the next few years contributed generously to it without taking a sixpence.

On January 11, 1865, the day after Annand assumed the editorship of the *Chronicle*, it published anonymously the first of Howe's "Botheration Letters." With plenty of leisure Howe had obviously been trying out his hand on the Quebec scheme, and when he left for

Boston at the end of January six additional letters had appeared in print. Letters 2, 5, 6, and 7 dealt with the constitutional structure of the Canada-to-be. Though Britain and the United States were supposedly the exemplars, Howe concluded that "this hybrid resembles nothing on this continent, or on the other. The fare presented to us is neither fish, flesh, nor good red herring." Britain had tried to work an Imperial Parliament in harmony with local legislatures, but had quickly swept them away. Under the Quebec scheme the experiment was to be tried again to satisfy the French Canadians; yet, just as under the Union Act they had controlled the government and legislature of Canada simply by sticking together, so they would succeed in doing under the new scheme. If thwarted, they would "back their Local Legislature against the United Parliament, and, in less than five years, will as assuredly escape from the Confederacy as Belgium did from Holland." The United States had achieved its prosperity under the old constitution of the states and all the resultant misery and bloodshed had resulted from an attempt to override state rights. Nonetheless, the Quebec scheme gave the provincial legislatures "scarcely more weight or dignity than the [Halifax] City Council," and he was certain that Tupper, Archibald, and McCully would not take a seat in them, "if offered free of cost and charges."

A legislative union would have no better results. In the United Kingdom its effect had been to drain Scotland of its wealth and population, and to enrich the country in which political power was concentrated. In Ireland the outcome was even worse: "The fox, when invited to the lion's banquet, paused when he saw all the tracks of the other animals leading into the den, and none of them coming back. Let us pause – *there* are millions of Irishmen's tracks to guide us, all going one way, and bones enough, God knows, mouldering all over the world to show what has become of the victims."[75] Although the precise conclusions to be drawn from these letters is unclear, Howe seemed to be pointing out the difficulty, perhaps the impossibility, of devising a properly balanced federal union and, at the same time, to be rejecting a legislative union in which the entities were substantially disparate in wealth and strength. Running through all his speeches and letters on Confederation was the fear that it would hand over to Canada the management of Nova Scotian affairs; that is why the Botheration Letters advocated a legislative union of the Maritime Provinces on the premise that Nova Scotia needed to be in a position of strength before she took another step.

Letters 3, 4, and 10 outlined the proper course for the province in the existing circumstances. Happy with her low tariff and sound currency, she ought not to let herself be drawn into the high protective duties of Canada, to the detriment of her trade with Britain, the United States, and the rest of the world. Perhaps, when the ICR was built, it might be possible to rub out the "divisional lines [of British America] by familiar intercourse." But under existing conditions, "*where there are no cohesive qualities in the material, no skill in the design ... unite what you will, and there is no strength.*" Nova Scotia would not be stagnant without union, for in the next twenty to thirty years it could see its population doubled and its railroad system extended; "let us work our destiny upon these lines, without running away, above tide-water, above the will-of-the-wisp at Ottawa, which will land us in a Slough of Despond."[76] In Letters 8 and 9 Howe dealt with the matter which, as much as any, would eventually bring him back into politics, the contention of McCully and Tupper that the existing legislature might implement Confederation without an appeal to the people. "Mr. McCully," he said, "may have the power to knock out his mother's brains, but the act, if done, would be murder, nevertheless."[77] In Letter 11 Howe could not resist poking fun at the Nova Scotia delegates who, with all their talents, "have got a good deal to learn." Indeed, they had been "done Brown" by George Brown, who had somehow or other got them to accept representation by population in the Commons without having to concede the American principle of equal representation in the Senate.[78]

The first eleven Botheration Letters had marshalled all the arguments Howe would ever use against the Quebec Resolutions, although later he would play down their constitutional aspects in favour of economic arguments. The tendency has been to attach great significance to them, to suggest that "they rallied opinion everywhere."[79] If they did, it was not because of their author's name, for few knew his identity until the end of February. Undoubtedly they irritated the Confederate press just as they delighted the *Chronicle*'s readers. Among the latter, however, they had the effect of reinforcing opinions already held, rather than of converting readers from another point of view. For the weight of evidence shows that Nova Scotians had already made up their minds before Howe chose to participate directly or indirectly. His part in the emergence of anti-Confederate sentiment was in fact a modest one and the oft-repeated statement that he roused his countrymen against the Quebec scheme is based largely on myth. Admittedly, however, the allusions, wit, style, and content of the letters afforded the knowledgeable unmistakable clues to their authorship, and as early as January 20 the *Evening Express* said it had "a shrewd suspicion who he is." For a week or two Howe did not observe the accelerating conflict at first hand, since he was absent in Boston discussing Fishery Commission matters with Hamlin. But even there he was keeping his eye on the Nova Scotian situation, especially on Jonathan McCully who – now the publisher of the *Unionist and Halifax Journal* – used an editorial from the *Novascotian* of May 24, 1838, to demonstrate that advocacy of union was among "the first acts of [Howe's] long and chequered political life."[80] That was too much for Howe, who telegraphed from Boston that he had been in Britain when the editorial was written. "Mr. Howe," added the *Chronicle*, "is a long way from home, but not so far that he cannot hear from and properly answer his traducers."[81]

Things were becoming too interesting for Howe to remain long in the United States, the more so because he wanted to watch Tupper's treatment of political union in the legislature. To a myriad of articles on Confederation in the *Chronicle* Howe undoubtedly contributed frequently, including perhaps an editorial of February 22 which came close to saying that he wrote the Botheration Letters. Immediately the *Unionist* intervened to inform the British government that an imperial officer was doing his utmost to defeat imperial policy. Why, replied the *Chronicle*, was the name of Howe – an imperial officer – being continually dragged into print and his viewpoint systematically misrepresented? Did not imperial officers "all over the world ... have to decide and to act in all sorts of emergencies on the spur of the moment?"[82] Perhaps this was Howe expressing his own exalted view of his office; perhaps he wanted all the more to get into print because of the intimation of McCully and Tupper that, since the colonial secretary favoured the Quebec scheme, the people should have no voice in the matter. Certainly one can imagine him wondering how Herbert Huntington would have reacted to such a suggestion; his "right leg, with a heavy boot at the end of it, would ... have commenced a series of gymnastic responses very edifying to behold."[83]

The *British Colonist*, Tupper's personal organ, reacted to the supposed identification of the author of the Botheration Letters by starting the myth – or at least initiating the charges – that Howe's vanity and egotism were determining his conduct on union. Until Tupper came along, it said, Howe had been "master of the situation." In helping to force him out of office in 1857, Tupper had reduced him to writing two books under another person's name to show that he was the "'ablest statesman' to be found in this or any other country." Later he had had to watch Tupper carry out two undertakings he himself had sought ineffectually to promote: compulsory assessment for education and a plan for intercolonial union. All that was "too much for Mr. Howe's vain and selfish nature to endure"; so he gave the complete lie to his own efforts to bring about union in 1861–62 and to his speech of August 1864 describing union as "the dream of his life."[84]

The Speech from the Throne opening the legislature on February 9, 1865 was noncommital on Confederation, affording Howe clear-cut evidence that Tupper was recognizing the state of feeling in Nova Scotia. Hence, in the last of the Botheration Letters on March 2, he sang a paean of praise for ordinary Nova Scotians who, though unaccustomed to investigating political questions, studied the Quebec Resolutions, jumped on the platform to confront the delegates, and so ventilated the question that the Quebec scheme might "now be considered as dead as Julius Caesar" in Nova Scotia. The electoral defeat of Tilley's Confederates in New Brunswick on March 6 simply confirmed this conclusion. Needing no longer to write for the *Chronicle*, Howe watched with secret pleasure as Tupper coped with a difficult situation. His temporary expedient, a return to a legislative union of the Maritimes, was not objectionable to Howe, but he must have noted that most of Tupper's speech supporting Maritime union was devoted to a defence of the Quebec Resolutions and he must have been pleased that enough of Tupper's supporters opposed those resolutions to prevent their being presented to the assembly.[85] By the end of March, except for desultory sniping, the fire had also gone out of the newspaper debate. To Howe Nova Scotia seemed safe for the moment and he could turn his attention elsewhere.

Nothing pressing or consequential took him to the United States in the second week of May, unless it was the roving commission of an imperial officer.[86] Following a few days with Hamlin in Bangor, he visited Yale and New Haven. There, fortuitously, he learned that the great army reviews that followed the Civil War – it had ended in April – would soon begin in Washington. By travelling without stops he arrived in time to see Grant's army march past "just as they came out of the field"; a little later he also saw Sherman's army and the 6th Army Corps, "altogether about 230,000 men, the greatest military spectacle of modern times." For him the scene was beyond the power of description. "It was no holiday pageant such as I have often seen in London or Paris but stern reality ... there was scarcely one man who had not been under fire, and the greater number had gone through many conflicts or had marched with Sherman from Chatanooga to Savanah." Howe met President Andrew Johnson and, for a day, sat in his booth sizing up the generals as they were introduced. Following a visit to the Virginian battlefields – "so long the Seats of War, and objects of such bloody contention" – he returned to Washington where he met Generals Grant and Meade, and visited the courtroom in which Lincoln's assassins were being tried. Elatedly he also reassumed the role of roving commissioner. The Detroit Board of Trade had invited representatives of the major cities of Canada and the United States to attend a convention early in July which would deal with matters of common concern to both countries, and the new British minister, Sir Frederick Bruce, thought it would be useful if Howe attended, apparently as an observer. This meant that he had some weeks to idle away between Washington and Detroit.

Slowly he made his way up the Shenandoah Valley to Harper's Ferry and the scene of John Brown's raid and capture – "the old fellow whose 'soul is marching on'." At Winchester he was fortunate enough to meet his son Fred before making his way to Harrisburg along the route taken by the Southerners when they marched into Maryland and Pennsylvania. "All this country," he prophesied, "will be classic ground and it was a great privilege to be able to see it just as war had left it." Little escaped him, whether it was "darkeys by the thousand having a complete Saturnalia" or disbanded northern and southern soldiers everywhere confronting each other: "the play of the passions was infinitely curious to a keen observer." After a few days at Cresson Springs, a watering place atop the Allegheny Mountains where he gossiped, ate wild strawberries and cream, and "did [nothing] else but drink the Waters," he made his way to Pittsburgh and later to Toledo, where he joined in celebrating the Fourth of July, even though "a display of heat lightning ... put all their fireworks to shame."

Meanwhile, warned by a fearful Foreign Office which knew the irrepressible Howe all too well, Sir Frederick Bruce instructed him belatedly to interfere in no way with the functions of the official Nova Scotian delegates at the convention and to limit himself to "the part of observer with a view to giving me useful information." But neither Bruce nor Lord Russell needed to fear, for the Nova Scotian delegates put Howe at their head and he could therefore participate freely "without assuming any official position or compromising Your Lordship."[87] To the convention's committee dealing with the Reciprocity Treaty, Thomas Ryan of Montreal and Howe presented the British American point of view and found both prejudice and ignorance. Because of the thinly veiled resentment at Britain's treatment of the North during the Civil War, Howe agreed with Bruce that the opposition to reciprocity was "as much political as economical."[88] But he also found opposition from special interests such as the lumbering interests of Maine and the coal and iron interests of Pennsylvania, and it took three days of argument before the committee accepted a resolution asking the president to negotiate a new reciprocity treaty.

By general agreement Howe presented the views of the fifty British American delegates to the whole convention on July 14. Worried that he would not be equal to the occasion because of fatigue and the oppressive heat of the room, he betook himself to a bar-room, where he joined some men drinking beer, "got them interested in his talk, spun yarns to them, lifted himself out of [his] depressed mood ... and filled his soul full of strength and ardour."[89] This diversion, he said afterwards, had much to do with the success of his speech. In content, its arguments were those of his letters to the *Albion*, but in its eloquence, persuasiveness, and deft mixture of emotion, humour, and reason, it rates among his best.[90] To those Americans who kept arguing that British Americans sympathized with the South, he again pointed out that hundreds of their sons had served with the North, few with their opponents. His son had been with Sheridan in all his great battles and no benefit Howe could possibly get from the Reciprocity Treaty could ever "compensate me or that boy's mother for the anxiety we have had with regard to him." At that point, "people stood up on their chairs, waved their handkerchiefs, tossed their hats, ... shouted themselves hoarse,"[91] and Howe came close to breaking down.

Next he scorned the idea that the end of reciprocity would force British Americans to seek annexation. "You know what you call Copperheads, and a nice life they have of it. Just such a life will the man have who talks treason on the other side of the line." Then, in his most serious vein, he proceeded, as Roy suggests, from a purely commercial allusion almost to the sublime:[92]

Some reference has been made to "elevators" in your discussions. What we want is an elevator to lift our souls to the height of this great argument. Why should not these great branches of the family flourish, under different systems of government, it may be, but forming one grand whole, proud of a common origin and of their advanced civilization? We are taught to reverence the mystery of the Trinity, and our salvation depends on our belief. The clover lifts its trefoil leaves to the evening dew, yet they draw their nourishment from a single stem. Thus distinct, and yet united, let us live and flourish.

Roy is quite wrong, however, in suggesting that Howe was so preoccupied with the Confederation issue and the fear of being unemployed if the Reciprocity Treaty were terminated, that he "set comparatively little store by his [oratorical] success." Actually he had dismissed intercolonial union as a dead issue and he seldom anticipated financial developments as long as eight months in advance. He called his speech "the greatest triumph of my life" and the "crowning oratorical triumph" of his career, inasmuch as forty newspapers reported it and their editorials almost invariably sang his praises.[93] The only sour note was in Nova Scotia, where the *Halifax Unionist* and the *British Colonist* both argued that anyone pleased with the outcome of the convention would have to be "thankful for very small favours." Would it not have been infinitely better, suggested McCully, if colonial interests had not been represented at all in Detroit.[94] In Hamilton, where Howe stayed with Isaac Buchanan for a few days, he revised the speech and had it printed and forwarded in typical Howe style to everyone of consequence. "All down through Canada I was welcomed as a benefactor, and every where pressed to stay."[95]

Meanwhile activities of varying kinds had been taking place in the Fishery Commission. As Howe had expected, the Foreign Office had found George Perley's statement of his father's accounts to be unacceptable; besides, Perley had twice "wrecked" appointments with Howe at Saint John, once through his not being in a condition to transact business. Hence, on his return to Halifax, Howe relieved Perley of his duties.[96] More significantly, because of the pro-Confederation policy of the British government, he would not use the sloop *Royalist*, awaiting him at Halifax, for his projected trip to Newfoundland. As early as January he had told Russell of his opposition to the Quebec scheme, sent him extracts from the Botheration Letters, and hoped that the British government would "shake itself clear of the odium of having counselled ... any such coup de main" as Confederation without genuine Nova Scotia assent.[97] In July Tupper and Henry, visiting England primarily on other matters, were told emphatically by Colonial Secretary Edward Cardwell that he would not let them revert to a legislative union of the Maritimes "unless it was taken up as a part of, and ancillary to, the scheme for the consolidation of the whole."[98] In turn, Tupper informed Cardwell that his chief difficulties with union in Nova Scotia were due to Howe, but that lately he had become much more quiet, and if he could be summoned to London, "*on business connected with the Reciprocity Treaty*, he might easily be converted into a supporter of Confederation."[99] Summoned by Russell, Howe left for England in August, only eight days after his return from Canada. But in suggesting that Howe's views might have softened, Tupper was quite mistaken. In a letter to Sir Frederick Bruce, Howe pointed out that, although he had always favoured union by a natural development – railroads first and social and commercial intercourse afterwards – the Canadians, who should know that even French girls wanting to be married "don't like to be ravished," started at the wrong end: "they tried by a sort of coup d'etat to overthrow in three months the Constitutions of former free Provinces, which were working successfully."[100]

For Howe it was an eight-day trip to Cork, during which, after three months of crowded activities, he was "not disinclined to lounge and sleep and take it easy for a while";[101] two days in seeing Dublin and its Exhibition; and then "the Wild Irish Line": by boat to Holyhead at nearly twenty miles an hour and on to London by train at sixty. The very day of his arrival he saw Russell at the Foreign Office and discussed reciprocity and colonial union. "It is evident they are very anxious to get my support to the measure, but I did not disguise my opinions and made a holy show of it before we were done."[102] Instructed to see Cardwell, Howe discovered that the colonial secretary would be away for a fortnight and so he could afford to be sick for a few days, until "a dose of Morrison" helped him to recover. To Russell and Cardwell it was soon apparent they had made a mistake in following Tupper's advice, for they could think of nothing for him to do but prepare two papers, in effect, at the British taxpayers' expense. Howe spent the following two months in making excursions around London and southern England and, almost incidentally, in writing the papers.

For ten days he lived at Gravesend, where he watched every kind of craft entering and leaving the Port of London and engaged in "most instructive contemplation of things new and strange." His major excursion began at Margate, "the Cockney's Summer paradise," and took him to Canterbury, where he revelled in the historical riches of the Cathedral: "you breathe an atmosphere of antiquity in these old places that everyone is conscious of when you get to them but which nobody can describe. How many hours have I lingered over Shakespeare's Henry the 4th, marvelling at the stately old Kings perplexities and laughing at the humors of Falstaff. Here the Monarch lay at my feet and Gadshill where the merry Knight robbed the travellers and was himself robbed in return, was not far off." His jaunt also took him to the Isle of Wight and the Westphals. Ryde Pier especially fascinated him, partly because half the yachts in England were sailing about it, and partly because it had brought together "the most marvellous collection of beautiful women that I ever saw in any part of the world. English women have a springy step, a joyous manner, a look of dignified yet courteous self possession which one sees occasionally elsewhere, but nowhere else out of England do you see a whole Pier full of women with these characteristics." At the Westphals' he "made a mighty onslaught on the Admiral's cold lamb and good sherry," and noted that his hosts were getting very feeble. "I think I have seen them for the last time."

By mid-September he had presented Cardwell with an elaborate paper on Confederation which "cut it up, root and branch," in fifty-four paragraphs filling seventeen sheets of letter paper.[103] He had also begun, at Russell's request, a paper on the organization of the empire. Finished by the end of September, it was "a formidable affair ... I have done it however to my own satisfaction."[104] The culmination of his thinking on the subject since 1846, it broke little new ground. But it did spell out more specifically than before how the colonies might impose both taxation and compulsory military service as a contribution to the defence of the empire.

A short social visit to Scotland intervened before Howe returned to Halifax in late November to learn, not to his surprise, of the death of his half-sister Jane, to whom he had been unburdening himself of his inmost thoughts for more than thirty years. "I am not exactly 'the last Rose of Summer left blooming alone'," he told her daughter Sarah, "but the last stem of a somewhat stately growth left standing amidst the mould of all the others." Although sometimes afflicted with loneliness, he took "comfort from the younger saplings springing up all round me."[105] Meanwhile some danger signs had appeared on the union scene. He attached little importance, however, to the victory of the Confederate Charles Fisher in a by-election in York county, New Brunswick, or the British government's sending off to Hong Kong Nova Scotia's lieutenant-governor, Sir Richard Graves MacDonnell, who had refused to become a tool either of the colonial secretary or of the governor general in forcing constitutional change. In London Howe had met MacDonnell's successor, Sir William Fenwick Williams, a native Nova Scotian and hero of Kars, and had described him as "a pleasant person ... full of Confederation [who] will do his best to carry it."[106] Unperturbed, he saw no reason why the assemblymen would change their minds and he was confirmed in his view of public attitudes by a by-election in Lunenburg on December 27, in which a Confederate Tory lost by 1,332 to 646 despite conduct on the part of Tupper that he considered execrable.[107]

Away from his family almost continuously for seven months, he hoped to have a month to himself free from controversy and bustle. But within two weeks of his return the *Reporter* painted a picture of him that went beyond the limit in nastiness. Supposedly unable to abandon "his meddling, demagogue propensities" and possessed by "a mean, pitiful jealousy" of men who ventured on great objects of which he was not a part, he was allegedly using "little minds" and hangers-on like Annand to defeat union.[108] Refusing to let himself be assailed in this "wanton and eccentric style," Howe replied that for seven months he had interfered, neither directly nor indirectly, in the Confederate debate and that Annand was "about the last man in the Province who would submit to any body's dictation." Was this not part of the "attempt to brow-beat and silence every man who asserted his right to think for himself" on Confederation? What made Howe most indignant was the *Reporter*'s effort to denigrate his own and Nova Scotia's political past. "I am not much ashamed of my contemporaries and fellow-workers, whether friends or foes"; except for failing to secure an educational system supported by compulsory assessment, "I accomplished everything that I ever seriously set about" and Nova Scotia had never rejected any of his principles or measures.[109] Not unexpectedly, Howe's letter was greeted with a spate of critical editorials, but he had had his say and said no more.

In his six or seven weeks at home he and Susan Ann talked over his prospects for the future. Both were concerned as he left for New York early in the year to complete the business of the Fishery Commission, which would expire with reciprocity on March 17, 1866. But he was almost ecstatic after a meeting in New York with William Morrell, who had just purchased the *Albion*, the "English" paper in the city, and offered him its editorship after March 31. Everything about the offer pleased him. Morrell proposed that the paper, hitherto a little stodgy, should reflect "a more genial spirit" and broader views of the kind that Howe had expressed at Detroit. No less pleasing was the suggestion that he might either contribute editorials and articles, live where he liked, and attend to other business, at $1,500 a year, or live in New York and edit the paper at $3,500 a year. So, if the British government gave him anything worthwhile, he would get the salary and, in addition, make $1,500 by light labour; otherwise, he and Susan Ann could live in New York in their own quiet way, save $1,000 a year towards paying their debts and leave their assets in Nova Scotia undiminished. "For this new and unexpected mercy I fervently thank God. It makes me feel more independent of all chances and casualties than I have done for many a day."[110]

Relieved in mind, Howe was off to Washington where, early in February, he and Hamlin began dealing with the Newfoundland and more southerly American rivers. In short order they had marked off the mouths of the Exploits, Gambo, and Terra Nova rivers in Newfoundland, and the Delaware and eleven smaller rivers in Maryland, which Howe had visited in the last two summers. "We have," he told Susan Ann, "a good share of business to show for our three years labours. We have acted in perfect harmony and agreed upon everything."[111] On March 19, two days after the expiry of the treaty, Howe made his last major report to Lord Clarendon, the foreign secretary, telling him that all field work had ceased and that charts showing the overall work of the commission were being prepared.[112]

Yet the Fishery Commission occupied the smaller part of Howe's time at Washington. His success at the Detroit Convention had led him to believe that political motives were by far the most important impediments to reciprocal trade arrangements. Yet, with the ending of the American Civil War and the diminution of political hostility, the Americans had not withdrawn their notice of the abrogation of the Reciprocity Treaty, an indication that economic forces were more important determinants of their behaviour than he had supposed.[113] Having failed to get agreement on negotiations for a new treaty, Russell now tried "the ingenious device," suggested by Lord Monck, of "using the parallel movements towards reciprocity and Confederation ... to reinforce each other." The theory was that, although separately the provinces could carry little weight at Washington, united they might strengthen their influence for reciprocity.[114] Accordingly, Galt and Howland from Canada, A.J. Smith from New Brunswick, and W.A. Henry from Nova Scotia journeyed to Washington towards the end of January to seek new arrangements. Seward, uninterested and about to absent himself, left them in the hands of the secretary of the treasury, who in turn referred them to the Ways and Means Committee of the House of Representatives and its veteran chairman, Justin S. Morrill of Vermont, an ardent protectionist. Because the committee's terms seemed utterly unreasonable, the provincial delegates did not stay long. Looking on but not consulted – and perhaps for that reason irked – Howe thought the business had been "fearfully bungled." Instead of putting facts before Congress, he said, "the Delegates discussed the subject with the Committee. When bluffed by [Morrill] they cleared out leaving everything to drift, and nobody here to sift the question and appeal from [Morrill] to Congress."[115]

Although Howe found many Americans still indignant because of the depredations of the *Alabama* and *Shenandoah*, and others who believed they could shake off the allegiance of British America by an illiberal trade policy, he was convinced that most members of Congress were so absorbed in the emancipation of negroes that they know nothing about the character and value of their northern trade. The "woeful amount of ignorance in both Houses," he told A.T. Galt, is "the greatest difficulty we have to contend with."[116] Deciding to play a circumspect role, he suggested to both Galt and the Halifax Chamber of Commerce that they send a couple of intelligent merchants to Washington to exercise influence quietly and to prepare for friendly adjustment if Morrill's bill failed in one House or the other. But neither replied positively, and he was thoroughly annoyed by the Halifax Chamber's request that he act for it: "now that the whole is in a mess I am not such a fool as to assume a task which can only be accomplished by a month's hard labor and at a cost of perhaps $1,000 in printing and social influence, very useful in engineering measures through Congress."[117]

He was not yet done, however; perhaps he could still "do more for the Provinces without hope of credit or reward than any member of the Delegation or anybody else."[118] Accordingly he submitted two more articles to the *Albion*, designed to dispel the ignorance surrounding trade relations with British America, and later distributed 500 copies to congressmen and newspapers all over the country.[119] But his naïve belief in the efficacy of his persuasive powers was all too evident in this instance, for the articles did nothing to remove the mountains that stood in the way of renegotiating a trade treaty. Nevertheless, when the Morrill tariff was defeated in the House of Representatives, he hoped that "the counsels of judicious men, who now understood the question [would] yet prevail"; so, on his return home, he would advise the government not to impose high retaliatory duties but instead to put provisions in their revenue acts allowing their duties to be varied by order in council, "should Congress, before the Session closes evince a more just and conciliatory spirit."[120]

As yet, he had made no decision as to his future. Still hoping for an imperial appointment, he had told Russell how useful he could be in giving the British government an overall view of the North American fisheries with suggestions for their improvement. But as time passed he became less hopeful of his prospects. The 12th of March found him "lonely, weary, vexed," and anxious for a week of personal freedom at home. Although half inclined to accept William Morrell's offer, he had got word from Halifax that steps were being taken behind the scenes to get the assembly to accept Confederation. "Poor old Nova Scotia, God help her, beset with marauders [i.e., Fenians] outside and enemies within, she has a hard time of it, and my mouth closed and my pen silent." Though moved to "fight the battle of my own country in [her] dark hours ... I, for the first time in my life, hesitate between duty and interests."[121] Personal interest seemed to prevail when, on March 20, his friend "Jerry" Northup received the telegram: "A free man. Have accepted M's offer."[122] Yet he came back to Halifax still not fully decided. All that was certain was that the fishery commissionership had lapsed.

## CHAPTER NINE

# "This Crazy Confederacy"

Howe was back none too soon. True, two days after his return, he asked Cardwell to inquire of Lord Clarendon, whom he did not know at all well, if his services might be used in a remodelled Fishery Commission or in the fishery service, since "I cannot afford to be idle."[1] But as it turned out, he did not even wait for a reply. In his absence discussion about Confederation had been, like an iceberg, almost submerged. Twice, however, on November 15 and January 19, Annand had used the *Chronicle* to suggest holding a new conference to draw up revised terms of union. Was he hoping that he and his colleagues might use it to produce a stalemate and hence prevent any kind of union? Or did he sense that some kind of union was inevitable and that he had better participate or lose any chance of sharing in the allocation of the "loaves and fishes"? In mid-March 1866 he was still weighing the second consideration and the failure to mention Confederation in the Speech from the Throne did not deceive him. As Lieutenant-Governor Williams put it, "My total abandonment of Confederation is too much like Punch even for [my opponents'] sincere belief ... They know what I was sent here for."[2]

Because of the Fenian scare, the Canadian government called out the militia on March 7, an action carrying consequences in its wake which would provide the reason, or the excuse, to bring Nova Scotia into Confederation. Almost immediately Williams reported a great change in public sentiment to the Governor General, Lord Monck; the latter responded by urging Williams to act without waiting for his counterpart in New Brunswick to do so. So on March 13 Williams suggested to Annand that he propose to Tupper the calling of a new conference on union in London, where the British government might act as an arbiter. But Annand, who had "nibbled at union"[3] earlier, now backed away. Playing for time, he asked the anti-Unionist A.J. Smith of New Brunswick if he was thinking of suggesting another conference, since, in that case, he would take the initiative in Nova Scotia.[4] Convinced, however, that the anti-Confederate lines would hold in New Brunswick, he turned down Williams's proposal. That is how the situation stood when Howe returned to Halifax on March 27.

None was a closer observer than he of the drama which unfolded rapidly in the weeks that followed. On April 3 William Miller, an independent assemblyman from Richmond who had previously opposed Confederation, "made William Annand's motion"[5] and proposed another conference on union. Although Tupper denied any previous communication with him, the *Chronicle* denounced the "very pretty piece of acting" and the "corrupting influences ... at work in the House of Assembly."[6] It was referring especially to Miller and Samuel McDonnell, a second anti-Confederate who had also announced his conversion. Both now proclaimed it "the duty of every man who desires to uphold British connexion – who is opposed to annexation – who has no sympathy with the Fenians ... to promote ... a union of the provinces."[7] From this moment there was fear, indeed consternation, in the anti-Confederate ranks that much of the assembly might be swept into the Unionist camp. Halifax had become excited when Williams called out the militia on March 17 because of the Fenian scare; it became even more so as preparations were made for Admiral Hope to proceed to the Bay of Fundy by warship, loaded with troops under General Doyle, to protect New Brunswick against the Fenians gathering at Eastport, Maine, under Doran Killian.

This was the juncture at which Howe took over the anti-Confederate cause and put "an end to the intrigue and the editorials."[8] Reluctantly and almost heartsick, he reentered the provincial politics he had forsworn, but not before he had sought unsuccessfully to get Williams and Adams G. Archibald – a Confederate, but still leading the Liberals in the assembly – to accept the principle of popular consultation before proceeding with union.[9]

It was, wrote Chester Martin, Archibald's determination to "resort to the *brutum fulmen* of an imperial statute after the stark refusal to submit the issue to the electorate ... which brought [Howe] into the field, horse, foot and artillery."[10] Then, and then only, did he address an open letter to the people of Nova Scotia.[11] Not minimizing the danger of the Fenians, he even feared they would not come alone. For, at a time when both the Republicans and Democrats were bidding for the million votes which the Fenians were said to control, "no human being ... can tell what may or may not arise ... out of these complications." Although past the age for military service, if the admiral detailed a ship for instructional purposes, he would be honoured to "present [himself] with a blue jacket on"; he could at least help to work a gun and demonstrate to others there were "no labors or perils which they were asked to confront which I am not willing to share." But though recognizing the danger, he was equally certain that a time when Nova Scotians should be unified was not the time to engage in acrimonious debates about constitutional matters: "my proposition is very simple. It is to let well enough alone ... Let us ... not destroy our sound constitution by eccentric innovations."

Howe's letter notwithstanding, the next day – April 10 – Tupper moved a resolution embodying Miller's suggestion. Almost at once Howe was back with a second letter to the people of Nova Scotia in which he asked if Tupper's course was prudent, safe, or decent. For the "slavish sycophant" who said that its people should be quiet because the queen, her ministers, the governor, the general, and the admiral all wanted union he had nothing but scorn. "Every Nova Scotian has the right, nay it is his duty, to stand up and defend the institutions of his country against them all."[12] Writing to Cardwell at the same time, he withdrew his request for another imperial appointment. It had been furthest from his mind, he said, to intrude himself into provincial politics, but the decision to press union at a time when the frontiers were threatened by invasion and to allow Nova Scotians no voice in the matter left him no choice.[13] Donald Creighton, seldom friendly to Howe, said he did it "rather pompously,"[14] but others might regard it as a simple, straightforward explanation of his decision.

In those days Halifax was a small place and Howe's intelligence brought him news of the steady stream of assemblymen to Government House, where wining and dining became a key part of Williams's strategy. Who could wonder, asked the *Chronicle*, that men like Caleb Bill and Mathurin Robicheau, "dazzled with the sight of the fringe and fittings supplied by the tax payers, ... bewildered with a hero's condescension, plied with wine and false promises ... consented to commit the treason which has rendered them infamous"?[15] William Miller, for all his professed patriotism and statesmanship, told Samuel McDonnell that "we ... had better get into line or we should be left out in the cold and lose all chance of obtaining any of the good positions."[16] But, outwardly at least, the argument that in a time of emergency Nova Scotians ought to accept the British government's view of what was best for their own protection was dominant, even though the *Acadian Recorder* dismissed it contemptuously as "lick-spittleism," "superfine loyalty," and running "the 'royal' machine too much."[17] The time had come, said Tupper, "when we must decide whether we shall be annexed to the United States or remain connected with the Parent state," while Hiram Blanchard, one of four

Liberals supporting him, fervently hoped he would "never live to see the Stars and Stripes floating over Citadel Hill."[18]

For Tupper it was crucial to win over sufficient Conservative members previously opposed to union to tip the balance. On April 17 six of them joined with the independent Miller to carry Tupper's resolution by thirty-one to nineteen. Typical of them was C.J. Campbell of Victoria, who stated that his objections of twelve months ago had "vanished like smoke" because of the need to "save us from annexation or from invasion."[19] Naturally the anti-Confederate press condemned the Confederates' use of timely circumstances to effect their ends. "The Fenians made their appearance at Eastport, and forthwith the Confederation resolution was tabled in our House of Assembly. A few days after the resolution was carried, and presto! the Fenians had evaporated and gone."[20] The evidence seems conclusive that a resolution for union could not have been carried in 1867 but for the Fenians. The resolution of April 17 would become Howe's greatest impediment in the months to come.

The vote taken, Howe addressed a third letter to the people of Nova Scotia which condemned the "wretched intrigue" by which "31 gentlemen" had taken steps to "annex this Province to Canada, without your counsel or consent ... For my part I shall sleep all the sounder, that before this act was done my protest against it was on record."[21] By the end of the month he had also addressed a letter to the people of Canada defending himself against the charges of inconsistency in their newspapers. For thirty years, he pointed out, he had opposed the idea of either a federal or a legislative union unless it was preceded by the development of political and social intercourse, but in recent years his efforts to achieve that end through an intercolonial railroad had been blocked by political deadlock in Canada – he was diplomatic enough not to blame the frailties of Canadian politicians. Surely, he said, Canadians would not "agree to force, by an act of Parliament, upon an unwilling people, great changes matured without their revision and passed without their consent."[22] Meanwhile the Nova Scotian Confederates looked on anxiously as Howe masterminded steps to defeat them: the making of common cause with Thomas Killam and the Yarmouth School from which he had long been estranged; the drawing up of an address to the Crown signed by eighteen assemblymen and five legislative councillors; the establishment of the League of the Maritime Provinces (usually called the Anti-Confederation or Anti-Union League) with himself as president, William J. Stairs and Patrick Power as vice-presidents, and William Garvie as secretary; and the circulation of a monster petition to show the feelings of ordinary Nova Scotians towards union. The Confederate press countered by picturing him as doing Doran Killian's work unasked.

Then he was off on a five-week speaking tour of the eight western counties, perfecting the country organizations of the league and setting in motion the gathering of names for the petition. The trip – beginning at Windsor on May 8 and ending at Chester on June 15 – was more a coronation than an attempt to win minds. Speaking to the already converted, he boasted he "could not find five hundred Confederates on the whole tour."[23] His audiences were especially responsive to his vivid description of the "wretched transaction" by which "thirty-one gentlemen" were converted, not like St Paul, "by light from Heaven," but by offers of judgeships, senatorships, and legislative councillorships: "one gentleman was not bagged till two o'clock in the morning – only half an hour before the division took place." By such means, he said, the conspirators "rushed this measure through at black midnight, with indecent haste after a debate of five days. Five days! Why, I have seen the Attorney General take two to deliver himself of a speech about the road grant."[24] The tour was most significant, however, for making clear the basic reasons for Howe's opposition to Confederation. Latter-day critics who accept unquestioningly the accusations of his contemporaries that his egotism and jealousy of Tupper led him to adopt a course entirely inconsistent with his past position have really demonstrated that they do not understand Howe. George Johnson, who knew him well in these years, became convinced that, above all else, his opposition was due to "the belief that Union would draw away the minds of the people of the British Isles & of Br North America from what he deemed the most vital question of the times – the organization of the Empire," indeed would prevent it from ever being realized.[25] This feeling was so strong that he even questioned the motives which had led to D'Arcy McGee's "death-bed repentance" and support of Confederation. "He could not forget that gentleman's antecedents, nor satisfy himself that his present movements were not tending to detach these Provinces from the parent empire."[26]

Under the new dispensation, Howe said, Nova Scotia would get a new capital in the backwoods of Canada, "with an Indian name, and any quantity of wilderness and ice in the rear of it – with a great chest, and nothing in it but the records of annual deficits." Imagine the effect of such a capital on a Nova Scotian. "Take [him] to Ottawa, away above tidewater, freeze him up for five months, where he cannot view the Atlantic, smell salt water, or see the sail of a ship, and the man will pine and die."[27] Of what possible use could this capital be to the commercial classes of Halifax, familiar with the trade of the world?

Was the outlook for Nova Scotia orators so bleak that they would sigh for a turbid river full of slabs and sawdust?

To those who argued that Ottawa would be the centre of a great Confederacy, Howe replied that he already belonged to one. The apostle Paul had boasted of his Roman citizenship and its benefits, and similarly so could he. "I am a British subject, and for me that includes free trade and a common interest with fifty Provinces, and two hundred and fifty millions of people, forming an Empire too grand and too extensive for Paul's imagination to conceive." Canada, he had been told, had invented a new flag with a beaver gnawing himself off a maple tree. "Verily we should be inferior animals, and our fur not worth much, if we were to knaw ourselves off of the great tree whose tap roots are in British Islands – whose limbs stretch far and wide over the universe – beneath whose majestic shade there are at once dignity and repose." For him "London [was] large enough ... London, the financial centre of the world, the nursing mother of universal enterprise – the home of the arts – the seat of Empire – the fountainhead of civilization. London, where the Lady we honor sits enthroned in her people's affections ... where Legislative Chambers the most elevated in tone and intelligence control the national counsels and guard the interests of the Empire."[28] Could Nova Scotians be blamed, then, for preferring London under the dominion of John Bull to Ottawa under the dominion of Jack Frost?

Here was the son of old John Howe speaking in the same accents he had been using since he wrote for the *Acadian* in 1827; here was the loyal Briton and Nova Scotian patriot, who in both roles found the proposals for union altogether abhorrent. He, who had always been a prime mover in great causes, may be criticized for allowing his local patriotism to exaggerate the evils that might befall his native province under union; for failing to recognize the feasibility of a united British America in the 1860s; and for not recognizing the utter impracticability of his proposals for the organization of the empire. But little credence should be given to "the hoary mythology which has perpetuated the charges of inconsistency, precipitate intervention, and bad motives foisted upon him by the partisanship of the Confederation era."[29]

Home in Dartmouth for barely three weeks, Howe left for Britain on July 5, the first of the British Americans to go that summer. As was her wont, Susan Ann offered no objections to what he considered his duty. By instruction of the Anti-Confederation League he was to demand that no scheme of union be adopted until first accepted by the people whose future it would affect. On landing at Cork he discovered that Lord Russell's government had fallen and had been succeeded by a Tory administration under the earl of Derby with his son Lord Stanley as foreign secretary and the earl of Carnarvon as colonial secretary. To him the change seemed to bode nothing but good: it had brought to power two men whom he knew well, Derby and Sir John Pakington, the first lord of the admiralty; it gave him unpledged men to deal with and hence a greater chance of fair play; it also permitted him a breathing space, since the new ministry would want to finish the session quickly.[30] In his usual style, he spent a few feverish days seeing as much as he could of southern Ireland. Almost with horror he wrote of the lot of the Irish peasant. "God help us, how little our people [in Nova Scotia] know of real poverty." He did not miss the opportunity to kiss the Blarney Stone, "a work of some difficulty as you have to kneel and lean over the lower wall of the opening which is wide enough to drop through ... Gentlemen are held by the tails of their coats and ladies by the crinoline but if anything gave way the 'art of sinking' in poetry would be nothing to the downward flight of eloquence that would be borne to the depths below."[31]

By the third week in July Howe was established in London, to be joined shortly by his long-time political ally William Annand. Unknown to himself, the massive effort he was about to make was destined to defeat from the start. No less than the Liberals, the leading Conservatives had become convinced of the need for British American union and Carnarvon, in particular, thought that from the imperial point of view it would best be completed that summer if possible. Indeed, he even had plans to pass a skeleton bill effecting the union and permitting the details to be filled in by order in council, and he abandoned them only when it became clear that the Canadian delegates would not arrive before Parliament prorogued on August 10.[32] Actually Howe's only hope of success – and it was Tupper's fear – was that action by the British Parliament might be postponed beyond May 1867 when an election was due in Nova Scotia. Great was Tupper's indignation, therefore, when the governor general, Lord Monck, thinking that the new government – whatever its attitude towards union – would seek a quick prorogation, kept the Canadian delegates at home. The Maritime delegates sailed on July 19 and, like Howe, had to keep kicking their heels in London when a protracted session of the Canadian Parliament, John A. Macdonald's taking to the bottle, and the revival of the Fenian scare prevented the first of the Canadian delegates from leaving for Britain until November 7. As a result, Howe's expected stay of three or four months became one of almost ten. During all that period he never missed reporting, by the fortnightly packet, to Stairs, a vice-president of the league, and writing more intimately to Susan Ann.

For the moment he decided to keep a low public profile and simply make his presence known to those who might serve his needs later. Late in July he addressed two long letters to the prime minister, Lord Derby,[33] which reflected a change in stance for a new audience. Contrary to Cardwell's view, he said, colonial union would have an adverse effect on imperial interests. Four years' examination of the American military machine had convinced him that Canada west of Quebec City was indefensible, especially in the absence of an intercolonial railroad. In contrast, the Maritimes could be defended as long as Britain retained control of the sea; further, they could provide the seamen to man the 100 ironclads which could permit the mother country to defend its fifty provinces and dependencies around the world. Was Britain well advised, then, to trifle with the loyalty of Nova Scotians by destroying their institutions against their will? Somewhat presumptuously, the second letter advised Derby not to commit his government to union as Cardwell had done, but to insist that those who wanted to disturb the existing order of things present a measure perfect in all its parts; that other British Americans in London have a chance to be heard; that several months' discussion take place in the colonies; and that only then, if circumstances dictated, should a measure be submitted to Parliament.

When the foreign secretary, Lord Stanley, thanked him for his services as fishery commissioner, Howe seized the opportunity to offer him advice, too, although not on union.[34] First, he had a threefold prescription for improving British-United States relations: settle the *Alabama* claims whatever the cost; improve conditions in Ireland so that Irish emigrants to the United States would be without the grievances which were reflected in the Fenian movement; and employ as British emissaries in the United States only those who were competent to seize "the numerous festive or public occasions ... to rub out a prejudice, or to vindicate the policy of Great Britain." Venturing also into British domestic affairs, he warned Stanley against the liberalization of the franchise that was being contemplated. "In gentlemanly bearing, attention to business, patient deliberation and sensitiveness," he pointed out, the American House of Representatives, elected on the basis of universal suffrage, was far inferior to the British Commons. Thus Howe, never an out-and-out democrat, was once again expressing the belief that anyone worth his salt could easily acquire the limited amount of property needed to exercise the right to vote. Hidden from view are the inmost thoughts of the British ministers whom an upstart from the colonies, admittedly a senior one, presumed to instruct on both domestic and foreign policy.

For six weeks Howe maintained a low profile, so much so that Cardwell wrote to Governor Williams, "I never heard (except from yourself) that Mr. Howe had come here at all."[35] When, on August 6, Annand and he sent Carnarvon their instructions from the league and a petition to the House of Commons signed by 18,000 Nova Scotians, the colonial secretary told them he did not wish to "antici-pate [his] discussion" of Confederation with the official delegates and promised a full hearing in due course.[36] That being exactly what they wanted, Howe was elated. "So far we have made no mistakes, and ... [Tupper et al.] have made a great one, by bragging of what they had done, before they had done anything."[37] He and Annand were tempted to reply when the *Times* called them a remnant of the inhabitants of British America who ought not to complain to the British Parliament if their legislature voted them into union.[38] But instead of being drawn into small wars, they decided to reserve their fire until they could "deliver a broadside, of heavy metal."[39] At the end of August Howe was off to Gravesend, away from the bustle of London, to produce a paper that he hoped would startle the govern-ment. Annand helped him to polish it and it was ready for circulation in pamphlet form just before mid-September. "This operation will cost our friends some money," he told Stairs, "but I know they will not grudge the expense," especially as it was "in many respects original and entirely overwhelming."[40]

The pamphlet, *Confederation Considered in Relation to the Interests of the Empire*,[41] expanded upon the first of his earlier letters to Derby. "The wisdom of Solomon and the energy and strategy of Frederick the Great," he said, would be needed to preserve the province of Canada even as it was. Yet Canada, with incomprehensible brashness, proposed to take over the four eastern provinces, the Hudson's Bay Company's territories, British Oregon and Vancouver Island. "The builders of Babel were only a little more ambitious than these Canadian politicians," and Bismarck and Louis Napoleon were "pigmies" compared to them. Such aspirations could only provide an excuse for American intervention, and he who had seen 250,000 troops march past the reviewing stand at the close of the Civil War had no doubt about the result. For Canada, then, the best course was to be "quiet, unobtrusive, ... [not] increasing the hazards which her defence involves, by any premature aspirations to become a nation, for which status at present she is totally unprepared." As for his own province, a forced marriage with Canada would result in thousands of Nova Scotians being reluctant to "fight for a domination which they repudiate and for a nationality they despise." Who could say that the republicans to the south would not take advantage of such a stupid error in policy? Would not time spent on schemes to break up the empire be better used in devising plans to "organize its vast intellectual and physical resources, and lift us above the atmosphere of doubt and apprehension?" In the months that followed Howe would continue to argue that British American union, under existing circumstances, was fraught with danger to the very existence of the empire, but he won few, if any, converts to that view in Britain.

The pamphlet in his hands, he worked feverishly to distribute it. First it went to cabinet ministers, influential members of Parliament, and leading colonials. "We shall let it do its work behind the scenes for a few days," he told Susan Ann, "and then launch it upon the broad waves of public discussion."[42] The second round went to the remaining members of Parliament, the leading newspapers, and, indeed, to anyone who might conceivably be of use to the Nova Scotian cause. To the Scottish editors he wrote that "old Scotland should stand by her namesake and see that she got fair play."[43] Because the *Times* was "so influential, that it is a natural misfortune to have it go wrong," he pleaded with its editor to say, at the very least, that "the Union should be voluntary if formed at all."[44] The first 500 copies being quickly exhausted, Howe ordered a second batch. "We shall ruin you all I fear with printing, and postage," he told Stairs, "but there was no other way to reach the governing classes here and to change the stream of public opinion."[45]

Then, late in September, he awaited the reaction. The London *Morning Star*, generally regarded as the organ of the radical MP, John Bright, insisted that the Nova Scotians' case was such that they ought not to be pushed into "an uncongenial union." When, in his reply, Tupper brashly signed himself "Prime Minister of Nova Scotia," he took a ribbing for it in Annand's rejoinder.[46] The London *Daily News*, also radical in sympathy, took much the same line as the *Star* and when another of Nova Scotia's official delegates, Jonathan McCully, chose to reply, he got a dressing down for leaving many questions unanswered.[47] *Lloyd's Weekly* asserted that Howe had easily put "the quarrelsome politicians of the Canadas" in their place; the London *Patriot*, organ of the Independents, called Confederation a "magnificent" but "premature" notion, and told the Canadians they were mistaken if they thought that Britain would pay for their defence and expansionary proposals; the *Evening Express* held that a province which could not defend itself against marauding bands was not in a position to "claim authority and power" over others.[48] In another way Howe and Annand sought to cast the Canadians in a bad light. To their friend Thornton Hunt of the London *Daily Telegraph* they sent a batch of editorials from Canadian newspapers arraigning the ministers of that province for intemperance, including one suggesting that during the last Fenian scare John A. Macdonald, the minister of militia, was "lying drunk – yes drunk – so drunk as to be incapable of performing any official act." They then forwarded the *Telegraph*'s stinging denunciation along with the Canadian editorials to Carnarvon, pointing out the impropriety of committing the government and defence of the Maritime Provinces to men "incapable of restraining tendencies utterly irreconcilable with ... vigilance, secrecy and prompt action."[49] Clearly it was to be a war in which no quarter was to be given.

Howe expected and received criticism from that part of the press that normally supported the Derby government, especially from the *Canadian News*, edited by the secretary of the Grand Trunk. Without even mentioning the pamphlet, the *Standard* argued that "the integrity of the British dominion in North America" was dependent on colonial union; the *Spectator* found the pamphlet activated by provincial jealousy and covering only a small portion of the case; the *London Review* suspected "party motives and jealousy below the surface," and could see nothing in union which would inflict "an appreciable injury on Mr. Howe or his constituents."[50] Yet, generally, Howe was satisfied with the results of his propagandist activity. "We have now got the rascals fairly before the people," he wrote Susan Ann,[51] and certainly he was more successful in having his position discussed in the British press than any Nova Scotian before him or since his time. Again, Annand and he thought it unwise to reply to their critics – to entangle themselves in "small wars with particular Newspapers"; better by far to "take high ground and enlarge rather than narrow the boundaries of discussion."[52] As usual with Howe on such occasions, he became too optimistic, too ebullient. "The Deacon [i.e., Annand] and I are confident in our ability to thrash the whole crew ... We have got the tide turning."[53] But though he had won considerable sympathy for himself in the British press, he should have realized it was not the crusading type of support that would have caused any government to have second thoughts about proceeding with union.

As the weeks passed by and the Canadians did not come, Howe fretted to Susan Ann that the official delegates had brought "over their wives at the public expense while you are left to look out of the verandah windows, and count the days till I come."[54] Although Sydenham Howe had decided upon a career in banking, he was worried about two of his three other sons, Fred and Joe, Jr; he hoped they would "turn up all right yet" and vowed to do what he could for them on his return. Denied a share in the entertainment of the official delegates, he had more than enough "private entertainment": an evening with Carlyle; dinner with the Fishmongers; and a delightful breakfast with an old friend, Edward Twistleton, and some chance acquaintances: Under-secretary Adderley; the celebrated geologist Charles Lyell; Dean Mitford, a son of the historian of Greece; and James Spedding, the editor of Bacon's works – together they made "a charming forenoon of it."[55]

In early October Howe decided to enlarge the boundaries of discussion by remodelling the paper he had prepared a year earlier for Lord Russell on the organization of the empire. By mid-month he was almost finished and expecting to "lose no credit by this second attempt to instruct the governing classes of this country." But if only he were rich enough to enter Parliament: "in five years we would have a scheme of Government sufficiently expansive to include the whole Empire."[56] Dominating the paper[57] was his attempt to spell out specifically how the colonies could impose both taxation and compulsory military service for the defence of the empire. Treat, he said, "the whole empire as the British Islands are treated, holding every man liable to serve the Queen in war, making every pound's worth of property responsible for the national defence." In colonies where direct taxes were unpopular, the tax for national defence might be imposed as an addition to their ad valorem duties. If some colonies wanted the privileges of British subjects without paying for them, it were better they were known "in a season of tranquillity ... rather than wait till war finds us unprepared and leaning upon presumptions in which there is no reality." Once the colonies had made contributions of this kind it would be difficult to deny them the participation in the councils of the empire he had long been demanding, perhaps through the sending of some members of their cabinets to the British Parliament. Would such proposals, he asked, not suit "the practical turn of thought ... of our people ... without disorganizing the political machinery already working so well." To Howe, devoted Briton and nonradical reformer, the organization of the empire appeared a much more natural alternative than "this Crazy Confederacy" that would lay rough hands on existing institutions.

Just as he was completing his second pamphlet, Tupper was answering his first in a 78-page letter to Carnarvon released on October 19. Becoming positively Burkian, he argued that if the Nova Scotian electorate were to be consulted on union and its General Assembly overruled, the province would be declared unfit to work its free institutions.[58] Following another of many councils of war,

Annand was deputed to answer Tupper and, to get out of his way, Howe went off on one of those fast-moving jaunts that, to him, went under the name of holidaying. In Portsmouth he chanced to see the *Tyrian* which had brought him on his first trip to England in 1838: "I could hardly believe that I had trusted my precious life in such a wretched Craft." He did not tarry long with Susan Ann's relatives, the Westphals on the Isle of Wight: she would "drive me over Ryde Pier in a month ... it is painful to see how much she exacts and how much he gives without a murmur."[59] At Southampton he got a copy of Annand's pamphlet, and although his first reaction was to describe it lukewarmly as "all right," he later said that Tupper's pamphlet would "not do much harm when Annand's gets into the right hands."[60]

As November progressed, Howe was elated at the reaction to his pamphlet on the organization of the empire. After the *Standard, Pall Mall Gazette*, two Hampshire papers, and even the *Canadian News* generally endorsed his views, he became hopeful they would finally prevail. "It may not be done in my mode or in my time, but when once the public mind of this country begins to move in the right direction, it keeps on moving."[61] Perhaps, too, the pamphlet would "create a diversion ... that may be fatal to Confederation" by delaying a decision on union until an election in Nova Scotia set matters right.[62] As another instrument of delay, he pressed a full investigation of union. "You appoint a Committee of Enquiry before a Railway or a Turnpike is sanctioned," he told Stanley; surely nothing less would be done in a matter involving the future of five provinces.[63] November brought its annoyances and setbacks as well. Previously favourable to Howe on Confederation, the *Star* – a strong advocate of an extended franchise in Britain – gave him a sharp rap over the knuckles after it had discovered, or been informed, that he had recently voted to restrict the Nova Scotia electorate. Philosophically he told Stairs that he had sustained "so many [blows] that another thump or two makes but little odds." He also became a little impatient with his friends in Nova Scotia. When they talked of the 40,000 signatures they had collected for the monster petition, he reminded them that the actual number was substantially less. He even read a lecture to the loyal, unobtrusive Stairs for letting his fortnightly letter out of his possession. "You have no idea of the delicacy and secrecy required in conducting such operations as we are engaged in, and how mischief may be done by the slightest imprudence."[64]

At long last, by the end of November, the Canadian delegates had established themselves at the Westminster Palace Hotel, near the Parliament Buildings, some distance from the Alexandria Hotel, overlooking Hyde Park, where the Maritime delegates were staying.

In less ostentatious quarters at 23 Savile Row, the Nova Scotia anti-Confederates had received reinforcements in the person of Hugh McDonald, MPP, "a raw green politician from Antigonish,"[65] whom Howe found congenial and competent, and William Garvie, the articulate, sharp-tongued, brilliant secretary of the Anti-Confederation League and ardent admirer of Howe, who had come to read law in Lincoln's Inn. Even after the London Conference got down to formal work on December 4, Howe could find out little of its proceedings. He told Stairs that "until they have agreed upon something we have nothing to attack, but we keep, through every channel we can occupy, operating in the meantime on public opinion."[66]

With the delegates in session, Howe and his colleagues thought it high time to present their case to Carnarvon in person. So, on the 18th, they "strode into his rooms with a consciousness that we had vindicated, before the Empire our right to be there, and that no Minister could venture to snub or bluff us off."[67] Howe noted with satisfaction their success in condensing their main points "vividly" into an hour and a half; he was equally pleased that Carnarvon had promised to read two long private letters he had written "from the heart" a few weeks earlier.[68] The first, to Sir John Hay,[69] had emphasized that the Nova Scotian movement against Confederation had been a spontaneous one in which he had played little part. Along Halifax's two miles of waterfront, scarcely seven merchants favoured it, and Enos Collins, aged ninety-two and the richest man in the province, had asserted that, if he were twenty years younger, he would take up his rifle and resist it. Yet Howe made it clear once again that his primary motivation was not mercantile considerations but his desire to remain within the empire. "I am a dear lover of old England and to save her would blow Nova Scotia into the air or scuttle her like an old ship." But if Britain would run no risk to maintain the old relations, would Nova Scotia choose Ottawa when she had lost London and could have New York? "We go in for the Empire one and indivisible but when the old ship is broken up we are not such fools as to trust our lives in a crazy craft in which we are certain to be drowned." Clearly Howe was saying he might prefer annexation to "a catamaran of a Confederacy."

In the more remarkable second letter to Lord Normanby, who, as Lord Mulgrave, had recently served as governor of Nova Scotia, Howe argued that his plans for the empire were "visionary" only because no one would grapple with them.[70] "But I can afford to wait. All I hope now is to set people thinking in the right direction." He had sought to educate them on many things: from responsible government to the systematic settlement of the poor in the colonies so as to reduce the hosts of Irishmen emigrating to the United States and thereby remove the possibility of Fenianism; in each case, he thought, time had proved him right. Disclaiming all thoughts of himself – "There is no position in this Confederacy, if it is formed, that I cannot win" – Howe said he was worried only about the dismemberment of the empire. When the colonies were formed into new nations, their old respect for mixed classes and orders would disappear; having neither kings nor peers, they would develop the contempt for them that prevailed in the United States and would become republics in short order. "How will it stand with England when all the English Speaking people, outside these two Small Islands, are Republicans, in close Sympathy with the millions of Democrats who are rising pretty near the Surface [in England] just now?" Concluding with a prophecy that Chester Martin thinks may have been "the worst and the most reckless of his career,"[71] he asserted he had bet four baskets of champagne, "one that Confederation will not be carried – another that, if it should be carried, in a Year after we shall elect our own President and send our Minister to Washington – and two that, in less than five years after the new Nationality is set up ... British America will be incorporated with the Republic. I hope sincerely that I may win the first but, if not, I am sure to win the other two."

Had Howe, once the advocate of popular causes, become highly conservative in later life? In fact, he had expressed much the same viewpoint in the *Acadian* of 1827 and it had remained largely submerged since that time because only seldom had something arisen to evoke it. He had never been much of a democrat and for him a choice between a thoroughly democratic system and a monarchical system which rested on a balanced distribution of powers among mixed classes and orders, and had stood the test of time was, to put it baldly, one between evil and good. But in making the likely dismemberment of the empire his chief reason for opposing Confederation, he actually played into the hands of the British authorities, who found that argument easy to answer.

In his meeting with Carnarvon Howe had laboured under severe physical disabilities. A wet, dark autumn, combined with the fatigue resulting from his compulsive urge to be doing things, had led to bronchial colds which he could not throw off. A great deal of reading and writing, much of it by candle-light or gaslight, caused first his right and then his left eye to become seriously inflamed. To a degree that was unusual for him, he began to feel sorry for himself. On his sixty-second birthday, the 13th of December, he treated Annand and McDonald to wine, but it was not a happy affair, indeed "the saddest day I have passed in England ... [and I] do not want to see any

more Birth Days without Home, Plumb Pudding and the children."
Especially perturbing was the news that Susan Ann had dispensed
with her domestic. Insisting that she ought to have one during the
winter months, he told her to want for nothing: "till I get back Jerry
[Northup] will cheerfully hand you any funds that you or Syd may
need."[72] It was another penalty he had to pay for opposing Confederation.

During the Christmas season, which he spent with Lord Overstone,
his "bronchital tubes were stuffed with cold and [his] eyes completely
gone," but he returned to London under adverse weather conditions
– temperatures of 10° below zero followed by eight inches of snow –
with his eyes "all right – [his] cough gone and [his] voice ... as clear as
a trumpet."[73] January saw the battle between the British Americans
renewed in the British press. "So the war rages," Howe wrote, and
although "[we have] only four Needle guns on our side to eighteen on
the other, we contrive to return their fire pretty well."[74] But for him
the only acts that now mattered were those of Carnarvon. The
colonial secretary had told him, over the holidays, that he would try to
do full justice to the arguments contained in his letters to Hay and
Normanby. A litte presumptuously, Howe then outlined the courses
he thought Carnarvon might pursue and was told that, whatever the
outcome of the Confederation debate, Carnarvon appreciated getting to know "one who has played so continuous & leading a part in
B. North America as yourself." Although Howe called it "a great
personal triumph,"[75] he might better have wondered if he was being
prepared in a nice way for an adverse decision already made.

Clearly he had expected to have an opportunity to comment upon
the official delegates' final proposals, but Carnarvon told him on
January 4, 1867, that they were in no shape to be made public. Could
Howe not "assume the Quebec Resolutions" and act accordingly?
Although Howe might have reminded him that the Nova Scotia
legislature had not accepted the Quebec Resolutions, he agreed to the
colonial secretary's suggestion in order to avoid "the delay and
annoyance of a cross fire of replies and rejoinders of which there
would be no end."[76] After another council of war the four Nova
Scotians decided on an elaborate paper that would "stagger and
convince the Ministry or ... instruct Parliament."[77] Then Howe was
off to Gravesend for ten days of writing with scarcely an hour of
relaxation. Each day he forwarded about fifteen foolscap pages for
correction by his colleagues; on his return he was surrounded by
scriveners who worked against time to get the paper into Carnarvon's
hands. The latter told him that the cabinet had not yet made up its
mind, but "the sooner that all objections and counter proposals are

before me the better." On the 21st "The Case of the Maritime Provinces" was completed. Although Howe had found it difficult to provide all the arguments for persons considering the subject for the first time and still write something new, he hoped it would be "an awkward document for the Ministry to take down to Parliament should they decide against us."[78]

How different it would be, he argued, when Maritimers who now were treading their quarterdecks with security became citizens of a "wretched confederacy whose 'drum beat' nobody ever heard, and which has not a war ship upon the ocean, or a minister or a consul with the slightest influence abroad"? Although the consolidation of people was supposedly a basic tendency of modern life, any of its good effects could be secured if the governor general summoned annually some ministers from each colonial cabinet to draft bills on matters requiring common action such as railroads and tariffs, and to determine each province's contribution to defence in men and money. In an accompanying letter to Carnarvon Howe suggested that no British politicians ought to object to Parliament delaying a union bill until the provinces approved the proposals: not the Whigs unless they unwigged themselves; not the Radicals, who wanted everyone to exercise the franchise meaningfully; and certainly not the Conservatives, who should resist the destruction of existing institutions without great deliberation.[79]

It took only a week for Carnarvon to make known his decision: despite Howe's "very able paper," he still believed strongly in the efficacy of British American union.[80] So on January 29 the crunch had come and Howe realized that he had few cards left to play. Even he doubted that he had managed to dramatize his case sufficiently to have much influence in Parliament. An old friend, worried by his defeatist attitude, told him that, despite his reverses, he could – before he reached the age at which Palmerston became prime minister – see his "power extended from the Atlantic to the Pacific." Almost despairingly, he turned to Lord Russell and begged him to help delay the bill until after the spring elections in Nova Scotia, instead of following a course totally at variance with the tenets of his past life.[81] For want of an alternative he also grasped at other straws. Perhaps the Derby government, tottering from its inception, might collapse; perhaps, since it was simply following its predecessor's policy, it might not be "very hearty in the cause" and its "followers might be left on the loose."[82] But he reckoned without Carnarvon and the government. Shaky on the key issue of the day, the extension of the franchise, they got it out of the way by repeated postponements, and "having nothing else ready" rushed the Confederation bill

through Parliament, allegedly with "unusual if not indecent haste."
As Howe saw it, the Little Englanders were having their way; British
politicians of all colours had become convinced that the Canadian
frontier was indefensible and that Britain would be powerless to keep
in check the massive American forces that might be launched against
it. "This conviction, not openly avowed in all cases," Howe concluded,
"underlay the action of all parties in both Houses" on the Confederation bill.[83]

Yet he was hardly prepared for the apathy and indifference of
both Houses. Told that the bill would be introduced in the Commons,
he was taken a little off guard when Carnarvon started it in the Lords,
allegedly to have the government's views presented more precisely
than if Under-secretary Adderley had done it in the Commons. In
accordance with normal procedure, Howe did not see the bill until
February 12, the day of its first reading in the Lords. But it made no
difference, for by this time he was confining himself to a single point:
"*let the Bill lie on the table till after the May elections in Nova Scotia. There
will then be two months to pass it if they are favorable, and it ought not to pass if
they are not.*"[84] Courteous to the end, Carnarvon sent personal
invitations to "see the show" in the Lords, and Howe and McDonald
were present at all the stages. For them second reading on the night of
the 19th was a distressing experience. At the outset about fifty of the
450 members were present as a compliment to Carnarvon; at the end
barely twenty were left to approve a bill which the colonial secretary
described as "one of the largest and most important measures which
for many years it has been the duty of any Colonial Minister ... to
submit to Parliament."[85] Playing down the significance of the Nova
Scotia petitions, Carnarvon asked what better evidence there could be
of the true feelings of Nova Scotians towards union than a vote of
their legislature. Calling the request for delay "a plan for indefinite
postponment" of union, he pointed out that the present stage had
been reached only after great difficulty, "and we may be sure that
many years will pass before any such proposal for Confederation
[would again be] submitted to Parliament."[86]

For the other speeches, mercifully short, Howe had nothing but
contempt.[87] Normanby asserted that the Nova Scotia petitions "represented the opinion of the agitators" and that the colonies, if they
wished, might become independent or seek annexation to the United
States since Britain derived no pecuniary benefit from them. The
aging Lord Russell laid stress on a pointless remark of Sir James
Kempt, governor of Nova Scotia some forty years earlier, while Lord
Monck relied on a quotation of William Pitt about parliamentary

supremacy which he took from one of Tupper's letters and, according to Howe, "talked nonsense with some fluency."[88]

The other stages in the Lords were no more edifying. On third reading Lord Campbell argued that Parliament was in justice bound to permit an appeal to the Nova Scotia electorate unless some great imperial necessity dictated otherwise, but receiving no support he did not press his amendment. In the end the bill received third reading on the 26th with "but 10 lords in their places" and after a debate that Howe thought "would not have done credit to a college union or a common debating society." How different from the debate on Irish tenures, where the lords "talked and listened eagerly."[89]

Howe's fortnightly letters to Stairs and Susan Ann had foretold certain defeat in the Lords but hoped for better things in the Commons where a few of its ablest members had promised "some powerful aid." But preparing Susan Ann for the worst, he told her he would fire his last shot in his country's defence and then, "with a clear conscience and a cheerful spirit ... commence the World again, and a Kind Providence will take care of us as it has hitherto always done."[90] The very day that the Confederation bill passed in the Lords it was introduced in the Commons and second reading set for two days later on February 28. To defend what Howe called "the same game of rapid manipulation,"[91] Adderley made the patently absurd defence that he wanted the bill to be placed quickly before the country and, as a concession, promised to let the debate continue for a second day, if necessary. One day was more than enough.

The debate in the Lords had been largely irrelevant and unmeaningful; that in the Commons was often a travesty. Of the bill's proponents, Howe spoke well only of Cardwell, on the opposition side of the House. Not a little outrageously, Adderley credited Howe with helping J.W. Johnston to get the first resolution on union through the assembly in 1854, a statement that was wrong on every count. No such resolution was passed at that time and Howe spoke, not on union, but on organization of the empire. Relying on equally false information from Tupper, Sir John Pakington baldly asserted that "no man in Nova Scotia was a more prominent advocate of the union than Mr. Howe." Edward Watkin of the Grand Trunk outdid them both by stating that Tupper had preached Confederation throughout Nova Scotia in the election of 1863: actually it was not before the voters in any way. Finally, exceeding all the others in fantasy, Baillie Cochrane declared that the province had been converted to Confederation after the governor of Maine opposed it.[92]

Howe placed his main reliance upon the advanced Liberal, John

Bright, with whom he had developed a genuine rapport. What bill affecting so large a portion of the empire, Bright asked, had been hurried through Parliament in the manner of this one? Had Nova Scotia been treated with the tenderness, the generosity, and the consideration it deserved at a time when its future was at stake? Although he conceded the constitutional right of the existing Nova Scotia legislature to initiate the change, was it of no little moment that it had not been elected on union and was it not hazardous to bind the province before its electors had pronounced on the subject?[93] Bright stood almost alone, however, and second reading passed without division. Garvie, who had been drumming up support among the MPs, was even more appalled than Howe that they did "not know the first thing about us and did not care to know." Especially annoying to him was John Stuart Mill, who was so bound up with female suffrage and "the Orange women in Westminster" that he had no time for Nova Scotia. Bitterly he noted that "the House got livelier and better filled when a dog tax bill came up [next] ... country gentlemen who could not maybe point out Nova Scotia on the map kept fox hounds subject to a tax [and that] interests them more keenly than a Canadian tariff."[94]

For the moment Howe was more restrained. He told Susan Ann on March 2 that he could at least lie down beside his father in the churchyard without losing his respect. He informed Stairs that he had a few more shots to fire in the closing stages of the bill, but obviously he put greater hope in the fall of the government. "At present the Ministry appears very shaky, and I should not be surprised if they were out within the next few days."[95] As it turned out, it was Howe's last-ditch plans, not the government, which collapsed. Hesitant about supporting a cause that was doomed to failure because most backbenchers would not desert their leaders, Robert Lowe backed out of speaking for Howe's position in committee. After deliberating two days, Edward Horsman refused to present the petition of 30,000 Nova Scotians because he did "not concur in their prayer." George Hadfield succumbed to pressure from Cardwell and Adderley, and withdrew his promise to move Howe's amendment that the Act of Union not be proclaimed until the legislatures of Nova Scotia and New Brunswick gave their consent following the next election. Sorrowfully Howe told Bright he was beginning to have "nearly as bad an opinion of the two Houses of Parliament as you have ... It does seem hard that 30,000 Englishmen, merely because they live outside of these Islands and have no representation cannot get the prayer of a Petition presented to the House of Commons by one independent member. There is, I suppose, nothing for it but to submit."

Accordingly, he told Bright to bother no further about protecting Nova Scotia's interests.[96]

The proceedings in committee angered Howe and Garvie in other ways. To rush through "a disagreeably dull measure which did not affect anybodys seat," the clerk read a whole batch of clauses at once, indeed only the numbers of the clauses, and "they passed, sure enough, without anybody worrying himself about their contents."[97] For the moment Howe contented himself with telling Susan Ann that "'we are routed, horse, foot and artillery,' this time," and with again expressing satisfaction to Stairs that he could lay his bones beside those of his kindred with the consciousness that he had been "true to the living and the dead."[98] But two weeks later, when the significance of the defeat had fully sunk in, the effect was nothing short of traumatic, which was certainly not surprising in the case of one who had always had an abiding faith in Parliament. To Susan Ann he confided that he had simply not been "prepared for the utter indifference, and manifest disposition to get rid of us, evinced by both Houses." British public men, he told Stairs, thought only of themselves, and "having made up their minds that the Provinces are a source of peril and expense to them – the prevailing idea is to set them adrift, to gradually withdraw British troops from them ... to leave them ... pass into the [American] Union if they prefer that solution of their difficulties."[99]

Idolizing Howe as he did, Garvie worried about him: "Poor Howe! the disaster tried his spirit very hard – very, very hard."[100] But, while still in England, Howe could at least gloat a little over the perturbation caused by the news of the Russian sale of Alaska to the United States. When British newspapers pondered if it meant a firm alliance between the two countries and if Russia would "sympathize whenever Jonathan is ready to absorb the 'new dominion'," Howe thought about republishing his prophecies that any attempt to build up a new nation beside the United States would lead to retaliatory measures. He concluded, however, that it would do no good since Britons were more excited about the Oxford-Cambridge boat race than "if British America were sunk in the sea."[101] Earlier he had even thought of asking to be heard at the bar of the Commons and had dismissed the idea for the same reason. Clearly he was being more than a little unfair to the British politicians. Although he could rightly blame them for both ignorance and apathy in colonial matters, most of them were not Little Englanders and did not want to abandon the empire connection. But they did expect a greater commitment by colonials to their own defence and they simply could not understand Howe's argument that in union there would not be strength. Obviously his predominant concern with the organization of the empire had made him discover pitfalls in union that were more illusory than real. In concentrating the Nova Scotian case on a concern that was uniquely his he may have committed a serious tactical error; certainly he could have made the British parliamentarians much more uncomfortable by a single-minded emphasis upon the injustice of forcing Nova Scotia into union against its will.

More than at any time since 1826 Howe faced an uncertain future. His personal finances, in reasonably good shape when he left the Fishery Commission, were again in a state of chaos. From Halifax his friends counselled him to "cease from any course of Public action ... which may be at a Sacrifice of your personal feelings and interests."[102] Pondering his next move, he lingered in England longer than he needed. But actually it was not much of a choice: "defenceless as our people must be for some time I am hardly at liberty to desert them now." So, if they still expected his aid and wanted him to go to Ottawa, he would not be found wanting; otherwise he would be freed from all obligations and in a position to "dispose of what remains of life to the best advantage." To Stairs, as earlier to Susan Ann, he emphasized that he had not sought or been offered preferment while in England, nor could he until relieved of "responsibilities which my countrymen may yet wish me to assume."[103] Late in April, as he left for home, he could not resist a Parthian shot at Stanley. Though "cured of a great deal of loyal enthusiasm," he would, nevertheless, retain his kindly feelings for the mother country, "even when separated, as I fear it is about to be from my own."[104]

## CHAPTER TEN

# Accepting the Situation

Thousands awaited Howe when RMS *China* berthed late at night on May 6 at Cunard's wharf in Halifax. At his request the reception was subdued out of respect to James Cogswell, president of the Halifax Banking Company, whom an errant wave had killed a day earlier. It did not take him long to find out what had been happening in his absence. He noted that the *Acadian Recorder* had been telling Sir William Frederick Williams to communicate the true state of public opinion to the Colonial Office: "If he refuses, the day will come, if he lives much longer, when he will wish he had."[1] After reflection Howe had decided that the next step must be to punish the Nova Scotians who had voted the province into union. That was the brunt of his message in Mason's Hall on May 9, supposedly to a committee of the anti-Confederate League, but actually to a crowded public meeting. Although made Canadians by an act of Parliament, he said, Nova Scotians should free themselves from the control of men no better than Cataline's Confederates or Benedict Arnold. "Why, Judas Iscariot did not ask to be folded to his Master's bosom, after he had betrayed him."[2]

At this juncture Howe accepted the fact of union and proposed that anti-Confederate MPs should go to Ottawa and "aid [the Canadians] to work the new system fairly," if the latter were so disposed. "For a time," he said, "we must follow their fortunes."[3] But he was outraged when John Young, the Montreal Reformer and publicist, told him it was everyone's duty to "accept the situation" and if all the Liberals stuck together, "the majority in the coming House of Commons will be theirs." Both parties in Canada, Howe replied, had exhibited "equal barbarity" towards Nova Scotia: "that Liberals and Reformers would so act never entered our heads to conceive." Hence

Nova Scotians would go to Ottawa "unpledged and be governed by circumstances after they get there."[4]

In three major public addresses during these weeks – in Dartmouth on May 22, in Temperance Hall, Halifax, on May 24, and at Truro on June 4 – Howe handled the Unionists without gloves.[5] The thirty-two traitorous assemblymen, he told Dartmouthians, had earned the halter or axe. "We may not even elevate them to the dignity of tar and feathers, but we can at least leave them on the stools of repentance to become wiser and better men." In Temperance Hall he allegedly "spouted treason" in a sentence which, with variations, he repeated elsewhere. "If the British forces were withdrawn ... and this issue were left to be tried out between the Canadians and ourselves, I would take every son I have and die on the frontier, before I would submit to this outrage." In Truro he humbled Adams Archibald in his own bailiwick by questioning his relations with Tupper. "Is there an honest woman in Colchester, if she had proclaimed another woman a strumpet, would breakfast with her, dine with her, sup with her, and sleep with her afterwards?"

Already an election campaign was under way, even though its exact date would not be known for several months. From the outset Howe feared that his vow to "punish the scamps" might fail if the Catholics, who had moved to the Conservatives in 1857, continued in that allegiance. Indignant that McCully and Archibald were placing the primary blame for the estrangement upon him, he sought to show that they were no less responsible than he. But the Antigonish *Casket* would not let him off the hook: "You are the only individual in Nova Scotia whose position, influence, and ability [could have given] the No-Popery cry a week's animation."[6] His chief concern, however, was with Archbishop Connolly of Halifax, with whom he had developed a friendly personal relationship despite a wide gulf on political and religious questions. Connolly, an out-and-out Confederate, told him to "punish the rascals," himself included, if he could, but begged him to do nothing to "excite our Catholic people ... already inflammable enough" or "Americanize" the province. "I will consent to anything but to become a Yankee." Howe replied that any rise of annexationist sympathy was due to those who had "unsettled established institutions & treated the population with contempt." But Connolly would not agree to remain "above the range of mere political controversy" and obviously he would intervene publicly in favour of Confederation.[7]

The Antis would have liked to pit Howe against Tupper in Cumberland, but fearing the possibility of defeat had him nominated in Hants instead. His success there was never in question, but there were serious doubts about the two Antis running for the provincial seats who, according to Howe, seemed to have been "selected for no other reason than because they lived at opposite ends of the county." To drag these men in, he said later, "I had to ride twice round the entire county, and address twenty meetings."[8] Tupper, perturbed by the publicity given Howe's speeches, challenged him to another meeting in Temperance Hall facing "the same men ... [before] whom you have ventured to traduce me in my absence." Although Howe, as the challenged party, claimed "the right to choose the ground," he forfeited any advantage by offering to debate with Tupper in Archibald's county of Colchester and in Cumberland itself.[9]

Accordingly the two men met head on in Truro on June 4 and on at least six other occasions between June 27 and July 13 while Howe was visiting every hamlet of any size in Cumberland. Asked to be a candidate for that county, he replied he would "like no better sport" than to "bowl the doctor out" if he were not committed elsewhere. But where could one find a better candidate than William Annand, his friend of thirty-five years? He had only to speak and Annand got the nomination.[10] Although Howe addressed few meetings outside of Hants and Cumberland, that was not surprising since the leader's speaking tour had not yet become institutionalized. Tupper, hard pressed by Annand, devoted all his energies to Cumberland, while Howe, who had often campaigned in other counties, saw no need to exert himself this time.

For good reasons Howe did not state exactly what he wanted, for at this stage he found it difficult to be explicit and, besides, he wished to keep his options open. It was likewise not surprising that other anti-Confederates spoke with differing voices. In Pictou Martin Wilkins wanted the legality of the British North America Act to be challenged; in Lunenburg the Antis were pledged first to repeal of the act and, that failing, to its amendment; in Yarmouth they did not want the union recognized even to the extent of sending MPs to Ottawa. These differences were, of course inevitable, since provincial party organizations did not exist and individual candidates were on their own. Howe's major difficulty was of another kind: a multiplicity of prospective candidates, including former Conservatives, eager to run on the anti-Confederate ticket. He had to be especially persuasive to induce the Pictou Liberals to accept his old enemy and unrecon-structed Tory, Martin Wilkins. He also had immense difficulties putting party affairs in order in Digby, but few in Queens, where he easily induced his old friend Lewis Smith to give way to a former Tory.[11]

Just before election day, September 18, Archbishop Connolly declared it was "a sacred day of conscience, to vote ... for THE WHOLE

UNION TICKET," and then asked "my whole Catholic people to follow my example."[12] Nevertheless, the results were almost all that Howe could have hoped. Although the Unionists carried Halifax City by 400 votes, they lost the whole county by over 200, thanks, wrote the archbishop, to "the one sided vote of a few bigoted Presbyterians" outside the city.[13] Tupper beat Annand by a mere 97 votes and managed to pull in one provincial running mate, H.G. Pineo, on his coattails; similarly the personal attractiveness of the Confederate Hiram Blanchard enabled him to win an assembly seat in Inverness. Otherwise the victors were all Antis, eighteen MPS and thirty-six MPPS.[14]

Returning to Halifax from Windsor, Howe was received much like "the old Roman Generals who had achieved a victory for the benefit of the Republic."[15] Almost beside itself, the *Colonist* declared the cavalcade to include "some of the most notoriously bad characters in the city, on a lot of broken-kneed animals which the knacker's yard should have claimed months ago."[16] Over the next few months the Unionist press tried all sorts of tacks to explain away their defeat. One was to suggest that anti-Confederation became "a sort of cave of Adullam. Into it flocked all who were discontented or in distress, or sore on account of fancied wrongs."[17] But although Tupper's act for the compulsory support of education had caused widespread discontent, the election of 1867, more than any other, was a referendum on one question – Confederation. The Unionists' second tack was to minimize the extent of their defeat. Of 52,000 voters, they said, only 20,000 had voted for the Antis, while 32,000 had either supported union or stayed home. "Is it right, then, to say that Nova Scotia has actually declared against union?"[18] But, as Howe indicated, his party had carried four counties by acclamation and ten others by extraordinary majorities, while in three of the four remaining counties no Confederate candidate had run.[19] Finally the Unionists argued that, although reason and fact favoured them, "dispassionate listeners were difficult to get at" because of Howe; they then told him to "do his damndest. THANK GOD, the Union is safe beyond the reach of [him] and all his treasonable pack." To secure repeal, let him "disport his graceful figure in the purlieus of Westminster ... for the rest of his life": it would achieve nothing.[20]

Until now the Antis had been agreed on only one thing, to punish the Unionists. But once they came to appreciate the magnitude of their victory, their newspapers spoke out spontaneously for repeal. On September 25 the *Eastern Chronicle* declared that the people had "practically instructed" their representatives to demand it. A day later the *Morning Chronicle* opened itself to the charge of treason by suggesting that, if the imperial authorities were just, "we should be freed from the connection forced upon us. If we be not, and that speedily we fear strange consequences." In May, at Temperance Hall, Howe had said that Nova Scotia might still "get clear of this scrape" if it had the right hand of fulcrum.[21] Having got it, he now warned Stanley that, unlesss redress was granted, "we shall cease to regard England as the fountain head of justice and begin to study foreign affairs on our own account." To Sir Frederic Rogers he intimated that "if the Queen's Government ... denies us justice ... there will be feelings engendered and scenes enacted here which both you and I would regret."[22] He did not mention repeal explicitly, but when the federal and provincial members caucused in Halifax on October 5 they decided not only to authorize the Anti MPs to go to Ottawa but to pursue repeal as well. "An infamous piece of deception," charged the *Colonist*; already Howe had deserted his election platform and adopted an entirely new one. "Is Nova Scotia prepared to enter on a suit for the repeal of the Union before it has had three months' trial?"[23] Howe took the position that Governor Williams, having badly misrepresented the feelings of Nova Scotians, should leave office at once. That suited Williams who, mission accomplished, wanted only to depart without incident; it had been understood in any case that he would soon be succeeded by Sir Hastings Doyle, commander of the troops in Halifax and a personal friend of Howe. Shortly after the election Doyle hoped that Howe, having given the Unionists "the most infernal licking a party ever got," would "not kick them when they are down." He also requested Howe, who "will no doubt pull the strings more or less," to recommend the men best suited for the Executive Council, including the leader of the government. Howe replied that "while guarding my own consistency and honor," he would do his best to "smooth your path" and "help you to do any good you can."[24]

In Ottawa John A. Macdonald was also sizing up the situation, inaccurately, as it turned out, because of faulty intelligence about Howe. After the election Archbishop Connolly told him not to be alarmed, since Howe could easily be "tickled by something worth acceptance under the Dominion." Jonathan McCully having said much the same thing, Macdonald became convinced that Howe could be quickly won over if he were handled suitably.[25] K.G. Pryke suggests that what he meant was "a firm handshake, a friendly smile and perhaps a bit of patronage."[26] Accordingly, Macdonald sought to persuade P.C. Hill, co-leader with Hiram Blanchard of the provincial government, not to let the ministry resign until actually voted out. Since a public reaction would take place as soon as Nova Scotians perceived the advantages of union, it would be well to have the votes of those who condemned it recorded on the *Journals*. "As Howe had had his revenge upon you, you should, like good Christians, try to take yours on him."[27]

To the Hill-Blanchard government Macdonald's advice was not only impracticable but even dangerous. For a ministry with only one executive councillor and one backbencher in the assembly to cling to office was clearly to invite disorder. Accordingly its first act, after Doyle assumed the governorship on October 28, was to offer its resignation. Following Howe's advice Doyle requested R.A. McHeffey, the only anti-Confederate MPP with previous ministerial experience, to head a new administration. Having left for Ottawa, Howe was not there for the dénouement. In his absence the anti-Confederate caucus adopted a hard line and expressed an "unalterable determination" to extricate the province from the BNA Act.[28] Obviously fearing that the moderate McHeffey was not suited to the needs of the day, it relegated him to an executive councillorship without office and chose William Annand, who had a seat in neither House, to head the new administration with the former Conservative Martin Wilkins as his principal colleague and attorney general. Nevertheless Howe justified everything he and the governor had done: Doyle had had no choice but to consult him, "the acknowledged Leader of the combined [anti-Confederate] movement," and he was right to have proposed McHeffey, a man without enemies and high in the confidence of the whole party, as the "best medium of communication" at a time when Annand did not have a seat in the legislature.[29]

Without office and pay for eighteen months, Howe turned to his personal affairs just before he left for Ottawa. For some time he had been living out of "old savings of one kind or another" and incurring new debts all the while. To meet some of them and to enable Susan Ann to maintain herself in his absence, he got Stairs to discount his note for $1,000. "I hope," he said, "when the wheel of better fortune comes round again to be able to repay all obligations except those of friendship which I trust between us will never be effaced."[30] In Ottawa he vowed to maintain his independence, "asking nothing and accepting nothing till Parliament decides for or against us," following which he would be "governed by circumstances after full consultation with our friends." Still confident of his own abilities, he told Susan Ann that, if "ever free to consult my own interests I can cut my way fast enough to the honours and profits of the Dominion."[31] But he spurned overtures to assume the leadership of the opposition in the Commons, partly because he was "not very familiar" with one of the languages being used, partly because most members opposing the government differed with him on Confederation.[32]

The House was full and the galleries crowded on November 8 when the spokesman of the major threat to the union took part in the debate on the Address.[33] Most of the speech would not have been new to Nova Scotians. Although Howe thought the skeleton of the BNA Act bad enough, the situation would be much worse when the Nova Scotian tariff, banking, and currency systems were assimilated to those of the Dominion. All that Nova Scotians "got in return was 80 cents a head – the price of a sheepskin in Nova Scotia." Perhaps the most striking thing about the speech was its "Little Canada" stance. He who had always expounded grandiose schemes pooh-poohed the idea of a new nation extending to the Pacific. Because Britain had been pouring its surplus population into foreign countries, she would be glad to get rid of the Red River colony. But Nova Scotians did not want its young men to defend a corner of the earth hundreds of miles away. "All the colonies had room enough for ten times their present population, and the acquisition of more territory would only be a source of weakness." Entirely satisfied with his speech, Howe declared that friends and foes alike agreed it was "worthy of our country and of the occasion."[34]

In his reply Tupper engaged in hyperbole and pictured Nova Scotia as being the greatest prospective beneficiary of Confederation because "Providence had given us all the elements of a great manufacturing industry." To prevent agitation from thoroughly unsettling the entire country and forestalling the introduction of capital, should Howe not adopt the patriotic course and let "the great ability he possesses" be put to better use?[35] All this led John A. Macdonald to state that Tupper had completely "used up our friend Howe," and that the latter, by not saying he would agitate for repeal, had indicated he would "by and by be open to reason."[36] But again he was too sanguine, for in his reply Howe deliberately emphasized that all the Nova Scotia Anti members, federal and provincial, were pledged to repeal.[37] Actually it was not Tupper who disturbed Howe – he had never taken the Doctor's oratorical efforts seriously – but D'Arcy McGee who, like Howe, was in his element expounding great causes eloquently and imaginatively. Originally admirers of each other, they had been driven apart on the Confederation issue. Although McGee warned Howe that he would be treating him harshly in the Throne speech debate, Howe nonetheless kept a dinner engagement and was sorry he did.

Resenting Howe's use of "your country" (Canada) and "my country" (Nova Scotia), McGee sternly reminded him that by his presence in the House he had acknowledged the Union and that he could not "be in the Union and out of it at one and the same time." The safety of any state, he continued, depended upon "the spirit and the unity" of its people and it was the duty of its public men to raise the public spirit. Howe and the Anti leaders in Nova Scotia were censurable on many grounds, but most of all because their election appeals "tended to beggar and belittle our public affairs; to estrange and render [the people] suspicious and skeptical." Even if the difficulties were "as high as the peaks of Etna or Tolima, or Illimani, yet ... the pure patriotic faith of an united people would be all sufficient to overcome [them]."[38] Seething, Howe awaited McGee's reappearance in the House to "give our Irish friend a skinning," but it was not to be. Shortly rumours would spread that McGee had a running sore in his foot, was breaking up, and might not return. "It would be horrid bad taste," Howe told Susan Ann, "to attack him while it is doubtful if he will live or die."[39]

Other incidents also displeased Howe. Almost at the outset the "noble 18" became seventeen when Stewart Campbell of Guys-borough went "over to the enemy, body and breeches." But perhaps it was just as well, for Campbell had been "sulky and reticent and communicated with nobody till he had taken his plunge."[40] Even more disconcerting to Howe was his inability to get his views before the public in the absence of a published Hansard. Because his first speech was "news," it was reported adequately, but thereafter he got meagre attention. He did not complain of the newspaper reporters who were doing their best. But Parliament met in a small town whose newspapers could not be expected to report the proceedings in the same way as their Montreal and Toronto counterparts. Some members like Macdonald, Tupper, and McGee wrote out their speeches for the local papers. "I cannot do this as mine were long and the labour, to say nothing of the cost of publishing them, would be too great."[41]

Nevertheless he had something to say almost every day and gradually worked himself into his new environment. Macdonald, he noted, spoke well, especially when he was angry, being "trenchant, animated and effective," while Cartier was "the most overrated man in the House. He screams like a seagull in a gale of wind, has a harsh, bad dictatorial manner and an illogical mind."[42] With almost fiendish delight Howe himself spoke on the bill to allow the Grand Trunk to issue new mortgage bonds having preference over most of its existing securities. The Railway Committee, he argued, should conduct a searching inquiry before it authorized another batch of securities which might result in "absolute ruin to those who held them."

Compare, he said delightedly, the record of the Grand Trunk with that of the public railways in Nova Scotia. "You never saw such ruffling of feathers," he told Susan Ann.[43]

He paid closest attention, however, to the purchase of the Hudson's Bay Company lands and the tariff. On the former he spoke at least four times, once to pay off "some fellows who had taken liberties with me" and once to answer Tupper, whose infrequent speeches were largely about Howe.[44] Almost everything, he thought, was wrong with the Hudson's Bay Company bill.[45] Because the company had done little to improve the condition of the Indians and had simply grown "rich and fat," it should be abolished along with slavery and the penal laws. Recently it had watered its stock to increase its sale price and London speculators would laugh derisively at "the poor French Canadians, the ignorant Bluenoses, and the penniless West Canadians" if they accepted the value that the company put on its lands. The bill also enabled Howe to vent his ire on contemporary British politicians. "No man was fonder of England than he. He drew his blood from her stock, replenished his mind with her history, ... he loved the soil upon which the old monuments of industry of his forefathers rested." But the England of the day lacked a Chatham and went "stumbling, blundering on at haphazard to cover up the blunders of [its] statesmen," who were "over anxious to get rid of us" completely. Personally he was opposed to "playing the game of England, by slipping into her shoes at the outset of the union ... If we are to take upon ourselves national obligations and national liabilities we should be treated like a nation." These would be his views of contemporary British politicians to the end of his days.

In justifying his "Little Canadianism," he admitted he had once had a view of a country extending from the Atlantic to the Pacific. "But the philosopher's stone was a favourite idea, and so was 'perpetual motion,' both of which were abandoned because they did not happen to turn out realities." Facts like a staggering debt, to be increased shortly by the building of the ICR, had cured him of his dreams. "We were asked to grow like Jonah's gourd, to grow up in a night, and to wither in a night by and by in shame and desolation." This time there was no McGee to chide Howe, but Tilley did the best he could. Accusing Howe of damaging Canada in the eyes of the world, he argued that 35,000,000 acres of land, acquired at a mere trifle per acre, would soon repay all the costs.[46]

The new tariff saw the light of day belatedly, delayed – it was alleged – until the Maritime members were ready to return home for Christmas. It bore out all of Howe's prophecies, although the failure to report the debates *in extenso* prevents a thorough analysis of the

Antis' criticisms. The general tariff, previously 10 per cent in Nova Scotia, was assimilated to the Canadian rate of 15 per cent, accompanied by duties on breadstuffs, stamp duties, and taxes on newspapers and bank circulation. Almost as an afterthought the minister of finance, Sir John Rose, defended his handiwork as a source of badly needed revenue. An independent Nova Scotia, he argued, would have been compelled to increase its tariff by a similar amount; besides, it was receiving $5.22 per capita from the Dominion compared with Canada's $4.50, a sum far in excess of its contribution. Rose was much less convincing in justifying the duties on flour, corn, and corn meal which, the Nova Scotians charged, were designed to protect the Ontario producer while bearing heavily on the poor.[47] Pointing out to a Newfoundland friend that all but three Maritime members had rejected the budget provisions, Howe warned that his province would likewise be "taxed and trampled on" if it let itself be "seduced by the arts of political schemers."[48]

Howe left Ottawa convinced that anyone who had heard him would realize he was "in earnest," and Macdonald perhaps confirmed it by saying he had "tried our patience extremely" and "talked a great deal of nonsense and some treason."[49] But if Howe spoke treasonably, nothing in the published debates indicates it. He returned home to find that newspaper reports on the tariff had roused intense excitement. Typically the *Citizen* charged that the new duties had been forced on the province "through the most infamous combination of treachery and tyranny, ... Heaven forbid that the Dominion Government should shower any more of its benedictions upon us!"[50] Howe did little to allay the excitement or discontent. Forty days in the Canadian Parliament, he said at Temperance Hall, Halifax, on January 13, had convinced him "we will be nothing more than bondsmen if the [BNA] act continues." Two days later at Brooklyn, Hants county, he pointed out that there was "not a public man in the mother country, who is not an idiot, who would [seek] to reimpose [the corn laws]. Yet in face of this great fact, and in outrageous violation of the settled policy of England, our Canadian taskmasters have fastened these bread taxes upon us."[51]

Clearly the tariff had evoked hostility well beyond the Unionists' fears. At the end of 1867 Governor Doyle reported the province "boiling over with Anti Confederate bile ... A feeling of annexation *they tell me* is gaining ground ... since the tariff arrived, and the food of the poor become taxed!"[52] According to Archbishop Connolly, Howe had tried to control the movement, but had had to "run helter skelter with his crowd of maniacs"; however, this judgment bears little resemblance to the facts. Determined to do nothing "inconsistent with

[his] character," Howe used all his powers to keep Nova Scotians "within legal and constitutional bounds" until a formal appeal for redress was made to Britain.[53] Naturally Doyle was fearful about having to meet an assembly containing only two Unionists among its thirty-eight members, "odds that would beat the Angel Gabriel if sent here to govern this Province!" But Howe told him that unless Lord Monck induced him to "play the Gordon game [in New Brunswick] over again," his provincial advisers would not press him to "do anything that a soldier or a gentleman cannot do without a forfeiture of self respect." As for himself, he promised to "sacrifice a great deal" before allowing Doyle to be injured, and he put this statement on record "that you may show it to me should I fail to keep my word."[54]

Undoubtedly Howe was in a quandary about his next step. Weary of the turmoil that for twenty months had caused him to neglect his personal concerns, he compared himself to Admiral Collingwood who, afloat for years in the Mediterranean, remained at his post until all was well.[55] Because his first speech at home – at the Mechanics Institute in Dartmouth on December 27 – was not publicly reported, its contents can only be gauged from McCully's letter to Macdonald, by no means an unbiased source.[56] But McCully was clearly right that Howe had agreed to head a repeal delegation to Britain, even though highly dubious of the prospects of success. He was also right that Howe was lukewarm about holding repeal meetings, but not, as was suggested, because of any lack of ardour for repeal itself. At his second public meeting, in Temperance Hall, Halifax, he argued that such meetings were no longer needed now that the Anti-Unionists had both leaders and organization. More telling, however, was his fear they might get out of hand. Until then, not "a head [had been] broken, not a pane of glass broken, not an outrage committed, no police ... required to keep the peace at the hustings," and he wanted to keep it that way.[57] But perhaps he was moved most by earlier comments in the British Commons and Lords that Nova Scotians were simply pawns in his hands and that his agitation of the province had created the anti-Confederation movement. "I am determined," he told his third meeting at Brooklyn, "when the question comes before the Imperial Parliament again, that this not be said."[58] So except for the three meetings, all organized by others, he stuck to his fireside.

Although these gatherings supported repeal and asked for a delegation to put the Antis' case before the British Parliament, Howe continued to warn his listeners about the gloomy prospects. Two years ago he would have sworn they could get redress. "I believed that the throne of England sat above the fountain of honour and of justice, that the House of Lords would do justice though the heavens should fall, that a man with a manly, honest case could go to the bar of the House of Commons and obtain fair play ... but if you ask me if I feel that confidence now, I do not." Although Englishmen were sensitive to injustice in the United Kingdom, they were "often strangely indifferent" to it elsewhere. Last year a million people had died of starvation in India, but Britons gave more thought to the twenty-seven people who fell through the ice and drowned in Hyde Park. Grimshaw, the jockey who rode the French horse *Gladiateur* to victory in the Derby, got more biographical notices on his death than would all British North American statesmen put together. Londoners would not be as startled if a province sank or melted in the Gulf Stream as if a single member of the Lords or Commons fell off Westminster Bridge and was drowned. From "this insular apathy and indifference to all outward interests" Nova Scotia had most to fear. "Will the British Parliament give the time necessary to review the facts, and ... have the magnanimity to repair the wrong? We shall see. In the meantime it is our duty to give them the opportunity."[59]

In private Howe outlined three alternatives if the appeal for redress failed: to work the existing system to its logical termination, independence; to drift on and, as bitter feelings increased in Nova Scotia, to shake off Canadian domination by force; or "to leave this country which I probably will." Publicly his somewhat menacing, enigmatic remarks on the future thoroughly perturbed Connolly and McCully. "Let no resistance be offered," he said, "until we get our answer from England." If unfavourable, a period of trial to public men and danger to the whole community would begin, since Nova Scotians were unlikely to submit "year after year to be taxed *ad libitum* by this Dominion Parliament" or "send men up to be outvoted and laughed at."[60] Clearly the gathering momentum for repeal was producing a more forceful Howe. And gathering it was, for without any urging from the centre and certainly none from Howe, twenty-six meetings were held in December and February, at least one in each county but Victoria. About one quarter approved the use of any means to gain repeal and one at Bridgeville, East River, Pictou county, called for the seizure of the customs offices if repeal was not granted. Although many demanded that the federal members not go again to Ottawa, the *Morning Chronicle* willingly let them make the decision: "we believe that they will do so wisely and well."[61]

At the opening of the provincial legislature on January 30, 1868, Attorney General Martin Wilkins presented a series of resolutions demanding repeal and containing some of the constitutional folklore for which he would become notorious, especially the contention that the British Parliament was legally incapable of passing the BNA Act. But even before the resolutions, or an address based on them, could be adopted, the Executive Council passed a minute appointing Howe as a delegate in order to expedite his passage to Britain; shortly it added Annand, Jared Troop, and H.W. Smith to the delegation. Only later did the assembly approve their selection and instruct the delegates to accept nothing but the restoration of the pre-1867 constitution of Nova Scotia. Before Howe left, Garvie had told him that official Britain hoped the Canadians would be successful in making them "all Stewart Campbells, and in stopping your mouths before you get as far as a formal appeal for Repeal." Naturally John A. Macdonald wanted the duke of Buckingham and Chandos, colonial secretary in the Disraeli administration formed after Derby's retirement, to be firm: otherwise, "the consequence will be that the professional agitators will keep up the agitation."[62]

The harbinger of others to follow, Howe left for Britain by the *City of New York* on February 14. To his delight Susan Ann could accompany him and he hoped that they might see Paris together. But her presence also increased his burden, since not only did he keep up his usual frenzied round of official activities, but he also spent his leisure in sight-seeing, theatre-going, and travelling with her in London's environs. Before the other delegates arrived he laid "the foundation for an outside airing of our case." The assembly's address, which had to be forwarded through the governor general, would be delayed and he thought it wise not to proceed with the petition of the anti-Confederate members, which could be presented directly, until he was fortified by "strong expressions of opinion by the independent press.[63] He concentrated on the newspaper editors with whom he had developed a rapport the previous year – Walker of the *Daily News*, Falvey of the *Hampshire Independent*, and Blanchard Jerrold of *Lloyd's Weekly* – and although he adapted his letters to the specific paper and editor, he usually included a copy of the petition and made reference to the results of the elections, the falsity of the data and arguments used to influence Parliament in 1867, the treatment accorded Nova Scotians in the Canadian Parliament's first session, and the indifference and apathy shown in Britain towards colonial matters.[64] In June, when he surveyed the results of his overtures to the press, he was generally satisfied. The *Times*, opposed to him in 1866, was silent for the moment and would later admit that Nova Scotia had a strong case. A not unsympathetic *Manchester Guardian*, supported generally by the *Manchester Examiner and Times* and the *Morning Advertiser*, held that "the true plan" for the colonies was to "help them out into the world with tender care" and to convince them "that they should lose no time in seeking an independent footing."[65]

Five newspapers altogether opposed him, led by a government organ, the *Standard*, which called him a "disappointed man," criticized his contentions that colonists were insensitively treated in Britain, and told him that "his statements should contain some elements of truthfulness." The *Examiner*, relying on misleading material circulated by Tupper and the Unionists, thought that Howe was "too sagacious a man to suppose, that he can all at once pull down the edifice of which he was one of the chief builders." The *Morning Herald*, after calling Nova Scotia "the petulant colony ... the 'wild Wales' of this England of the West," told its people to overcome their "natural drawbacks" by willingly uniting with "a community more rich and more enticing." The *Saturday Review* was certain that the intelligence of Nova Scotia supported the union and that it took "an agitator like Mr. Howe to convince an ill-informed populace that they had been made the victims of a nefarious conspiracy." The *Spectator* was emphatic that "we are not going to alter Imperial laws of the highest importance under orders from Halifax." Although Howe and his colleagues sought to meet these criticisms, they experienced difficulties of various kinds: the *Review*, for example, never inserted replies and the *Standard* seldom deviated from the government line.[66]

Otherwise, said Howe, the London newspapers gave the Antis "invaluable aid." The *Daily News* suggested that the only way out of "the inconsiderate statute of last year" was justice and the *Morning Star* commented sternly on the "unjustifiable ... indecent haste" of Parliament in 1867. Although the British government could not retreat with honour, said the *News of the World*, "yet retreat is the only action to be taken consistent with justice." The *Glowworm* was convinced that any advantages in Confederation could be achieved without the complete absorption of a colony against its will; the *Daily Telegraph* demanded that Nova Scotians be shown "there was a determination to render them impartial justice"; *Lloyd's Weekly* had no doubt that "the most dismal prophecies of the non-union delegates have been already fulfilled"; the *Sun* concluded it was contrary to British practice to "rule any State in a manner unwelcome to its people."[67] The provincial press was even stronger in denouncing, as Howe put it, "the foolish coup d'état by which we were swindled out of our independence." Thus the *Leeds Mercury* blamed Parliament for acting on insufficient information and "attempting to legislate for a country of which they know so little," while the *Glasgow Sentinel* argued that the loyalty of the most loyal of colonies should not be frittered away, especially because of its value to the navy.[68]

Even as Howe dealt with the press he was also appealing to MPs whom he had previously found sympathetic: Robert Lowe, Henry Fawcett, Thomas Hughes, and especially John Bright, to whom he wrote: "Your advice and aid will be very precious to us now and I know we will have both." In mid-March he reported everyone in the Commons "up to his eyes in the Irish [Church disestablishment] debate" and on the 16th he stayed late to hear "the great speakers," Gladstone and Disraeli, deal with the question. He had no desire to see the colonial secretary until the assembly's resolutions and address arrived at the Colonial Office. In this instance it was a "reverse of the old saying that 'the longest way round is the shortest way home'," since March was over before the first of these documents arrived through the governor general. Then, on April 3, the duke of Buckingham granted an interview to all the Nova Scotian delegates. To Howe British officialdom was now at its conciliatory best, seemingly all too conscious that its acts of the previous year were precipitate and anxious to get out of its dilemma as best it could. In this instance the duke not only engaged them in a two-hour preliminary discussion but also assured them that their views would be presented to the cabinet.[69]

By this time it was also apparent that the opposition press in Nova Scotia had been right and that a delegation of four was unnecessary. Clearly Howe and Henry W. Smith, perhaps the best legal mind in the assembly, could easily have carried on by themselves without Jared Troop, undistinguished in his talents, and William Annand, who was using the trip to further his business interests. Of especial interest to Howe was the arrival of Charles Tupper, sent by John A. Macdonald to "shadow" him. The choice had occasioned difficulties on several fronts. A.T. Galt declined to accompany Tupper on the ground that he was not the right man to deal with Nova Scotia.[70] After the Liberals Blake and Holton charged that Tupper's mission was an insult to the province Macdonald framed his order in council to make it clear that Tupper's primary objective was to provide information to the British government, not to engage Howe in public debate; he also instructed Tupper to "adopt the most conciliatory tone with your Nova Scotia friends."[71] But he could not prevent Dr T.S. Parker, the Liberal member for Wellington Centre – Macdonald called him that "sneak" Parker – from moving for Tupper's recall. D'Arcy McGee replied that "a family matter" ought to be left within the family and that Tupper was therefore the appropriate choice.[72] Gradually, however, Macdonald was realizing the failings of his Nova Scotian sources of information and henceforth he would take more and more of the pacification of Nova Scotia into his own hands.

Howe had anticipated Tupper's presence and treated it philosophically. Early in April they had an hour's talk, in which, writes K.G.
Pryke, they sought to outbluff each other.[73] Their perceptions of the
exchange differed materially. According to Howe, Tupper suggested
that the Canadians would offer any terms if the Antis laid down their
arms and then the two of them "combined, might rule the Dominion"; thereupon Howe "chaffed him all around the compass." Of the
same meeting Tupper reported that he had offered to combine his
fortunes with those of the Antis to ensure full recognition of Nova
Scotia's claims but that Howe, though deeply impressed, feared his
own party might abandon him.[74] To Tupper's credit he was genuinely
anxious for a rapport with Howe, something that had not developed
in their twenty years' acquaintance. Although his letters to Macdonald undoubtedly exaggerated his contribution to the unfolding
panorama of events, the British government welcomed him at a time
when "the efforts [that] Howe and Company were making through
the press, and members of Parliament, occasioned a good deal of
anxiety." But contrary to the wishes both of Tupper and the Colonial
Office, Macdonald still insisted that Tupper "not come in conflict with
[Howe] before the public if you can avoid it."[75]

In his fortnightly report of April 9 Howe told of 2,000 copies of the
Nova Scotia case being sent to the leading newspapers and all the
members of the Commons and Lords. He had also submitted
Attorney General Wilkins's constitutional opinions to eminent counsel, Sir Roundell Palmer and William Vernon Harcourt, who replied
almost at once there could be no doubt of the legal capacity of
Parliament to pass the BNA Act. The Nova Scotians were also
considering the merit of trying to have their case presented at the bar
of the Commons and engaging Harcourt to do it.

At Easter, during the long parliamentary recess, Howe took Susan
Ann to Stonehenge, Winchester and Salisbury Cathedrals, and
Magdalen College, and then for several days to the duke of
Buckingham's seat at Stowe for meetings that had been "arranged"
with Tupper, although not by Howe. Of these meetings Howe wrote
or said little, knowing that his fellow delegates and his friends in
Halifax were suspicious of his contacts with Tupper. In contrast, the
latter had much to say, although he was clearly engaging in wishful
thinking when he told Macdonald: "If there is any faith in men I think
I may consider the matter, if judiciously arranged by you, *settled*."[76]
At the most Howe was exploring possibilities in case he eventually had
to concede defeat, but that time was not yet.

On his return to London Howe suffered a recurrence of sore eyes
and Susan Ann had to read him the *Times* and do a good deal of

copying. He was elated, nonetheless, by the "widespread and effective support" he was receiving in the press and by the election of an anti-Confederate in a provincial by-election in New Brunswick.[77] He was also pleased that by late April the delegates had agreed upon a final plan of action. If consent was forthcoming, Harcourt would present their case at the bar of the Commons and they were already "priming and loading" him. After numerous meetings with Bright at the Reform Club he and Howe had concluded that the government itself would take no action on the Antis' demands; that Parliament also would do nothing without some kind of inquiry into the facts; that a parliamentary investigation would be quickest and best; and that Bright should try to get an early debate on the Nova Scotian petition.[78]

But these plans went all for naught. Unexpectedly the colonial secretary instructed the delegates to meet him on May 2 before the cabinet made its decision, and on that day Howe and Smith confronted him, Adderley, and Elliot at the Colonial Office. To Howe it was obvious from the outset that Buckingham would not agree to an investigation without strong parliamentary pressure; clearly he had accepted Tupper's assurances that Ottawa would repeal the taxes which Nova Scotia found obnoxious and supposedly "leave [it] without substantial grievances." All that Howe and Smith could do was prophesy a stern reaction in Nova Scotia to any compromise that would deprive it of the right of self-determination.[79] Although Buckingham promised an answer in a few days, it was not forthcoming. At a time when the Disraeli ministry was tottering on the Irish Church disestablishment issue Nova Scotia had low priority. Not until May 8 did it become clear that the government would not resign and an election would be postponed until autumn.

Even then Parliament did not deal with Nova Scotia as Howe had hoped it would. Because of the pressure of other public business and the Whitsuntide holidays Bright could not get an earlier day for the debate than June 16. Since repeal would obviously not be granted without an investigation, Howe did not think he was departing from his instructions in agreeing that Bright should simply demand an inquiry, preferably by an on-the-spot royal commission to obviate the need of bringing witnesses from Nova Scotia. But he was beginning to lose hope. "In the present state of parties, with the utter indifference displayed on all questions except that all engrossing one upon which the fate of the Ministry depends," the government's reply would undoubtedly be unfavourable.[80] From Halifax his son Sydenham reported rumours that he had capitulated and was accepting Dominion office; he replied unequivocally that he could "not desert our country till her fate is decided, and when it is, I fear she will want me more than ever"; yet it was "no joke, with a family and no fortune, to be putting wealth and honours on one side for years at my time of life."[81]

Howe knew that the rumours came from two sources, one being Lieutenant-Governor Doyle who, recently in England, had shown Adderley some of Howe's letters which seemed to indicate he would "accept the situation" if repeal were rejected.[82] But the main source was Tupper who, unable to participate in public discussion, was telling scores of public men that Howe would submit tamely and enter the federal cabinet when Nova Scotia's demands were turned down. Tupper even half persuaded Lord Campbell to stop looking after Nova Scotia's case in the Lords until Howe convinced him that failure to grant redress would "weaken the power of the Crown" in North America.[83] Asked by Bright about the possibility of violence in the province, Tupper replied that "the worst revolt" would be to "see Howe become a member of Sir John's cabinet within six months." But he did not impress Bright as he thought he had, since Bright would tell the Commons somewhat disparagingly that Tupper had "a persuasive tongue ... and ... an ambition ... not willing to be confined ... within the comparatively narrow limits of ... Nova Scotia."[84]

Tupper had another "go" at Howe, but it is uncertain who took the initiative. On May 21, following "some wonderful tricks" by a Japanese troupe at the Lyceum, Howe drove Tupper home in his cab and, according to Tupper, invited him for breakfast; yet Susan Ann's diary states explicitly that Tupper wished to "have some *talk* with Joseph." No less different were their versions of the exchange of views. According to Tupper, both agreed that the interests of all required Howe to "take hold with us," but "we must handle the subject with great delicacy." He added that Mrs Howe "goes with me strongly," but nothing in her diary or the Howe Papers indicates that the Howes reacted in this manner.[85]

For much of May the pressure was off Howe and he could give more attention to Susan Ann: on the 12th, her sixty-first birthday, they attended a performance of *Faust* at Covent Garden and on the 13th a reception at Chandos House. Late in the month the Northups arrived and on the 27th – Derby Day – they all went to Epsom, where Susan Ann marvelled at the sums spent on the favourite, the Marquis of Hastings's *Lady Elizabeth*. Then the two couples were off to France, despite Susan Ann's lack of enthusiasm. "I am not anxious to see Paris – but yield to Joseph's wish who is very desirous I should see all I possibly can while I am in Europe."[86] On the way back they went to Ryde, where they found that Lady Westphal had died a week earlier and the admiral was in such great distress that Susan Ann remained with him a few days.

Arriving in London on June 12, Howe discovered Buckingham's dispatch of eight days earlier which, though conciliatory, rejected the contention that the BNA Act had been passed without proper consultation, called on "loyal" Nova Scotia to recognize that the union was "important to the interests of the whole empire," and requested the Dominion Parliament to "relax or modify any arrangements [on taxation, regulation of trade, and fisheries] which may prejudice the peculiar interests of Nova Scotia, and of the Maritime portion of the Dominion."[87] Though expected, it made Howe gloomy about the prospects in the Commons since "the decision of the Government would probably be followed by a rigid 'whip up' of its adherents – who would be reinforced by that Section of the Whigs led by Mr. Cardwell."[88] Leaving nothing to chance, Tupper, despite his instructions from Macdonald, arranged for the *Canadian News* to publish his reply to Howe in the Dominion Parliament and for a copy to be sent to each member of the British Commons just before the debate came off. "Had not this step been taken," he boasted, "the division would have been very different, as I have been kept muzzled, while the other side have been in full cry."[89]

All the Nova Scotian delegates along with Northup and Garvie were in the gallery of the Commons on the evening of the 16th. The earnest mood of the House contrasted markedly with its "flippant indifference in 1867," and over 300 were there to hear Bright argue that the BNA Act had been passed upon "representations extravagantly coloured," if not "absolutely untrue." Never had so important a measure been adopted with such "unseemly haste," and yet it was said that "there is no remedy in this Parliament which did ... the injustice." To build up "a great State by making a victim" of Nova Scotia was no less objectionable because it was done to "meet certain difficulties in Canada or in the Colonial Office." Every person in the colonies should "feel that the Crown had not been a Crown of tyranny, but a Crown of just government to them." For Howe it was a "masterly statement," the more so as Bright's facts, which he had supplied, were impeccable and unchallengeable.[90]

In contrast, Adderley was guilty of a monstrous perversion of the facts in suggesting that union had been actively agitated for fourteen years in Nova Scotia and that in the election of 1863 "all parties were so unanimous ... that it was not even raised on the hustings." Almost as faulty were his arguments that during the recent campaign Howe had promised to give the union a fair trial and that the voters were not nearly as opposed to Confederation as they seemed since they were also expressing an opinion on Tupper's unpopular school act. Resorting altogether to hyperbole, he contended that Nova Scotia, instead of having no say in policy-making, "appeared to have dominant influence, and at this moment to rule the policy of the Dominion Parliament. Every Act that had yet been passed was in favour of Nova Scotia." It would have been possible, Howe wrote, to correct the "palpable mistakes" and "fallacious reasoning," but the night was "so far advanced, [that] further debate would not in our opinion have materially varied the decision."[91]

As Howe expected, the Whig Cardwell joined the Tory Adderley in rejecting the demand for an investigation. Indeed, only four members joined Bright in speaking favourably for the petitioners and he would not have divided the House had it not been for the nature and tone of Adderley's remarks. Neither he nor Howe was surprised that he was voted down by 183 to 87. Howe's only solace was that "the most stirring intellects and conspicuous leaders of public opinion" in a moribund Parliament had shown sufficient independence to vote against the official leaders of their parties.[92] Lord Campbell did not get a day for debate in the Lords until July 6 and then could not prevail over the duke of Buckingham, who argued that an investigation would "excite false hopes," or over the earl of Carnarvon who, in defence of his handiwork, suggested that "time, which changes so many things, ... will heal the irritation."[93] The Nova Scotians were not even there to hear them, having left for home two days earlier.

While still in England, Susan Ann wondered "where this trouble will all end ... I pray it may not lead to bloodshed."[94] Her husband was certain the Nova Scotian Antis would not tamely acquiesce as Tupper had prophesied. "If I know them," he told one correspondent, "they will draw their bonnets over their brows & fight on at all events till the meeting of the next Parliament." To a Nova Scotian executive councillor, Robert Robertson, he outlined the possibilities – outright capitulation; open insurrection and intrigues with foreign countries; creation of a deadlock through the resignation of the Executive Council; passive resistance in the form of refusing to do military service or pay duties – and found them all unsatisfactory or hazardous. The best course, he thought, was to remain united for another few months, hoping that in the reformed British Parliament the combination between Cardwell and Adderley might be broken up and Bright would have a seat in the cabinet; "if so, we are pretty sure to win."[95] As in 1867, the Nova Scotian delegates did not leave without a Parthian shot in the form of a protest which contrasted Parliament's treatment of the 700,000 Protestants of Ireland with that of 370,000 Nova Scotians. A few nights earlier, on Irish Church disestablishment, the House of Lords was crowded – "Royal Princes on the cross-benches, a goodly array of Bishops in lawn sleeves around the woolsack, and of noble ladies, richly attired, raining influence from the galleries." In the previous year, when Nova Scotia was voted into Confederation, only ten Lords were present. "A good many historic delusions were dissipated on that day."[96] It was another poignant illustration of Howe's thorough disillusionment with the British politicians of the day.

The Halifax to which Howe returned contained, in Tilley's words, "inflammable material *every where*"; the *Chronicle* was even suggesting openly that Nova Scotians might "have to take the matter in their own hands, and set themselves free."[97] More than a little worried, A.W. Savary, MP for Digby, warned Howe that, if the *Chronicle* continued to discuss annexation and countenance physical resistance, "it will soon drive all loyal & respectable men out of our ranks."[98] Howe, fatigued physically and mentally after two years of continuous exertion, showed his own frustration when two Cumberland Antis asked him to help defeat Tupper in the ministerial election which would follow his expected appointment to the cabinet. "Some of our friends think that I am made of wrought iron, never want rest and am never to wear out? ... [They] fancy that to ride round a large County and tear your lungs to pieces on platforms and in barns is a pleasant pastime for an old fellow of 63. I wish they would try it."[99]

The day after he returned home – on June 16 – Howe met the executive councillors and leading anti-Confederates in Annand's office and told them that "without some new and startling movement on our side of the water" another delegation to England would be futile.[100] Earlier he had suggested a joint demand of the Maritimes for a union of their own, but Robert Robertson had already gone to New Brunswick unofficially and drawn a blank. Presaging the break that was to come with Howe, Annand, fond of delegations to London for his own purposes, wanted another following the British election, but all the meeting could come up with was a council of war of federal and provincial members to be held on August 3 shortly before the legislature was to resume its sittings.

Most of the teething problems of the new Dominion having been settled, John A. Macdonald had more time to devote to Nova Scotia, the major running sore that was left. Already aware of the inaccuracy of the reports of McCully and Tupper on Nova Scotia, he was now to be given an example of the latter's lack of judgment. Writing from England, Tupper stated that if, on his return, he found Howe's course unchanged he would go through the province drumming up support for union; he hoped however, that this would be unnecessary, since, if Howe were given the refusal of a few choice offices, "I am *sure* he will accept."[101] Macdonald was nothing if not horrified. Even before Tilley and Archibald informed him of the abhorrence of Tupper in much of Nova Scotia, he had concluded that his suggestions were a recipe for conflagration. So, on Tupper's arrival in Halifax, he found a request from the prime minister to postpone his public meetings and a suggestion that he should not even write to Howe, for if the latter acted spontaneously it could not be alleged that his action had been "preceded by any offer of advancement for himself or his friends of any kind."[102]

In the end Tilley, not Tupper, determined Macdonald's course. Breakfasting at Howe's home two days after his return, he was told that although any Antis who accepted office would be branded traitors, nonetheless "the reasonable men wanted an excuse to enable them to hold back the violent and unreasonable of their own party." Hence great good might result if discussions were opened between the leading Antis and the Dominion government, at which the latter would make proposals. The best opportunity, Howe thought, would be immediately prior to the August convention of anti-Confederates, and Macdonald's presence offered the best chances of success. Tilley urged the prime minister to make the most of the opportunity at a time when Howe "appears disposed to act rationally ... Men of less influence and ability may attempt violent means, but if *he* is firm, *they* can do but little."[103] Archibald was no less convinced that Howe and his friends wanted something to excuse them for not taking more radical steps. "In a question of this kind – one in which the well being – almost the existence of the union – is involved – a pecuniary concession is nothing to the Dominion."[104]

Pressed also by Tupper, Macdonald decided to go to Halifax even though the *Acadian Recorder* advocated that he be treated roughly. This was much too much for Howe: "If we have lost our constitution let us preserve our manners ... Are we so strong that we can afford to outrage the public sentiment of the whole world by reckless disregard of all the usages of civilized diplomacy?"[105] His intervention, he told Garvie, "startled the blood and thunder people" and "ensured for the Missionaries safe passage to and fro"; he was delighted that "the high and mighty" were being compelled to come to Halifax and that they would owe "their security from insult to that great rebel whom for three years they had labored to crush."[106] Little else pleased him. The difficulty of keeping the Antis working in harmony increased day by day. Newfoundland was reported to be thinking about entering

Confederation and Provincial Secretary Vail had been as unsuccessful at Charlottetown as Robertson at Fredericton. "If the other Maritime Provinces would rally round us we could force the enemy back and obtain security for all,"[107] but those prospects were bleak.

Hoping to "strike off the tallest head," Macdonald met Howe alone on August 2 shortly after he arrived in Halifax and thereby "created immense jealousy among the locals."[108] Howe made it clear that he would continue to press for repeal as long as it offered any hope of success, while Macdonald indicated he would follow the colonial secretary's advice and seek an accommodation, hoping that Howe would press Nova Scotia's case from within the cabinet. Howe made his usual reply that such a course would lead to his being charged with desertion and destroy his usefulness.[109] The precise details of the convention, which began the next day, are in dispute, but Howe's friend, E.M. McDonald, editor of the *Citizen*, was surprised most of all that, although the delegates had been back for two months, the provincial government had come up with neither a policy nor even the shadow of a suggestion; as usual, "all eyes turned to Mr. Howe for advice."[110]

Once again he outlined all the possibilities, including one that "if 'the locals' were prepared to strike work, resign their offices and repudiate the act I would resign and go to the Country with them!" The suggestion, he discovered, was "very distasteful to the Departmental folk, who wanted to hold their offices, cry out for repeal, and throw the responsibility of a compromize on the Dominion men."[111] Later it would be debated whether he had made the proposal, and, if he had, how seriously. But undoubtedly he made it, since, before it became the subject of controversy, he put considerable emphasis on it in a letter to Garvie. At the convention he also revealed the details of his conversation with Macdonald. As a result, Annand went to Government House and suggested to Doyle that any proposals of Sir John should be made through the "local" government, only to be told that Macdonald's official intercourse must be with the federal members from Nova Scotia. It was just another incident in a growing split between the "Dominion men" and the "locals," the latter anxious to maintain the perquisites of office, content to worsen their bad relations with Ottawa, and keen to blame the failure to get repeal on the federal MPs. Howe could see all sorts of personal motives at work in widening the breach: Martin Wilkins's indignation that Howe had taken action to prove that Wilkins's law was nonsense; the jealousy of Annand and Troop, aroused by the fact that he, not they, had been invited to the colonial secretary's estate at Stowe; and Annand's annoyance at his opposition to another delegation to England, where the former might concoct "another grand Company scheme" to enrich himself.[112]

The convention having accomplished little in two days, it appointed a committee to make proposals. Despite the opposition of the "locals" that committee agreed, on Howe's casting vote, to hear Macdonald, Cartier, Kenny, and Mitchell and it accorded them "sufficient courtesy" to permit Sir John to state generally what he was prepared to do and express his willingness to consider any specific propositions. On receiving the committee's report, the convention did no more than pledge itself to repeal within the law and constitution, to which, Howe later wrote scornfully, "nobody attached any importance."[113] Before Macdonald left, however, he agreed to send Howe a letter after prorogation in Nova Scotia, containing terms agreed between them, which, though marked "private," he might show to his friends, with the hope of winning them over and inducing some of them, along with Howe, to take office. That was the major accomplishment of Macdonald's mission to Halifax.

Howe returned to his books – always "an unfailing resource, after the stormy hours 'which try men's souls'" – full of scorn for "the blood and thunder" people who wanted to coerce everybody into a scheme of passive resistance or another delegation. To one who proposed a particularly extreme course he replied that "a gunboat with 100 marines and a flying battery of artillery" would soon make him see things differently.[114] Forces were already in train which would permit a move in a new direction. A.W. McLelan, the Anti MP for Colchester, had come to believe that the province would never again get the Dominion in as favourable a bargaining position and the only obstacles to an adjustment were Annand and the *Chronicle*. Asked by an anonymous writer in the *Acadian Recorder* to "speak out" on his intentions, Howe replied he would act "upon my own independent judgment, irrespective of clamour or dictation from any quarter."[115] Macdonald had left Halifax wondering if the assembly, which had done none of the ordinary business of the province since the election, might refuse to work the constitution. Howe watched, too, as the Executive Council passed a minute and the assembly a series of resolutions condemning the colonial secretary's dispatch. He was amused, and certainly not perturbed, when Wilkins, not yet admitting defeat on his own peculiar brand of constitutional law, gave it a new twist by arguing that, since the preamble of the BNA act stated that Nova Scotia wished to be federally united, the act itself – resting as it did on a palpable falsehood – was necessarily invalid.[116] When Blanchard challenged him, he replied that unless the province's grievances were speedily remedied the legislature would take matters into its own hands. "A tariff bill would be passed, and the Collectors of Customs instructed to obey it ... If these means won't avail we'll appeal to another nation."

This was too much for Lieutenant-Governor Doyle, who inquired if he had uttered these "disloyal sentiments." Wilkins replied that he was "incapable of entertaining or expressing" that kind of sentiment and, on the governor's insistence, agreed to have his disavowal published.[117] Although Macdonald thought he could discern Howe's "directing hand in this matter," Howe denied having anything to "do with the correspondence, which the General managed adroitly."[118] Doyle was not yet done with the incident. The assembly having passed a vote of censure on him for having called Wilkins to task, he "*forced them to expunge*" it, apparently on the threat of dissolution, "so now we have *kissed* & made friends again!"[119] Showing his scorn of the "locals," Howe said he did "not believe in making treasonable Speeches one day nor in eating them the next, nor in censuring a Governor and then shrinking from the inevitable alternative – a dissolution."[120] He again indicated his distaste when he refused, because of Wilkins's uncomplimentary reference to the delegates, to appear at the bar of the House with the other delegates on September 14 to receive its thanks, even "although ... within 5 min$^s$ walk" of its environs.[121] He was also perturbed by the honour accorded Gen. Benjamin Butler and his Congressional reciprocity committee on their visit to Halifax, especially after Butler suggested that reciprocity could not be secured under the existing order; for Howe it was proof positive of the visit's "purpose, scarcely disguised, of encouraging the annexationist feeling."[122] Both he and Macdonald breathed sighs of relief when the General Assembly prorogued on September 21 without further incident.

Anything but sanguine, Doyle feared that "the people of the Country are 'a head' of our friend Joe, & that he will have great difficulty in restraining them." If the *Morning Chronicle* continued to fulminate treason, he did not see "how we are ever to get the Country quiet."[123] Howe was not nearly as concerned about the *Chronicle*, which still prophesied that his "white hairs will be as an oriflamme ... in the glorious war" of liberation, as about the slanders coming "out of the Province Bldg. on the meanest and most contemptible of motives." One of them pictured the British government saying to him: "You quiet Nova Scotia and we will take care of you."[124] To the merchant Robert Boak he stated unequivocally that he had received offers from neither the Dominion nor British governments and that his intention was to stand independent from them and the provincial government so that if he eventually had to act on his own judgment he would be "perfectly untrammelled by all considerations except those of public duty." To proposals that the provincial government reimburse the merchants for financing the delegation of 1866–7, his reaction was that they were entitled to it on public grounds; to suggestions that they in turn recognize his services, he conceded he was "not rich enough to refuse their gift," but he would take it only for past services, not for the pursuit of some future policy of which he did not approve.[125]

During September Macdonald wrote to Howe four times,[126] always indicating that he had taken Nova Scotia under his special care. He missed no opportunity to stress the great injury done to the province by a state of affairs in which, if he failed to fill offices in the province, he was charged with neglect of duty, and if he appointed union men, he was accused of insulting the majority of the people. In the first letter (September 4) he hoped that Howe would soon be in a position to recommend a Nova Scotian for the Railway Board; in the second (September 15) he stated that he had appointed a *locum tenens* until Howe could see his way clear to making a nomination; he also needed a Nova Scotian to fill a Senate vacancy and another – "a first rate Lawyer" – to sit on the commission for the assimilation of the statute law. In the third (September 21) he emphasized that he had left the three directorships of the penitentiary service unfilled until disorganization had appeared in several prisons, "another instance in which Nova Scotia suffers from the unhappy position of affairs!"

Howe's one letter to Macdonald during the month exhibited more than a little despondency.[127] It was unfortunate, he thought, that Macdonald had been unable to make definite propositions to the committee of the convention, since, as a result, "matters have drifted here for a month until the excitement has increased, and the cry for repeal or annexation, is heard all over the Province." With prorogation in sight, could Sir John not send his proposals in writing? Howe would show them to a few of his friends and then forward their views to Macdonald. This process would at least exhaust the resources of friendly negotiation and the British government would know at what point the differences were irreconcilable. Macdonald replied that their agreement was to postpone his letter until prorogation, and to give it more weight he would consult his colleagues when they reassembled; however, it would be only a repetition of what he had said before the committee and what was already known to the provincial ministry. As a prod, he expressed confidence, from first-hand reports, that Howe had only to declare that "the present Constitution should have a fair trial, and your will will be law. All your own friends, all the moderate antis, and the whole union party will rally round you and you must succeed."[128] But certainly not Howe, and probably not Macdonald, really believed it. Indeed, Howe told Sir John bluntly that, until the federal government adjusted the financial grievances on equitable principles, "I could not recede a step, and nobody would follow me if I did. Give me a fair case to our people, and the business is more than half done."[129]

Macdonald's letter of October 6, though marked "private," was written in such a way that Howe could show it to whomever he willed. It insisted that the Nova Scotia MPs deal with constitutional and nonfinancial matters in the Dominion Parliament, but that the federal minister of finance, Provincial Treasurer Annand, and others might take up financial, taxation, and commercial questions, which, it promised, would be treated "not in a rigid but in the most liberal spirit." Once again Macdonald pointed out that Nova Scotia was suffering serious hardship by not being fully represented in the federal cabinet. Could Howe not follow the course of Daniel O'Connell who, though he spared no effort to repeal the union of England and Ireland, did not stand aloof in Parliament, but gave general support to the government of the day and secured some say in the administration of Irish affairs.[130]

Although Macdonald was playing for high stakes, his insistence on delaying appointments for Nova Scotians until Howe made up his mind was not sitting well with his own followers. From Tupper, Archibald, and McCully had come complaints that they had not even enough influence to appoint a tide waiter, but Sir John would concede nothing to any of them. "Now, my dear Doctor," he told Tupper, "... If I appointed a Union man to office now, it would be a breach of faith on my part, would give Howe an opportunity of throwing himself back again into the arms of the violent Antis." Telling Archibald he could not give Howe an excuse for cutting off negotiations, he urged him to "exert all your influence with our friends to keep quiet for a time." While admitting the "anomalous" situation to McCully, he was adamant about not losing the chance of "getting the rational portion of the Anti-Union party to accept the situation ... for the sake of rewarding a few friends."[131] To each of his correspondents he emphasized that leaving vacancies for Howe to fill was a fundamental part of his plan to win over Nova Scotia or at least split the Antis.

For Howe, Macdonald's letter had immensely more personal consequences. Although he told Annand about its arrival, he did not ask him to read it since he and his government were bent on repeal and nothing else. To let Macdonald know exactly where he stood, he made it clear he was still for repeal if he could get it. But he fully realized that Gladstone, who would likely be prime minister after the next election, had already voted against Nova Scotia twice. If the new British Parliament refused an investigation, it would be very difficult to stem the public tide in Nova Scotia unless the federal government offered "large and substantial measures of reparation." That, he explained, was why he took the risk of opening a correspondence with Macdonald, of showing it to the Dominion MPs, and a few judicious friends, and of admitting its existence openly. As a result, he was being asked every day if he "accepted the situation as the phrase goes." Because Macdonald's letter indicated a spirit of fairness and because Annand refused to go to Ottawa to discuss financial matters, he was sending copies of speeches by McLelan and Annand setting forth Nova Scotia's financial claims. Would Sir John Rose, the federal minister of finance, and his deputy examine them to determine the extent of agreement? As for following O'Connell's course, he was not in a "very enviable" position, but he preferred to hold it for the moment. "The responsibilities resting upon me are not light, and I can only relieve myself of them by maintaining ... a position of personal independence."[132]

In a follow-up letter Howe asked to be told with dispatch where he and the province stood. Sir John Rose, he hoped, would quickly confirm or disprove the impression that from a condition of great prosperity and light taxation Nova Scotia had become highly taxed with no funds to spare. "Do not hang fire, but send forward your dissection of Annand's and McLellan's [sic] statement without delay." Macdonald should also ensure that immediately after the election the British government would declare its policy on Nova Scotia quickly and emphatically so that men's minds would not remain unsettled.[133] Meanwhile Howe was finding that his dealings with Macdonald were not being regarded with favour by the Anti MPs. Even the moderate Hugh McDonald of Antigonish wondered how the federal members could justify to the country the opening of negotiations until the provincial government had its answer from Britain, while A.G. Jones of Halifax warned that the Antis must continue to present a bold front and not show signs of weakness "until the people themselves see ... the utter hopelessness of getting Repeal."[134]

To gauge his future course Howe apparently resorted to extraordinary means early in October, when he spoke extemporaneously in Pictou county at the opening of the Drummond Colliery and its accompanying seven miles of railway. Newspaper reporters did not know what to make of a speech which alternated between extolling the glories of the Dominion and castigating the means used to force Nova Scotia into it. In a spirit of fun George Johnson presented his friend Howe in the garb of a Unionist in an article in the *Reporter*. Howe circulated it among his friends and interpreted the replies to mean that by good management he could win in Hants county as a member of Macdonald's cabinet. Such, says Johnson, was the device which he used to "turn as sharp a corner as he ever turned in his whole political career."[135]

More and more the differences between him and the "locals" were coming into the open. To Howe it appeared from time to time that the *Recorder* and *Chronicle* were publishing slanders "often covertly and sometimes directly aimed at me, the object being to frighten me into silence or make me come into line and favor a delegation ... then they praised me a bit and tried to make the public believe there was no difference between us."[136] He made no reply until John Stiles, writing from Washington under the name "Saxon" (the *British Colonist* called him "the Washington correspondent of the repeal organs of the province"), had a letter published in the New Glasgow *Eastern Chronicle* on October 21 in which he asked if Howe had accepted the situation and suggested that, if repeal could not be secured, complete independence or annexation was not impracticable. That went altogether too far for Howe; at a time when Britain and the United States were well on the way to settling their disputes, could Nova Scotia, he asked, expect assistance from the United States in defying Britain? How easy it would be to seal Nova Scotian ports hermetically! What would happen to Nova Scotia's greatest glory, its fleet of ships? "Are we prepared to lose them?"[137]

In an attempt to patch up the differences Annand, Robertson, and the Pictou assemblyman, Dr George Murray, met with Howe and agreed that the attacks on him would cease, that those Antis who wished might pursue their own repeal policy without him, and that he might receive written submissions from Macdonald and test his sincerity. But the attacks did not stop and when a former judge, the eighty-two-year-old John George Marshall, questioned his dealings with Macdonald and his integrity itself, he thought he would be "a dastard and a fool to allow this system of bullying and defamation to go on."[138] So between November 6 and 27 he wrote five letters which, in attempting to answer Marshall, "Justitia," "Saxon," Annand himself, and others, sought primarily to justify his behaviour to the public.[139] Containing little that was new, they continued to emphasize that nothing he was doing prevented him from advocating or accepting repeal and that in testing the sincerity of the Canadians he was simply attempting to find an alternative to fall back on if the local government failed to secure repeal. He struck a highly sensitive chord in the "locals" when he described their reaction to his proposal at the convention that the Executive Council should resign and along with the Dominion members seek reelection. "Not a man rose to second it, or to give to Nova Scotia her last chance of a peaceful and loyal repeal of the Union." Angry denials followed and a minute of council of November 10 categorically stated that "no proposition in the terms and to the extent mentioned by Mr. Howe was made by that gentleman."

Despite increasing pressure from Macdonald, Howe would not be hurried. The prime minister was mistaken, he said, in assuming that he could lead the Antis as he liked; although he might take office and carry his own county he could "not at present carry the country." Just as Mirabeau "played with a Revolution and lost time till it was too late to save the nation," so Macdonald had lost time in not treating Nova Scotia with the proper spirit and now, after a bad start, his only course was to go as far as he could in allaying discontent.[140] Throughout December, as Howe remained silent, the wheels of fortune turned completely in Macdonald's favour. To the Annand government's minute of council hinting at a change in status for Nova Scotia if repeal should fail, the outgoing colonial secretary, the duke of Buckingham, replied acerbically that, knowing the loyalty of Nova Scotians, he was quite content to let them "determine the circumstances under which they will be disposed to withdraw their allegiance from the British crown, and the means to which they will be prepared to resort for effecting that withdrawal."[141] More to the point, there could be no doubt about the stance of the newly established Gladstone government which, except for John Bright, consisted largely of proponents of Confederation, and Macdonald was already pressing it for a quick statement of its position.

The failure of repeal a foregone conclusion, Howe for all practical purposes "accepted the situation" when he wrote to Macdonald on January 4, 1869. But in telling Sir John that victory was "fairly in the cards," it was not so much a victory for himself and Nova Scotia as for the prime minister who had, in fact, "cut off the tallest head." In two ways Howe indicated his willingness to come to terms: his agreement, in company with McLelan, to meet Sir John Rose at Portland later in the month and his desire to play a major role in awarding the federal patronage in Nova Scotia; it was unwise, he agreed, to "continue the system of giving all places to a minority of the population."[142] Perhaps understandably, an exuberant Macdonald boasted of the "composite measure *per saltum*" he hoped to carry at the next session: "What a glorious programme it would be ... with Nova Scotia pacified, Newfoundland voluntarily joining & the acquisition of Hudson's Bay."[143]

During the preceding three months Howe's patience with the "locals" had been wearing thin and he was now in a position to display his contempt for them. What, he wondered, would they do next? Certainly not engage in a general strike as he had earlier suggested, since that involved sacrifices which he was confident they would not make. Seeing that he was determined to go to Portland, the Dominion MPs E.M. McDonald and A.G. Jones suggested that he take Provincial Secretary Vail with him and thus neutralize and wear down the hostility of the "locals." Having convinced him against his will, they then told him that Vail could go only on the lieutenant-governor's invitation, not on Howe's. The latter's "temper then got up ... if [the local gentlemen] did not choose to accept an invitation merely because it came through his hands, he '*would see them d...d*' before they should get one through any other source."[144] On January 14 he and McLelan went to Portland without Vail and two days later they were on their way to Ottawa where, Howe said, "we shall stay till we have closed up everything. What we do will remain a profound secret till Parliament meets."[145]

By the 28th he reported that negotiations had closed "triumphantly." Not only had a debt of $1,188,750 been wiped out, but $166,734 per annum was to be added to the provincial revenues for ten years, of which "$78,036 per annum is to remain payable forever ... So far so well."[146] What Howe did not say was that the attempt to base the increased payments to Nova Scotia upon equitable considerations had foundered in a welter of calculations and that in the matter of subsidies and debt allowances Nova Scotia had got nothing more than New Brunswick had received in 1867. Nonetheless Howe counted it a real achievement for two reasons. By the standards of the day "better terms" had added substantially to the revenues of the province and by going even as far as he did in breaching the financial terms of Confederation Macdonald was inviting all-out attacks by the Ontario Grits. Meanwhile, on January 13, the Canadian government had learned by telegram that the Gladstone government would entertain no proposals for repeal. On the 30th, the day on which the dispatch arrived in Ottawa, Howe was sworn into the Dominion cabinet as president of the council, even though he had given assurances before leaving home that he would not take office until his friends in Halifax agreed. E.M. McDonald recognized the inevitable: "At first he declined. It was hinted that if he did not go into the govt. Tupper would, and could easily carry Cumberland with 300 or 400 majority. McLellan [*sic*] joined John A. in urging him ... Thus pressed on all sides, he at last gave way."[147]

But were Macdonald and Howe serving even their own best

interests? Had Howe taken the moderate Vail to Portland, the latter might have been persuaded to accept the inevitable and carried others like him; more importantly, had Howe not completed the "better terms" agreement on his own and not entered the cabinet immediately, but instead had returned to Halifax in a conciliatory manner, laid all his cards on the table, argued that he had secured the best possible deal, and at least appeared to let his associates participate in the settlement, he might have won over the moderates and split them off from the extremists. Macdonald, of course, had always overestimated Howe's ability to carry most of the anti-Confederates with him and believed that his "conversion" presaged the end of his own troubles in Nova Scotia. Howe knew it was not so, but, as earlier in his disputes with the Baptists and the Catholics, he had decided that enough was enough, that he would stand no more of inanity, harassment, and blatant self-seeking. He would take the decision by himself and let the Annands, the Marshalls, and the extremist assemblymen do their worst. Unfortunately for him and Macdonald this mode of proceeding ensured that the great bulk of the anti-Confederates would be induced to "accept the situation" only by a process of slow attrition.

Before mid-January the Anti press had got wind of Howe's negotiations and was in full flight against him, "Mr. Sextus Tupper," and "Mr. Tarquinius Macdonald." Under the driving force of A.G. Jones the Nova Scotia Repeal League had come into being by month's end and the *Chronicle* was hoping it would say, "We will not endure Union with Canada, we shall pay no taxes to the Dominion Government, except when we are forced to by the bayonets."[148] Generally Howe was pictured as standing "alone in the silent, gloomy places outside of the pale of popular favour"; even "if he had the lyre of Amphion, or the magical pipe of the Pied Piper of Hamelin," he could not "command a following in Nova Scotia sufficient to justify any one in putting him at the head of a party."[149] That, of course, was the rub. Both Howe and Macdonald had gambled, not only that he could win reelection in Hants, but that he could establish a sufficient Confederate (Conservative) presence to ensure at least a reluctant acceptance of the status quo. To the accomplishment of that objective he would now turn.

## CHAPTER ELEVEN

# Pacifying the Antis

Buoyantly, and "with a very good feeling towards the Union party," Howe returned to Halifax with little delay. In warning him that Parliament might prove balky in dealing with "better terms" if Nova Scotia remained "sulky and recalcitrant," Sir John A. Macdonald had even dared to hope that Annand would at long last submit to the inevitable.[1] But the *Chronicle* quickly dashed his hopes by heaping scorn on Howe, the man who one year would have died for his country on the Tantramar marshes and the next concluded an agreement which, for ten years, would bring the province "the paltry pittance of $67,653, equal to eighteen cents a head of our population." Thinking of the ministerial election he would have to run, the *Recorder* turned poetic: "Oh, Joe, oh, Joe, you'll get your faring / In Hants they'll smoke you like a herring."[2]

For E.M. McDonald, editor of the *Citizen* and Queen's printer, Howe's defection had created an awful dilemma. In Howe he saw occasional rashness and wrongheadedness, but honesty of purpose and energy in action; in Annand insincerity, a wavering imbecility of purpose, and the certain loss of everything. So, behind the scenes, he urged the "locals" to forget about punishing Howe, to accept "better terms" as a first instalment, and to press for additional constitutional changes. Having failed because of "wounded official vanity [and] a stubborn pride in the League," and believing that Howe's defeat would be a disaster to Nova Scotia and that support by the Tory *Colonist* and *Reporter* would do him harm, McDonald concluded that only the *Citizen* would help him "and therefore it must."[3] Yet, knowing that opposition to Annand involved sacrifice for himself and his family, he equivocated for three weeks. When, on March 2, 1869, he came out unambiguously and blamed the carrying of Confederation on Annand's "secret intrigue" with Governor Williams in 1866, retribution was sharp and swift; the next day H.W. Blackadar of the *Recorder* was Queen's printer and sharing the government printing with Annand.[4]

Other than Stairs and Northup, few Halifax notables went along with Howe; the merchants in particular hardened their attitude against him and the Dominion. Doyle could hardly describe the bitter feelings of Howe's old friends, who thought they had been "dragged ... into the mud and left sticking there." If only Howe had taken them into consultation and endeavoured to win them over through conciliation. Almost beseechingly, he begged the prime minister to lend Howe every assistance "'*coute qui coute*,' for, if he is reelected [his enemies] *must* give up the Ghost."[5] Actually Macdonald needed little encouragement; he had invested too much of his time and energy in pacifying Nova Scotia to let it all go for naught, particularly when it might imperil the entire edifice of which he had been the chief architect. His ability over a short time to make himself *au courant* of Nova Scotian politics and politicians, and his skill in forging a united effort from disparate elements simply through correspondence were masterly. Although Tupper's conduct at this juncture was entirely circumspect, McCully and Blanchard, fearful that Howe's election would permit him to "absorb all the patronage," were almost willing to sacrifice him and Nova Scotia. Did they not realize, Macdonald wondered, that if Howe were defeated, the federal government might have to grant the Nova Scotia patronage to Annand and hence "leave the Union Party out in the cold *en permanence*"?[6]

Such were the waters swirling behind the scenes when Howe arrived in Halifax on February 8. Within a few days he had written a lengthy election card for circulation throughout Hants, seeking to justify his conduct by restating the facts as he knew them. To the *Chronicle* he was hard put to "make shabby conduct appear respectable." Why should Nova Scotia accept a one-man arrangement: "we want no Emperor Howe"? Had "the foul vulture ... been turned into a swan by the tip of Howe's wand"?[7] Publicly Howe complained that his enemies had organized Hants against him even before he could explain his conduct; they had, in fact, nominated Monson H. Goudge, a country storekeeper, on February 10, the day before he set foot in the county. At his own organizational meeting he noted the absence of old friends and the presence of new ones. Clearly the electors of Hants, strong in their political loyalties, faced a real dilemma. The old Conservatives were being asked to vote for a man whom many of them believed was "less likely to do right than the devil himself." The old Liberals found it equally hard to support someone whom two years earlier they had elected to "whale Confederates."

Tupper and Confederates could give him little outward help since their very presence in the county would have aroused animosity. Besides, he refused to be indebted to his old rivals: "The lion scorned all aid. It must be Joe Howe that elected Joe Howe, and not Joe Howe and somebody else."[8]

To promote his campaign he used the Hants County *Gazette*, a narrow sheet resembling the program of a boat race with which his journalist aide George Johnson "bombarded the county with ... journalistic pom-pom." The tactics of his opponents became clear in the first public meeting at Windsor on February 13 when they put up Goudge, Jones, and Annand in turn to oppose him and he felt obliged to answer each of them. "Intellectually the labor was not great ... but the hard part of it was, to make three speeches in a cold barn of a Court House and to sit for hours in an atmosphere but a few degrees warmer than that of the street ... Could I stand the strain of this severe work in mid winter?"[9] Time and again his opponents would quote his old speeches at him and he would reply that Tupper could beat them at that kind of game any day. "These [changes of position] continually occur in a free country where men's views must vary with changing circumstances."[10]

Between February 13 and March 2 there was a meeting almost every night in a different polling district, and although he usually had to fight "a whole batch of fellows" all by himself his confidence steadily increased. From Cheverie he wrote to Doyle: "No matter what the enemy says I have taken their measure and *shall beat them handsomely.*"[11] But his opponents' plan to grind him down finally succeeded. At Welsford he found it "terrible work to make two long speeches, of an hour each ... in a large Drill Shed with doors opening at both ends every five minutes." Although his "chest and bronchial tubes felt the strain badly," he went on the next day to Nine Mile River where, unable to endure the pain in his back, he wrapped himself in his sleigh blanket and lay at the back of the platform. To George Johnson it almost seemed as if his "opponents were literally dancing over his prostrate form" and he quickly took advantage of the audience's sympathy when it became his turn to speak. "In a few moments he had by sheer force of will over-come the physical pain he suffered and from being a woe-begone specimen of humanity had become transformed till his face in the excitement shone like an angel's."[12] Then, having "wiped out [his opponents'] slates," he collapsed and lay in a farm house for a week before he could return home for four weeks to recuperate.

Unprecedented snowstorms cut off the "backwoods of Canada" from the outside world for almost a fortnight in late February and early March, but even so Macdonald lost no opportunity to assist Howe. He told Archibald that, although Howe could not "be seen too much in such suspicious company as that of you & Tupper ... where there is a will there is a way to meet!"; at his urging Tupper himself handled Howe's conversion with suitable delicacy in the *Colonist* and Howe happily acknowledged that both Tupper and Archibald had "acted with loyalty & discretion."[13] Macdonald also saw to it that Howe's campaign was adequately financed, urged on all the while by Governor Doyle, who told him bluntly that "nearly 130, if not more, ... will vote for the highest bidder, and the sinews of war ought to be forthcoming." Howe himself stated publicly that the Halifax merchants might try to defeat him by bribery, but that he "could send a telegram which would bring me two pounds – for every one that they can raise" – "an indiscreet speech," Macdonald said, "but as he made it, we must try to justify his statement."[14]

The Antis had at their disposal £2,000 which the merchants had contributed towards the delegates' expenses in 1867 and which the assembly had returned to them. This sum, said Howe, "is now to be solemnly dedicated to my defeat with whatever else they can raise" and "when men are angry they give much more than in their charitable moods."[15] But Macdonald's confidence that his friends in Ottawa and Montreal would counter Howe's enemies "with some liberality" was justified, for Sir John Rose raised $1,425 in Montreal; Macdonald drew $11,575 from the government's secret service fund; and, according to Alexander Mackenzie, a levy of $1,000 was imposed on each cabinet minister. K.G. Pryke estimates that, if Mackenzie was right, Howe's campaign may have cost as much as $30,000, a sum so staggering that Tilley though he might be unseated for bribery.[16]

With Howe's concurrence the 20th of April became the date of by-elections in Hants, Yarmouth, and Richmond.[17] By the 6th he could resume his series of meetings but with a difference. His voice unfit for lengthy public discussion, his friends took up most of "the drudgery of replying to all the windy attacks of the Leaguers emissaries"[18] and he resorted mainly to written attacks upon his worst tormentors: Goudge, "born to measure tapes and laces, not to rule Provinces or to conduct revolutions"; Jones, who at Nine Mile River "stood over me more than an hour declaiming, without having the common decency to enquire if I was ill"; and Annand, who equated patriotism with "trafficking in the Crown Estate, ... getting up bubble companies, and cheating honest people out of their money."[19] The day before the election Boak, West, Duggan, and other Leaguers arrived from Halifax with £1,000, half of it allegedly destined for Maitland. Wanting to prepare Susan Ann for the worst, Howe told her that if the eastern districts broke down under this unprecedented expenditure, she might expect bad news. "Have no fears for me. I am prepared for either result and the minute it is known will smoke a cigar and turn my thoughts to the future with a calm pulse."[20]

He need not have worried. Although his earlier majority was cut, the margin of victory was still a comfortable 383. Within a fortnight he was off to Ottawa, determined, he said, to "do my share of work, and thoroughly master the public business of the Dominion." By May 13 he was participating in debates, though "rather indistinctly ... his voice apparently still weak in consequence of his recent illness."[21] With trepidation he supported the British government's insistence on a salary for the governor general that seemed large compared with the American president's. To the Liberals he pointed out that "a walk up Broadway" would "satisfy any one that they would search there in vain for republican simplicity" of the kind they wanted. Perhaps the Parliament buildings at Ottawa might savour of monarchy, but half the members lived "in lodgings in a style of republican simplicity, which might satisfy almost any one."[22]

By far his greatest difficulty was with the resolutions for Canada's acquisition of the North-West Territories. Alexander Mackenzie, who singled him out as his chief target, argued that one who had strongly opposed this proposition the previous year ought to be excluded from a cabinet which was pursuing it further. Howe replied that the policy had been proceeded with earlier despite his opposition and that he did not hold himself responsible for its adoption at that time. Nor did he accept responsibility for the revolutionary act of Confederation, and "if it were to be made a rule that none of us opposing Confederation ... should ever enter the Cabinet, then Nova Scotia would have very slight representation there."[23] Repeating a long-held view, he contended that parties ought not to be "constant institutions" which bound men in unchanging loyalties in opposition to their consciences. As he saw it, "Parties form and reform, fuse and divide in all free Countries as opinions change, and new issues and exigencies arise." He was certain, too, that "the great Party now forming" in Nova Scotia would govern for some time and "the fools who have tried to crush me, will ... find themselves, before long, crushed under its weight."[24]

In the most contentious measure of all, the provision of "better terms" to Nova Scotia, Howe left the leading role to others because he wanted the act of reparation to be a free-will offering without special pleading on his part. But again Mackenzie led him to intervene by alleging that only one Nova Scotian – Howe himself – had "accepted the situation." Contradicting him, Howe pointed out that as a result of "better terms" most Nova Scotians now felt they "could speak for themselves," unbound by instructions from the Repeal League, and that thousands had "made up their minds to give the dominion a fair trial." To justify his sitting in the same cabinet with those he had accused of "all sorts of crimes," he argued that he needed to give "a guarantee to ministers that he would share the responsibility" of "better terms" and to Parliament that he would use them to win the people over to accepting the new order.[25] Nonetheless, the Ontario Grits gave the government a bad time. "On one division we had but a majority of 19 [even] with 8 Cabinet Ministers and 14 Nova Scotians to vote for them. Had our men remained at home as they were advised to do – or had I not gone into the Cabinet there would not have been a ghost of a chance of getting one Dollar voted."[26]

Sitting in Parliament from four o'clock until midnight, Howe found, was not the best prescription to cure his bronchitis or build up his constitution. His position was rendered all the easier because Macdonald made sure that every promise he had given Howe was honoured. The presidency of the council being a sinecure, he could devote himself to bringing Nova Scotia into line by using patronage to the best advantage. It was the smaller offices, not the judgeships or senatorships, that served his purposes best. His practice was to ask for and accept the recommendations of Nova Scotian MPs for those offices, provided they were reasonably cooperative. Only W.H. Chipman of Kings thoroughly aggravated him; since he had been consulted in the appointment of even the meanest way-office keeper, Howe simply could not understand his hostility, especially as he was not "aware of any thing having been done in [his] County to give offence."[27] Otherwise Howe managed to establish civil relations with most of the Nova Scotians members.

But he could be blunt when he needed to be. He told William Ross, the MP for Victoria, that he could accept no further recommendations for fish wardens, there already being too many, and informed James McKeagney of Cape Breton county that he had already "crowded a great many Nova Scotians" into the Revenue Department and "a dozen old friends [were] wanting places ... that I cannot provide for"; he rejected all objections of civil servants to the low salary scale, pointing out that his son Sydenham had given up a salary of $1,000 to become his secretary at $600. To one who complained that being compelled to live in the woods fifteen miles from civilization prevented his being married, he replied that "the best training for a bride is to rough it in the bush a bit and ... conform to the circumstances in which professional duty places her husband." In one instance he insisted so strongly that the directorship of prisons in Nova

Scotia should go to a Conservative who had supported him vigorously in the by-election but who was unsuited to the position that Macdonald refused to overrule him in favour of the better qualified son-in-law of Charles Tupper.[28]

Missing nothing the Antis did at the spring session of the Nova Scotia legislature, he congratulated Amos Purdy, a deserter from their ranks, for having "badgered them right well": it only needed "two or three more good fellows at your back to whip them out of their 'boots'."[29] He also praised Doyle for cramming the "Lumps of loyalty" down the Antis' throats and for making them "more supremely ridiculous." But Doyle spurned any suggestions that he take "energetic measures" to overthrow the government, since he had no constitutional reason to dismiss it and since Howe's victory had permitted the governor to *"speak out"* in terms he had hitherto dared not use. "I *complimented* them upon the *Patriotic* fight they had made! and asked them what move they now had, except to take Nova Scotia from General Doyle, which they knew they *could* not do, or to get the Yankees to help them, which they were quite aware meant war with England."[30] A little later the prime minister, intent on breaking up the Antis, again broached the possibility of appointing Martin Wilkins to the bench. Would he not, if he "took the shilling," lose any "objection to play our game here"?[31] But neither Howe nor any other Unionist wanted to go that far.

A fortnight of complete rest following the session of 1869 made "a new man" of Howe and brought back "a good deal of the fun and deviltry which used to inhabit this tenement of clay." It also revived his old zest to see new things and new places, this time "the leading features of Ontario."[32] But Sir John had other plans for him, the assumption of the secretaryship of state for the provinces and a major responsibility for the transfer of the North-West Territories and the establishment of Manitoba as a province. Pleased with the change from a sinecure to an office of importance, he started out in mid-August, on his own initiative, for the North-West, which nobody in the Macdonald cabinet had yet visited. "To a degree it was right, to a degree ironical," suggests W.L. Morton, "that the first champion of 'provincial rights' in the history of the Dominion" should be given his new responsibilities; jokingly Howe said he wanted to find out "if there were jobs for Nova Scotians out there."[33] As usual, the *Chronicle* turned its choicest sarcasm on him. At a time when the governor general was to visit Halifax, Howe had gone to Thunder Bay. "Joseph lost his pluck when he turned his coat. He had no mind to face the terrible merchants of Halifax, who had injured him so much."[34] On

September 19 he wrote optimistically that he was sixty miles west of St Cloud, Minnesota, and hoping to reach the Red River at Abercrombie, North Dakota, three days later.[35] But he was twenty-two days out of St Cloud before he finally got to Fort Garry in the second week of October, for, despite the stout Canadian horses, the summer floods had soaked the prairies badly and prolonged the trip. Fortuitously for him, as it turned out, he had become well acquainted with six young Canadian business men under E. Sanford, all bound for the Red River. Even at Abercrombie, 315 miles distant from Fort Garry, Howe and his party had heard rumours that William McDougall, named to be the first lieutenant-governor of Manitoba, would not be allowed to enter the territory, but they themselves were everywhere received courteously and hospitably.

At Fort Garry Howe declined every invitation of accommodation, wanting above all to retain a completely independent position. It did not take him long to size up Dr J.C. Schultz and his "Canadian Party," and the deep suspicion with which they were viewed by the Indians and half-breeds. Schultz's group, he concluded, were the same kind of "loyal people" who, in times past in Nova Scotia and the Canadas, had "claimed all the loyalty, all the intelligence and all the respectability, and held that the masses of the people counted for nothing"; like their counterparts they had also "assumed all the airs of the superior race."[36] Painstakingly he talked to the leading men of every interest so far as he could ascertain them. Discovering to his surprise that not one Canadian privy councillor had ever seen or read the records of the colony's council, the governing body of the district of Assiniboia, he spent two days digesting them. Because Ottawa had no copies of the colony's statutes, he took copies back for the minister of justice and the cabinet.

Though uninformed at the outset, he was "not long in ascertaining that all was not so serene" as had been supposed.[37] He left Governor William MacTavish of the Hudson's Bay Company with the impression that he was a "shrewd clear headed man" who "very soon made out his whereabouts" and would be "able to set some of his colleagues right in their ideas about Red River."[38] While still at Fort Garry, he told Macdonald that his visit had been "opportune and useful," that he had "cleared the air a good deal" and dispelled "any amount of absurd rumours ... I have done my best to give McDougall a fair start. All will now depend on his tact, temper and discretion."[39] On the return journey, marked by "bitter cold weather and much exposure," he met McDougall and his party east of Georgetown, Minnesota, "facing sleet and wind enough to cut their throats."[40] Nonetheless, he would later have to defend himself for not taking time to enlighten

McDougall on the situation he would face. Amazing to him was the great cavalcade of carriages and the number of women and children in McDougall's train. To Howe it appeared as if he was going out as "a great satrap paying a visit to his Province, with an amount of following, a grandeur of equipage and a display of pomp that was enough to tempt the cupidity of all the half-breeds in the country ... That, I say, was his first blunder, and a great blunder it was."[41]

To assist McDougall, Howe did elaborate in detail his impressions of the various elements of the Red River society in a letter from St Paul on October 31. The new governor, he suggested, should not patronize Dr Schultz, Charles Mair, the exponent of Canada First, and their "little clique of persons at war with the more influential elements of society." But the Canadians generally, if treated fairly, could be used to form the basis of his government until immigration added to their numbers. It was to be hoped that the half-breeds, if counselled wisely by their priests, could also be incorporated into the political system; in the case of the Indians, however, because they repudiated any suggestion of the land being sold by the Hudson's Bay Company, it might be necessary to conclude some form of treaty.[42]

Unfortunately for Howe, he was having to deal with a man whom G.F.G. Stanley suggests might purposely have been chosen had Canada wanted to stir up trouble in the North-West. "Cold and intractable in his dealings with his colleagues, McDougall was not the man to handle a difficult situation with patience and understanding ... He did not know the half-breeds at all."[43] On the very day Howe wrote to him, he was blocked at the American border by Métis organized by Riel. On receiving the news, Howe advised him to exercise his judgment as circumstances dictated and warned him that he was in no position to exercise legal authority until he had received a proclamation formally annexing the territory.[44] Told by McDougall that Fort Garry was in Riel's hands, Howe replied that the matter had been referred to the British government and in the meantime he was to avoid collision with the insurgents and not to violate the neutrality laws of the United States.[45] Already McDougall was finding villains in Governor MacTavish, whom he accused of "weakness and imbecility," and in some of his councillors, suspected by him of complicity in the insurrection.[46] On December 7 Howe told him that the government was sending the Rev. J.B. Thibault and Charles de Salaberry to help put down the "unlawful assemblage" on the Red River and obtain access for the Canadian authorities, and that Donald Smith, the Hudson's Bay agent at Montreal, would go out as a special commissioner to help MacTavish restore order at Fort Garry. Meanwhile the authority of the Hudson's Bay Company would remain unimpaired.[47]

Only after sending this letter did Howe receive McDougall's of November 20, which once again castigated the local authorities for failing to establish communication with him. But of immensely more import to Howe was the charge that his "remarks, while at Fort Garry, are repeated from mouth to mouth, and construed into an approval of [the insurgents'] present attitude of 'resistance to tyranny,' and defence of their rights."[48] Indignantly Howe denied that he had ever said anything which would countenance breaches of the law or prevent the establishment of the Dominion's authority. At no time had he even seen Riel, Father Ritchot, or anyone connected with the insurrection, and everywhere he had given assurances that the colony would shortly be granted provincial status and its young men be drawn without distinction of blood into the federal public service.[49]

Meanwhile McDougall was making blunder after blunder. On December 1 he issued a proclamation announcing the transfer of the territory to Canada and his appointment as lieutenant-governor, a document that was both worthless and illegal; a little later he issued a commission to Col. John Dennis to raise a force to put down the insurrectionists, a mission beyond that officer's power to fulfil. A horrified Howe could only tell him that none of these acts had been authorized and might have brought in the Indians with "fearful consequences." Accordingly his duty was plain: to exercise no authority in the name of the Dominion and to remain in Pembina until he had been ordered to assume the government.[50] Early in 1870 McDougall was back in Ottawa in disgrace. But he would have his innings too.

After mid-January George Brown and the *Globe*, strongly siding with Dr Schultz and the Canadian party, put the blame for the Red River disaster generally upon the government and specifically upon Howe. Throughout the colony, they said, he had exhorted all and sundry to stand out against the introduction of Canadian rule until they could make good terms as the price of their consent.[51] In Nova Scotia the Liberal press had a field day at Howe's expense. "Treachery," it said, summed him up; he was "just the man" to attempt the mischief of which he had been accused. His "chaff" might well have helped to promote the Red River insurrection: "he nearly raised a rebellion in Nova Scotia, talked rhodomontade about dying in a mud puddle, and then shirked off to the government camp and sold himself. The old fellow will get his due yet."[52] While William McDougall was feeding his grievances to the *Globe* in three public letters, Howe was telling the prime minister that McDougall's attempt to clear himself by putting the blame for his failure on "any and every body that he can with any colour of pretence" was only natural in "a man of his temperament" and that "the absurd stories published in the 'Toronto Globe,' originated in [his] loose and unguarded utterances." The failing of the cabinet, if any, was to have placed "too great a reliance on [his] foresight and discretion"; if a "conspiracy" against the government of Canada had existed in the Red River colony, McDougall should have discovered it since he had had his officers working there all the previous summer.[53]

Fortunately for Howe he had any number of witnesses to refute the charge that he had been "uttering all sorts of treason in some mysterious way." At his hotel in Fort Garry he shared the one parlor with the Canadian businessmen, Sanford and Turner, and had had little private conversation, "nine out of ten times these two gentlemen being present ... and heard every word he spoke."[54] Similarly, as he travelled through the colony, his driver Alcock was privy to his conversation with all sorts of people. So, when the Toronto *Globe* published a biting editorial against Howe on January 17, Turner gave "a flat and unqualified denial" to any suggestion that he had uttered disloyal sentiments or given encouragement to the disaffected to resist union with Canada. When George Brown (Howe called him "the mean son of a gun") not only refused to print Turner's letter but followed up his first editorial with a stronger second one, Turner had his reply published in the Hamilton *Spectator* of January 19. In thanking him, Howe ventured the opinion that the "lies, made out of whole cloth, have come out of Schultz & Morris nest of worthies."[55]

Once again, the allegations against Howe were unending but he always had his defendants. The "old fellow" Alcock published the names of Howe's travelling companions and the persons he visited to demonstrate that no one would have ventured to talk treason in their presence, while Sanford and Captain Kennedy sent letters to a somewhat relenting Brown vindicating Howe's conduct in specific instances.[56] Late in February, in the Commons, Howe denied that he had used a single expression that could be construed as an invitation to insurrection. Nor should anyone blame him for not halting "on the open prairie that bitter morning" to hold a lengthy conversation with McDougall: "when there were women and children concerned, it would have been barbarous to have stopped the cavalcade." Besides, "looking back at all that he had done," he did not think things would have been "much better if they had stopped for an hour or two."[57]

Later in the session, when Howe was forced to defend more than once the government's policy on Manitoba,[58] he could not avoid dealing with further accusations against himself, including one that he had drunk champagne with Riel: "I never saw Riel in all my life, and I never drank champagne either with him or with anybody at Red

River. In fact, I do not believe that there was a bottle of champagne in the Territory fit to drink." When Alexander Mackenzie – again seeming to delight in harsh treatment of Howe – called Sanford "a Yankee annexationist," Howe insisted that "every word" and "every thought" of his companion had indicated "a warm regard" for Canada's interests in the North-West. To charges that he himself had pulled down "the British flag or somebody's flag with 'Canada' upon it" he indignantly replied that he had neither torn it down nor ordered anyone else to do it.

To Howe it was more than a little astounding that Brown and Mackenzie should take McDougall, Schultz, and the "loyalist party" of the Red River as the special objects of their admiration; it was even amusing that they praised McDougall, who only a year earlier had been their bête noire for having deserted the Liberal party in 1867. For them he had the medicine to set them writhing. Riel, he said, might be "a bar-room loafer," but he had "brains enough to coop [the loyalist party] up in [Schultz's] house, and then to drive them into Fort Garry like a flock of sheep ... with all their professions of loyalty not one of them fired a shot for Canada." Yet these were the men whom McDougall wanted to put in his council, while leaving out the descendants of the original settlers of the soil – a veritable "act of madness." Proudly Howe declared that he could put his public dispatches in a brief pamphlet and bequeath them to his children as "honourable testimony of the way in which their father acted in these trying, harassing and difficult circumstances."

For a time, in Howe's words, the government had "rocks, shoals and quicksand all around us," made all the worse by the passions aroused in Ontario by the murder of Thomas Scott and by the breakdown of Sir John A. Macdonald. But in his time of trouble, all the Nova Scotian MPs "acted like bricks" and the opposition made it rather easy for him: although the government was highly vulnerable on at least two points – its ignorance, largely through its own failing, of the actual state of affairs on the Red River and the appointment of so unsuitable a person as governor – Mackenzie and the Grits chose not to concentrate on them. "My speech," wrote Howe, "knocked McDougall off his legs, and ... his own measure in opposition to us ... was beaten by a decisive majority of 120 to 11."[59] Not yet finished, McDougall shortly published "a masterpiece of invective" in the form of eight letters addressed to Howe, whom he called "the chief abettor, if not the chief instigator" of the Red River insurrection.[60] Fortunately for Howe, few took McDougall seriously. It may have been suspected, and rightly too, that Howe had told the discontented to use the same constitutional means he had always employed to remove ills. But neither Macdonald nor any of his party gave the slightest credence to McDougall's arraignment of him, nor do present-day historians like Stanley and Morton. "Howe, who might have done much to check the Canadian expansion he had once opposed," writes Morton, "loyally sought to prepare a peaceful way for it. He had made his bargain in January 1869, and he kept it."[61] All too obviously, the charges against Howe were originally the concoctions of Schultz and "the loyalist party," who, spurned, sought revenge on the one who had spurned them.

For Howe the trip to the North-West had far-reaching consequences of another kind. He had forgotten he was "no longer a Boy" and that his "constitution of iron" was beginning to fail.[62] His voice barely lasted out the session and he ended it excessively fatigued. Though quickly recovering, he was never the same again. For the rest of 1870 he kept careful watch over the North-West, but his problems eased after May when A.G. Archibald became lieutenant-governor of Manitoba and used his good common sense to bring calm to the new province. On Howe's instructions he prepared a land settlement plan for consideration by the cabinet. Only once did Howe become a little perturbed, but, as he expected, the report that Archibald had issued warrants against Riel and O'Donoghue with orders to shoot if they resisted proved to be unfounded.[63] Howe's portfolio including oversight of the Indians, his Nova Scotian opponents were highly amused when he intervened in a dispute between the Indians of Caughnawaga and the white residents of the area. "Mr. Howe is to go to Caughnawaga as the great pacificator, to smoke the pipe of peace with his Indian brethren. At last he has found a chance for glory."[64]

To get Nova Scotia to accept the new order remained Howe's first concern. As part of the Confederation agreement, the Dominion government had taken over the Nova Scotia Railway (Halifax to Windsor, Truro, and Pictou), and towards the end of 1869 he became alarmed at a mounting series of protests when its new general superintendent, the New Brunswicker Lewis Carvell – a businessman and not a politician – raised its carrying charges sufficiently to meet both the operating expenses and the interest on the original cost. Nova Scotians demanded that the lines they had built themselves should be run, "not as a work commercially profitable, but as a special cheap convenience to the people who use it."[65] Thinking "the best answer he could give ... was to get Carvell out," Howe had managed it by mid-January 1870; he had also seen to it that "half the increased tolls put on the Waggons [were] to come off and arrangements ... made to carry freights at cheap [rates] from Richmond into the City."[66]

But patronage remained his handiest weapon to get the Nova Scotian MPs to give reasonable support to the government. Senior appointments to the judiciary were somewhat troublesome, since so many of the MPs were lawyers and only two vacancies existed. Howe could easily satisfy A.W. Savary of Digby, who recognized his lack of seniority and who wanted only to be assured that Stewart Campbell with his small practice and little reading in the law did not get one of them. Howe also gave little consideration to James McKeagney, the member for Cape Breton county, an unending searcher after patronage and borrower from him to the extent of £30 or £40 – "see what it is to be poor!!" As usual, he paraded before Howe his contribution to the party in eight elections and the gratification his appointment would give to Nova Scotia's 80,000 Catholics. Howe was much more taken with Hugh McDonald of Antigonish, his companion in London in 1866–7, whose knowledge of the law put McKeagney to shame and whose influence among eastern mainland Catholics was undoubted.[67] So, although Howe told the minister of justice, Sir George-Etienne Cartier, that Senators J.W. Ritchie and Jonathan McCully, one a Conservative and the other a Liberal Confederate, would make excellent judges, he also asked him to keep in mind McDonald, whose religious group had never got an appointment to the Supreme Court even though it controlled the elections in two eastern counties and largely influenced the results in four others. Ritchie and McCully secured the judgeships, but Sir John A. Macdonald himself gave an assurance that McDonald would not be forgotten in the event of another vacancy.[68] When McCully thanked Howe for overlooking their recent estrangement, the latter replied he had no personal feelings to indulge: "we had a good deal that was pleasant to remember and whatever there was of an opposite character it was a duty to forget."[69] The handling of the judgeships probably contributed little to making Nova Scotia rest more easily in the Canadian federation, but at least they were dealt with in a manner which prevented rifts with the MPs and hence a setback in reconciliation.

In dealing with the smaller offices Howe had much more positive results in 1870. Simply stated, his policy was to treat the Anti members fairly, "hoping to bring them all right." In January he gave Alexander Campbell, the postmaster general, the names of ten Nova Scotian MPs whose advice on appointments he might take without reference to himself.[70] By the year's end, apart from Isaac Le Vesconte of

Richmond, who was drunk more often than not and hence unreliable, all but three were giving the government "fair support." The exceptions were James Carmichael of Pictou, always extreme and now almost openly annexationist; the unbending A.G. Jones of Halifax; and the running mate whom he influenced, Patrick Power. The result was to ease Howe's own burden since he simply referred an applicant to his own MP: "as Representative of the County the place is at [his] disposal." He still had to deal with office-seekers from Hants and when necessary he did not pull his punches. To one who acted as if Howe had personal knowledge of his capabilities for all sorts of employment he replied bluntly: "I have no such knowledge." Sometimes he simply said he had "no chance to employ one out of twenty of those who apply."[71] To supplicants generally he made it clear he would be no party to breaking established procedures, especially in the awarding of contracts. "They are not given as a matter of grace and favour, but invariably to the Lowest Tender ... If Grant's tender is the lowest he will get the contract as a matter of course. If not I could not give it to him if he was my own Brother." Though he was prepared to assist those who supported the new political combination, "I abhor the system of turning poor devils out of office, which has disgraced both parties in Nova Scotia."[72]

In addition to patronage, Howe also had help from the Ontario Grits, albeit unwittingly. Annoyed to the teeth because Edward Blake had insisted that Nova Scotia's "better terms" were a final settlement, the *Chronicle* told the Nova Scotia members to be "careful ere they discharge King Wolf, that King Tiger is not about to mount his throne."[73] The new climate in Nova Scotia was evidenced in the results of federal by-elections. In September 1869 Archibald had no difficulty in being elected in Colchester;[74] in May 1870 L.DeV. Chipman, returned for Kings as an Anti in his father's place, declared he would go to Ottawa "untrammelled" and prepared to serve Nova Scotia's best interests; and in July Tupper was returned for Cumberland by acclamation after his appointment to the cabinet. To crown it all, in November F.M. Pearson defeated an out-and-out Anti, perhaps even annexationist, in Colchester and though nominally an Anti himself, he went to Ottawa with perfect freedom to support the Dominion government.

Later in 1870 a provincial by-election in Halifax which pitted the Confederate Philip Carteret Hill against William Garvie caused Howe much soul-searching. From the outset he advised against "getting drawn into a heavy contest" which Hill could not win "unless Old [Enos] Collins shells out in power of money."[75] Personally he refused to interfere because of the services and sympathy which Garvie had accorded him for four or five years. Although Garvie too was somewhat restrained, he insisted on holding Howe responsible for "his dogs," Northup and E.M. McDonald, who, he alleged, hounded him throughout the county.[76] When Garvie lost by fourteen votes, Howe could not help feeling sorry for him even though he had "acted like an Ass" and considered "abuse of old friends ... a sure Card."[77] For the merchants Duffus, Boak, and Esson he had no sympathy at all. "They have found out that money is not brains. Annand has used and humbugged them all and no wonder now that they are savage."[78] A little philosophically he conceded that a handful of votes could have defeated the Confederates and caused them to lose much of the prestige gained by their federal victories. Nonetheless, "we have run six elections, in five large central Counties, and my Compromise and action in 1868 has been sustained, though all the influence of the Local Government has been exerted against me."[79] To him obvious signs of the enemy's demoralization were the *Eastern Chronicle*'s criticism of the provincial government for not taking his advice in 1868 to "*stop the Executive Machinery*" and the Antigonish *Casket*'s comment that Annand and Wilkins could not elect a man from one end of Nova Scotia to the other.[80] For the return of comparatively normal conditions in provincial politics he could claim more than a little of the credit. More and more he was becoming convinced that his policy of maintaining a reasonable rapport with the Dominion members while letting the "locals" stew in their frustration would win out in the end. For the Anti members to give a "fair support" to the Macdonald administration in return for the disposition of patronage automatically meant a separation of sorts from the "locals," and for their followers to turn to them for Dominion offices meant an ever-widening acceptance of the federal régime.

Into Howe's own life also came greater tranquillity than he had enjoyed for a long time. To him it was a pity that finally, when he had time to devote to his family, he saw little of them. Ellen, married to the capable Cathcart Thomson, lived in Halifax, but Howe could at least make good use of him and Northup as his unofficial agents there. Sydenham, "having proved his capacity up here" and after recently marrying his cousin Fanny McNab, had returned to Halifax to take charge of the accounts of the Maritime Provinces for the federal Department of Finance. Bill, "a very fine fellow, ... steady and industrious," was serving as Howe's private secretary, but Joe and Fred were still causing him concern. The former had quit the sea and for the moment was roughing it in the bush on Manitoulin Island and supporting himself; Fred had returned from the United States and was working for the Grand Trunk at Sarnia for $400 a year, just enough to live on, but with a hope of promotion.[81] By the end of 1870 Susan Ann, with her husband's help, had completed furnishing their modest house at the corner of Queen and Metcalfe streets and he reported "Mother ... once more surrounded by her own traps, which are all good of their kind without being extravagant."[82] They went out little in society, but spent their evenings reading, he taking ten or twelve volumes at a time from the Parliamentary Library. When tired of that, they played whist or backgammon. Late in June they left for an extended stay in Nova Scotia, his mouth "beginning to water already at the thought of the Cods Heads and Shoulders and Broiled Haddocks" that he intended to devour.[83] Essentially it was a time of meeting old friends with little intervention in politics. As the year ended, the Howes had Christmas dinner and parties for Nova Scotians in Ottawa, but he would much "rather have had [his] children and grandchildren around an old fashioned Plum Pudding."[84]

At about the same time he was offering a loan to his niece Sarah, Jane's daughter, who was proposing to open a bookstore at Digby in the spring. "I would make it a gift but Aunt's future is yet very uncertain, and I have never been able to save enough to make it secure." When an acquaintance in Halifax died with "a pile of money," he would say ruefully: "What a 'good old gentlemanly vice' avarice is. I fear it is too late in the day for me to take to it."[85] Almost too late he was taking whatever steps he could to put his finances in order. With care he and Susan Ann had set themselves up in Ottawa without incurring any debt; besides, he had paid back in full the money he had borrowed years ago from James McNab. Through Northup he also put the screws on Annand – "the rascal deserves no forbearance at the hands of either of us"[86] – and, perhaps to their surprise, got $1,368 almost at once and a promise of the balance of $500 shortly.

During the winter of 1870–1 Howe took extremely good care of himself, "getting along in the old way ... one day ... like another – Work, Dinner, Backgammon, a Walk, a Cigar & Book & Bed."[87] Although he had given up concerts, lectures, and balls, he occasionally accepted an invitation to dinner and, to repay their hosts and hostesses, he and Susan Ann had a dinner party of their own on their forty-third wedding anniversary, their most cheerful in years. Among the guests were a Chipewyan clergyman, who said grace in Indian, and a grandson of Joseph Brant, who spoke six or seven languages. To add to his pleasure, he occasionally had Northup send him a few dozen of his port wine and Bauld and Gibson's whole rum; once he requested a few of the largest codfish in the market: "We get no fish here but Haddock, which in winter are earthy and not fit to eat."[88]

As the session of 1871 approached, he felt in better health than he had in the past two years. But he had no illusions about his prospects: "I shall never have the strength I had, but by husbanding what is left may work on for a few years."[89] Even if the spirit was willing, he made little contribution to the session's debates. Two of his infrequent interjections were aimed at A.G. Jones, whose antipathy for him seemed to increase with time; why, he wondered, should Jones "bring up day after day, topics which were only calculated to create irritation, without doing good." Once his tormentor Alexander Mackenzie "made a stab at his vacant chair" by repeating a traitorous remark he was alleged to have made in the North-West, but he simply called it "a low invention and a disreputable falsehood," and let it go at that.[90]

More and more the limits of his physical endurance were being brought home to him. In the closing weeks the midnight sessions of the Commons helped to bring on a "frightful cold" which laid him low for a fortnight. Yet he enjoyed vicariously the government's successes to which he had contributed little. Gleefully he wrote of the "woeful thrashing" of the opposition by ninety-one to thirty-five on the session's first vote of nonconfidence. Even better, the only Nova Scotians to vote against the government were Jones and Carmichael – a clear sign that the province had taken another step towards full pacification.[91] No less satisfying to him was "the marriage of British Columbia with Canada"; never, he said, was "a measure of so much magnitude and importance ... carried in so short a time by a small body of gentlemen working together so unostentatiously and with perfectly good faith." By June eight to ten survey parties were already at work and he had taken steps to begin the geological survey of the province.[92] Regretfully, he admitted, speakers other than he had had to carry the bill through Parliament.

Most of Howe's departmental duties during 1871 had to do with Archibald and Manitoba. Almost imploringly, Howe enjoined the lieutenant-governor not to treat with Riel in any way; he also tried to get him the kind of military force he needed: "a small mounted corps ... who can go rapidly about if wanted." No more than before did he believe that a through railway to Manitoba was a possibility, but he looked to one beginning at Pembina that would connect with the American roads.[93] Twice he expressed regret at Archibald's actions. Once it was because he was apparently giving countenance to the wholesale appropriation of large tracts of land by the half-breeds. The regulations, Howe reminded him, prevented anyone from securing more than 160 acres without special permission.[94] Much more worrisome was the renewal of the Fenian raids, and he was greatly relieved when an invasion by Riel's co-conspirator, W.B. O'Donoghue, was quickly defeated and O'Donoghue himself captured. But the incident brought even greater worries. Riel had chosen the opportunity to assemble an "army of observation," apparently ready to fall upon the rear of the Canadian forces if O'Donoghue was successful. Howe's reports were that Archibald had overlooked Riel's strange conduct and had actually shaken hands with him. Did he not appreciate that "murder is murder any where, and [Riel's] taking of human life [in the case of Thomas Scott] without any paramount necessity and in cold blood, is rarely pardoned without atonement by a civilized community"? Did he not realize it had thrown the powerful Orange organization of Ontario, upon which so much of Macdonald's support rested, into a frenzy for almost two years? Could he not see that the sequel would be angry debate in Parliament and a likely defection of Ontario members?[95]

Not at all satisfied with Archibald's explanation that Riel and his men had been "euchred," Howe read him a lesson on the political facts of life. Riel's game, he said, was "neither to fight, nor to join O'Donague [sic]. It was to shake hands with the governor, and force an Amnesty." Surely it was folly to talk about the magnanimous treatment of political offenders in England; "we have hardly got to this elevation of sentiment in Canada." Even so, Canada had been highly generous in its handling of the North-West and its troublemakers: "we have given the Community a free Constitution, and to the Half Breeds a million and a half of land, and all this in less than a year after the outbreak." Indeed, so much had been overlooked that Edward Blake and the Ontario Liberals had swept to victory because of the failure to punish the Red River offenders; likely they would introduce a resolution condemning Archibald's actions in the Ontario House and carry it without opposition. Sir John Macdonald even believed that his Ontario members would desert him en masse in a similar vote; worse still, the effect might be disastrous for the Conservatives in the next federal election.[96] Come what may, however, Howe had decided he would contest that election if the people of Hants wanted him; by that time, he hoped, Blake's government would have had "six months to commit mistakes and disappoint supporters, and long before that we may be stronger than we think."[97]

Though he had no part in its negotiations, Howe found the Washington Treaty of 1871 highly disturbing, confirming as it did his complete loss of faith in the current crop of British politicians. More and more he wondered if it was worth while being part of the empire.

Britain's determination to settle the *Alabama* claims, he thought, had led to a complete sacrifice of Canadian interests. Not only had the Americans avoided compensating Canada for its losses in the Fenian raids, but they had won the right to use the Canadian fisheries in return for free trade in fish and monetary compensation, and not the wider reciprocal trading privileges that Howe had wanted. To Sir John Rose he intimated that he had expected British politicians to buy their peace at Canada's expense. "Bit by bit England gives North America away, and the feeling is becoming widespread here that the sooner we join that Branch of the British family that is not afraid of the other the better for us all." Even with the governor general he did not mince his words, calling the conduct of the British commissioners and the imperial government "hasty, selfish and unfair ... almost ... pusilanimous."[98]

Even the reaction in Nova Scotia was highly disappointing to him. From "Ned" McDonald he learned that, because of the free trade in fisheries, not five merchants in Halifax were opposed to the treaty and Patrick Power was actually hoping for a fall session and early ratification so that fishermen and fish dealers could benefit quickly from the American market.[99] Surprised and disconcerted, Howe replied that, whatever the reaction of the fishing trade, the agricultural, coal, and lumber counties could not possibly sustain the treaty. But when he sounded out the other Nova Scotian MPs he got anything but the unequivocally negative response he hoped for, except perhaps from Coffin of Shelburne, who complained because Canadian rights were being treated as an equivalent for the *Alabama* depredations with which Canadians had nothing to do. Dr Forbes of Queens wrote of "a feeling of indifference upon Dominion questions" and Dr Cameron of Inverness knew little of the treaty except what he read casually in the press; Killam of Yarmouth supported it wholeheartedly; Le Vesconte of Richmond thought it was "not all we had a right to expect, still it is better than none"; Hugh McDonald of Antigonish was dissatisfied, but would "make some sacrifice before seeing you defeated."[100] Clearly no concerted opposition to the treaty would emerge in Nova Scotia and by the end of 1871 Howe was left with only the faint hope that Congress might make changes in the tariff favourable to Canada. "But I have no faith in the rascals, and they may, as they did last year, ... fall back upon their old duties."[101]

Politically Nova Scotia continued to show movement in Howe's direction during 1871. Although a contributed editorial in the *Chronicle* declared that "manifest destiny" decreed the province's "absorption into the United States by voluntary annexation, or by harsher means," Doyle noted that his advisers had permitted more loyal sentiment than usual in the Speech from the Throne and even the word "Dominion," to which hitherto "they never would allow the *slightest reference* to be made."[102] Nonetheless, when the Antis called an election for May 16, the *British Colonist* said disdainfully that their basic principles were "'eternal hate' to Canada; detestation of Canada; 'stubborn unyielding resistance to Canada'."[103] As usual, Howe had any number of invitations to participate, but declined, knowing that a public campaign in the open air would completely "knock me up." But to those who had "defamed" him for nearly three years, including some "who would never have been anything but for [his] assistance," he promised a lesson in better manners.[104]

It took the form of five letters addressed to the people of Nova Scotia from Ottawa, timed for late April and early May to achieve maximum benefit in the election.[105] The first two gave "a skinning" to Annand, Wilkins, and "the little knot of worthies" who had taken liberties with him in his absence. Although most industrious men of his own age were affluent, even "rolling in wealth," he had never bought an acre of land nor invested a pound for his family, never trafficked in gold mines or timber lands, never enriched himself by abusing the knowledge he possessed. If, however, he sifted through Annand's gold mining, coal mining, and public printing operations and could not show he had abused his trust as a public officer, "then my pen is naught." As for Wilkins, he had accepted the prothonotary-ship and could "pass the rest of his days in swearing witnesses to do what he never did himself – 'to tell the truth, the whole truth, and nothing but the truth'." As for minor worthies like Thomas Morrison and Jared C. Troop, they had "not sixpence-worth of patriotism or honour to divide among them" and were elected only "on the strength of a tide-wave which not a man of them had the ability to create." Clearly Howe's diminished physical strength had not weakened his power of invective. Although the third and fourth letters effectively showed up as "buncombe" Annand's charges that he had advocated "but feebly the anti-confederate cause," the fifth was much less successful in demonstrating that he had not taken the negotiations for better terms unfairly out of Annand's hands.

Nothing better illustrated the whirligig of Nova Scotia politics than the fact that the *British Colonist* and *Express*, a little earlier the critics of Howe's every political act, published these letters between April 24 and election day. The *Colonist* exulted that "the lash of their old master touches the Annandites to the quick," while the *Express* was certain that the letters would "quicken that process of dissolution that has been going on among the Anti-Confederates." In their turn, the *Citizen* – no longer edited by "Ned" McDonald – scorned Howe's writing as the "last infirmity of [a] noble mind" and the *Chronicle* called him "A Voice from the Grave." Later, in much nastier vein, it published three letters of "Nemesis," which accused him of being as "prodigal of his principles as of his Bank Notes ... Is it any wonder ... that in consummating ... treachery, his health gave way?"[106] Howe thought of replying, but gave up the idea when the election results exceeded his highest hopes. The election of thirteen Conservatives, up from two, meant that Annand would be kept in line in the next assembly. Even more satisfying to Howe, the electors had got rid of all "the wild men" who had been pushing Annand to extremes. "Dr. Murray, who could not hear the answer to a plain question put by himself in the Convention will have time now to improve his hearing, and Dr. Brown, Dickie, Chambers, Kidston, Ryerson and others are properly punished for their folly." In Hants he was delighted to see "those ungrateful rascals Lawrence and Young on the flat of their backs." What would Elkanah Young do with his "figured waistcoat" now?[107]

For Howe the election brought indignant letters from his supporters in Nova Scotia protesting that federal MPs who had been granted the disposition of patronage had worked to reelect the Annand government. But he remained adamant that he could not dictate their conduct in the provincial elections and that as long as they gave a "fair support" to the federal government, he could not refuse to "consult them about the patronage of their counties whether they came from Ontario, Quebec, or Nova Scotia."[108] Pryke suggests that the campaign "clearly indicated that the 'better terms' agreement of 1869, which Macdonald had promoted as a means of cementing a coalition between the confederates and the 'compromisers,' was not working as anticipated" and that the practical result of the agreement was to "prevent the federal party from taking any concerted action in provincial politics."[109] But it is highly doubtful that Macdonald, and even more so that Howe, viewed their relationship with the Anti MPs as a coalition in the sense that Professor Pryke conceives it or, in fact, as a coalition at all. Certainly for Howe the election results meant that the pacification of Nova Scotia was practically complete. With most of its federal members giving a "fair support" to the government, "we can afford to laugh at all the rest."[110]

In other respects patronage followed the usual routine in 1871. The lengths to which applicants went to press their claims never ceased to amaze Howe. One got old Admiral Westphal on the Isle of Wight to forward his application; another had testimonials sent from all over the world recommending him for an office for which Parliament had not even provided the money. For Howe it was burden enough to have to make appointments in Hants, to the departments in Ottawa, and to senior offices such as judgeships, and a relief not to have to deal with the other Nova Scotian counties. Delightedly, and despite the railings of the locals, he had named to the Senate the old Tory Ezra Churchill, who had fought for him "like a brick" in the Hants by-election.[111] The $250-a-year lighthouse keeper's position at Burntcoat, because it afforded "a capital chance to make a farm" at the same time, elicited an incredible number of applicants and in desperation he left it to "Ned" O'Brien, his agent in Hants county, to make a recommendation. Without anyone's advice he sought an office for a cousin of Susan Ann. "It is devilish hard for me to see [him] with six children starving when every week something is given to fellows in whom I have no earthly interest."[112] At Ottawa he even got a position for "young Sargent," whose father and uncle, when assemblymen in the 1830s, had "voted fifty times against the liberties of their country." But he had a wife and three children and "I do not visit the sins of the father upon the son as good Christians usually do."[113] Refusing to let the climate of Ottawa "freeze his affections," he let scarcely a week go by without doing something for a Nova Scotian at home or in Ottawa. At Christmas dinner he entertained young Butler, Ussher, Sutherland, and Harrington, all Nova Scotians with "livings provided ... by [his] exertions."[114]

Despite his frailness, he continued on the go. His granddaughter Mary Thomson had spent almost a year with him and Susan Ann, during which she recovered her health, learned some French, improved her musical abilities, and saw as much as most people of central Canada and its social life. Before bidding her farewell, her grandparents took her to Niagara Falls, the Welland Canal, and then by steamer to Montreal, "shooting the rapids through the Thousand Isles."[115] But this was only preliminary to another trip he dearly wanted to make, but which he viewed with misgivings: an invitation to deliver the oration at a gathering of the Howes in Massachusetts on September 1. Deciding to do it in easy stages, he spent a few days in the Eastern Townships with Judge Christopher Dunkin at Brome before giving his speech at Framingham near Boston. Much more than the "simple and good-humoured introduction to the business of the day" he said it would be, it demonstrated that his intellectual vigour was in no way impaired.[116] Archivists ever since have used one of its truisms: "A wise nation preserves its records, gathers up its muniments, decorates the tombs of its illustrious dead, repairs its great public structures and fosters national pride and love of country, by perpetual reference to the sacrifices and glories of the past." Typically he suggested that if the saints in Heaven were hovering "over the innocent reunions of their kindred, my father's spirit will be here, gratified to see that the family, divided by the Revolution, is again united, and that his son, to use the language [of Burns], is 'respected like the lave'." But could not these meetings help to draw together, not only single families, but the great family that the revolutionary war divided into three branches? If it was wise to gather the Howes together, how much more important was it to unite the three great branches of the British family in "a common policy, as indestructible as their language, as enduring as the literature they cannot divide."

After returning to Ottawa, Howe went to the Saguenay on Indian business and, as might be expected, expressed awe at Capes Trinity and Eternity. "On bends of the river walls of rock nearly three times as high as Blomidon, rose straight out of the water like a wall."[117] Much of the autumn he divided between Hants county and Halifax, where Governor Doyle and he could not resist a few merry evenings exulting in their victory over Annand and Wilkins. But delighting him most of all was the prosperity of the province. Mackerel, scarce for some time, had "rolled in upon the coast in endless abundance"; wheat-growing, long suspended because of the weevil, had begun again, and ship-building was active once more. His "better terms" agreement had averted direct taxation, and "the Locals are left without a grievance of sufficient magnitude to outweigh the general prosperity of the country."[118] What more could be asked?

During 1871 Howe's personal and family problems remained much as they were. After Joe "came off" the Manitoulins in the spring, he was off to Manitoba, and although his father gave him money to buy land, he feared the young man would never settle down. Fred had written from Sarnia of daily "sets to" with his employer and of likely loss of employment again.[119] To help Sarah launch her bookstore, Howe sent $200 as a loan and a box of government reports, almanacs, and pamphlets. "Auntie," he told her, was content that he help her in this way.[120] But he was still worried about leaving Susan Ann badly off. So, when her uncle, Admiral Westphal, made her a present of £100 stg, he added a similar amount of his own and invested the total in 6 per cent Dominion bonds to provide her with ready cash in case of his death. Yet still finding it difficult to turn down requests for aid, he could not allow the "old fellow" in Hants who wanted money for the Mosherville church to go empty-handed. As usual, he showed the greatest kindness to Edward's children. A son Johnnie lived with him in Ottawa until he found work for him. Upon his sister Mary, still in Maitland, "her affectionate grandfather" impressed the importance of penmanship, explaining that it alone would tell whether letters came from "painstaking and accomplished girls or women, or from careless and slatternly persons."[121]

In mid-January 1872 Howe reported himself in fair health for "an old fellow," but having to do what he had never done before, "take some care of himself."[122] Nonetheless, on February 22 he addressed the YMCA in Ottawa and caused the greatest stir he would all year.[123] Critical as usual of the attitude of British politicians towards the empire, he had become even more convinced of the existence of a drift towards separation. Not only had the British government treated Canada badly in the Washington Treaty, but it was also removing its troops from Canada, except for those in Halifax, and, according to his information, they were even taking their gun carriages and sentry boxes with them. Although his speech was largely inspirational – Canadians faced challenges greater than any he had "ever heard or read of, in ancient or modern times ... We cannot afford to have a laggard, an idler, or a coward" – he could not stifle his resentment at "England's recent diplomatic efforts to win her own peace at the sacrifice of our interests," nor forbear saying that the time was "rapidly approaching when Canadians and Englishmen must have a clear and distinct understanding as to the hopes and obligations of the future."

Few of Howe's speeches drew more widespread and continuing comment than this one. The *Novascotian* joined the *Acadian Recorder* in picturing him as craving to be at the centre of "*high melodrama*"; "politically very much out at [the] elbows" for the moment, and unable to prattle again about shedding "the precious blood of himself and his interesting family" on the Tantramar Marsh, he seized upon independence as the basis of a new agitation.[124] The Toronto *Globe* concluded that "Annexation ... an old Tory device ... must be the one and only logical result of Mr. Howe's reasoning"[125] and it joined with other opposition papers in Quebec and Ontario in suggesting that he could no longer remain in the cabinet. In letters intended to reach the British government the prime minister took a very strong line, freely conceding that Howe had made a fool of himself, that although he had "outlived his usefulness," he had "not lost his powers of mischief." But since Nova Scotia was still "a slumbering volcano," he would not require him to resign. Instead, he would treat the speech as "evidence of his senility & nothing more," indicate strong disapprobation of its contents, and require him to suppress the pamphlet which reproduced it.[126]

Nevertheless, Macdonald, himself smarting under his treatment at

Washington, may have inwardly relished what outwardly he could not approve. Not in the least penitent, Howe continued to send out his pamphlet to all and sundry with the comment that it contained "a good deal of good advice to our young men and no treason." Partisans, he said, were fighting over it, "as they are apt to do over any thing I write or say. But here, as at home, I say what I think, and rightly read I am sure there is not a line in the Lecture that is not true."[127] To Governor Doyle he expressed unabashedly his annoyance about the folly of general colonial policy. Although he had been wrong about the removal of the sentry boxes and gun carriages, the withdrawal of the British troops who used them "shakes the confidence of every loyal man and encourages every Independent and Annexationist in these noble Provinces."[128]

When Howe's old foe Alexander Mackenzie opened the session of 1872 by criticizing his language as "the most extraordinary ... ever used by a Minister of the Crown, and ... utterly unwarranted," it looked as if the government might be in trouble. Macdonald defended Howe as best he could: he also regretted the withdrawal of British troops and he could find nothing disloyal in Howe's speech; indeed, it was "the wailing cry of a loyalist fearing that the colony was going to be forsaken."[129] Later, when Howe spoke on the Treaty of Washington, the situation had so altered that he could assume the offensive. Strangely, the provocative part of his speech and pamphlet turned out to be "more important" in Britain than at home. There the *Standard* had reproached the government for providing the grounds for Howe's fears and the *Spectator* had congratulated him for showing that in the colonies "our centripetal policy ... is considered [to be] ... purely selfish." Put on the defensive, the *Times* declared that it was "not we who would set about the disintegration of this great Empire."[130] Undoubtedly Howe could claim some credit for the pro-colonial newspaper reaction, although he went too far in the Commons in suggesting that he "had changed all that"; he also had grounds for boasting that "the little Pamphlet which at first startled a good many people ... is now in British America almost universally approved."[131]

Otherwise Howe's participation in the business of the House was minimal in 1872. He performed a few departmental duties such as piloting the estimates of the Geological Survey through the Commons and occasionally he defended the quality of his nominees for high office, but he was not even there when the session closed. A severe winter and nightly sessions of Parliament had led to prolonged coughing, palpitations, and swelling about his feet and ankles, and early in June he had left for Atlantic City with Susan Ann, "with but slender hopes of ever seeing Ottawa again." Rest, sunshine, and warm baths cured his coughing and "saved his lungs, but did nothing for the dangerous swellings in his legs until "a skilful [Boston] physician" effected a marked improvement over a three-week period.[132] He was still recuperating in the United States when Macdonald had Parliament dissolved for an election in which Howe could not participate.

So on July 8 he addressed a letter to the electors of Hants, putting the disposal of his seat in their hands. In a second letter two weeks later he defended his "acceptance of the situation" and of membership in the cabinet.[133] Otherwise the "better terms" agreement might not have got through Parliament and Nova Scotia might not have avoided direct taxation, or secured sixty substantial federal appointments, or made headway towards securing a fair share of civil service positions at Ottawa. Seeing that the province could not get out of Confederation, he had sought to make her "count for something within it. And she has counted for some thing." By this time Nova Scotia's Anti press had accepted the federal political regime to the extent of advising its readers to "choose the Blake and Mackenzie party in preference to the designing faction ... now ... denying us an honest, vigorous and economical government."[134] At dissolution it called on Nova Scotians to destroy the Cartier-Macdonald administration as a means of getting rid of Howe and Tupper. The former, it said, had been "sucked dry like an orange" and would be discarded "like the empty rind" when it suited Macdonald's purpose. "Hants ought to be up and doing" and help "put an end to the profligate reign of corruption at Ottawa."[135]

But on nomination day, the 8th of August, Howe was returned unopposed, "one of the favoured few," complained a correspondent of the *Acadian Recorder*, "who can do as they please and yet retain their public position."[136] Although the newspapers disagreed strongly on the overall results in Nova Scotia, Jones and Power were beaten in Halifax, and, to all appearances, ten of the twenty-one members were out-and-out supporters of the government compared with one in 1867. "Repeal, Annexation, Grittism, bogus Reform, Rougism, are all wiped out," exulted the *British Colonist*; "... [a] good day's work done on the 15th August, 1872." When, a fortnight later, Howe arrived in Halifax, looking "a little bleached, but otherwise ... healthy," some wondered if "old Joe's sickness was only a *ruse*, intended to gain sympathy and avert Opposition in Hants County."[137]

Six pleasurable weeks in Nova Scotia made Howe as well as he ever would be. All solicitude, Macdonald told him that there was no need for him to return early to Ottawa since the cabinet was doing only routine business. Nor did he need to "hazard [his] health" by staying there during the next winter now that the government had a safe majority.[138] Nonetheless, before October was out, Howe was at his desk performing what were, in fact, routine duties. Dealing with patronage was never-ending, but less arduous with the establishment of set procedures; however, Howe continued to make a few exceptions, once in getting an office for a son of Michael Tobin at Archbishop Connolly's request. "Mike," said Howe, would not have left the government had he been a member and he was pleased to give a lift to a family which had fallen on bad times.[139]

This year Howe was especially concerned with looking after sitting or defeated members. For senior appointments he had an unmistakable preference for MPs over civil servants. The latter "run no risks and pay nothing for the support of Government"; the former "give their lives to the public, run costly elections, spent a great deal of money in hospitality or in the relief of the destitute among their constituents. This class of persons have the strongest claims upon Government."[140] To Hugh McDonald, reelected in Antigonish, he again gave assurance of the first vacancy in the Supreme Court. "We have been waiting for one of the Judges to break down with old age, and to have the decency to retire. They have done neither." For James McKeagney, defeated in Cape Breton, he sought a superior court vacancy in Manitoba, even though he did not consider him qualified for one in Nova Scotia, and a little hesitantly Macdonald honoured his request. But when A.W. Savary of Digby wanted a second vacancy in Manitoba, Howe said jokingly that "they would think us too modest, if we were to claim *two* out of *three* judges in a distant Province"; however, "your turn will come some of these days." One member had to take second place to other considerations: Ray of Annapolis did not get the senatorship he wanted; instead it went to Henry Kaulback who, certain not to win the Lunenburg seat, was induced in this way to make way for his brother Edwin, who at least had a chance to be elected.[141]

Howe's letter-book, always a mixture of governmental, political, and personal matter, contains a larger proportion of personal letters in 1872. As usual, he stated again and again the "great drawback" of living in Ottawa: "our fireside is dreary, during the long Canadian winters, for want of the chicks that ought to make it merry."[142] He contrived, of course, to do what he could for family and friends. He enjoined Joe, still in the West, to "hold on to your land. Do not sell an acre of it." Although he had $600 ready for Sydenham if he needed it, he advised against his buying a house. His own mistake, he said, had been to buy property before he could pay for it. "You now have all the comforts of life about you, and widening a crib to hold two Babes instead of one will not cost ten dollars." He also cautioned "Syd" against putting money into life insurance: "of all the swindles of modern times the greatest are Life Insurance Companies ... The best life Insurance is the investment of ones savings in Government Securities, Bank Stock, or Mortgages on Real Estate."[143] To Robert Fitzrandolph, who had married Sophia Austen, the daughter of his half-sister Jane, he gave warnings about "some scheming Yankees" who, in the pretext of establishing hemlock bark factories, had ruined two of his best friends; be careful, he said, or "they will take the eyes right out of your head." To his grandson James Thomson, who had lost all his trappings in a fire aboard ship on a trip to Spain, he sent $10 accompanied with his usual advice: "Improve your handwriting till you can write like copperplate without lines, spell correctly, and express yourself gramatically [sic] and be assured that hard work is the secret of success in every occupation."[144]

To others, whatever their status, he spoke his mind as the occasion warranted it. He told Principal Dawson of McGill that in writing letters that might be shown to cabinet ministers he ought not to "forget that the imperative mood is apt to give offence." He dealt harshly with the nephew of a Presbyterian minister who hoped to use his uncle's influence with Howe to supply goods to the government without tender. Aghast at a suggestion that would "degrade his uncle, and involve [himself] in a transaction that would ... be a violation of [his] oath of office," Howe replied angrily that he hoped to "return to Nova Scotia with hands as clean as they were when [he] left it."[145] With leisure on his hands he was contemplating a third volume of speeches and letters to bring the Annand volumes up to date and considering an offer of John Lovell to publish his poems, although he wondered if they were worth it. "I have been too much engaged in the rapid currents of political life to write much or to write well." Still they might make a small volume of 200 to 250 pages.[146]

Unknown to himself, his presence in the cabinet was limiting the prime minister's freedom of action in several ways. Sir John wanted to accord recognition in the form of CMGs to Tupper, Tilley, and Campbell, but thought better of it because "it would grievously wound Mr. Howe." Since the latter's life "hangs on a single thread," he wanted to make certain that no "act of [his] should snap it." Accordingly he decided to let the matter drop "until Howe is disposed of."[147] More worrisome to him was the burdensome nature of Howe's portfolio. Shortly Alexander Morris would be succeeding Archibald as lieutenant-governor of Manitoba, and before he left the policy for that province and the North-West would have to be settled in intensive discussions that might overtax Howe physically, if not mentally. In his dilemma Macdonald turned to Tupper. Could he get Howe to write him a note requesting less onerous duties: "Let me not appear as asking him to take this step, as I would not hurt Howe's *amour propre* for anything."[148] But because Howe returned "looking much stronger and better in every way," apparently Tupper balked at the idea. As a result, Howe would have to effect his own removal; perhaps he would see for himself that his best course was to become lieutenant-governor of Nova Scotia.

## CHAPTER TWELVE

# The Last Journey

"Disposing" of Howe was not on the mind of the prime minister alone. Even the opposition papers in Nova Scotia agreed that something should be done for him, "now [as they put it] that he is old, broken in health, and ... impaired in intellect." But they were insistent that a governorship was not for one who had got himself "ignominiously bought, and paid for" and then put "the finishing touch to the ruin of his reputation" by making himself troublesome to the prime minister.[1] In September 1872 Howe left the question open: under no conditions would he replace his friend Hastings Doyle before the latter served out his full term the following May, or before the House met and "floored" the opposition in the debate on the address.[2]

If Macdonald expected him to do no more than go through the motions during his last months in Ottawa, he was wrong in one instance. Always sceptical of the schemes of private railway contractors, Howe pondered early in December whether to go along with the proposals for railway building developed by Sir Hugh Allan and apparently accepted by the cabinet. Concluding that they would be "a surprize to Parliament and the country, and fraught with consequences deeply injurious to the best interests of the Dominion," he was prepared to resign "rather than throw over, for the sake of office, my conscientious convictions."[3] Though dissuaded from that course, he had decided by the end of the year that his health would not let him hold a ministerial office much longer and that the governorship, for a variety of reasons, offered the best prospects: it would provide adequately for his family for five years; it would let him spend his remaining years among his nearest and dearest; it would crown his public life with the highest position open to him in Nova Scotia.[4]

Macdonald himself must have realized the undesirability of choosing someone as representative of the queen who was almost anathema to many of the political leaders in his province. As the appointment became more and more likely, the *Acadian Recorder* took the lead in saying it would be "an insult of such magnitude that it never would or could be forgiven or forgotten ... The 'meanest thing that crawls' need not envy him in the enjoyment of his new dignity."[5] But despite his worries about Howe's reception in Nova Scotia the prime minister had little choice: it was clearly time for Howe to go; he had to be provided for; only the governorship would not make heavy demands and yet would have great prestige.

Howe himself gave short shrift to the Antis who objected to his appointment. Dismissing two particularly obdurate "worthies" as being all too conscious of their base ingratitude towards him, he intimated that "even they shall have nothing to complain of." Most of his compatriots, he was sure, recognized that his forty years of public service had earned him the office. Admittedly some might genuinely fear he would "violate [his] own principles by treating them unfairly," but they would be "mistaken in this, as in every thing else." Surely if anyone understood the principles of responsible government he did. If the present ministers retained their majority, they could carry on unhindered. "Should they break down it will not be my fault." He had never treated anyone who was civil and courteous with rudeness or unfairness, and "it is too late for me to begin now."[6]

Though the "locals" could not prevent Howe's appointment, they had other ways to harass him. When he learned that Annand was trying to have the British garrison in Halifax take over Government House, he replied indignantly: "They shall not if I can help it ... I have my feelings about the matter and am determined to live in Government House from which Mamma and I were excluded for years and where we so often met black looks and cold shoulders."[7] Nothing came of it, but it was only one of several worries. From Sydenham, who was acting as his emissary in Halifax, he finally learned to his relief that the provincial government would allocate the usual allowance of $800 for gas and fuel at Government House. But would it also provide the $1,250 for his private secretary? "They may reduce the Secretary's salary but it will be a mean thing if they do."[8] Again he was right that they would not for fear it might be regarded as a personal attack on him. Accordingly he arranged six months' leave from the federal public service for his son William to act in that capacity.[9]

Most worrisome of all, could he afford to be lieutenant-governor? Unwittingly he had supported "overpaying" the governor general, little knowing that the lieutenant-governors were being "starved," perhaps a natural outcome of John A. Macdonald's conception of the diminished role of the office. In Ontario Howland had had to draw heavily from an ample private income; Archibald had spent $6,000 more than he received during his short stay in Manitoba; and in Quebec City Belleau gave only one ball a year and no dinners. Perhaps Wilmot had "come out square" in New Brunswick, but only because Fredericton was a small town without garrison or squadron and hence without great need to entertain. Because Halifax was a garrison and naval town and a port of call for mail steamers which often brought distinguished visitors, "the duties of hospitality could not be withheld without lowering the position to humiliation." Nonetheless, the governor's official income prior to Confederation, a salary of £3,000 stg with substantial perquisites, had been practically cut in two. Doyle, with his military allowances and private income, could carry on much as before, but for Howe it was out of the question.[10]

The always sympathetic Doyle offered to explain to the federal government that it must either augment the governors' incomes or reconcile itself to their living and entertaining in quite a different style. But although Howe believed the government might eventually yield to pressure from all the provinces, he doubted if any change would be in time to affect him. To Doyle he confided his intentions. By living in lodgings for five or six years Susan Ann and he had paid off their debts and preserved the "little property" he had earned at his profession before he entered public life; under no conditions would he use it up and "endanger [his] personal independence for an hour ... to please anybody." Nor would he ask for any increase in salary, but simply "spend all that I receive." Admittedly the contrast in style between him and Doyle would be extreme, but "the people will soon get used to it."[11]

The timing of Howe's departure from Ottawa was to depend upon his health and the government's success in the first divisions of the new Parliament. To his own surprise he continued to perform his departmental and council duties without ill effects. An occasional dose of medicine and careful dieting apparently helped to counteract the same dangerous symptoms which had threatened his life in the previous year. He also found port and rum in moderation to be useful and, the port in Ottawa being undrinkable, he once sent an urgent request to his son-in-law Thomson in Halifax to replenish his supply with two dozen bottles. During the last few weeks in Ottawa he filled his letters with nostalgic references to the past. To Falvey of the *Hampshire Independent* he wrote: "God bless old Southampton say I from the bottom of my heart. The City and its beautiful surroundings with all the cheerful faces that gathered round me there in 1851, are ever present to my mind." Expecting never to see Doyle again, he promised always to retain "the memory of a friendship, unalloyed [by] one disturbing element." Asked for a favour by his nephew William, son of his half-brother David and the only member of his family to support him in the struggle for responsible government, he said it gave him "infinite pleasure" to help one with whom his heart had "beat in unison, ... in all the vicissitudes of my active public life." Reminiscing on the death of Susan Ann's cousin, he intimated, in the words of Thomas Moore:

> I feel like one who treads alone,
> Some banquet-hall deserted,
> Whose lights are fled, whose garlands dead,
> And all but he departed.[12]

Towards the end his participation in departmental and parliamentary business was slight. Once a worried Macdonald wrote to him about a statement of Alexander Morris that the provisions of the treaties with the Indians were not being carried out,[13] but the records indicate little else of significance. Howe said little in the Commons, his last utterance being a short comment on April 4. But the session brought him a great disappointment, since the government majority of forty that he had expected never materialized. On the first division, a minor one relating to the seating of an Ontario member, it was only sixteen, with five Nova Scotians voting against the government and four abstaining. "A few of our fellows acted in an absurd and thoughtless manner ... weakening us, and giving aid and comfort to the enemy." Apparently a combination of factors, especially the lack of consultation, had denied the government the "fair support" he expected from the Nova Scotians. Although more of them came into line in the second division on March 19, "one or two of them I will never trust again."[14]

Again Howe stayed in Ottawa too long, reluctant to leave, he said, "while there was a single Nova Scotian adrift." When he finally got away in mid-April, there was snow and ice along the track in Vermont and New Hampshire and cold east winds in Boston. Worse still, the Boston physician who had helped him the year before was unavailable and his substitute did him no good. He arrived in Halifax "pretty well used up," indeed, "trembling between life and death."[15] Nonetheless, he was sworn in as lieutenant-governor on the 10th of May. Annand absented himself in the United States, but Provincial Secretary W.B. Vail read the commission and the rest of the Executive Council were all Howe could have wished, "quiet but cordial." Among the general public a few old friends gave him black looks and crossed the street to avoid meeting him, but time, he believed, would be a great healer. Quite unworried, he assured Macdonald he would behave circumspectly and apprehended no difficulties.[16]

Spring, he anticipated, would soon burst upon Halifax and then, if anything was left to build on, he hoped to get right again. He went on carriage drives two or three times and during the last week of May he seemed better than he had been for some time. He gave a lengthy interview to his friend and admirer, George Johnson of the *Reporter and Times*, but overdid it on the 28th with a drive to Deer's Inn at Preston, ten miles from Dartmouth, that left him utterly fatigued. For some time intense pain had forced him to sit up at least three nights a week, unable to lie down or to sleep. On the last evening of the month he alternately walked the floor of his study and sat in his chair, watched over anxiously by Susan Ann and his son William. At 4:30 a.m. on Sunday, June 1, he was persuaded to go to bed, but collapsed on the way and died within ten minutes, conscious to the end. The *Chronicle* described the cause of death, if anything other than a general breaking down of the constitution, as an ailment of the liver.[17]

In keeping with Howe's scepticism concerning formal, organized religion, the only service was a short one in an upper room of Government House for relatives and close friends on June 3, the day of the funeral; it was conducted by the Rev. J.K. Smith, of Fort Massey Presbyterian Church, to which Susan Ann adhered. Six thousand marched in the procession from Government House to Camp Hill cemetery, watched by twenty thousand others. One onlooker, nine-teen-year-old William Critchton Harris, wrote that everything was "carried out on as grand a scale as possible." For him, however, one thing threw "dampers over the whole procession ... one of those lumbering death carts, which looked like a machine for carrying a loathsome patient to a small-pox hospital, and seemed better fitted for such work than anything else."[18]

For a moment all the bitterness of the immediate past was forgotten. It was not surprising to have the *Evening Express* call Howe "our greatest man" and to suggest that in the United States he would have been at least vice-president and in Britain ranked with John Bright. But for the *Chronicle* to state that "no British North American approached him in breadth of statesmanlike views" was a startling overnight change on its part.[19] Yet even in death he provoked controversy. The *British Colonist*, and more particularly the *Reporter and Times*, could not resist pointing a finger at Howe's "murderers"; "it was the cruel inhumanity of a bitter, needless, reckless, vindictive, political struggle in Hants in 1869 which produced the three years' physical torture, the three years of sleepless, agony-enduring nights, the blanched cheeks and the shrivelled look." Many would apostrophize the silent corpse: "'Thou are the ruins of the noblest man that ever lived in the tide of times' in Nova Scotia, and 'these are thy butchers'."[20] Angrily the *Chronicle* castigated these attempts to take advantage of its decision to follow the maxim, *de mortuis nil nisi bonum*. Had it not conceded that Howe had been "the head and front of all the great political changes in Nova Scotia"? Unrepentant, it insisted that, if the Hants election of 1869 were to be fought over again, it "and the party which it supports would do as they did then."[21]

In the two or three days following Howe's death the Halifax press explained his success as well as anyone has ever done it. Rightly much of it was attributed to his ability to transfer, although necessarily in diluted form, his overpowering enthusiasm to others. In part, he could persuade and excite his listeners and readers because of the vast store of information he had amassed on any proposal he advocated. "[It] came as the result of much consuming of the midnight oil, as the result of many hours snatched in early morn from inviting repose. [It] came ... by dint of much seeking, because of ardent wooing."[22] Partly it was due to the force of his speeches and writings, with their grace and aptness of illustration, once again dependent on his industry. His happy quotations were not picked up at random, but dug out of the mass of English literature and stored in his capacious mind until they could be used. His style of writing was "no haphazard, slap dash [one], slipped into and out of easily as a man slips into and out of his slippers – it was fashioned and stamped ... only after such labor as would daunt the most eager aspirant for literary honors."[23] But it gave him full command of "terse simple Anglo-Saxon," and was reinforced by his early delvings into "Shakespeare and the other 'wells of English undefiled'."[24] Even his oratory did not come full-blown, but was perfected, in the 1830s, in the seclusion of a quiet grove.

Some of it also came naturally. He may have been defective in some ways as a poet, but he had the poet's instinct for simile, analogy, and drawing inspiration from the slightest things. And it all added up to his being able to move, perhaps even manage, Nova Scotians more than anyone before or since.

He touched you with a tender word and you softened – even if you were an opponent ... He tickled you with a humorous story – and you laughed even though you came to be angry. He flashed before you some daring simile and you felt dazzled – even though your critical taste disapproved. He flung in at random some miraculously happy quotation from some rich treasure-house of English literature – and you could not help admiring the culture of the man, even though the next moment he would offend you with a vulgarism.[25]

This crudity, a product of his apprentice days, provided his opponents with a continuing ground for criticism, but it never damaged him with a people whom he got to know better than any Nova Scotian of his or any day. Whatever his foibles and frailties, he continued to evoke "the music of popular applause." He knew "how to call it out, how to manage it, how to enjoy it. It was his thanks, his pay, his inspiration; it was what he most desired."[26]

For, like his father, he had not "an itchy palm," no desire to build up possessions in money or property; without exaggeration he could say that when he had money it was all the better for those who had not. He died poor – so poor that Susan Ann had to depend partly on the beneficence of her children until the legislature of Nova Scotia granted her an annuity in 1885[27] – while many around him grew rich because of him. Yet he did not receive the recognition he deserved for his pecuniary disinterestedness because of a peculiar twist of character. Seemingly because he was Joseph Howe who was wont to sacrifice himself for the public good, he believed he need not be as circumspect as other men in his relations with government. In the matter of the excise office accounts in the 1840s he behaved not much differently than his Tory predecessors; later his opponents grossly exaggerated the building up of a Joseph Howe compact of office-holders from among his own relatives. But in both instances his seeming lack of care for the impression his conduct might create in the public mind left him more vulnerable to attack than he needed to be.

Howe's ability to move Nova Scotians did not mean that he held the province in the palm of his hand. For the most part single-handedly, he built up the Reform party in Nova Scotia and established its pre-eminence. But when party lines hardened the Tories were only barely in a minority and the Liberal victories in the four elections between 1848 and 1859 were always by relatively small margins. Hence another of Howe's quirks was sufficient in itself to keep or place his party in opposition on two occasions. Normally long-suffering in the face of continuing personal attacks, he would suddenly explode in righteous indignation, brush aside moderation and temperateness, and seek, through his unexcelled power of invective, to blast his enemies into oblivion. It happened in the early 1840s when he so alienated the Baptists that he cost his party a certain victory by a single seat in the election of 1843. It happened again in 1857 when he so shocked the sensibilities of Catholics that their members and sympathizers in the assembly transferred power to the Conservatives without benefit of an election. The quirk operated once more in 1869 when, after suffering long-continued annoyance and harassment at the hands of the "locals," he decided he had had enough of them, and spurned their joining in the negotiations with the Dominion government, except as he called the tune. This time the price he paid was to make the pacification of the province more difficult.

Clearly Howe was a master propagandist and influencer of public opinion, and he knew it. Indeed, his confidence reached the point of believing that, even with limited facilities or opportunities, he could move mountains. Unrealistically he thought he could influence larger jurisdictions with the same ease as at times he did little Nova Scotia – hence his disappointment in 1855 at the failure of his direct appeal to the American public for sympathetic understanding of the British cause in the Crimea. But considering the odds against him, he had remarkable success in gaining newspaper and other support in Britain in 1851, 1866–7, and 1868. The colonial secretaries who granted him a free hand in testing and moving public opinion may have had second thoughts when his successes complicated their own problems.

In putting his viewpoints before the public Howe was accused both of inconsistency and of indulging in fantasy. Because he believed that political parties ought to re-form as issues and circumstances changed, and that in the process former friends might become foes and former antagonists become colleagues, he multiplied the possibilities of being charged with somersaulting. Yet because he generally adhered to a few basic principles his career was freer from serious contradictions than was the conduct of most politicians of his day. His alleged inconsistency on Confederation was largely in the minds of those who knew neither the man nor his priorities. He could, much more legitimately, be charged with too great a susceptibility to grandiose projects. It is not true as sometimes alleged that the only figures he understood were figures of speech. Unquestionably he could present financial statistics of the greatest complexity with competence and understanding, and his own weak financial position resulted not so much from mismanagement as from compassion for unfortunates. But although no British American of his day, or no Nova Scotian of his or any day, surpassed him in "breadth of statesmanlike views," he was altogether carried away at times by some of the schemes he advocated and he anticipated results from them that were more fanciful than realistic. He accepted the Atrato Canal project largely because of his faith in its promoters, who in turn were interested in him only as publicist and propagandist. Even if all of Nova Scotia had been as fertile as the Annapolis Valley – something he at times seemed to take for granted – he was engaging in high-flown fancy to expect that the misfits of London could successfully pioneer its soil. He magnified beyond all reason the development which a railway from Halifax to Quebec would bring in its wake. He seemed not to understand that, even if the flow of public opinion in Britain had not been away from the idea of a more closely integrated empire, his own proposals for its government were unrealizable and unworkable.

Howe carried his concept of growth and development, so much a part of him, over to the after-life. Cynics who scoffed at the depth of his religious experience and equated his lack of membership in any formal religious body with unbelief, had no access to his diaries, which are replete with thanks to the Creator for His mercies, and which depict a man, sometimes immodest elsewhere, humbling himself before the Almighty. Two weeks before he died he suggested that development was everywhere the result of death. When the grub shivered and trembled, the golden-winged butterfly sprang into existence. So was it with man. "The Great Author of Life was wise and good, and having impressed the great fact of 'development' upon Nature, had, by so doing, bidden man to conclude that he too was to obey the same law. Not leaving man to find his own way to a sound conclusion by the dim light of reason, He had provided the blazing sun of revelation."[28] Though unlike his father in some ways, he lived and died with the same simple faith in an all-wise Creator.

The unforgettable all-pervading characteristic of Howe is his exuberant, ineradicable, almost inexhaustible energy. Months of almost unceasing and sometimes disappointing activity might leave him weak and dispirited, but not for long. Shortly he would rebound with new stores of energy, perhaps to continue the old quest on a new tack, perhaps to venture into fresh and untrodden fields. So it was in the greatest disappointment of his life – the repeated rebuffs of his many attempts to have his concept of empire recognized and the apparent decision of British politicians to loosen rather than tighten the imperial tie – and in his greatest disillusionment – the failure of British parliamentarians to take more than a fleeting, almost indifferent glance at Nova Scotia's pleas on the question of political union. Those who heard and saw him on his return from Britain in 1868 and those who today read his letters and speeches of those months might conclude that he had cut a pathetic figure. But if so, it was not for long. Before the YMCA at Ottawa he made it clear that he had become a Canadian fully and unconditionally, and delighted in the prospects of his new country. "There never was [one] with so many natural resources flung broadcast before so limited a population ... Canada cannot afford to have one drone in the intellectual hive."[29] None would have liked more than he to make himself a powerful spokesman of Canadian possibilities as he had been of so many causes in the past. It would have been just the kind of challenge to enable him to leave "upon the history of his country the stamp of his energy."[30] None could have met it with greater vision, enthusiasm, or vigour.

# Notes

CHAPTER ONE

1 Words undoubtedly written by Howe for the Speech from the Throne opening the Nova Scotia legislature in 1849. See *JHA*, Jan. 18, 1849, p. 205.

2 Buller to Howe, Mar. 24, 1848, in Chester Martin, ed., "The Correspondence between Joseph Howe and Charles Buller, 1845–48," *Canadian Historical Review* 6 (December 1925): 327.

3 Howe to Buller, May 4, 1848, ibid., p. 329.

4 Ibid., pp. 329–30n1.

5 Howe to unknown, Mar. 15, 1848, "Howe Letters," p. 99.

6 Howe to Buller, Feb. 12, 1848, in Martin, "Correspondence," p. 326.

7 Not until 1863 did a Nova Scotian premier present the resignation of his ministry immediately after his party's defeat at an election.

8 *Novascotian*, Mar. 6, 1848.

9 Ibid., Mar. 13, 1848.

10 All excerpts from the debate on the judges bill are taken from the *Sun*, Mar. 22, 1848.

11 11 Vic., c. 23.

12 *Sun*, Apr. 3, 1848.

13 The bill would have produced savings of £3,910 6s. 3d. cy up to Jan 19, 1848.

14 For details see *Novascotian*, Apr. 3, 1848.
15 Speech of Mar. 25, *Sun*, Mar. 31, 1848.
16 Ibid., Apr. 3, 1848.
17 Speech of Mar. 31, ibid., Apr. 10, 1848.
18 Ibid., Apr. 7, 1848.
19 Speech of Mar. 31, *Novascotian*, Apr. 17, 1848.
20 Ibid.
21 The result was the bizarre situation in which, when the council was in Committee of the Whole, with Rudolf in the chair and the Tory president voting, the lord bishop's vote carried every division against the government, whereas when the president was in the chair and Rudolf supported the government, the committee's report was rejected and the government's proposal upheld notwithstanding the bishop's vote. See *Acadian Recorder*, Apr. 1, 1848.
22 Ibid.
23 *Novascotian*, Apr. 10, 1848.
24 *Journals of the Legislative Council*, Apr. 6 and 7, 1848, pp. 79, 81.
25 Speech of Mar. 21, *Sun*, Mar. 24, 1848.
26 Speech of Mar. 28, *Novascotian*, Apr. 3, 1848.
27 Howe to Buller, May 4, 1848, Martin, "Correspondence," p. 329.
28 Speech of Mar. 18, *Sun*, Mar. 24, 1848.
29 Speech of Mar. 18, *Times*, Mar. 28, 1848.
30 Howe to Buller, May 4, 1848, Martin, "Correspondence," p. 329.
31 Grey to Harvey, June 20, 1848, *JHA*, 1849, App. 4, pp. 84–5; ibid., June 24, 1848, App. 7, p. 121.
32 Ibid., June 23, 1848, App. 6, pp. 108–10.
33 Ibid., June 19, 1848, PANS, RG 1, vol. 87, doc. 98, pp. 128–46. The sections critical of Harvey are omitted in the extracts published in the *Journals*. See *JHA*, 1849, App. 10, pp. 141–5.
34 Howe to Buller, July 21, 1848 (private), JHP, vol. 6, pp. 215–6. Howe pointed out that Sir Rupert George was then in England, while Mr Justice Bliss had been there all winter: "Both I suspect have been busy at the Colonial Office."
35 Address of Executive Council to Harvey, Apr. 20, 1848, *JHA*, 1849, App. 10, pp. 138–41.
36 Ibid., July 20, 1848, pp. 146–8.
37 Grey to Harvey, Nov. 15, 1848, ibid., p. 148.
38 Address of Executive Council to Harvey, July 21, 1848, ibid., App. 6, pp. 111–4.
39 Grey to Harvey, Nov. 15, 1848, ibid., pp. 116–8.
40 Des Barres to Howe, Sept. 11, 1848, JHP, vol. 1, pp. 281–4; ibid., Nov. 6, 1848, pp. 289–91.
41 Draft of letter to George, Feb. 27, 1848, JHP, vol. 10, pp. 260–2; Howe to George, May 12, 1848, ibid., vol. 6, pp. 207–8.
42 Howe to Crosskill, May 12, 1848, *Royal Gazette*, May 17, 1848.
43 Howe to Harvey, n.d., JHP, vol. 10, pp. 84–99.
44 See note appended to Fairbanks's letter of Oct. 26, 1848, JHP, reel 24, item 208.
45 *Sun*, Mar. 20, 1848.
46 *Acadian Recorder*, Mar. 18, 1848.

47 For draft copy see JHP, vol. 10, pp. 264–5.
48 Howe to Henry Troop, July 9, 1849, ibid., vol. 35, n.p.
49 Howe to Peter Bonnett, May 1, 1849, ibid.
50 Howe to unknown, May 8, 1848, ibid.
51 Howe to W.A. Henry (private), May 9, 1848, ibid.
52 Howe to Slocumb (private), Jan. 6, 1849, ibid.
53 *Acadian Recorder*, Apr. 15, 1848.
54 *Novascotian*, June 19, 1848.
55 *Acadian Recorder*, June 24, 1848.
56 See letter from "One of Yourselves," *Novascotian*, Oct. 9, 1848.
57 Speech of Jan. 19, *Novascotian*, Jan. 22, 1849.
58 Speech of Feb. 1, ibid., Feb. 12, 1849.
59 Grey had agreed that the legislature need not provide further for Sir Rupert George, who had been granted a retiring pension, or for J.W. Johnston, who had voluntarily accepted a reduction in the attorney general's salary and taken credit publicly for his sacrifice. Grey to Harvey, June 19, 1848, *JHA*, 1849, App. 10, pp. 143–4.
60 Speech of Mar. 8, *British Colonist*, Mar. 10, 1849.
61 Speeches of Mar. 8, ibid., Mar. 13 and 20, 1849.
62 *Novascotian*, Feb. 19, 1849.
63 Ibid.
64 Speech of Jan. 29, *British Colonist*, Feb. 1, 1849.
65 Speeches of Jan. 29 and 30, ibid., Feb. 1 and 3, 1849.
66 Speech of Feb. 1, ibid., Feb. 6, 1849.
67 Speech of Jan. 30, ibid., Feb. 1, 1849.
68 Speech of Feb. 24, *Novascotian*, Apr. 16, 1849.
69 Ibid.
70 Speeches of Feb. 23 and 26, ibid., Apr. 16 and 23, 1849.
71 *British Colonist*, Mar. 8, 1849. The derogatory reference to Henry alludes to his desire to be "spoon-fed" in the matter of patronage.
72 Trotter to Howe, Sept. 14, 1849, JHP, vol. 1, pp. 319–20; Howe to Trotter, Oct. 12, 1849, ibid., vol. 6, pp. 229–31.
73 *British Colonist*, Mar. 20, 22, and 24, 1849.
74 Howe to Huntington, May 2, 1849, JHP, vol. 35, n.p.
75 Quoted in *British Colonist*, Feb. 27, 1849.
76 Ibid., Jan. 25, 1849.
77 Speech of Jan. 19, *Novascotian*, Jan. 22, 1849.
78 *British Colonist*, Jan. 25, 1849.
79 *Novascotian*, May 7, 1849.
80 *British Colonist*, Apr. 17, May 3 and 10, 1849.
81 Chisholm, 2:20; for letter to Moffatt, see ibid., pp. 21–9.
82 Howe to Hamilton Merritt, May 21, 1849, JHP, vol. 10, pp. 100–106; Howe to J.S. Hogan, Oct. 29, 1849, ibid., vol. 6, pp. 232–9.
83 *British Colonist*, May 12, 1849.
84 *Novascotian*, June 26, 1848.
85 *British Colonist*, May 12, 1849.
86 Ibid., May 12 and 17, 1849.
87 Harvey to Grey, Feb. 8, 1849, *JHA*, 1858, App. 51, p. 376.
88 Grey to Harvey, Feb. 23, 1849, ibid., pp. 377–8.
89 Howe to Henry Troop, July 9, 1849, JHP, vol. 35, n.p.

90 *Novascotian*, Mar. 26, 1849.
91 Harvey to Grey, Mar. 9, 1849, *JHA*, 1858, App. 1, pp. 379–83. The disproportion in the five counties was as follows:

|  | Tories | Reformers |  | Tories | Reformers |
|---|---|---|---|---|---|
| Hants | 33 | 14 | Cumberland | 30 | 16 |
| Kings | 32 | 13 | Lunenburg | 20 | 5 |
| Annapolis | 35 | 7 |  |  |  |

92 Grey to Harvey, May 21, 1859, ibid., pp. 387–8.
93 *British Colonist*, June 12, 1849.
94 Ibid., Feb. 13, and June 26, 1849.
95 *Novascotian*, Oct. 22, 1849; *Morning Chronicle*, Nov. 27, 1849; *British Colonist*, Dec. 25, 1849.
96 *JHA*, Mar. 31, 1849, p. 402.
97 *Novascotian*, May 7, 1849; *British Colonist*, May 19, 1849.

CHAPTER TWO

1 *British Colonist*, Mar. 12, 1850.
2 Speech of Mar. 9, *Novascotian*, Apr. 29, 1850.
3 *Sun*, Apr. 3, 1850.
4 Speech of Jan. 30, *Novascotian*, Feb. 4, 1850.
5 *British Colonist*, Feb. 5, 1850.
6 Speech of Feb. 4, *Novascotian*, Feb. 11, 1850.
7 Speech of Feb. 19, ibid. (extra), Feb. 28, 1850.
8 *Acadian Recorder*, Feb. 23, 1850.
9 *Novascotian*, Mar. 11, 1850.
10 Harvey to Grey, June 4, 1850, *JHA*, 1851, App. 6, p. 10.
11 Speech of Feb. 23, *Novascotian*, Mar. 11, 1850.
12 Grey to Harvey, July 15, 1850, *JHA*, 1851, App. 6, p. 11. See also J.M. Beck, *The Government of Nova Scotia* (Toronto: University of Toronto Press, 1957), p. 139.
13 Speeches of Mar. 4, 5, 6, 1850, Chisholm, 2: 34–48.
14 Ibid.
15 *British Colonist*, Mar. 9, 1850.
16 Speech of Jan. 18, *Novascotian*, Jan. 21, 1850.
17 *Acadian Recorder*, Mar. 9, 1850. For resolutions see *JHA*,, Mar. 27, 1850, pp. 600–1.
18 Johnston's speech of Mar. 19, *British Colonist*, Mar. 27, 28, and 30, 1850.
19 Speech of Mar. 20, 1850, Chisholm, 2: 53, 57, 65, 67.
20 *Acadian Recorder*, Mar. 23, 1850.
21 Speech of Feb. 26, *Novascotian*, Mar. 18, 1850.
22 *JHA*, 1850, App. 17, pp. 56–7.
23 *Novascotian*, Jan. 14, 1850; *British Colonist*, Jan. 10, 1850.
24 Howe to unknown, Apr. 26, 1850, JHP, vol. 6, pp. 252–5.
25 Speech of Mar. 1, *Novascotian*, Mar. 25, 1850.
26 Speech of Feb. 26, ibid., Mar. 18, 1850.
27 Speeches of Feb. 28 and Mar. 1, ibid., Mar. 25, 1850.

28 *British Colonist*, Mar. 21, 1850.
29 Howe to unknown, Apr. 26, 1850, JHP, vol. 6, pp. 252–5.
30 Speech of Feb. 28, *Novascotian*, Mar. 25, 1850.
31 Young to Harvey, July 3, 1850, PANS, RG 1, vol. 259, item 54.
32 See reports of council meetings, July, 2 and 9, 1850, ibid., item 53.
33 *JHA*, 1850, App. 83, pp. 249–50.
34 Speech of Feb. 2, *Morning Chronicle*, Feb. 5, 1853.
35 Speech on fifth day of debate, *Novascotian*, May 21, 1849.
36 *British Colonist*, Feb. 5, 1850.
37 Speech of Mar. 25, *Sun*, Apr. 29 and May 1, 1850.
38 Speech of Mar. 26, ibid., May 3, 1850.
39 Ibid., Apr. 3, 1850.
40 Ibid., May 15, 1850.
41 Howe to Harvey (probably), Aug. 22, 1850, JHP, vol. 35, n.p.
42 *Sun*, Sept. 2, 1850.
43 Chisholm, 2: 94. He was not above a little deception when he stated that he had composed his resolution on the spot.
44 Howe to Harvey (probably), Aug. 22, 1850, JHP, vol. 35, n.p.; Harvey to Grey, Aug. 29, 1850, *JHA*, 1851, App. 40, pp. 130–2.
45 Harvey to Grey, *JHA*, 1851, App. 40, pp. 132–3.
46 Chisholm, 2: 99–104.
47 Howe to Susan Ann at sea, Nov. 5, 1850, "Howe Letters," p. 106.
48 Ibid., Nov. 28, p. 109.
49 Ibid., Nov. 24, p. 108.
50 Howe to Grey, Nov. 25, 1850, *JHA*, 1851, App. 40, pp. 133–44.
51 Diary, Nov. 29, 1850, JHP, vol. 66, p. 26.
52 Ibid., Dec. 1, p. 28. In his *Letters to Lord John Russell* (1846), Howe had proposed colonial representation in the British Parliament, but not through executive councillors, and for the purpose of defending colonial interests rather than initiating "a vigorous colonial policy."
53 Howe to Susan Ann, Dec. 18, 1850, "Howe Letters," p. 110; Diary, Dec. 3, 1850, JHP, vol. 66, pp. 28–9.
54 Howe to Grey (private), Dec. 4, 1850, JHP, vol. 6, pp. 292–325.
55 Grey to Howe (private), Dec. 12, 1850, ibid., vol. 1, pp. 410–2; Diary, Dec. 13, 1850, ibid., vol. 66, pp. 38–9.
56 Howe to Grey (private), Dec. 16, 1850, ibid., vol. 6, pp. 328–39.
57 Diary entry of Jan. 26, 1851, summarizing events from Dec. 18 to Jan. 25, ibid., vol. 66, p. 43; Howe to Susan Ann, Dec. 18, 1850, "Howe Letters," p. 110.
58 Diary, Dec. 28, 1850, JHP, vol. 66, pp. 48–53.
59 Ibid., Dec. 30, 1850 and Jan. 6, 1851, pp. 54–5 and 62–3.
60 Ibid., Jan. 10, 1851, p. 65.
61 On the day of the speech Mayor Richard Andrews of Southampton took him to its charitable institutions, where he saw a host of young people whom he wished he might take to Nova Scotia, far "removed from the necessities of either poverty or vice." *Hampshire Independent*, Jan. 18, 1851.
62 See Chisholm, 2: 141–56.
63 Howe to Susan Ann, Jan. 17, 1851, "Howe Letters," p. 111; Smyth to Mrs Howe, Jan. 17, 1851, ibid., p. 112.

64 Capt. Hale to Howe, n.d., JHP, vol. 5, pp. 364–5; A.B. Richards to Howe, Feb. 5, 1851, ibid., vol. 1, pp. 502–5; Harvey to Howe, Feb. 4, 1851, ibid., pp. 494–6.
65 Howe to Susan Ann, Jan. 17, 1851, "Howe Letters," p. 111; Howe to Grey, Jan. 15, 1851, JHP, vol. 6, pp. 475–80.
66 Howe to Grey, Jan. 16, 1851, Chisholm, 2: 119–40.
67 Howe to Harvey, Jan. 17, 1851, "Howe Letters," p. 111.
68 Grey's memorandum on Howe's letter of Jan. 16, 1851, JHP, vol. 24, pp. 366–71. As usual, Howe promptly struck out the passages that offended Grey.
69 Grey to Howe (confidential), Feb. 12, 1851, ibid., vol. 1, pp. 564–5.
70 Diary, Feb. 13, 14, 15, 1851, ibid., vol. 66, pp. 82–5.
71 Ibid., Feb. 21, 22, 1851, pp. 91–3.
72 Ibid., Feb. 26, 1851, pp. 99–103.
73 See Sydenham Howe to J.A. Chisholm, Dec. 17, 1908, JHP, reel 22.
74 Howe to Stanley, Feb. 28, 1851, ibid., vol. 6, pp. 586–7.
75 Hawes to Howe, Mar. 10, 1851, ibid., vol. 36, pp. 313–31.
76 Diary, Mar. 11, 1851, ibid., vol. 66, pp. 118–9; Howe to Keating, Mar. 13, 1851, ibid., vol. 36, pp. 385–94; Chisholm, 2: 160–2.
77 Howe to Grey, Mar. 17, 1851, ibid., vol. 36, pp. 337–54; Grey to Howe (private), Mar. 18, 1851, ibid., pp. 355–60.
78 Diary, Apr. 10, 1851, vol. 66, p. 139.
79 Acadian Recorder, Jan. 4, 1851; McCully to Howe, Feb. 11, 1851, JHP, vol. 1, pp. 544–59.
80 Morning Chronicle, Feb. 18 and Mar. 1, 1851.
81 British Colonist, Apr. 26, 1851.
82 Speech of Mar. 6, ibid., Mar. 29, 1851.
83 McCully to Howe, Feb. 11, 1851, JHP, vol. 1, pp. 544–59.
84 Ibid., p. 547.
85 British Colonist, Feb. 6, 1851.
86 McCully to Howe, Feb. 11, 1851 (with addendum of Feb. 13), JHP, vol. 1, p. 551; Harvey to Howe (private), Feb. 13, 1851, ibid., pp. 578–81.
87 Paraphrase of speech in Novascotian, Mar. 24, 1851.
88 Howe to Grey, Sept. 30, 1852, JHP, vol. 36, pp. 690–2; British Colonist, Apr. 3 and 5, 1851.
89 Acadian Recorder, Apr. 26, 1851; Morning Chronicle, Apr. 29, 1851.
90 Howe to Harvey, n.d., JHP, vol. 10, pp. 53–4. The removal was not accomplished without a wholesale washing of dirty linen in public. See letters of Young, Uniacke, and Henry in the British Colonist between May 13 and 20.
91 Chisholm, 2: pp. 167–84.
92 Ibid., pp. 205–11.
93 Howe to freeholders of Halifax county, Sun, July 30, 1851.
94 See Howe to electors of Nova Scotia, Morning Chronicle, Aug. 19, 1851.
95 Howe to Grey (private), Aug. 5, 1851, JHP, vol. 6, pp. 742–4; speech at nomination meeting in Halifax, Sun, Aug. 11, 1851.
96 British Colonist, Sept. 20, 1851; Morning Chronicle, Aug. 23, 1851.
97 Howe to Peto, Betts and Brassey, Sept. 4, 1851, JHP, vol. 6, pp. 746–7.
98 Howe to electors of Nova Scotia, Morning Chronicle, Aug. 19, 1851.
99 Howe to constituency of Cumberland county, ibid., Sept. 9, 1851.
100 Chisholm, 2: 222.

101 Howe to Archibald, Oct. 1, 1851, *Novascotian*, Oct. 6, 1851.
102 A.B. Richards to Howe, Sept. 5, 1851, JHP, vol. 1, pp. 817–26.
103 M.H. Perley to Howe (private), Aug. 2, 1851, ibid., pp. 778–81; Head to Howe (private), Sept. 20, 1851, ibid., pp. 827–30.
104 Howe to Peto, Betts and Brassey, Oct. 2, 1851, ibid., vol. 6, pp. 754–6; Howe to Grey, Oct. 2, 1851, ibid., vol. 36, pp. 528–31. Grey assured him he would do everything possible to discourage Archibald. Grey to Howe (private), Oct. 16, 1851, ibid., vol. 1, pp. 864–5.
105 Speeches of Nov. 8 and 11, *Novascotian*, Nov. 17 and 24, 1851.
106 Speech of Nov. 15, ibid., Dec. 22, 1851.
107 Speech of Nov. 24, ibid., Dec. 29, 1851.
108 *Morning Chronicle*, Dec. 2, 1851; Howe to unknown, Dec. 4, 1851, PANS, "Howe Letters," p. 116.
109 Head to Howe (private and confidential), Dec. 9, 1851, JHP, vol. 1, pp. 921–4.
110 Howe to unknown, Dec. 4, 1851, "Howe Letters," p. 116.

CHAPTER THREE

1 Grey to Harvey, Nov. 27, 1851, *JHA*, 1852, App. 10, p. 37.
2 Ibid., Jan. 9, 1852, pp. 47–9.
3 Howe to Harvey, Dec. 24, 1851, ibid., p. 43.
4 Speech of Jan. 22, 1853, *Morning Chronicle*, Jan. 27, 1853.
5 Howe to Grey (private), Feb. 5, 1852, JHP, vol. 36, pp. 659–62.
6 *British Colonist*, Jan. 24 and 29, 1852.
7 Howe to Hincks, Jan. 5, 1852, JHP, vol. 7, p. 1; Howe to Grey (private), Feb. 5, 1852, ibid., vol. 36, pp. 659–62.
8 Hincks to Howe (confidential), Feb. 2, 1852, ibid., vol. 2, pp. 20–3.
9 Speech of Feb. 2, *Morning Chronicle*, Feb. 5, 1852.
10 *Morning Chronicle*, Feb. 7, 1852.
11 Speech of Feb. 5, ibid.
12 Speech of Feb. 6, *Novascotian*, Feb. 16, 1852.
13 Harvey to Grey, Apr. 4, 1850, *JHA*, 1852, App. 22, p. 158.
14 Speech of Feb. 19, *Novascotian*, Mar. 1, 1852.
15 *Morning Chronicle*, Mar. 9, 1852.
16 *British Colonist*, Jan. 27 and Feb. 21, 1852.
17 Ibid., Feb. 28, 1852.
18 Howe to Harvey, Feb. 24, 1852, JHP, vol. 7, pp. 8–11.
19 Election card, *Morning Chronicle*, Mar. 6, 1852.
20 Ibid., Mar. 20, 1852.
21 *British Colonist*, Mar. 2, 1852.
22 *Eastern Chronicle*, Mar. 19, 1852.
23 Letter in *Morning Chronicle*, Mar. 30, 1852.
24 Letter in *British Colonist*, Apr. 17, 1852.
25 Grigor to Howe, Mar. 1, 1852, JHP, vol. 2, pp. 33–8.
26 Howe to Hincks, Feb. 29, 1852, ibid., vol. 7, pp. 16–19.
27 Speech of Jan. 22, 1853, *Morning Chronicle*, Jan. 27, 1853.
28 Howe to Hincks, Apr. 29, 1852, JHP, vol. 7, pp. 24–31.
29 Howe to Derby (private), June 24, 1852, ibid., vol. 36, pp. 684–8.
30 Ibid.; also Howe to Grey, Mar. 31, 1852, ibid., vol. 7, pp. 20–3.
31 Howe to Smyth, June 24, 1852, ibid., vol. 36, pp. 677–9.

32 Howe to Andrews, June 24, 1852, ibid., pp. 680–3.
33 *British Colonist*, July 1, 15, 24, 29 and Oct. 2, 9, 1852.
34 Bell to Howe, Nov. 15, 1852, JHP, vol. 2, pp. 95–7.
35 *Morning Chronicle*, Sept. 28 and Oct. 5, 1852; *British Colonist*, Oct. 2, 1852.
36 *British North American*, Sept. 15, 1852.
37 *British Colonist*, Nov. 4 and 13, 1852.
38 Bell to Howe, Nov. 15, 1852, JHP, vol. 2, pp. 95–7.
39 Speech of Jan. 22, *Morning Chronicle*, Jan. 27, 1853.
40 Diary, Oct. 28 and 29, 1852, JHP, vol. 66, pp. 144–5.
41 Ibid., Oct. 29 and Nov. 6, pp. 146–7, 151. Publicly Howe said he "enjoyed for ten days the courteous and friendly intercourse" of Jackson. Speech of Jan. 22, *Morning Chronicle*, Jan. 27, 1853.
42 Diary, Nov. 18, 1852, JHP, pp. 146, 163.
43 Smyth to Howe, Nov. 18, 1852, ibid., vol. 2, pp. 108–18.
44 Howe to Derby (private), Nov. 27, 1852, ibid., vol. 7, pp. 52–53; James A. Roy, *Joseph Howe: A Study in Achievement and Frustration* (Toronto: Macmillan, 1935), p. 179.
45 Howe to Brown et al., Dec. 28, 1852, JHP, vol. 7, pp. 86–8.
46 Speech of Jan. 22, *Morning Chronicle*, Jan. 27, 1853.
47 Speech of Jan. 27, ibid., Jan. 29, 1853.
48 Speeches of Feb. 1 and 2, ibid., Feb. 3 and 5, 1853.
49 Ibid., Feb. 8, 1853.
50 Howe to le Marchant (private), Feb. 7, 1853, JHP, vol. 7, pp. 90–104.
51 Speech of Feb. 10, *Morning Chronicle*, Feb. 26, 1853; ibid., Feb. 8, 1853.
52 Speech of Feb. 12, ibid., Mar. 1, 1853.
53 *British Colonist*, Feb. 12, 1853.
54 *JHA*, Feb. 19, 1853, pp. 267–8.
55 Ibid., Feb. 23–24, 1853, pp. 275–9.
56 In justification, he pointed out that the opposition, although too weak to carry anything, was "strong enough to obstruct, with the aid of five of our usual supporters who represent distant Counties off the tracks, all successful legislation." Howe to Sykes, Sheffield, and King (private), Mar. 17, 1853, JHP, vol. 7, pp. 110–1.
57 Speech of Mar. 22, *Morning Chronicle*, Apr. 9, 1853.
58 Speeches of Mar. 14 and 21, ibid., Mar. 26, and Apr. 7, 1853.
59 16 Vic., cc. 1 and 2.
60 *Sun*, Mar. 26, 1853; *Morning Chronicle*, Apr. 12, 1853.
61 Howe to Sykes, Sheffield and King, Mar. 17, 1853, JHP, 7:110–1; speech at Amherst, June 29, *Novascotian*, July 18, 1853.
62 Speech of Jan. 29, *Morning Chronicle*, Feb. 1, 1853.
63 Speeches of Jan. 25 and 26, ibid., Jan. 29, 1853.
64 Speech of Mar. 5, *Novascotian*, Mar. 21, 1853.
65 Speech of Jan. 27, *Morning Chronicle*, Jan. 29, 1853. Morton replied that with Howe's "vaunted physical strength and that of [his] children, legitimate or illegitimate," he had nothing to do, but that he had "yet to learn that the qualifications that befit a prize fighter are also a recommendation for a Statesman." *British Colonist*, Jan. 29, 1853.
66 Speech of Jan. 28, *Novascotian*, Feb. 9, 1853.
67 Quoted from the *Hamilton Spectator* in *British Colonist*, Mar. 12, 1853.
68 *British Colonist*, Feb. 17, Apr. 19, 28; May 19; June 9, 1853.

69 Speech of June 29, *Novascotian*, July 18, 1853.
70 A little earlier, when bills of the previous session withdrawing the permanent grant to King's College and disestablishing the Church of England (actually part of the Revised Statutes of 1851) were held up in Britain, William Annand (speech of Jan. 31, *Morning Chronicle*, Feb. 3, 1853) complained that "we have not yet responsible government in Nova Scotia." In the second instance Howe was accused by Hibbert Binney, the Anglican bishop of Nova Scotia, of "wilful misrepresentation" for suggesting that Binney had intervened against the bill in England. He had, in fact, intimated that the bill was of little consequence since the "Establishment," though nominally recognized, had been "practically ignored." Binney to le Marchant, Mar. 2, 1853, JHP, vol. 30, pp. 83–6.
71 *British Colonist*, June 21, 1853.
72 Ibid., Sept. 15, 1853.
73 See Jackson to le Marchant, Sept. 30, 1853 and to Hincks, Sept. 23, 1853, *JHA*, 1854, App. 4, pp. 67–8.
74 *Morning Chronicle*, Oct. 15, 27 and Nov. 5, 1853.
75 *Novascotian*, Feb. 27, 1854.
76 Debate of Feb. 7, *British Colonist*, Feb. 9, 1854.
77 Debate of Feb. 4, ibid., Feb. 7, 1854. To no avail Howe also asked the assembly not to disfranchise the Indians: "when I meet an Indian on the passage to the other world, I do not want him to tax me with not only having robbed him of his broad lands, but of having wrested from him the privilege of voting." Debate of Feb. 13, ibid., Feb. 18, 1854.
78 Debate of Jan. 31, ibid., Feb. 2, 1854.
79 For speech see Chisholm, 2: 268–95.
80 Perhaps for the first time Howe was suggesting that Grey had defaulted on the guarantee for this reason.
81 Commonly found in Howe's speeches and letters of these years was the idea that continued deference to the anticolonials would eventually produce internal difficulties in Britain itself.
82 Perley to Howe, Mar. 3, 1854, JHP, vol. 2, pp. 243–5.
83 *Acadian Recorder*, Mar. 4, 1854.
84 Speech of Feb. 1, *British Colonist*, Feb. 4, 1854.
85 Speech of Feb. 16, *Novascotian*, Mar. 6, 1854.
86 Speech of Feb. 15, ibid., Feb. 27, 1854.
87 *Sun*, Feb. 20, 1854.
88 Speech of Feb. 27, *British Colonist*, Mar. 7, 1854.
89 Jackson to le Marchant, Mar. 3, 1854, *Novascotian*, Mar. 20, 1854.
90 *British Colonist*, Mar. 28, 1854.
91 In addition to Wilkins the "flies" were Elkanah Young (Falmouth) and Benjamin Smith and Nicholas Mosher (Hants county).
92 *British Colonist*, Aug. 29, 1854.
93 Speech of Feb. 15, *Novascotian*, Feb. 27, 1854. The daughter, Ellen, his oldest surviving child, had married Cathcart Thomson in October 1851.

CHAPTER FOUR

1 Howe to unknown, Apr. 19, 1854, "Howe Letters," p. 117.
2 McKeagney to Young, Apr. 15, 1854, PANS, William Young Papers, MG 2, box 733, item 377.

3  *Acadian Recorder*, May 20, 1854.
4  *British Colonist*, Apr. 6, 1854.
5  Ibid., Apr. 6 and 8, 1854.
6  *Acadian Recorder*, Apr. 8, 1854.
7  *Sun*, Apr. 7, 8, 13 and May 15, 1854.
8  *Morning Chronicle*, May 16, 1854.
9  *Sun*, May 17, 1854.
10  Howe to unknown, Apr. 19, 1854, "Howe Letters," pp. 117–8.
11  Ibid., p. 118.
12  Ibid. Howe, the Nova Scotian patriot *par excellence*, added: "Perhaps I would if she was wanted to defend Nova Scotia, for whose sake I do not know the thing I would not attempt."
13  *Sun*, July 8, 1854; *Acadian Recorder*, May 6, 1854.
14  *Novascotian*, July 24, 1854.
15  See commissioners' first report, JHA, 1855, App. 17, pp. 142–4. An embankment of solid stonework crossing an arm of Bedford basin on the second section required 100,000 tons of rock filling alone.
16  Speech of Mar. 27, *Novascotian*, Apr. 17, 1854.
17  See Godley to Howe, Sept. 5, 1854, JHP, vol. 2, pp. 296–302; Howe's answer to Godley is contained in Howe to Adderley, Nov. 4, 1854, ibid., vol. 7, pp. 162–89.
18  Ibid.
19  Illustrating his feelings of insecurity, Young asked Johnston, his foe of many years, to accompany him. He hoped "we will find something more to say to each other than on a former occasion where the mutual silence was so remarkable & so edifying." Young to Creighton, May 2, 1854, William Young Papers, box 733, item 409. Hincks stated bluntly that "the thing is absurd ... [Johnston's] object will be [to] *block you* if he can." Hincks to Young (confidential), June 5, 1854, ibid., item 462.
20  Young to Chandler, June 10, 1854, ibid., item 474.
21  Hincks to Young (confidential), June 5, 1854, ibid., item 462.
22  Speech of Dec. 5, *British Colonist*, Dec. 14, 1854.
23  Speech of Dec. 6, *Novascotian*, Dec. 18, 1854.
24  JHA, Dec. 11 and 12, 1854, pp. 573–9.
25  Speech of Feb. 15, *Novascotian*, Mar. 5, 1855.
26  Speech of Feb. 16, Mar. 19, 1855. Fred and Sydenham, then attending Horton Academy, both wanted the cadetship, but only the latter fell within the prescribed age of twelve to fifteen.
27  Speech of Feb. 21, 1855, Chisholm, 2: 299–304.
28  JHA, Feb. 28, 1855, p. 648.
29  B. Wier to Howe, Apr. 4, 1855, JHP, vol. 18, p. 332.
30  See Richard W. Van Alstyne, "John F. Crampton, Conspirator or Dupe?," *American Historical Review* 41 (April 1936): 493–5.
31  J. Bartlet Brebner, "Joseph Howe and the Crimean War Enlistment Controversy between Great Britain and the United States," *Canadian Historical Review* 11 (December 1930): 305.
32  Ibid., 306.
33  Le Marchant to Herbert, Mar. 1, 1855, JHP, vol. 18, pp. 63–5.
34  Rabbi Dr Moses J. Burak to the author, May 27, 1965.
35  Howe to le Marchant (confidential), Mar. 12, 1855, JHP, vol. 18, pp. 91–105.
36  Ibid.

37 Ibid., Oct. 9, 1855, vol. 19, pp. 109–11.
38 Brebner, "Howe and the Enlistment Controversy," p. 307.
39 See Van Alstyne, "Crampton, Conspirator or Dupe?," pp. 495–6. Carlisle's opinion was enclosed in Crampton to Howe, Mar. 11, 1855, JHP, vol. 21, pp. 40–2.
40 Howe to Crampton, Mar. 16, 1855, ibid., vol. 18, pp. 146–51.
41 Howe to le Marchant (confidential), Mar. 15, 1855, ibid., pp. 134–44.
42 Ibid.
43 Ibid.; see also diary of trip, Mar. 12, 1855, ibid., vol. 66, pp. 186–7. "Crimping" was the practice of entrapping men for service in the army or navy.
44 Howe to Crampton (confidential), Mar. 15, 1855, ibid., vol. 18, pp. 134–44.
45 Howe to Crampton (confidential), Mar. 17, 1855, ibid., pp. 159–66.
46 Howe to Russell, Mar. 15, 1855, ibid., pp. 119–31; diary, Mar. 24, ibid., vol. 66, p. 209.
47 Howe to Palmerston (confidential), Mar. 21, 1855, ibid., vol. 18, pp. 223–34.
48 Howe to le Marchant (confidential), Mar. 15, 1855, ibid., pp. 134–44.
49 Crampton to Howe, Mar. 22, 1855, ibid., pp. 256–7; le Marchant to Howe, Mar. 22, 1855, ibid., pp. 258–60.
50 Howe to Crampton, Mar. 24, 1855, ibid., pp. 271–3.
51 Diary, Mar. 22, 1855, ibid., vol. 66, pp. 203–4.
52 Brebner, "Howe and the Enlistment Controversy," p. 313.
53 Diary, Mar. 24, 1855, JHP, vol. 66, p. 206.
54 Diary, Mar. 25, 1855, ibid., p. 211; Howe to le Marchant (confidential), Apr. 4, 1855, ibid., vol. 18, pp. 315–21.
55 Brebner, "Howe and the Enlistment Controversy," p.315n2.
56 Van Alstyne, "Crampton, Conspirator or Dupe?," p. 497.
57 Howe to le Marchant (confidential), Apr. 4, 1855, JHP, vol. 18, pp. 315–21.
58 Ibid.
59 Ibid., Mar. 26, 1855, vol. 21, pp. 66–72.
60 Brebner, "Howe and the Enlistment Controversy," p. 309.
61 For details see diary, JHP, vol. 66, pp. 213–35.
62 Howe to Crampton (confidential), Apr. 9, 1855, ibid., vol. 18, pp. 360–72. Hertz added further to Howe's difficulties by involving a mad Englishman named Perkins in his ventures. Howe concluded that his main object was to extort money as the price of his silence.
63 Diary, Apr. 4 or 5, 1855, ibid., vol. 66, p. 175.
64 Howe to Crampton (confidential), May 4, 1855, ibid., vol. 18, pp. 540–6.
65 Diary, April[?] 1855, vol. 66, pp. 167–9.
66 Howe to le Marchant (confidential), Apr. 10, 1855, ibid., vol. 18, pp. 356–8.
67 Howe to Crampton, Apr. 11, 1855, ibid., pp. 376–8; Howe to unknown, Apr. 14, 1855, "Howe Letters," p. 128.
68 Ibid., p. 130.
69 For a copy of the letter, see JHP, vol. 18, p. 337.
70 Diary, Apr. 6, 1855, ibid., vol. 66, p. 172.
71 Howe to editors of New York *Herald*, Apr. 7, 1855, ibid., vol. 23, pp. 404–8.
72 Howe to le Marchant, Apr. 2, 1855, ibid., vol. 18, pp. 295–306.

73 Mathew (apparently) to Howe (confidential), Mar. 29, 1855, ibid., pp. 286–9.
74 More than once vessels were ordered for recruits who failed to materialize. During Howe's expedition westward "Tommy" Tilestone, acting as arbitrator, agreed to pay Captain McNeil of the *Louisiana* $1,000 because of Angus McDonald's inability to provide the passengers he had promised. Tilestone to Howe, Apr. 30, 1855, ibid., vol. 18, pp. 489–90. Howe was indignant, maintaining that McNeil had not fulfilled his part of the bargain.
75 *British Colonist*, Apr. 12, 1855. Noting that the Halifax papers were "filled with gasconade," Howe added: "If I am not in the Tombs the fault is not theirs." Diary, n.d., JHP, vol. 66, pp. 164–5.
76 Howe to unknown, Apr. 14, 1855, "Howe Letters," p. 129.
77 Howe to Head (confidential), Apr. 14, 1855, JHP, vol. 18, pp. 391–8.
78 Brebner, "Howe and the Enlistment Controversy," pp. 319 and 319n2.
79 Howe to Crampton (confidential), Apr. 26, 1855, JHP, vol. 18, pp. 521–38.
80 See letters of Susan Ann Howe, ibid., vol. 2, pp. 379–406, esp. p. 389.
81 Wier to Howe, Apr. 4, 1855, ibid., vol. 18, p. 332.
82 Howe to unknown, Apr. 14, 1855, "Howe Letters," p. 129.
83 Brebner, "Howe and the Enlistment Controversy," p. 320.
84 Howe to le Marchant, May 8, 1855, JHP, vol. 21, pp. 145–60.
85 Le Marchant to Russell, May 10, 1855, ibid., vol. 18, pp. 570–4.
86 Turnbull to Howe, May 10, 1855, ibid., pp. 628–9.
87 See Van Alstyne, "Crampton, Conspirator or Dupe?," p. 498.
88 Ibid., p. 502.
89 Brebner, "Howe and the Enlistment Controversy," p. 321.
90 See second letter of Howe to Van Dyke, Nov. 6, 1855, JHP, vol. 20, pp. 58–77.
91 Howe to Smolinski, June 2, 1855, ibid., vol. 19, pp. 3–4. Howe stated that the lieutenant-governor had asked him to withdraw his earlier letter, "the powers conferred by [it] being unusual and susceptible of misapprehension abroad."
92 Van Alstyne, "Crampton, Conspirator or Dupe?," pp. 500–2.
93 Turnbull to Howe, May 28, 1858, JHP, vol. 18, pp. 681–2; de Korponay to Turnbull and Wilkins, May 12 and 22, 1855, ibid., pp. 649, 675–8.

CHAPTER FIVE

1 *British Colonist*, June 9, 1855. Was not Young, it asked, the same person who had threatened Howe with a *capias* for a private debt just as he was preparing to board a steamer for Britain a few years earlier?
2 Johnston's letter to the people of Nova Scotia, ibid., May 8, 1855.
3 *Acadian Recorder*, Jan. 20, 1855.
4 Young to the people of Inverness county, *Novascotian*, May 7 and 14, 1855.
5 *Acadian Recorder*, Apr. 28, 1855.
6 Included among the Tories was James McKeagney of Cape Breton, formerly a Liberal, who did not support the government in the new House.
7 *Morning Chronicle*, May 31, 1855.

8 *British Colonist*, May 31, 1855.
9 Ibid., June 2, 1855.
10 Ibid., Jan. 25, 1855.
11 *Acadian Recorder*, June 9, 1855.
12 Howe to Baring Bros, June 20, 1855, JHP, vol. 7, pp. 246–57.
13 Baring Bros to Howe, Aug. 16, 1855, ibid., vol. 2, pp. 547–51.
14 Howe to Wilkins, Aug. 17, 1855, ibid., vol. 68, pp. 111–7.
15 Le Marchant to Howe, Aug. 16, 1855, ibid., vol. 2, pp. 557–68; William Walsh to Howe, July 9, 1855, ibid., pp. 453–6.
16 Letter from London, Aug. 27, 1855, ibid., reel 23.
17 Letter from Calais (no. 3), Aug. 26, 1855, ibid.
18 The personal vignettes and reactions are to be found in letters from Calais (nos. 2 and 3), ibid.
19 Letter from Calais (no. 1), Aug. 25, 1855, ibid.
20 He did join the ladies in making conundrums, a fad of the day. One of his own was: "Why is Cardinal Wiseman's nose like the castle of Edinburgh? Because it's on an Eminence."
21 See Elliot to Howe with accompanying memorandum, Sept. 7, 1855, JHP, vol. 2, pp. 582–9.
22 Howe to Susan Ann, Aug. 31, 1855, JHP, reel 23, item 47.
23 Diary, Sept. 27, 1855, ibid., vol. 51, p. 3.
24 James A. Roy, *Joseph Howe* (Toronto: Macmillan, 1935), p. 200.
25 J.M. Beck, "Joseph Howe: Opportunist or Empire-Builder?," *Canadian Historical Review* 41 (September 1960): 189.
26 D.G. Creighton, *Dominion of the North* (Boston: Houghton Mifflin, 1944), p. 250.
27 Howe to Russell (confidential), Mar. 15, 1855, JHP, vol. 7, pp. 194–211; Russell to Howe, Apr. 10, 1855, ibid., vol. 2, pp. 416–8.
28 Supra, pp. 68–9.
29 Howe to Sir Denis le Marchant, July 4, 1855, JHP, vol. 7, pp. 234–6.
30 Howe to Russell, July 3, 1855, ibid., pp. 224–33.
31 Beck, "Opportunist or Empire-builder," p. 190.
32 See G.P. Gooch, ed., *The Later Correspondence of Lord John Russell, 1840–75* (London: Longman, Green, 1925) 2: 187.
33 Howe to Russell (confidential), July 11, 1855, JHP, vol. 7, pp. 275–8; Russell to Howe, July 13, 1855, ibid., vol. 2, pp. 478–9.
34 McGeachy to Howe, Aug. 15, 1855, ibid., pp. 539–42.
35 Bigg to Howe, July 13, 1855, ibid., p. 471.
36 For Hincks's pamphlet see Francis Hincks, *Reminiscences of His Public Life* (Montreal, 1884), pp. 228–50; for Howe's reply see Chisholm, 2: 311–27.
37 Howe to Molesworth, Sept. 4, 1855, *JHA*, vol. 7, pp. 356–71.
38 Molesworth to Howe, Sept. 7, 1855, ibid., vol. 2, pp. 578–81.
39 Hincks, *Reminiscences*, pp. 366–7.
40 R.S. Longley, *Sir Francis Hincks* (Toronto: University of Toronto Press, 1943), pp. 234–41.
41 Howe to Molesworth, Sept. 10, 1855, JHP, vol. 7, pp. 375–9.
42 Roy, *Howe*, p. 202.
43 Howe to Sydenham Howe (personal), July 24, 1855, JHP, reel 23, item 154.
44 Diary, Dec. 24, 26, 29, 1855, ibid., vol. 51, pp. 59, 60, 63.

45 Perley to Howe (private), Jan. 13, 1855, ibid., 2: 342–5.
46 Howe to Fisher, Oct. 10, 1855, ibid., vol. 7, pp. 398–406.
47 These letters are scattered throughout JHP, vol. 2.
48 Russell to le Marchant, June 22, 1855, ibid., vol. 21, pp. 230–1. Earlier (May 23) he had asked that Howe not be sent again to the United States.
49 Howe to le Marchant, June 4, 1855, ibid., pp. 197–200.
50 Howe to Wilkins, Feb. [?], 1856, ibid., vol. 19, pp. 216–24; Howe to Crampton, Mar. 20, 1856, ibid., pp. 234–47.
51 Howe to Turnbull, Feb. 25, 1858, ibid., pp. 383–4.
52 Howe to le Marchant, Feb. 8, 1858, ibid., pp. 351–60.
53 For letter see ibid., pp. 89–94.
54 For the letters see ibid., vol. 20, pp. 43–57 and 58–77.
55 Crampton to Howe, Nov. 10, 1855, ibid., pp. 7–11.
56 Howe to Crampton, Jan. 5, 1856, ibid., vol. 19, pp. 198–203; Howe to Clarendon, Mar. 27, 1856, ibid., pp. 254–5.
57 Le Marchant to Howe, n.d., ibid., vol. 5, pp. 140–1; for letter to Roebuck see ibid., vol. 19, pp. 250–1.
58 Howe to Gladstone, July 30, 1856, Chisholm, 2: 329–46.
59 Gladstone to Howe, Jan. 25, 1857, ibid., p. 346.
60 *British Colonist*, Feb. 21, 1856.
61 McCully to Howe, Aug. 30, 1855, JHP, vol. 2, pp. 570–3.
62 *Acadian Recorder*, Mar. 8, 1856; see portrait by Charles Rohan (pseud.), ibid., June 7, 1856; Young to G.C. Laurence, Mar. 18, 1876, PANS, William Young Papers, MG 2, box 734, item 778.
63 Assembly *Debates*, Mar. 4 and 5, 1856, 107–8, 118–9.
64 *Acadian Recorder*, Mar. 8, 1856.
65 Le Marchant to Young (confidential), Mar. [?], 1856, William Young Papers, box 734, item 762.
66 *Presbyterian Witness*, Mar. 29, 1856.
67 Young to G.C. Laurence, Mar. 18, 1856, William Young Papers, box 734, item 778; Young to Perley, Apr. 25, 1856, ibid., item 839.
68 Howe was at McLeod's bedside when he died within a few weeks; later he sent his mother the most compassionate of letters and a brooch containing a lock of her son's hair, winning her gratitude for deigning to "pity the burning tears and broken heart of a poor decrepit old widow." Howe to Mrs McLeod, Apr. 16, 1856, *JHA*, vol. 7, pp. 439–41; Mrs McLeod to Howe, May 13, 1856, ibid., vol. 2, pp. 721–4.
69 Howe to Messrs McDonald & Simpson, May 27, 1856, ibid., vol. 68, pp. 205–8.
70 Diary, Mar. 3, 1856, ibid., vol. 51, pp. 123–4.
71 Young to Howe, July 23, 1856, William Young Papers, box 734, item 962.
72 Howe to Wilkins, May 19, 1856, JHP, vol. 68, pp. 176–83.
73 Ibid., June 5, 1856, pp. 219–22.
74 *British Colonist*, June 5 and 7, 1856.
75 Letter to *Morning Chronicle*, June 10, 1856. The Protestant religious press had for years treated Catholicism and Irish Catholics with varying degrees of contempt, but had never engaged in an all-out crusade of this kind.
76 *Acadian Recorder*, June 14, 1856.
77 *Daily Sun*, June 18, 1856; *Presbyterian Witness*, June 7 and 14, 1856.

78 Locke to Young, July 1, 1856, William Young Papers, box 734, item 934.
79 Young to McKeen, July 22, 1856, ibid., item 961.
80 John McKinnon to Howe, July 4, 1856, JHP, vol. 2, p. 757.
81 Bishop MacKinnon to Howe, Oct. 1, 1856, ibid., pp. 774–5. In reply Howe lamented that the province should be "eternally in a fever about something which happened in Ireland half a century ago, especially since Nova Scotia exhibited "a spirit of moderation, courtesy and fairness towards Catholics" not exceeded in any Christian country. "Though often annoyed with these people I did not rebuke them until they outraged all decorum." Howe to MacKinnon, Oct. 10, 1856, ibid., vol. 7, pp. 459–62. The files of the *Catholic* for 1856 are missing.
82 An outraged *Presbyterian Witness* (July 19, 1856) believed that a committee of its stature could have got Howe elected without his participation.
83 See Howe's speech, *Novascotian*, Sept. 15 and 22, 1856.
84 Young to Hugh Munro, Aug. 15, 1856, William Young Papers, box 734, item 1013; McKeen to Young, Aug. 26, 1856, ibid., item 1038; McLelan to Young, Dec. 29, 1856, ibid., box 735, item 1232.
85 Le Marchant to Howe, Aug. 21, 1856, JHP, vol. 2, pp. 758–60.
86 Howe to Blackwood, Nov. 15, 1856, ibid., vol. 7, pp. 467–76.
87 *Presbyterian Witness*, Dec. 13, 1856.
88 "Talk of the Town," *Acadian Recorder*, Dec. 20, 1856.
89 Ibid.
90 Excerpts from the Halifax *Catholic* in Howe's letter published in the *Morning Chronicle*, Dec. 27, 1856.

CHAPTER SIX

1 Letter in *Morning Chronicle*, Dec. 27, 1856.
2 For one explanation of Howe's conduct see George Johnson biography of Howe, PAC, George Johnson Papers, folder 6, pp. 149–53.
3 *Morning Chronicle*, Jan. 22, 1857.
4 Howe suggested that Young had confirmed this principle for Nova Scotia in his declaration of Apr. 30, 1855.
5 Fulton to Young, Jan. 20, 1857, PANS, William Young Papers, MG 2, box 736, item 1256; Blanchard to Young (private), Jan. 27, 1857, ibid., item 1265.
6 Young to Archibald (private), Jan. 8, 1857, ibid., item 1249. Archibald to Young, Jan. 16, and Feb. 5, 1857, ibid., items 1253 and 1270.
7 Quoted in *British Colonist*, Feb. 10, 1857.
8 Howe to J.H. Anderson, Feb. 8, 1857, JHP, vol. 7, pp. 487–93.
9 Assembly *Debates*, Feb. 9, 1857, pp. 28–9.
10 Ibid., Feb. 11, 1857, 45–51.
11 Ibid., Feb. 16, 1857, 91–106.
12 *Acadian Recorder*, Feb. 14, 1857.
13 Excerpt from the *Catholic* in *Daily Sun*, Feb. 14, 1857.
14 The Catholics were Bourneuf, Fuller, Martell, McKeagney, McKinnon, Robicheau, Smyth, and Tobin. The Protestant Liberals were John Wade, who followed, he said, the course most calculated to "arrest the demon of religious discord" (*Debates*, p. 68), and self-seeking W.A. Henry, who,

representing Sydney county with a population of 11,500 Catholics and 2,000 Protestants, could not be induced to "enter into an alliance for the persecution of the Catholic or any other body" (ibid., p. 56).

15  Ibid., Feb. 9, 1857, p. 28.
16  Howe to half-sister Jane, Dec. 4, 1857, "Howe Letters," p. 119.
17  McDonald to Howe, Mar. 10, 1857, JHP, vol. 2, pp. 867–8; Sprott to Howe, Feb. 18, Mar. 9 and 16, 1857, ibid., pp. 838–41, 859–61, and 869–72.
18  Howe to Binney, Mar. 3, 1857, ibid., vol. 7, pp. 501–3.
19  For the letter and the editorial, see Morning Chronicle, Mar. 5 and 7, 1857.
20  Assembly Debates, Mar. 7, 1857, p. 155.
21  Binney to Howe, Mar. 3, 1857, JHP, vol. 2, pp. 851–4.
22  Howe to Binney, Mar. 5, 1857, ibid., vol. 10, p. 219.
23  Acadian Recorder, Mar. 7, 1857.
24  Nicholas Meagher, The Religious Warfare in Nova Scotia, 1855–60 (Halifax: n.p., 1927), p. 24.
25  Review of Meagher's book, Canadian Historical Review 8 (September 1927): 258.
26  George Johnson biography of Howe, George Johnson Papers, folder 6, p. 151.
27  British Colonist, Mar. 28, 1857.
28  Ibid., Apr. 1, 1857.
29  Howe to Rev. G. Sutherland, May 12, 1857, JHP, vol. 7, pp. 513–6.
30  Assembly Debates, Apr. 9, 1857, pp. 190–3.
31  McNab, long connected politically, as well as by marriage, with Howe, had, in effect, deserted his party to succeed Howe as chief railway commissioner.
32  For Tupper's letters see British Colonist, Sept. 8 and 15, 1857; for Howe's letters see Morning Chronicle, Sept. 8, 10, and 19, 1857.
33  Daily Sun, Apr. 9, 1857.
34  See correspondence in JHP, vol. 2.
35  Howe to half-sister Jane, Dec. 4, 1857, "Howe Letters," p. 119.
36  Ibid.
37  Morning Sun, Jan. 22, 1858.
38  Morning Chronicle, Mar. 6, 1858.
39  Acadian Recorder, Apr. 3, and May 15, 1858.
40  British Colonist, Mar. 11, 1858.
41  JHA, Feb. 15, 1858, p. 424; debates of Feb. 10 and 11, Novascotian, Feb. 22, 1858.
42  Assembly Debates, Mar 1, 1858, pp. 108–9.
43  Ibid., Feb. 17, 1858, pp. 53–7.
44  Morning Sun, Mar. 17, 1858.
45  Assembly Debates, Feb. 24, 1858, p. 95.
46  Ibid., Feb. 24 and 26, 1858, pp. 96, 103.
47  Speech of June 8, 1859 at Bridgetown, Novascotian, June 27, 1859.
48  Morning Sun, June 4, 1858.
49  Ibid., June 11, 1858.
50  Speeches of Mar. 20, Novascotian, Mar. 29 and May 3, 1858.
51  Ibid.
52  Ibid., Acadian Recorder, Mar. 27, 1858.

53 *British Colonist*, Jan. 28, 1858.
54 *Morning Sun*, Mar. 19, 1858. Howe's old apprentice and political friend, Richard Nugent, who had been associated with Ritchie in publishing the *Sun*, had died in March while undergoing medical treatment in New York.
55 Ibid., Feb. 3, 1858.
56 Speech on declaration day, *Morning Chronicle*, Aug. 14, 1858.
57 *Novascotian*, Aug. 9 and 16, 1858.
58 Howe to le Marchant, Nov. 29, 1858; JHP, vol. 7, pp. 578–82.
59 Beck, "Howe: Opportunist or Empire-Builder?," p. 194.
60 Howe to Derby, June 16, 1858, JHP, vol. 7, pp. 530–9.
61 W.L. Grant, *The Tribune of Nova Scotia* (Toronto: Glasgow, Brook, 1920), p. 128; Howe to Bridges, Nov. 29, 1858; to Derby, Nov. 29, 1858; to Merivale, Nov. 29, 1858; and to Bulwer-Lytton, Nov. 27, 1858, JHP, vol. 7, pp. 574–7, 589–92, 583–8, and 566–70.
62 Russell to Howe, Jan. 8, 1859, ibid., vol. 2, pp. 954–5; James A. Roy, *Joseph Howe* (Toronto: Macmillan, 1935), p. 213.
63 Roy, *Howe*, p. 213; Derby to Howe (private), Jan. 17, 1859, JHP, vol. 2, 958–60; Howe to Sir Denis le Marchant, Mar. 10, 1859, ibid., vol. 7, pp. 610–2.
64 Carnarvon (for Bulwer-Lytton) to Howe, Feb. 15, 1859, ibid., vol. 2, pp. 962–3.
65 *Novascotian*, Nov. 29, 1858.
66 Ibid., Aug. 30, 1858.
67 See pamphlet of Frederick M. Kelley, *The Union of the Oceans by Ship Canal, without Locks, via the Atrato Valley* (New York, 1859).
68 See memo of agreement, Jan. 18, 1859, JHP, vol. 29, pp. 310–3.
69 See letters in JHP, vol. 31.
70 *Novascotian*, Feb. 7, 1859.
71 *Acadian Recorder*, Jan. 29, and Feb. 5, 1859.
72 Assembly *Debates*, 1859, pp. 100–1; *Acadian Recorder*, Feb. 19, 1859.
73 Ibid., Feb. 4, 1859, 11–13. Scornfully the *Acadian Recorder* (Feb. 5, 1859) pointed out that a footman, coachman, cook, or other minor functionary had ordered the lowering of the flag.
74 For the details which follow see *Novascotian*, Feb. 14, 1859.
75 *Acadian Recorder*, Feb. 19, 1859.
76 Except for the western district of Halifax, the voters within each county were to participate in the election of an equal number of members.
77 *Novascotian*, Feb. 28, and Mar. 7, 1859.
78 *British Colonist*, Mar. 1, 1859.
79 Ibid., Mar. 8, 1859.
80 *Novascotian*, Mar. 28, 1859.
81 *JHA*, Apr. 1, 1859, p. 117.
82 Howe to constituents of Annapolis, *Evening Express*, Apr. 25, 1859.
83 "Such an unsightly thing I never saw disfiguring a public edifice in any part of the world ... That which Mr. Johnston has reared, like most of the castles he has built in the air, terminates in smoke." Howe's speech of June 8 at Bridgetown, *Novascotian*, June 27 and July 4, 1859.
84 See *Acadian Recorder*, Apr. 9, 1859.
85 Ibid., Apr. 23 and 30, 1859.
86 *Evening Express*, May 23, 1859.

87  Howe to Macleod, Mar. 9 and 29, 1859, Correspondence of Rev. Hugh Macleod, PANS, D.C. Harvey Papers (uncat.), MG1.
88  Howe to Susan Ann, n.d., JHP, vol. 10, pp. 152–4; ibid., May 12, 1859, vol. 7, pp. 623–4.
89  *Morning Chronicle*, May 14, 1859.
90  *Novascotian*, June 27, 1859.
91  Howe to Serrell, May 26, 1859, JHP, vol. 31, p. 56 o-p.
92  Serrell to Howe, May 19, 1859, ibid., p. 56AA.
93  *Morning Chronicle*, July 5, 7, 9, 12, 16, 1859.
94  Howe to Serrell, May 26, 1859, JHP, vol. 31, p. 56 o-p.
95  Roy, *Howe*, p. 216.
96  Kelley to Howe, Aug. 29, 1859, JHP, vol. 31, p. 56II.

## CHAPTER SEVEN

1  *Novascotian*, June 20, 1859.
2  Howe to Susan Ann, June 16, 1859, JHP, vol. 7, pp. 632–4.
3  *Novascotian*, June 27, 1859.
4  Howe to Russell, Aug. 10, 1859, JHP, vol. 7, pp. 659–71.
5  Newcastle to Russell, Aug. 26, 1859, ibid., vol. 2, pp. 1002–4; Howe to Newcastle, Dec. 15, 1859, ibid., vol. 7, pp. 672–9.
6  Howe to Mulgrave (confidential), August 1859, ibid., vol. 7, pp. 639–56.
7  For a full discussion see J. Murray Beck, "The Nova Scotia 'Disputed Election' of 1859 and its Aftermath," *Canadian Historical Review* 36 (December 1955): 293–315.
8  Speech of Feb. 27 at Windsor, *Novascotian*, Mar. 12, 1860.
9  Speech of Jan. 30, ibid., Feb. 13, 1860.
10  *Acadian Recorder*, Apr. 21, 1860.
11  Speech of Feb. 27, *Novascotian*, Mar. 12, 1860.
12  *Novascotian*, Mar. 12, 1860. The attacks on politicians at this juncture were similar to those that convulsed the province during the earlier "war to the knife." Howe headed the Liberals under attack, much of it devoted to charges that he would stoop to any tactic to secure and retain office; there was also an attempt, as noted below, to injure him through the prominence given to the recent death of his illegitimate son Edward.
13  Speech of Feb. 27, ibid., Mar. 12, 1860.
14  In each case the assembly first chose fifteen members by lot from those eligible to serve; then the two parties to the case each struck off four members, leaving seven to try it.
15  *Acadian Recorder*, May 12, 1860.
16  *British Colonist*, Feb. 11, 1860.
17  Beck, "'Disputed Election'," p. 305.
18  Speech of Mar. 27, *Novascotian*, Apr. 16, 1860.
19  Speech of Apr. 24, ibid., May 7, 1860.
20  *Acadian Recorder*, Aug. 25, 1860.
21  *Novascotian*, Sept. 17, 1860.
22  Speech of Feb. 27, ibid., Mar. 12, 1860.
23  Speech of Apr. 9, ibid., May 7, 1860.
24  *Novascotian*, May 7, 1860.
25  Speech of Apr. 9, ibid., May 7, 1860.

26 *Novascotian*, Aug. 13, 1860.
27 *Acadian Recorder*, July 28, 1860.
28 *Morning Chronicle*, June 26, 1860.
29 Beck, "'Disputed Election'," p. 306.
30 Howe to Newcastle, Aug. 15, 1860, JHP, vol. 7, pp. 693–703.
31 Whelan to Howe, Apr. 14, 1860, ibid., vol. 3, pp. 11–18.
32 See the commissioners' interim report dated Oct. 1, 1860, ibid., vol. 65, n.p.
33 Howe to Mulgrave, Jan. 4, 1861, *JHA*, 1861, App. 2: Constitutional Questions, p. 39.
34 Mulgrave to Newcastle, Jan. 8, 1861, ibid., pp. 39–40.
35 Johnston to Newcastle, Jan. 8, 1861, ibid., pp. 41–2; *Minute of Executive Council*, Jan. 10, 1861.
36 Diary, 1861, JHP, vol. 48, pp. 91–2.
37 *Acadian Recorder*, Feb. 2 and Mar. 23, 1861; *British Colonist*, Mar. 30, 1861.
38 Speech of Feb. 9, *British Colonist*, Feb. 21, 1861.
39 Assembly *Debates*, Feb. 7, 1861, p. 51.
40 Ibid., Jan. 31, 1861, pp. 7–8.
41 24 Vic., c. 7 and c. 13.
42 Howe to Tilley (private), Nov. 9, 1860, JHP, vol. 7, pp. 706–8.
43 Assembly *Debates*, Feb. 4, 1861, p. 28.
44 Diary, 1861, JHP, vol. 48, pp. 90–1.
45 Assembly *Debates*, Mar. 19 and 21, 1861, pp. 258–78.
46 Howe to Mulgrave, Mar. 30, 1861, JHP, vol. 8, pp. 42–55.
47 *JHA*, 1861, App. 9: Tangier Mines, p. 3.
48 *Yarmouth Herald*, June 13, 1861.
49 For Howe's account of the trip to Yarmouth and Digby see diary, 1861, JHP, vol. 48, pp. 94–121; for Roy's comments see *Joseph Howe* (Toronto: Macmillan, 1935), p. 230.
50 For an account of the stay at Rothesay, JHP, vol. 48, pp. 122–33.
51 For the report see Assembly *Journals* (P.E.I.), 1862, App. o.
52 Frank MacKinnon, *Government of Prince Edward Island* (Toronto: University of Toronto Press, 1951), p. 119.
53 Howe to Newcastle, July 10, 1861, JHP, vol. 8, pp. 95–7.
54 For Howe's reports of Sept. 4 and Oct. 28, 1861 to Mulgrave see *JHA*, 1862, App. 2: Nova Scotia Gold Fields, pp. 10–15, 20–23.
55 Ibid.
56 Diary, 1861, JHP, vol. 48, pp. 147–8.
57 Howe to Ross, Aug. 14, 1860, ibid., vol. 7, pp. 689–92.
58 *JHA*, Apr. 15, 1861, p. 128.
59 Howe to Nelson, July 2, 1861, JHP, vol. 8, pp. 86–9.
60 Diary, 1861, ibid., vol. 48, p. 157.
61 Delegates to Mulgrave, Oct. 24, 1861, *JHA*, 1862, App. 9, pp. 5–7.
62 For the account of the western trip see ibid., 7; also diary, 1861, JHP, vol. 48, pp. 164–95.
63 Delegates to Mulgrave, pp. 5–7.
64 Diary, 1861, JHP, vol. 48, p. 88.
65 Howe to Mulgrave, Nov. 30, 1861, ibid., vol. 8, pp. 150–9.
66 Vankoughnet, Howe, and Tilley to Newcastle, Dec. 2, 1861, *JHA*, 1862, App. 9, p. 9.

67 The excerpts which follow are from the Oldham speech as reported from the *Manchester Guardian* in the *Morning Chronicle*, Dec. 28 and 31, 1861.

68 Smyth to Howe, Dec. 20, 1861, JHP, vol. 3, pp. 255–78.

69 *British Colonist*, Dec. 31, 1861.

70 Howe to Barings, Dec. 31, 1861, JHP, vol. 8, pp. 166–77; Howe's report to Mulgrave, Apr. 5, 1862, *JHA*, 1862, App. 9, p. 15. For details of formation of the association, see ibid., pp. 19–25.

71 See Howe to Tilley, Jan. 19, 1862, JHP, vol. 8, pp. 182–224.

72 Howe to Gray, Jan. 20, 1862, ibid., pp. 226–36.

73 Roy, *Howe*, p. 223.

74 Gray to Howe, Nov. 12, 1861, JHP, vol. 3, pp. 144–54.

75 Howe to Tilley, Jan. 19, 1862, ibid., vol. 8, pp. 182–224.

76 Debate of Feb. 27, *Morning Chronicle*, Mar. 1, 1862.

77 Debate of Mar. 8, ibid., Mar. 11, 1862; see also *JHA*, 1862, App. 18: Sheriff of Cape Breton, p. 27.

78 Debate of Mar. 20, *Morning Chronicle*, Mar. 29, 1862.

79 Ibid.

80 He also threw the opposition into a frenzy by stating that he had written to the judges and to Newcastle, through Mulgrave, to ascertain their views on the proposed reduction in salaries.

81 Speech of Mar. 26, *British Colonist*, Mar. 27, 1862.

82 *Morning Chronicle*, Apr. 1, 1862; Mulgrave to Newcastle, Apr. 3, *JHA*, 1863, App. 11: Civil List, p. 5.

83 Howe to Shaw (private), Apr. 4, 1862, JHP, vol. 8, pp. 268–71; Shaw to Howe (private), Apr. 5, 1862, ibid., vol. 3, pp. 404–6.

84 Speech of Apr. 10, *Morning Chronicle*, Apr. 17, 1862.

85 See, e.g. *Acadian Recorder*, Apr. 12, and May 24, 1862.

86 Mulgrave to Newcastle, Apr. 3, 1862, *JHA*, 1863, App. 11: Civil List, pp. 5–7.

87 Speech of Mar. 21, *Novascotian*, Apr. 29, 1861.

88 Howe to McKinnon and McDonald, May 28, 1862, JHP, vol. 8, pp. 292–5; McDonald to Howe (confidential), June 7, 1862, ibid., vol. 3, pp. 442–5.

89 McKinnon to Howe, June 27, 1862, ibid., vol. 3, pp. 462–4; Howe to McKinnon, June 18, 1862, ibid., vol. 8, pp. 301–3.

90 *Acadian Recorder*, Mar. 14, 1863.

91 Howe to Newcastle, Apr. 17, 1862, JHP, vol. 8, pp. 276–83.

92 Newcastle to Mulgrave, Apr. 12, 1862, *JHA*, 1863, App. 5: Inter-Colonial Railway, p. 2.

93 *Acadian Recorder*, May 17, 1862; *British Colonist*, Aug., 21, 1862.

94 Report of Howe and McCully to Mulgrave, Oct. 16, 1862, *JHA*, 1863, App. 5: Inter-Colonial Railway, pp. 4–6; Howe to Newcastle, Sept. 13, 1862, JHP, vol. 8, pp 316–9.

95 Chisholm, 2: 372–83. The militia bill, prompted largely by the Trent affair, would have added substantially to defence costs.

96 For excerpts from the Canadian papers see *Acadian Recorder*, Oct. 4, 1862.

97 *Morning Chronicle*, Oct. 4, 1862; *British Colonist*, Nov. 6, 1862.

98 Macdonald to Howe (private), Oct. 18, 1862, JHP, vol. 3, pp. 521–4.

99 See Howe's report to Mulgrave on the negotiations, Feb. 10, 1863, *JHA*, 1863, App. 5: Inter-Colonial Railway, pp. 9–15.
100 W.L. Morton, *The Critical Years: The Union of British North America* (Toronto: McClelland and Stewart, 1964), p. 123.
101 Howe to Under-Secretary Rogers, Dec. 19, 1862, *JHA*, 1863, App. 5, pp. 14–15.
102 Howland and Sicotte to Newcastle, Dec. 23, 1862, ibid., pp. 17–25.
103 Howe to unknown, Dec. 13, 1862, JHP, reel 23.
104 This reference to his speaking and social engagements, and the ones which follow, are in a letter to his half-sister Jane, January 1863, *Report of PANS*, 1953, App. B, pp. 16–19.
105 Howe to Adderley, Dec. 24, 1862, Chisholm, 2: 408–9.
106 Smyth to Howe, n.d. [prob. 1861 or 1862], JHP, vol. 5, pp. 429–32.
107 Tilley to Susan Ann Howe, Nov. 29, 1862, ibid., reel 23.
108 Howe to Angela Burdett-Coutts, Nov. 12, 1862, ibid., vol. 8, pp. 328–35.
109 Howe to Newcastle, Sept. 2, 1862, ibid., vol. 12, pp. 113–6; Howe to Russell, Sept. 2, 1862, ibid., vol. 8, pp. 312–4.
110 Howe to Newcastle, Dec. 1, 1862, ibid., vol. 12, pp. 117–22.
111 Howe to half-sister Jane, January 1863, *Report of PANS*, 1953, App. B, p. 17.

CHAPTER EIGHT

1 Howe to Newcastle, Jan. 20, 1863, JHP, vol. 8, pp. 485–90.
2 Howe to J.S. Macdonald, Jan. 13, 1863, ibid., pp. 480–4.
3 *British Colonist*, Jan. 22, 1863.
4 Speech of Feb. 12, *Morning Chronicle*, Feb. 14, 1863.
5 Ibid.
6 Speech of Feb. 13, ibid., Feb. 17, 1863.
7 Speech of Feb. 16, ibid., Feb. 19, 1863.
8 Speech of Mar. 16, ibid., Mar. 21, 1863.
9 Speech of Mar. 11, ibid., Mar. 17, 1863.
10 George Patterson, *The History of Dalhousie College and University* (Halifax, 1887), chap. IV.
11 Speech of Mar. 23, *Morning Chronicle*, Mar. 26, 1863.
12 Ibid.
13 *British Colonist*, Apr. 4, 1863.
14 Howe to le Marchant, Oct. 23, 1863, JHP, vol. 37, n.p.
15 Speech of Mar. 19, *Morning Chronicle*, Mar. 24, 1863.
16 Speech of Mar. 23, ibid., Mar. 26, 1863.
17 Speech of Apr. 6, supplement to ibid., Apr. 7, 1863.
18 *British Colonist*, Mar. 21 and Apr. 2, 1863.
19 Speech of Apr. 6, supplement to *Novascotian*, May 4, 1863.
20 For Pineo's defence see letter in *Morning Chronicle*, Apr. 25, 1863.
21 Tilley to Howe, Jan. 15, 1863, JHP, vol. 3, pp. 621–8.
22 Ibid. (private), Jan. 28, 1863, pp. 641–51.
23 *British Colonist*, Feb. 26, 1863.
24 *Morning Chronicle*, Mar. 21, 1863.
25 Speech of Apr. 18, 1863, *British Colonist*, Apr. 21, 1863.
26 Ibid.

27  Howe to Newcastle, Apr. 30, 1863, JHP, vol. 8, pp. 518–21.
28  James A. Roy, *Joseph Howe* (Toronto: Macmillan, 1935), p. 243.
29  Howe to Angela Burdett-Coutts (strictly confidential), Feb. 19, 1863, JHP, vol. 8, pp. 500–9.
30  Ibid., Mar. 5, 1863, pp. 510–7.
31  Ibid., May 14 and Mar. 5, 1863, pp. 530–6 and 510–7.
32  *British Colonist*, May 16, 1863; *Morning Chronicle*, May 19, 1863.
33  *British Colonist*, May 5, 1863.
34  *Acadian Recorder*, May 23, 1863.
35  Howe to Andrews, Nov. 25 and Dec. 24, 1863, JHP, vol. 37, n.p.
36  Howe to le Marchant, Oct. 23, 1863, ibid.
37  Sprott to Howe, Mar. 17, 1863, ibid., vol. 3, pp. 737–40.
38  For account of the trip see diary, 1863, ibid., vol. 55.
39  Howe to Lady North, Nov. 12, 1863, ibid., vol. 37, n.p.; JHP, vol. 55, pp. 36–7.
40  Howe to Angela Burdett-Coutts, Nov. 12, 1863, ibid., vol. 37, n.p.
41  Howe to Russell, Oct. 14, 1863, ibid., vol. 13, pp. 89–93.
42  Howe to Sir Gaspard le Marchant, Oct. 23, 1863, ibid., vol. 37, n.p.
43  For description of the trip and the later move to Fairfield see Howe to half-sister Jane, Oct. 22, 1863, *Report of PANS*, 1953, pp. 21–2.
44  For an account of Howe's residences see J.P. Martin, *Dartmouth Free Press*, July 27, 1967.
45  Howe to Angela Burdett-Coutts, Oct. 29, 1863, JHP, vol. 37, n.p.
46  Howe to Rev. H.L. Owen, Nov. 25, 1863, ibid.
47  *Morning Chronicle*, July 23, 1863.
48  Howe to Watkin, Nov. 27 and Dec. 1863, JHP, vol. 37: n.p. Earlier in the year, in another railway matter, the New Brunswick Court of Chancery had found in favour of John Shortridge's son-in-law and his partners.
49  Howe to Lyons (private), Jan. 30, 1864, ibid., vol. 8, pp. 542–4; Howe to Hammond (private), Feb. 2, 1864, ibid., vol. 37, n.p.; Hammond to Howe (private), Mar. 11, 1864, ibid., vol. 12, p. 226.
50  For copies of letters to the *Albion* see ibid., vol. 13, pp. 96–116.
51  JHP, vol. 55, p. 52.
52  Howe to le Marchant, Mar. 30, 1864, ibid., vol. 37, n.p.
53  *Acadian Recorder*, Apr. 30, 1864; Roy, *Howe*, p. 254.
54  JHP, vol. 55, p. 54.
55  Howe to Annand, July 8, 1863 and May 20, 1864, ibid., vol. 37, n.p.
56  For account of trip to the U.S.A. and its sequel see JHP, vol. 55.
57  Howe to Sir James Hope, Sept. 20, 1864, ibid., vol. 37, n.p.
58  Howe to Perley, Sept. 8, 1864, ibid., vol. 12, pp. 339–47.
59  See, e.g., *Morning Chronicle*, Nov. 21, 1863.
60  For exchange of letters see Chisholm, 2: 434–5.
61  Hammond to Howe, Aug. 24, 1864, JHP, vol. 12, pp. 324–5.
62  *Acadian Recorder*, Aug. 13, 1864.
63  While there was some disagreement on Howe's exact words, he never disputed this account, published in *Morning Chronicle*, Aug. 16, 1864.
64  Speech of June 4 at Truro, ibid., June 7, 1867.
65  George Johnson biography of Howe, PAC, George Johnson Papers, folder 6, p. 209; its source was Edward Palmer. See also Peter B. Waite, *The Life and Times of Confederation* (Toronto: University of Toronto Press, 1962), p. 105n7.

66 *Morning Chronicle*, Aug. 4, 1864.
67 See Waite, *Life and Times of Confederation*, p. 199.
68 See J. Murray Beck, *Joseph Howe: Anti-Confederate*, Canadian Historical Association booklet no. 17 (1965), p. 8.
69 Ibid., p. 4.
70 *Acadian Recorder*, Dec. 28, 1864.
71 George Johnson biography of Howe, PAC, George Johnson Papers, folder 6, p. 213.
72 Howe to the electors of Hants, no. 2, *Halifax Citizen*, Apr. 8, 1869.
73 Speech of May 9, 1867 in Mason's Hall, *Morning Chronicle*, May 15, 1867.
74 Speech of May 8, 1866 at Windsor, ibid., May 19, 1866.
75 Botheration Letters nos. 2 and 7, *Morning Chronicle*, Jan. 13 and 27, 1865.
76 Ibid., nos. 3 and 10, Jan. 14 and Feb. 8, 1865.
77 Ibid., nos. 8 and 9, Feb. 1 and 3, 1865.
78 Ibid., no. 11, Feb. 10, 1865.
79 Waite, *Life and Times of Confederation*, p. 213.
80 *Unionist*, Jan. 25 and 30, 1865.
81 *Morning Chronicle*, Feb. 4, 1865.
82 *Unionist*, Mar. 3, 1865; *Morning Chronicle*, Mar. 4, 1865.
83 Botheration Letter no. 8, *Morning Chronicle*, Feb. 1, 1865.
84 *British Colonist*, Feb. 28, and Mar. 2, 1865.
85 Two months earlier he had told Lord Russell he doubted if the Confederates could carry any of the eighteen counties. Howe to Russell, Jan. 19, 1865, JHP, vol. 8, pp. 571–8.
86 Howe kept no diary of the trip but later recounted it to Sarah, daughter of his half-sister Jane. Howe to Sarah, Dec. 10, 1865, *Report of PANS*, 1953, pp. 23–7.
87 Bruce to Howe (most private), July 13, 1865, JHP, vol. 4, pp. 36–8; Howe to Russell, July 21, 1865, ibid., vol. 12, pp. 413–22. The Nova Scotia delegates were W.J. Stairs, B.W. Salter, Thomas Killam, T.D. Archibald, and R.P. Grant.
88 Bruce to Howe, July 14, 1865, JHP, vol. 4, pp. 39–41.
89 "G.J.'s Reminiscences of Howe," p. 11, G.M. Grant Correspondence, folder 1, in PAC, George Johnson papers.
90 For the speech see Chisholm, 2: 438–55.
91 "G.J.'s Reminiscences of Joseph Howe," p. 11.
92 Roy, *Howe*, pp. 260–1.
93 Ibid., p. 262; letter of Howe, July 17, 1865, in extracts by Sydenham Howe, PAC, George Johnson Papers, folder 3, p. 41. Nothing said about the speech more delighted him than the remarks of a Detroit policeman, a former Halifax Irishman: "Oh! blood an ouns, wasn't I glad to hear the sound of your voice once more. I knowed what was coming and went down to the Convention early and got a good place, and wasn't it fun to see the Yankees all shouting like devils." Howe to Sarah, Dec. 10, 1865, *Report of PANS*, 1953, p. 27.
94 Halifax *Unionist*, July 21, 1865; *British Colonist*, July 27, 1885.
95 Howe to Sarah, Dec. 10, 1865, *Report of PANS*, 1953, p. 27.
96 When Perley protested, Howe replied: "I have reason to know that your nearest and dearest friends deeply regret what has been painfully obvious to a much wider circle." Howe to Perley, Aug. 31, 1865, JHP, vol.

12, pp. 430–5. For some time, too, the American secretary of state, Seward, had been complaining of the prolongation of the commission's work.

97  Howe to Russell, Jan. 19, 1865, JHP, vol. 8, pp. 571–8.
98  Report of the delegates, *JHA*, 1866, App. 4, p. 2.
99  Cardwell to Russell, July 15, 1866, Public Record Office, Russell Papers, 30/22, vol. 26.
100  Howe to Bruce (private), Aug. 1, 1865, JHP, vol. 8, pp. 602–5.
101  For details of trip see second letter to Sarah, Dec. 11, 1865, *Report of PANS*, 1953, pp. 27–31.
102  Howe to Susan Ann, Aug. 18, 1865, "Howe Letters," p. 179.
103  Ibid., Sept. 13, 1865, p. 180.
104  Ibid., Sept. 30, 1865. The paper was modified and printed in pamphlet form in 1866 and reprinted in Chisholm, 2: 492–506.
105  Howe to Sarah, Dec. 10, 1865, *Report of PANS*, 1953, p. 23.
106  Howe to Susan Ann, Sept. 30, 1865, "Howe Letters," p. 181.
107  A week before the election Tupper had published a dispatch from Cardwell suggesting that "the Union of the Provinces would afford the best hope of obtaining" a new reciprocity treaty. *Royal Gazette*, Dec. 20, 1865, containing Cardwell to Williams, Nov. 24, 1865.
108  Halifax *Evening Reporter*, Dec. 5, 1865.
109  Howe to editor of *Reporter*, ibid., Dec. 9, 1865.
110  Howe to Susan Ann, Jan. 15, 1866, "Howe Letters," pp. 186–7. Howe's friend Northup told him that, although it was "a very desirable [opening] to fall back on," Russell and Cardwell would surely "do what they ought." Northup to Howe, Jan. 20, 1866, JHP, vol. 4, pp. 82–3.
111  Howe to Susan Ann, Feb. 12, 1866, "Howe Letters," p. 188.
112  Howe to Clarendon, Mar. 19, 1866, JHP, vol. 13, pp. 126–7.
113  Donald C. Masters, *The Reciprocity Treaty of 1854* (London: Longmans, Green, 1973), p. 155.
114  Ibid., pp. 164–5.
115  Howe to Susan Ann, Mar. 6, 1866, "Howe Letters," pp. 190–1.
116  Note to Galt, Mar. 8, 1866, JHP, vol. 9, pp. 18–21.
117  Howe to Susan Ann, Mar. 6, 1866, "Howe Letters," pp. 190–1.
118  Ibid.
119  In February he had contributed other material to the *Albion*, including four articles for the series "John Bull to Brother Jonathan."
120  Howe to Clarendon, Mar. 20, 1865, JHP, vol. 12, pp. 479–86.
121  Howe to Susan Ann, Mar. 12, 1866, in extracts by Sydenham Howe, George Johnson Papers, folder 3, 46 B.
122  "Howe Letters," p. 192. He did not say whether it was the full- or part-time offer.

CHAPTER NINE

1  Howe to Cardwell (private), Mar. 29, 1866, JHP, vol. 12, pp. 487–9.
2  Williams to Gordon, Mar. 7, 1866, Lieutenant Governor's Telegraph Book, no. 13, PANS, RG 2, vol. 36.
3  Peter B. Waite, *The Life and Times of Confederation* (Toronto: University of Toronto Press, 1962), p. 228.
4  Annand to Smith, Mar. 20, 1866, *Morning Chronicle*, Mar. 2, 1869.

5 Waite, *Life and Times of Confederation*, p. 269n37.
6 *Morning Chronicle*, Apr. 4, 1866.
7 Assembly *Debates*, Apr. 3, 1866, p. 189.
8 Howe to electors of Hants, no. 2, *Halifax Citizen*, Apr. 8, 1869.
9 Howe to Sir John Hay, Nov. 12, 1866, JHP, vol. 9, pp. 199–210; Howe to Cardwell (private), Apr. 12, 1866, ibid., pp. 22–31.
10 Chester Martin, *Foundations of Canadian Nationhood* (Toronto: University of Toronto Press, 1955), p. 357.
11 Letter of Apr. 9, *Morning Chronicle*, Apr. 10, 1866.
12 Ibid., Apr. 12, 1866.
13 Howe to Cardwell (private), Apr. 12, 1866, JHP, vol. 9, pp. 22–31. This letter crossed Cardwell's reply to his earlier one, which stated, not encouragingly, that Clarendon would consider any suggestion of how his "services would be useful in ... the Fisheries." Cardwell to Howe (private), Apr. 14, 1866, ibid., vol. 12, pp. 491–4.
14 D.G. Creighton, *The Road to Confederation* (Toronto: Macmillan, 1964), p. 360.
15 *Morning Chronicle*, Oct. 24, 1867.
16 George G. Patterson, *Studies in Nova Scotian History* (Halifax: Imperial Publishing Co., 1940), pp. 110–1.
17 *Acadian Recorder*, Mar. 7, 1866.
18 Assembly *Debates*, Apr. 10 and 16, 1866, pp. 222, 245.
19 Ibid., Apr. 16, 1866, pp. 240–1.
20 *Morning Chronicle*, May 8, 1866.
21 Ibid., Apr. 19, 1866.
22 Ibid., May 1, 1866.
23 Howe to Isaac Buchanan, June 20, 1866, "Howe Letters," pp. 193–4.
24 Speech of May 8 at Windsor, *Morning Chronicle*, May 19, 1866.
25 George Johnson biography of Howe, PAC, George Johnson Papers, folder 6, 245A.
26 *Yarmouth Tribune*, May 23, 1866.
27 Speech at Barrington, *Morning Chronicle*, June 9, 1866.
28 Ibid.
29 J. Murray Beck, *Joseph Howe: Anti-Confederate*, Canadian Historical Association booklet no. 17 (1965), p. 19.
30 Howe to Stairs, July 13 and 20, in Lawrence J. Burpee, ed., "Joseph Howe and the Anti-Confederation League," *Transactions of the Royal Society of Canada*, sec. 2, ser. 3, 9 (March 1917): 425–6.
31 For an account of his Irish tour see the letters to his son William, Aug. 8, 11, and 13, 1866, JHP, reel 23, items 167, 168, 169.
32 Creighton, *Road to Confederation*, pp. 396–7.
33 Howe to Derby, July 24 and 30, 1866, JHP, vol. 9:48–56, 66–71.
34 Howe to Stanley (private), Aug. 20 and 21, 1866, ibid., pp. 82–99 and 100–8.
35 Cardwell to Williams, Sept. 1, 1866, quoted in Kenneth G. Pryke, *Nova Scotia and Confederation: 1864–74* (Toronto: University of Toronto Press, 1979), p. 34.
36 Elliot to Howe, Aug. 16, 1866, Burpee, "Anti-Confederation League," p. 429.
37 Howe to Susan Ann, Aug. 18, 1866, "Howe Letters," p. 196.
38 *Times*, Aug. 18, 1866.

39 Howe to Stairs, Sept. 10, 1866, Burpee, "Anti-Confederation League," pp. 431–2.
40 Ibid.; also Howe to Susan Ann, Sept. 10, 1866, JHP, reel 23, item 77.
41 See Chisholm 2: 468–92.
42 Howe to Susan Ann, Sept. 10, 1866, JHP, reel 23, item 77.
43 Howe to Stairs, Sept. 28, 1866, Burpee, "Anti-Confederation League," pp. 432–3.
44 Howe to editor of the *Times* (private), Sept. 17, 1866, JHP, vol. 9, pp. 135–7.
45 Howe to Stairs, Sept. 28, 1866, Burpee, "Anti-Confederation League," pp. 432–3.
46 London *Morning Star*, Sept. 21, 26, 29, 1866.
47 London *Daily News*, Sept. 21, 24, 29, 1866.
48 *Lloyd's Weekly*, Oct. 7, 1866; London *Patriot*, Oct. 4, 1866; *Evening Express*, Oct. 2, 1866.
49 Howe and Annand to Carnarvon, Oct. 3, 1866, JHP, vol. 9, pp. 171–81; London *Daily Telegraph*, Sept. 29, 1866.
50 *Standard*, Oct. 13, 1866; *Spectator*, Oct. 6, 1866; *London Review*, Oct. 6, 1866.
51 Howe to Susan Ann, Sept. 29, 1866 (letter no. 2), JHP, reel 23, item 81.
52 Howe to Stairs, Oct. 12, 1866, Burpee, "Anti-Confederation League," pp. 434–5.
53 Howe to Susan Ann, Sept. 29, 1866 (letter no. 1), JHP, reel 23, item 80.
54 Ibid., Oct. 25, 1866, item 84.
55 Ibid., Sept. 29, 1866 (letter no. 1).
56 Howe to Stairs, Oct. 12, 1866, Burpee, "Anti-Confederation League," pp. 434–5.
57 See Chisholm, 2: 492–506.
58 Charles Tupper, "A Letter to the Earl of Carnarvon" (London, 1866); see also J.M. Beck, *The Government of Nova Scotia* (Toronto: University of Toronto Press, 1957), p. 148.
59 Howe to Susan Ann, Oct. 25 and 26, 1866, JHP, reel 23, items 84 and 85.
60 Howe to Stairs, Nov. 9, 1866, Burpee, "Anti-Confederation League," pp. 435–6.
61 Howe to Susan Ann [?], Nov. 9, 1866, "Howe Letters," p. 202; *Standard*, Nov. 8, 1866; *Hampshire Independent*, Nov. 10, 14, and 21, 1866; *Pall Mall Gazette*, Nov. 17, 1866.
62 Howe to Stairs, Nov. 9, 1866, Burpee, "Anti-Confederation League," pp. 436–7.
63 Howe to Stanley (private), Nov. 14, 1866, JHP, vol. 9, pp. 182–9.
64 Howe to Stairs, Nov. 9 and 23, 1866, Burpee, "Anti-Confederation League," pp. 436–7 and 443–4.
65 T.T. Vernon Smith Diary, entry of Dec. 1, 1866, PANS, MG 1, vol. 1001, no. 2, 269.
66 Howe to Stairs, Dec. 8, 1866, Burpee, "Anti-Confederation League," pp. 444–7.
67 Howe to Susan Ann, Dec. 22, 1866, JHP, reel 23, item 87.
68 Howe to Stairs, Dec. 21, 1866, Burpee, "Anti-Confederation League," pp. 447–8.
69 Howe to Hay, Nov. 12, 1866, ibid., pp. 437–9.

70 Howe to Normanby, Nov. 22, 1866, ibid., pp. 439–43. The letter was in reply to Normanby's views that union would enable the colonies to defend themselves better and preserve their ties with Britain, and that colonial representation in the British Parliament was something "which neither you nor I shall ever see carried out." Normanby to Howe, Nov. 21, 1866, JHP, vol. 5, pp. 226–41.

71 Martin, *Foundations of Canadian Nationhood*, p. 359.

72 Howe to Susan Ann, Dec. 22, 1866, JHP, reel 23, item 87. Northup was one of his closest Halifax friends.

73 Ibid., n.d., item 150.

74 Howe to Stairs, Jan. 5, 1867, Burpee, "Anti-Confederation League," pp. 449–50.

75 Carnarvon to Howe (private), Jan. 1, 1867, JHP, vol. 4, pp. 263–5; Howe to Susan Ann, n.d., ibid., reel 23, item 150.

76 Carnarvon to Howe (private), Jan. 4, 1867, JHP, vol. 4, pp. 266–7; Howe to Carnarvon, Jan. 7, 1867, ibid., vol. 9, pp. 281–3. Carnarvon was being disingenuous, to say the least, since he was following John A. Macdonald's advice not to publicize the resolutions until an actual bill was presented to Parliament and thus make it more difficult for Howe to launch an attack. See Pryke, *Nova Scotia and Confederation*, p. 39.

77 Howe to Stairs, Jan. 19, 1867, Burpee, "Anti-Confederation League," pp. 451–2.

78 Carnarvon to Howe (private), Jan. 18, 1867, JHP, vol. 4, pp. 268–9; Howe to Stairs, Jan. 19, 1867, Burpee, "Anti-Confederation League," pp. 451–2. The "Case" was published in the *Morning Chronicle*, Feb. 16, 18, 19, 20, 1867.

79 Howe to Carnarvon (private), Jan. 21, 1867, JHP, vol. 9, pp. 289–96.

80 Carnarvon to Howe, Jan. 29, 1867, ibid., vol. 4, pp. 272–3.

81 Trelawny Saunders to Howe, Feb. 14, 1867, ibid., vol. 4, pp. 277–84; Howe to Russell (private), Feb. [?], 1867, ibid., vol. 9, pp. 297–302.

82 Howe to Stairs, Mar. 2, 1867, *Report of PANS*, 1957, pp. 27–9.

83 Ibid.; also Howe to Stairs, Mar. 15, 1867, Burpee, 456–9.

84 Howe to Stairs, Feb. 15, 1867, Burpee, "Anti-Confederation League," pp. 455–6.

85 *Parl. Debates* (Lords), Feb. 19, 1867, col. 557.

86 Ibid., col. 572. Of Carnarvon's speech Howe said that it reminded him of the man in the farce: "I'll kill you like a gentleman, you shall die without a groan." Speech of May 24 in Temperance Hall, Halifax, *Morning Chronicle*, May 29, 1867.

87 Howe to Stairs, Mar. 2, 1867, *Report of PANS*, 1957, pp. 27–9.

88 Ibid.; *Parl. Debates* (Lords), Feb. 19, 1867, cols. 576b–582.

89 Speech of May 24 in Temperance Hall, Halifax, *Morning Chronicle*, May 29, 1867. Perhaps to relieve his frustration, Howe wrote out the speech (it never saw the light of day) he would have delivered had he sat in the Lords. Contrasting its conduct on the BNA bill with that on one "involving the honor or the property of a single Peer," he told its members not to be surprised if the Nova Scotians elected to go to Ottawa came instead to London to press for the repeal of an act "for the rapid passage of which there is neither precedent nor necessity." See "The Speech that was not spoken," JHP, vol. 26–1, pp. 230–46.

90 Howe to Stairs, Feb. 15, 1867, Burpee, "Anti-Confederation League," pp. 455–6; Howe to Susan Ann, Feb. 15, 1867, "Howe Letters," pp. 205–6.
91 Howe to Stairs, Mar. 2, 1867, *Report of PANS*, 1957, pp. 27–9.
92 *Parl. Debates* (Commons), Feb. 28, 1867, 1165, 1187, 1188, 1192.
93 Ibid., 1180–5.
94 Garvie to Stairs [?], Mar. 15, 1867, Burpee, "Anti-Confederation League," pp. 461–3.
95 Howe to Susan Ann, Mar. 2, 1867, "Howe Letters," p. 207; Howe to Stairs, Mar. 2, 1867, *Report of PANS*, 1957, pp. 27–9.
96 Horsman to Howe, Mar. 3, 1867, JHP, vol. 4, pp. 289–91; Howe to Bright, Mar. 8, 1867, JHP, 10: 180–3. In appreciation, Howe sent Bright the two volumes of his *Speeches and Public Letters*, "the record of a life as stormy as your own." Admittedly, "they are too heavy to read," but he had nothing else to send except good wishes. Howe to Bright, Feb. 22, 1867, ibid., vol. 9, pp. 354–6.
97 Garvie to Stairs [?], Mar. 15, 1867, Burpee, "Anti-Confederation League," pp. 461–3.
98 Howe to Susan Ann, Mar. 15, 1867, "Howe Letters," p. 208, and to Stairs, Mar. 15, 1867, Burpee, "Anti-Confederation League," pp. 456–9.
99 Howe to Susan Ann, Mar. 28, 1867, "Howe Letters," p. 208, and to Stairs, Mar. 29, 1867, Burpee, "Anti-Confederation League," pp. 460–1.
100 Garvie to Stairs [?], Mar. 15, 1867, Burpee, "Anti-Confederation League," pp. 461–3.
101 Howe to Stairs, Apr. 13, 1867, *Report of PANS*, 1957, pp. 30–1.
102 Stairs to Howe, Mar. 28, 1867, Burpee, "Anti-Confederation League," pp. 459–60. A little later (April 11) Stairs added: "you have a perfect right to mark out your own path" (ibid., pp. 463–4), and Northup advised him to "*shape your own course as you may deem best having already sacrificed so much for the country*" (Apr. 11, 1867, JHP, vol. 4, pp. 297–8).
103 Howe to Stairs, Apr. 12, 1867, in extracts by Sydenham Howe, George Johnson Papers, folder 3, 50.
104 Howe to Stanley, Apr. 25, 1867, JHP, vol. 9, pp. 362–5.

CHAPTER TEN

1 *Acadian Recorder*, Mar. 11, 1867.
2 Speech of May 9, *Morning Chronicle*, May 15, 1867.
3 Ibid.
4 Young to Howe, May 3, 1867, JHP, vol. 4, pp. 307–8; Howe to Young, May 11, 1867, ibid., vol. 9, pp. 366–8.
5 For these speeches see Chisholm, 2: 508–20; *Morning Chronicle*, May 29 and June 7, 1867. By now Howe had increased the number of "traitorous" assemblymen from thirty-one to thirty-two, to include a Confederate who had not voted in the division of April 17, 1866.
6 Speech of May 24, *Morning Chronicle*, May 29, 1867; editorial from the *Casket* quoted in *British Colonist*, June 13, 1867.
7 Connolly to Howe, May 22, 1867, "Howe Letters," pp. 213–4; Howe to Connolly, May 23, 1867, ibid., pp. 215–6.

8  Letter of May 2, 1871, *British Colonist*, May 9, 1871.
9  Tupper to Howe, May 30, 1867, JHP, vol. 4, pp. 313–4, 315; Howe to Tupper, May 30 and 31, 1867, ibid., vol. 9, pp. 370–1, 372–3.
10  *Morning Chronicle*, July 18, 1867.
11  Letter of May 2, 1871, *British Colonist*, May 9, 1871. For general discussion see Kenneth G. Pryke, *Nova Scotia and Confederation* (Toronto: University of Toronto Press, 1979), esp. pp. 49–55.
12  *British Colonist*, Sept. 17, 1867.
13  Connolly to John A. Macdonald, Sept. 25, 1867, PAC, Macdonald Papers, vol. 116, pp. 46982–9.
14  Two delegates to Quebec, Archibald and Henry, were easily beaten, the latter losing by 1,238 to 390 in Antigonish.
15  *Acadian Recorder*, Sept. 25, 1867.
16  *British Colonist*, Sept. 24, 1867.
17  Ibid., Oct. 3, 1867.
18  *Evening Express*, Oct. 28, 1867.
19  Howe to Stanley (private), Sept. 25, 1867, JHP, vol. 9, pp. 374–86.
20  *Evening Express*, Oct. 28, 1867; *British Colonist*, Sept. 21, and Oct. 8, 1867.
21  Speech of May 24, *Morning Chronicle*, May 29, 1867.
22  Howe to Stanley (private), Sept. 25, 1867, JHP, vol. 9, pp. 374–86; Howe to Rogers (confidential), Sept. 26, 1867, ibid., pp. 390–3. From England William Garvie argued that the Antis could make their strongest case by sending a delegation to Britain as quickly as possible. Garvie to Howe, Oct. 12, 1867, JHP, vol. 4, pp. 345–60.
23  *British Colonist*, Oct. 8, 1868.
24  Doyle to Howe (confidential), Oct. 1, 1867, JHP, vol. 4, pp. 336–42; Howe to Doyle, Oct. 5, 1867, ibid., vol. 9, pp. 394–8.
25  Connolly to Macdonald, Sept. 25, 1867, Macdonald Papers, vol. 116, pp. 46892–9; McCully to Macdonald, Sept. 20, 1867, ibid., pp. 46968–75; Macdonald to P.S. Hamilton (private), Oct. 8, 1867, ibid., vol. 514, p. 48.
26  K.G. Pryke, "Nova Scotia and Confederation, 1864–70" (PH D thesis, Duke University, 1962), p. 145.
27  Macdonald to P.C. Hill (private), Oct. 7, 1867, Macdonald Papers, vol. 514, pp. 34–7.
28  For their "Declaration of Independence" of November 7 see *Morning Chronicle*, Nov. 9, 1867. Howe expected "a row about it" in Ottawa. Howe to Susan Ann, Nov. 18, 1867, "Howe Letters," p. 221.
29  Howe to Doyle (private), Jan. 15, 1868, JHP, vol. 37, n.p.
30  Howe to Stairs, Oct. 19, 1867, ibid., vol. 9, pp. 402–6. En route to Ottawa, Howe addressed two workingmen's societies in Montreal, where he boasted of the ten years he had spent in learning a trade and expressed pride in "the order to which I belong." *Morning Chronicle*, Nov. 11 and 12, 1867.
31  Howe to Susan Ann, Nov. 30 and Dec. 1, 1867, "Howe Letters," pp. 223–4.
32  House of Commons *Debates*, Nov. 8, 1867, 10.
33  Ibid., 10–13.
34  Howe to Susan Ann, Nov. 9, 1867, "Howe Letters," p. 220.
35  House of Commons *Debates*, Nov. 8, 1867, 13–20.
36  Macdonald to P.C. Hill, Nov. 11, 1867, Macdonald Papers, vol. 514, pp. 243–4.
37  Speech of Nov. 11, *Morning Chronicle*, Nov. 18, 1867.

38  House of Commons *Debates*, Nov. 14, 1867, 66–76.
39  Howe to Susan Ann, Nov. 16 and Dec. 1, 1867, "Howe Letters," pp. 220, 224.
40  Ibid., Nov. 18, 1867, p. 221.
41  Ibid., Nov. 18 and 22, 1867, pp. 221–2; House of Commons *Debates*, Dec. 10, 1867, 232.
42  Howe to Susan Ann, Nov. 22, 1867, "Howe Letters," p. 222.
43  Ibid., House of Commons *Debates*, Nov. 25, 1867, 127–8, 130–1.
44  Howe to Susan Ann, Dec. 7, 1867, "Howe Letters," p. 224.
45  See speech of Nov. 18 in *Morning Chronicle*, Nov. 25, 1867; also House of Commons *Debates*, Dec. 4, 6, 11, 1867, 183–6, 205–8, 249–50.
46  Ibid., Dec. 6, 1867, 208.
47  House of Commons *Debates*, Dec. 12, 13, *Morning Chronicle*, Dec. 23, 1867.
48  Howe to Musgrave, Jan. 7, 1868, JHP, vol. 37, n.p.
49  Letter of May 2, 1871, *British Colonist*, May 9, 1871; Macdonald to Connolly, Dec. 31, 1867, Macdonald Papers, vol. 514, pp. 318–9.
50  *Weekly Citizen*, Dec. 21, 1867.
51  *Morning Chronicle*, Jan. 17, 1868; *Citizen*, Feb. 11, 1868.
52  Doyle to Macdonald, Dec. 31, 1867, Macdonald Papers, vol. 114, pp. 46183–6.
53  Connolly to Macdonald, Feb. 19, 1868, ibid., vol. 116, pp. 47093–102; Howe to Musgrave (of Aylesford), Jan. 11, 1868, JHP, vol. 37, n.p.
54  Doyle to Macdonald, Dec. 31, 1867, Macdonald Papers, vol. 114, pp. 46183–6; Howe to Doyle (private), Jan. 13, 1868, JHP, vol. 37, n.p. Although he wrote in the strictest confidence, Howe was actually weakening his own position, since at least inferentially Doyle's letters to Macdonald revealed Howe's thinking at any particular juncture.
55  Speech of Jan. 13, *Morning Chronicle*, Jan. 17, 1868.
56  McCully to Macdonald, Dec. 28, 1867, Macdonald Papers, vol. 116, pp. 47041–4.
57  Speech of Jan. 13, *Morning Chronicle*, Jan. 17, 1868.
58  Speech of Jan. 15 at Brooklyn, *Citizen*, Feb. 11, 1868.
59  Ibid.; speech of Jan. 13, *Morning Chronicle*, Jan. 17, 1868.
60  Howe to Musgrave (of Aylesford), Jan. 11, 1868, JHP, vol. 37, n.p.; speech of Jan. 13, *Morning Chronicle*, Jan. 17, 1868.
61  Pryke, *Nova Scotia and Confederation*, p. 65; *Morning Chronicle*, Mar. 9, 1868.
62  Garvie to Howe, Jan. 1, 1868, JHP, vol. 4, pp. 375–86; Macdonald to McCully (private), Feb. 29, 1868, Macdonald Papers, vol. 514, pp. 549–52.
63  Howe to Sydenham, Mar. 14, 1868, "Howe Letters," pp. 135–7.
64  See Letters to the editors, JHP, vol. 38, n.p.
65  *Manchester Guardian*, Apr. 14, 1868; *Manchester Daily Examiner and Times*, Feb. 22, 1868; *Morning Advertiser*, Apr. 18, 1868.
66  *Standard*, Feb. 3, 1868; *Examiner*, May 2, 1868; *Morning Herald*, Mar. 17, 1868; *Saturday Review*, May 2, 1868; *Spectator*, Mar. 14, 1868. See Howe's comment on the press in letters to J.W. Cudlip, Apr. 25, 1868, "Howe Letters," pp. 233–5, and Charles F. Bennett, June 27, 1868, JHP, vol. 38, n.p.
67  *Daily News*, Mar. 23, 1868; *Morning Star*, Mar. 17, 1868; *News of the World*,

Mar. 22, 1868; *Glowworm*, Apr. 9, 1868; *Daily Telegraph*, Apr. 18, 1868; *Lloyd's Weekly*, Mar. 15, 1868; and *Sun*, Mar. 27, 1868.
68 Howe to Cudlip, Apr. 25, 1868, "Howe Letters," pp. 233–5; *Leeds Mercury*, Apr. 9, 1868; *Glasgow Sentinel*, Mar. 21, 1868. Newspapers in Southampton, Birmingham, Belfast, Dublin, and Limerick added their concurrence.
69 Howe to Bright, Mar. 6, 1868, JHP, vol. 38, n.p.; Howe to Sydenham, Mar. 14, 1868, "Howe Letters," pp. 135–7; Howe et al. to Vail, Mar. 28 1868, JHP, vol. 38, n.p.
70 Tupper alleged other motives. See Tupper to Macdonald, Apr. 9, 1868, E.M. Saunders, *Life and Letters of the Rt Hon Sir Charles Tupper*, 2 vols. (London: Cassell, 1916), 1:162–4.
71 Macdonald to Tupper, Mar. 23, 1868, ibid., pp. 161–2.
72 House of Commons *Debates*, Apr. 6, 1868, 467–71. "A beautiful speech it was," wrote Macdonald, and "within an hour afterwards he was a corpse," struck down by an assassin. Macdonald to Tupper (confidential), Apr. 30, 1868, Macdonald Papers, 514:693–7. Howe was "right glad, that I did not deliver the philippic I had prepared for him at Ottawa." Howe to Sydenham, Apr. 9, 1868, "Howe Letters," p. 232.
73 Pryke, *Nova Scotia and Confederation*, p. 67.
74 Howe to Sydenham, Apr. 9, 1868, "Howe Letters," p. 232; Tupper to Macdonald, Apr. 9, 1868, Saunders, *Tupper*, p. 163.
75 Tupper to Macdonald, Apr. 9, 1868, Saunders, *Tupper*, p. 163; Macdonald to Tupper, Apr. 30, 1868, ibid., pp. 167–9.
76 Tupper to Macdonald, Apr. 18, 1868, in Sir Charles Tupper, *Recollections of Sixty Years in Canada* (London: Cassell, 1914), pp. 79–81.
77 Howe to John W. Cudlip, Apr. 25, 1868, "Howe Letters," pp. 233–5.
78 Howe to Sydenham, Apr. 25, 1868, ibid., p. 236; Howe to Vail, Apr. 26, 1868, JHP, vol. 38, n.p.
79 Howe et al. to Vail, May 8 1868, ibid.
80 Ibid., May 22, 1868.
81 Howe to Sydenham, May 23, 1868, "Howe Letters," p. 238; Howe to Purdy, May 23, 1868, ibid., p. 237a.
82 Howe to Adderley, June 13, 1868, JHP, vol. 9, pp. 424–7.
83 Tupper to Macdonald, May 26, 1868, Tupper, *Recollections*, pp. 91–4.
84 Sir Charles Tupper, *Political Reminiscences* (London: Constable, 1914), p. 47; Tupper to Macdonald, May 2, 1868, Saunders, *Tupper*, pp. 165–7; *Parl. Debates* (Commons), June 16, 1868, 1665.
85 Susan Ann Howe diary, entry of May 22, 1868, JHP, reel 22; Tupper to Macdonald, May 26, 1868, Tupper, *Recollections*, pp. 91–4.
86 Susan Ann diary, entry of May 30 [?], 1868, JHP, reel 22.
87 Buckingham and Chandos to Monck, June 4, 1868, *JHA*, 1968, App. 10: Repeal Delegation, pp. 49–51.
88 Howe et al. to Vail, June 19, 1868, JHP, vol. 38, n.p.
89 Tupper to Macdonald, June 20, 1868, Saunders, *Tupper*, pp. 171–2.
90 *Parl. Debates* (Commons), June 16, 1868, 1658–76; Howe et al. to Vail, June 19, 1868, JHP, vol. 38, n.p.
91 *Parl. Debates* (Commons), June 16, 1868, 1677–86; Howe et al. to Vail, June 19, 1868, JHP, vol. 38, n.p.
92 Howe et al. to Vail, June 19, 1868, JHP, vol. 38, n.p.
93 *Parl. Debates* (Lords), July 6, 1868, 690–701.

94  Diary, June 16, 1868, JHP, reel 22.
95  Howe to Charles F. Bennett, June 27, 1868, ibid., vol. 38, n.p.; Howe to Robertson, June 20, 1868, ibid., vol. 9, pp. 428–40.
96  For the protest see *JHA*, 1868, App. 10: Repeal Delegation, pp. 52–7.
97  Tilley to Macdonald (private and confidential), July 17, 1868, Macdonald Papers, vol. 115, pp. 46636–66; *Morning Chronicle*, July 8, 1868.
98  Savary to Howe, July 20, 1868, JHP, vol. 4, pp. 437–40.
99  Howe to Bliss and Morse, July 23, 1868, JHP, vol. 38, n.p.
100 Howe to Garvie, Dec. 31, 1868, *Report of PANS*, 1948, pp. 38–43.
101 Tupper to Macdonald, June 20, 1868, Tupper, *Recollections*, pp. 94–7.
102 A second letter made the same point, but was couched in such terms that Tupper might show it to Howe if he thought it advisable. Macdonald to Tupper, July 4, 1868 (private), and ibid. (confidential), Macdonald Papers, vol. 514, pp. 986–94.
103 Tilley to Macdonald, July 17, 1868, ibid., vol. 115, pp. 46636–66.
104 Archibald to Macdonald, July 17, 1868, ibid., pp. 46667–77.
105 *Acadian Recorder*, July 29, 1868; Howe to *Morning Chronicle*, July 31, 1868, Chisholm, 2: 537–8.
106 Howe to Garvie, Aug. 14, 1868, *Report of PANS*, 1948, pp. 35–8.
107 Howe to John Livingstone, Aug. 1, 1868, JHP, vol. 9, pp. 462–5.
108 Howe to Garvie, Aug. 14, 1868, *Report of PANS*, 1948, pp. 35–8.
109 Macdonald to Monck (confidential), Sept. 4, 1868, in Sir Joseph Pope, *Memoirs of Sir John Alexander Macdonald* (Ottawa, 1894), pp. 29–34.
110 McDonald to Garvie, Dec. 25, 1868, *Report of PANS*, 1948, pp. 44–52.
111 Howe to Garvie, Aug. 14, 1868, ibid., pp. 35–8.
112 Ibid., Dec. 31, 1868, pp. 38–43.
113 Ibid.
114 Howe to "Ned," Aug. 12 and 17, 1868, JHP, vol. 38, n.p.
115 McLelan to Howe, Aug. 21, 1868, ibid., vol. 4, pp. 451–6; Howe to editor of *Morning Chronicle*, Aug. 25, 1868, Chisholm, 2: 538–40.
116 *JHA*, Aug. 14, 1868, pp. 52–5.
117 D.C. Harvey, "Incidents of the Repeal Agitation of Nova Scotia," *Canadian Historical Review* 15 (March 1934): 48–56.
118 Howe to Macdonald (confidential), Oct. 8, 1868, JHP, vol. 9, pp. 522–9.
119 Doyle to Macdonald (private), Sept. 15, 1868, Macdonald Papers, vol. 14, pp. 46197–204.
120 Howe to Boak, Sept. 26, 1868, JHP, vol. 9, pp. 508–16.
121 Howe to Wilkins, Sept. 14, 1868, ibid., vol. 38, n.p.
122 Howe to Macdonald, Sept. 15, 1868, ibid., vol. 9, pp. 477–95.
123 Doyle to Macdonald, Sept. 15, 1868, Macdonald Papers, vol. 114, pp. 46197–204.
124 *Morning Chronicle*, Sept. 12, 1868; Howe to Boak, Sept. 26, 1868, JHP, vol. 9, pp. 508–16.
125 Howe to Boak, Sept. 26, 1868, JHP, vol. 9, pp. 508–16.
126 Macdonald to Howe (confidential), Sept. 14, 1868, ibid., vol. 4, pp. 457–60; Sept. 16, 1868 (private and confidential), ibid., pp. 469–71; Sept. 21, 1868 (private and confidential), Macdonald Papers, vol. 514, pp. 1128–9; Sept. 26, 1868 (confidential), JHP, vol. 4, pp. 472–8.
127 Howe to Macdonald (confidential), Sept. 15, 1868, JHP, vol. 9, pp. 477–95.
128 Macdonald to Howe (confidential), Sept. 26, 1868, ibid., vol. 4, pp. 472–8.

129 Howe to Macdonald (confidential), Oct. 8, 1868, ibid., vol. 9, pp. 522–9.
130 Macdonald to Howe (private), Oct. 6, 1868, ibid., vol. 4, pp. 481–9.
131 Macdonald to Tupper (confidential), Oct. 27, 1868, Macdonald Papers, vol. 515, pp. 54–8; Macdonald to Archibald (confidential), Oct 27, 1868, ibid., pp. 51–3; Macdonald to McCully (confidential), Oct. 8, 1868, ibid., vol. 514, pp. 1203–5.
132 Howe to Macdonald, Oct. 21, 1868, JHP, vol. 9, pp. 543–55.
133 Howe to Macdonald (private), Oct. 27, 1868, ibid., pp. 588–95; Howe to Rose (private), Oct. 19, 1868, ibid., pp. 531–6.
134 Hugh McDonald to Howe, Oct. 24, 1868, "Howe Letters," pp. 250–1; A.G. Jones to Howe, Oct. 19, 1868, ibid., pp. 183–5.
135 "G.J.'s Reminscences of Joseph Howe," PAC, George Johnson Papers, folder 1, 14–16.
136 Howe to Garvie, Dec. 31, 1868, *Report of PANS*, 1948, pp. 38–43.
137 Letter to *Eastern Chronicle*, Oct. 24, 1868, Chisholm, 2: 543–6.
138 Howe to Ross, Dec. 7, 1868, JHP, vol. 38, n.p.
139 His letters of Nov. 6, 9, 16, 23, and 27 appeared in the *Morning Chronicle* of Nov. 7, 11, 18, 24, and 28, 1868.
140 Howe to Macdonald (confidential), Nov. 16, 1868, JHP, vol. 9, pp. 596–618.
141 Buckingham and Chandos to Officer administering the Government of Canada, Dec. 8, 1868, *JHA*, 1869, App. 1: Confederation, pp. 1–2.
142 Howe insisted particularly that Martin Wilkins not be appointed to the judiciary and Macdonald promised to "play Master Wilkins like a trout!" Howe to Macdonald (confidential), Jan. 4, 1869, JHP, vol. 9, pp. 640–7; Macdonald to Howe (confidential), Jan. 12, 1869, ibid., vol. 4, pp. 622–7.
143 Macdonald to Howe (confidential), Jan. 12, 1869, JHP, vol. 4, pp. 622–7; Macdonald to Tupper (confidential), Jan. 2, 1869, Macdonald Papers, vol. 515, pp. 351–4.
144 McDonald to Garvie, Mar. 11, 1869, *Report of PANS*, 1948, pp. 52–6.
145 Howe to Susan Ann, Jan. 16, 1869, "Howe Letters," p. 259.
146 Ibid., Jan. 28, 1869, pp. 259–60.
147 McDonald to Garvie, Mar. 11, 1869, *Report of PANS*, 1948, pp. 52–6.
148 *Morning Chronicle*, Jan. 29, 1869.
149 Ibid., Jan. 19, 1869.

CHAPTER ELEVEN

1 Macdonald to Tupper (private), Feb. 1, 1869, PAC, Macdonald Papers, vol. 515, pp. 512–3; to Langevin (private), Jan. 25, 1868, ibid., pp. 473–4; to Tupper (confidential), Jan. 28, 1869, ibid., pp. 485–90.
2 *Morning Chronicle*, Feb. 2 and 3, 1869; *Acadian Recorder*, Feb. 18, 1869.
3 McDonald to Garvie, Mar. 11, 1869, *Report of PANS*, 1948, pp. 52–6.
4 Doyle hoped that the prime minister might "carve out something to keep [McDonald's] pot boiling!" Doyle to Macdonald (private), Feb. 12, 1869, Macdonald Papers, vol. 114, pp. 46374–82.
5 Doyle to Macdonald, Feb. 3, 12 (private), 25 (private), 1869, ibid., pp. 46350–3, 46374–82, 46390–413.
6 Macdonald to Tupper, Feb. 15, 1869, ibid., vol. 515, pp. 566–8.
7 *Morning Chronicle*, Feb. 12 and 13, 1869.

8 "G.J.'s Reminiscences of Joseph Howe," PANS, George Johnson Papers, folder 1, 18.
9 Ibid., Howe to Macdonald, Mar. 19, 1869, Macdonald Papers, vol. 115, pp. 46853–67.
10 See speeches in *Citizen*, Feb. 18, 1869.
11 Howe to Doyle, Feb. 21, 189, "Howe Letters," p. 262. His meetings were at Hantsport, St Croix, Brooklyn, Avondale, Burlington, Kempt, Cheverie, Walton, Noel, Maitland, Kennetcook, Welsford, and Nine Mile River.
12 "G.J.'s Reminiscences," George Johnson Papers, folder 1, 19.
13 Macdonald to Archibald, Mar. 16 (private) and Apr. 12 (confidential), 1869, Macdonald Papers, vol. 515, pp. 730–2 and 779–80; Tupper to Macdonald, Feb. 1, 1869, Sir Joseph Pope, *The Correspondence of Sir John Macdonald* (Toronto: Oxford University Press, 1921), p. 86; Howe to Macdonald, Mar. 23, 1869, Macdonald Papers, vol. 115, pp. 46891–5.
14 Later Doyle would write: "The highest bidder I hear will win." Doyle to Macdonald, Mar. 5 (private) and Mar. 30 (confidential), 1869, Macdonald Papers, vol. 114, pp. 46427–34 and 46450–3; Macdonald to Doyle (private), Mar. 15, 1869, ibid., vol. 515, pp. 723–8.
15 Howe to Macdonald, Mar. 20, 1869, JHP, vol. 38, n.p.
16 For details see Kenneth G. Pryke, *Nova Scotia and Confederation* (Toronto: University of Toronto Press, 1979), pp. 91–2.
17 Macdonald had set the Yarmouth election for an earlier date before he realized that the certain anti-Confederate victory there might hurt his party's chances in the other two counties. Unwittingly Martin Wilkins, whose domestic law was no better than his constitutional law, came to his aid by arguing that the Nova Scotian election law required the three by-elections to be held on the same day. When, as a result, the returning officer for Yarmouth returned the writ unexecuted, he effectively undid the federal government's tactical error.
18 *Citizen*, Apr. 6, 1869. The series included meetings at Elmsdale, Gore, Upper Rawdon, South Rawdon, and Mount Uniacke.
19 Ibid., Apr. 6 and 8, 1869.
20 Howe to Susan Ann, Apr. 19, 1869, "Howe Letters," pp. 263–4.
21 Howe to Doyle, July 7, 1869, JHP, vol. 9, pp. 665–82; House of Commons *Debates*, May 13, 1869, 301.
22 House of Commons *Debates*, May 20, 1869, 408–10.
23 Ibid., May 28, 1869, 475–9.
24 Howe to Stairs et al., Apr. 28, 1869, JHP, vol. 9, pp. 662–4; Howe to Morse, Apr. 25, 1869, ibid., vol. 38, n.p.
25 House of Commons *Debates*, June 12 and 16, 1869, 752–3, 809–10, 826–7.
26 Howe to Doyle, July 7, 1869, JHP, vol. 9, pp. 665–82.
27 Howe to W.H. Chipman, Dec. 20, 1869, ibid., vol. 39, pp. 150–3.
28 See ibid. for letters to Ross, July 3, 1869, pp. 47–8; to McKeagney, Sept. 6, 1869 (twice), pp. 108 and 111; and Keating, July 2, 1869, pp. 38–9; Pryke, *Nova Scotia and Confederation*, pp. 101–2.
29 Howe to Purdy, June 11, 1869, "Howe Letters," p. 267a.
30 Howe to Doyle, July 7, 1869, JHP, vol. 9, pp. 665–82; Doyle to Macdonald, June 25, 1869, Macdonald Papers, vol. 114, pp. 46454–65.
31 Macdonald to Doyle (private), Nov. 10, 1869, Macdonald Papers, vol. 516, pp. 409–10.

32 Howe to Doyle, July 7, 1869, JHP, vol. 9, pp. 665–82.
33 W.L. Morton, *The Critical Years: The Union of British North America* (Toronto: McClelland and Stewart, 1964), p. 239.
34 *Morning Chronicle*, Aug. 20, 1869.
35 Some Americans he met at St Paul wanted help in building a line northward to Fort Garry and westward to the Pacific, but Howe was noncommittal.
36 House of Commons *Debates*, May 9, 1870, 1467–8.
37 Ibid., 1466.
38 See G.F.G. Stanley, *The Birth of Western Canada* (Longmans, Green: London, 1936), p. 64.
39 Howe to Macdonald, Oct. 16, 1869, Macdonald Papers, vol. 115, pp. 46899–902.
40 Howe to Susan Ann, Oct. 31, 1869, "Howe Letters," p. 266.
41 House of Commons *Debates*, May 9, 1871, 1465.
42 Howe to McDougall (private), Oct. 31, 1869, JHP, vol. 9, pp. 693–8.
43 Stanley, *Birth of Western Canada*, p. 65.
44 Howe to McDougall, Nov. 19, 1869, Sessional Paper no. 12, 1870, pp. 14–15.
45 Ibid., Nov. 29, 1869, pp. 32–3.
46 McDougall to Howe, Nov. 13, 1869, ibid., pp. 37–8.
47 Howe to McDougall, Dec. 7, 1869, ibid., pp. 42–3.
48 McDougall to Howe, Nov. 20, 1869, ibid., pp. 50–2.
49 Howe to McDougall, Dec. 11, 1869, ibid., pp. 58–9.
50 Ibid., Dec. 24, 1869, pp. 83–6.
51 Quoted from the *Globe*, *Acadian Recorder*, Jan. 22, 1870.
52 Ibid., Jan. 24, 1870; *Morning Chronicle*, Feb. 4, 1870.
53 Howe to Macdonald, Jan. 22, 1870, JHP, vol. 9, pp. 703–7.
54 House of Commons *Debates*, Feb. 21, 1870, 82.
55 Turner to Howe with enclosure, Jan. 21, 1870, JHP, vol. 9, pp. 708–9; Howe to Turner, Jan. 29, 1870, ibid., vol. 40, pp. 28–9.
56 Howe to Sanford, Feb. 12, 1870, ibid., vol. 40, pp. 52–3; Howe to Turner (private), Mar. 28, 1870, ibid., pp. 127–9.
57 House of Commons *Debates*, Feb. 21, 1870, 85.
58 For his major speech, the longest he would give in the Commons, see ibid., May 9, 1870, 1462–80.
59 Howe to Sydenham, May 21, 1870, JHP, vol. 40, pp. 169–73.
60 Stanley, *Birth of Western Canada*, p. 64. McDougall's work was *The Red River Rebellion: Eight Letters to Joseph Howe* (Toronto, 1870).
61 Morton, *Critical Years*, p. 240; Stanley, *Birth of Western Canada*, pp. 64–5.
62 Howe to Westphal, Jan. 14, 1873, "Howe Letters," pp. 315–6.
63 Howe to Archibald (private), Oct. 27, 1870, JHP, vol. 40, pp. 258–9; ibid. (private), Nov. 24, 1870, vol. 39, pp. 319–20.
64 *Morning Chronicle*, Sept 22, 1870.
65 Ibid., Jan. 24, 1870.
66 Howe to Rev. John Cameron, Jan. 20, 1870, JHP, vol. 40, pp. 7–9; to Ned O'Brien, Mar. 24, 1870, ibid., pp. 114–5.
67 Savary to Howe (private), May 30, 1870, ibid., vol. 4, pp. 702–9; McKeagney to Howe (private), June 17, 1870, ibid., pp. 710–7; H. McDonald to Howe (confidential), July 18, 1870, ibid., pp. 720–6.
68 Howe to Cartier (private), May 18, 1870, ibid., vol. 9, pp. 711–6; Macdonald to Howe (private), Oct. 24, 1870, ibid., vol. 4, pp. 740–1.

69 Howe to McCully, Oct. 24, 1870, ibid., vol. 9, pp. 717–9.
70 Howe to A. Campbell, Jan. 28, 1870, ibid., vol. 40, pp. 21–2.
71 See, e.g., Howe to Mrs Sinclair (private), Jan. 28, 1870, ibid., pp. 24–5.
72 Howe to unknown, Dec. 26, 1870, ibid., vol. 39, p. 428; Howe to Bliss, Apr. 25, 1870, ibid., vol. 40, pp. 156–7.
73 *Morning Chronicle*, Feb. 18, 1870.
74 When Howe introduced him in the Commons, the *Chronicle* (Feb. 19, 1870) reminded him of his statement that he would sooner touch the hand of a dead Irishman who had fought honestly for his country than that of the "betrayer" Archibald.
75 Howe to Northup, Oct. 19, 1870, JHP, vol. 40, pp. 229–30, and to "Ned" McDonald, Oct. 19 and Nov. 3 (private), 1870, ibid, pp. 240–1 and 269–71.
76 Speech of Nov. 4, *Morning Chronicle*, Nov. 9, 1870.
77 Howe to Thomson, Dec. 27, 1870, JHP, vol. 39, pp. 371–2, and to E.M. McDonald, Dec. 7, 1870, ibid., pp. 366–7.
78 Ibid.
79 Howe to Northup, Dec. 12, 1870, ibid., pp. 385–7, and to Jane Sangster, Dec. 7, 1870, ibid., pp. 360–4.
80 Howe to E.M. McDonald, Dec. 3, 1870, ibid., pp. 347–8.
81 Howe to Thomson, Dec. 25, 1870, ibid., pp. 424–5.
82 Howe to Sydenham, Nov. 7, 1870, ibid., vol. 40, 274–81.
83 Howe to Stairs, June 23, 1870, ibid., pp. 206–8.
84 Howe to Thomson, Dec. 17, 1870, ibid., vol. 39, pp. 408–9.
85 Howe to Sarah, Dec. 12, 1870, ibid., pp. 376–7 and to Thomson, Dec. 17, 1870, ibid., pp. 408–9.
86 Howe to Northup, May 14, 1870, ibid., pp. 258–9.
87 Howe to Mary Howe, Aug. 7, 1871, ibid., pp. 949–53.
88 Howe to Northup, Jan. 31, 1871, ibid., p. 484.
89 Howe to Sydenham, Feb. 2, 1871, ibid., pp. 492–5.
90 House of Commons *Debates*, Apr. 6, 1871, 970; ibid., Apr. 13, 1871, 1082–3.
91 Howe to Archibald (private), Mar. 13, 1871, JHP, vol. 39, pp. 565–6.
92 Howe to Helmeker, June 21, 1871, ibid., pp. 816–9.
93 Howe to Archibald (private), Jan. 3, 1871, ibid., p. 438; ibid. (private), Mar. 13, 1871, pp. 565–6; ibid. (private), Feb. 7, 1871, pp. 497–8.
94 Ibid. (private), Nov. 4, 1871, vol. 9, pp. 729–45.
95 Ibid.
96 Ibid (private), Dec. 26, 1871, pp. 746–60.
97 Howe to Rev. John Cameron, Nov. 17, 1871, ibid., vol. 41, pp. 68–70 and to Thomson, Dec. 27, 1871, ibid., pp. 156–65.
98 Howe to Rose, June 26, 1871, ibid., vol. 39, pp. 833–5, and to Lisgar (private), Aug. 22, 1871, ibid., vol. 9, pp. 725–8.
99 E.M. McDonald to Howe, June 13, 1871, ibid., vol. 4:733–6.
100 Howe to E.M. McDonald, Aug. 7, 1871, ibid., vol. 39, pp. 934–7; Coffin to Howe, Sept. 2, 1871, ibid., pp. 799–802; Cameron to Howe (private), Sept. 20 1871, ibid., pp. 803–4; Le Vesconte to Howe, Aug. 30, 1871, ibid., pp. 787–9; Hugh McDonald to Howe, Sept. 7, 1871, ibid., pp. 794–8.
101 Howe to Thomson, Dec. 27, 1871, ibid., vol. 41, pp. 156–65.
102 *Morning Chronicle*, Jan. 30, 1871; Doyle to Mcdonald (private), Apr. 6, 1871, Macdonald Papers, vol. 114, pp. 46577–84.

103 *British Colonist*, Apr. 20, 1871.
104 Howe to L.C. Longley, Apr. 8, 1871, JHP, vol. 39, pp. 594–5, and to A.B. Fletcher, May 15, 1871, ibid., p. 649.
105 For the letters see Chisholm, 2:599–619.
106 *British Colonist*, May 13, 1871; Evening Express, May 3, 1871; *Weekly Citizen*, Apr. 29, 1871; *Morning Chronicle*, Apr. 26 and May 3, 9, 11, 1871.
107 Howe to "Ned" O'Brien, June 10, 1871, JHP, vol. 39, pp. 720–6.
108 Howe to D. McCurdy, June 10, 1871; to J.R. Creed, June 9, 1871; to John Campbell and others, June 8, 1871; and to Rev. H. Girroir, Aug. 2, 1871, JHP, vol. 39, pp. 736–7, 704, 705–6, and 904–5.
109 Pryke, *Nova Scotia and Confederation*, p. 129.
110 Howe to Northup, June 10, 1871, JHP, vol. 39, pp. 718–9.
111 Howe to Sydenham, Feb. 2, 1871, ibid., pp. 493–5.
112 Howe to Northup, June 8, 1871, ibid., pp. 689–91.
113 Ibid., Nov. 24, 1871, vol. 41, pp. 90–1.
114 Howe to Thomson, Dec. 27, 1871, ibid., pp. 156–65.
115 Ibid., June 8 and 19, 1871, vol. 39, pp. 692–3 and 792–3.
116 Chisholm, 2:619–30.
117 Howe to Mary Howe, Aug. 7, 1871, JHP, vol. 39, pp. 949–53.
118 Howe to Archibald (private), Nov. 4, 1871, ibid., vol. 9, pp. 729–45.
119 A stern father severely reprimanded him only to discover later that his employer had no complaints about his work. Howe to Fred, Mar. 2 and June 14, 1871, ibid., vol. 39, pp. 532–3 and 757–8.
120 Howe to Sarah, Jan. 17 and Feb. 7, 1871, ibid., pp. 453–4 and 501–3. Shortly afterwards Sarah married John Dakin and Howe requested the first offer of refusal of her business to set up someone else.
121 Howe to Mary Howe, Dec. 28, 1871, ibid., vol. 41, pp. 182–3. At Christmas Howe gave her "liberty to draw for what you require, you can supply your own wants."
122 Howe to Alex. James (private), Jan. 17, 1872, ibid., p. 239.
123 Chisholm, 2:631–41.
124 *Acadian Recorder*, Mar. 2, 1872; *Morning Chronicle*, Mar. 5, 1872.
125 Quoted from the *Globe* in the *Acadian Recorder*, Mar. 16, 1872.
126 Macdonald to Rose (private), Mar. 5, 1872, Macdonald Papers, vol. 520, pp. 320–3; to Lisgar (private and confidential), Mar. 14, 1872, ibid., pp. 393–6.
127 Howe to Humphrey Howe, Mar. 12, 1872, and to Ross, Mar. 25, 1872, JHP, vol. 41, pp. 346 and 364–5.
128 Howe to Doyle, Apr. 5, 1872, ibid., pp. 379–81.
129 House of Commons *Debates*, Apr. 12, 1872, 20, 54–6.
130 For this opinion of the effect of Howe's speech and the newspaper quotations see Goldwin Smith, *The Treaty of Washington, 1871: A Study in Imperial History* (Ithaca: Cornell University Press, 1941), p. 112n31, and House of Commons *Debates*, May 10, 1872, 486.
131 Ibid., Howe to A.B. Richards, June 7, 1872, JHP, vol. 41, pp. 493–5.
132 Howe to Westphal, Jan. 14, 1873, "Howe Letters," pp. 315–6.
133 See *British Colonist*, July 27, 1872.
134 *Morning Chronicle*, Jan. 8, 1872.
135 Ibid., July 26, 1872.
136 *Acadian Recorder*, Aug. 13, 1872.
137 *British Colonist*, Aug. 17, 1872; *Acadian Recorder*, Aug. 31, 1872.

138 Macdonald to Howe (private), Sept. 21, 1872, Macdonald Papers, vol. 521, p. 519.
139 Howe to Connolly, Jan. 22, 1872, JHP, vol. 41, pp. 256–8.
140 Howe to Alexander Campbell, Jan. 15, 1872, ibid., pp. 222–5.
141 Howe to Savary (private) and E.M. McDonald (strictly confidential), Oct. 22, Dec. 11, and Mar. 1, 1872, ibid., pp. 509–10, 571, 324–7.
142 Howe to Milne, May 20, 1872, ibid., pp. 461–2.
143 Howe to Joe, Jr, Oct. 21, 1872, ibid., pp. 506–7 and to Sydenham, Jan. 15 and 30, 1872, ibid., pp. 219–21 and 276–7.
144 Howe to Fitzrandolph, May 11, 1872, JHP, vol. 41, pp. 435–6; to Thomson, Nov. 8, 1872, ibid., pp. 531–3.
145 Howe to Dawson, Apr. 23, 1872, ibid., p. 402; to Rev. John Cameron, Apr. 24, 1872, ibid., pp. 409–11.
146 Howe to Lovell, Dec. 16, 1872, ibid., pp. 577–8.
147 Macdonald to Dufferin (private), Sept. 19, 1872, Macdonald Papers, vol. 521, pp. 473–6.
148 Macdonald to Tupper (private), Oct. 9, 1872, ibid., pp. 666–7.

CHAPTER TWELVE

1 *Morning Chronicle*, Aug. 27, 1872; *Acadian Recorder*, Nov. 18, 1872.
2 Howe to Macdonald, Sept. 16, 1872, PAC, Macdonald Papers, vol. 115, pp. 46936–9; Howe to Savary (private), Oct. 22, 1872, JHP, vol. 41, pp. 509–10.
3 Howe to Macdonald, Dec. 6, 1872, Macdonald Papers, vol. 115, pp. 46940–2.
4 Howe to Westphal, Jan. 14, 1873, "Howe Letters," pp. 315–6, and to Joe, Jr, Jan. 8, 1873, JHP, vol. 42, pp. 23–6.
5 *Acadian Recorder*, Jan. 18 and Feb. 8, 1873.
6 Howe to J.W. Longley, Jan. 30, 1873, JHP, vol. 42, pp. 55–7; and to Doyle, Jan. 13, Feb. 3 (private), and Apr. 19, ibid., pp. 33–9, 58–60, 168.
7 Howe to Sydenham, Mar. 3, 1873, ibid., pp. 104–11.
8 Ibid., Mar. 15, 1873, pp. 124–9.
9 He also urged Sydenham not to buy a house, but to husband his capital and take a suite of rooms in Government House, thereby saving rent and taxes.
10 Howe to Doyle, Jan. 13 and Feb. 19, 1873, JHP, vol. 42, pp. 33–9 and 84–7.
11 Ibid., Jan. 13, 1873, pp. 33–9.
12 Howe to Falvey, Mar. 9, 1873; to Doyle, Apr. 17, 1873; to William Howe, Apr. 2, 1873; and to Ross, Feb. 25, 1873, JHP, vol. 42, pp. 114–5, 168, 141, 98–101.
13 Macdonald to Howe (private), Feb. 22, 1873, Macdonald Papers, vol. 522, pp. 838.
14 Howe to Sydenham, Mar. 15, 1873, JHP, vol. 42, pp. 124–9. For details see Kenneth G. Pryke, *Nova Scotia and Confederation* (Toronto: University of Toronto Press, 1979), pp. 148–50.
15 Howe to Macdonald, May 23, 1873, Macdonald Papers, vol. 115, pp. 46943–8.
16 Ibid.
17 *Reporter and Times*, June 2, 1873; *Morning Chronicle*, June 2, 1873.

18 Robert C. Tuck, *Gothic Dreams: The Life and Times of a Canadian Architect William Critchton Harris 1854–1913* (Toronto: Dundurn Press, 1978), p. 23.
19 *Evening Express*, June 3, 1873; *Morning Chronicle*, June 2, 1873.
20 *Reporter and Times*, June 4, 1873.
21 *Morning Chronicle*, June 2 and 10, 1873.
22 *Reporter and Times*, June 4, 1873.
23 *Evening Express*, June 3, 1873.
24 *British Colonist*, June 3, 1873.
25 *Evening Express*, June 3, 1873.
26 Ibid., June 5, 1873.
27 The yearly payment was a modest $500. 48 Vic., c. 40.
28 See report of interview in *Reporter and Times*, June 2, 1873.
29 Chisholm, 2:641.
30 Quoted from the Montreal *Gazette* in *Reporter and Times*, June 6, 1873.

# Note on Sources

The basic Howe records are seventy volumes of original papers held by the Public Archives of Canada, which are available on twenty-one reels of microfilm in the Public Archives of Nova Scotia. Other original papers of Howe are in the Harvard University Library and are available on reels of microfilm (reels 22, 23, and 24) in PANS. Usually considered as an integral part of the Howe record are the George Johnson Papers, held in PAC and available on a single reel of microfilm in PANS. A large selection of Howe's writings and speeches after 1848 is to be found in the second volume of Joseph A. Chisholm's two-volume edition of *The Speeches and Public Letters of Joseph Howe*. Some private letters are available in PANS in a typewritten collection by Joseph A. Chisholm, herein designated "Howe Letters." Letters to and from Howe are also contained in "Correspondence between Joseph Howe and Charles Buller, 1845–8," edited by Chester Martin, in the *Canadian Historical Review*, vol. 6; "Joseph Howe and the Anti-Confederation League," edited by Lawrence Burpee, in *Transactions of the Royal Society of Canada*, 1917; and *Report* of PANS for 1948, 1953, and 1957. Other correspondence, at least indirectly related to Howe, is to be found in the William Young Papers (PANS), especially boxes 733 to 736; the John A. Macdonald Papers (PAC), especially volumes 114–16, 514, 515, and 520–2; *Correspondence of Sir John Alexander Macdonald*, edited by Sir Joseph Pope; E.M. Saunders's *Life and Letters of the Rt. Hon. Sir Charles Tupper*, vol. 1; and Sir Charles Tupper's *Recollections of Sixty Years in Canada*.

Of the Nova Scotia newspapers the ones consulted most were the *Novascotian* and the *Morning Chronicle*, which were friendly to Howe until he "accepted the situation" and thereafter hostile. Other Halifax newspapers of use were: *Acadian Recorder, British Colonist, British North American, Citizen, Evening Reporter, Presbyterian Witness, Reporter and Times, Royal Gazette, Sun*, and *Times*, some of which also reversed their attitudes towards Howe on the question of Confederation; among the county papers used were the *Eastern*

*Chronicle* (New Glasgow), *Yarmouth Herald,* and *Yarmouth Tribune.* For the attitudes of the British press towards Nova Scotia and Confederation, the following London newspapers were consulted in the branch of the British Museum at Colindale: *Daily News, Daily Telegraph, Evening Express, Examiner, Glowworm, Lloyd's Weekly, London Review, Morning Advertiser, Morning Herald, Morning Star, News of the World, Pall Mall Gazette, Patriot, Saturday Review, Spectator, Standard,* and *The Times*; among the provincial newspapers of use were the *Glasgow Sentinel, Hampshire Independent, Leeds Mercury, Manchester Daily Examiner and Times,* and *Manchester Guardian.*

The principal Nova Scotia government documents used were the *Debates and Proceedings* of the House of Assembly, the *Journals* of the Legislative Council and the House of Assembly, the *Minutes* of the Executive Council, and the statutes. Howe's speeches in the Canadian House of Commons are found in the *Debates,* 1869 to 1873; his correspondence relating to his trip to the North-West in 1869 is contained in No. 12 of the *Sessional Papers* for 1870. The speeches of British parliamentarians on the enactment of the British North America Act and the attempt to have it repealed are to be found in *Parliamentary Debates* (House of Lords), and *Parliamentary Debates* (House of Commons) for 1867 and 1868.

Although the main reliance is on primary sources, the positions taken by James A. Roy in *Joseph Howe: A Study in Achievement and Frustration* are frequently used for purposes of evaluation. Judgments on Howe's part in recruiting for the Crimean War are found in Richard W. Van Alstyne's "John F. Crampton, Conspirator or Dupe?" (*American Historical Review,* vol. 41) and J.B. Brebner's "Joseph Howe and the Crimean War Enlistment Controversy between Great Britain and the United States" (*Canadian Historical Review,* vol. 11). Howe's search for office and his part in the disputed election controversy are dealt with in the author's "Joseph Howe: Opportunist or Empire-Builder?" (CHR, vol. 41) and "The Nova Scotia 'Disputed Election' of 1859 and its Aftermath" (CHR, vol. 36). Of use in treating the question of Confederation were Peter B. Waite's *The Life and Times of Confederation*; Kenneth Pryke's *Nova Scotia and Confederation: 1864–74*; and the author's *Joseph Howe: Anti-Confederate* (Canadian Historical Association booklet no. 17) and "Joseph Howe and Confederation: Myth and Fact" (*Transactions of the Royal Society of Canada,* 1964). G.F.G. Stanley and W.L. Morton respectively provide judgments on Howe's trip to the North-West in *The Birth of Western Canada* and *The Critical Years: The Union of British North America.*

# Index